PUZZLING STORIES

PUZZLING STORIES

THE AESTHETIC APPEAL
OF COGNITIVE
CHALLENGE IN FILM,
TELEVISION AND
LITERATURE

Edited by Steven Willemsen and Miklós Kiss

berghahn
NEW YORK · OXFORD
www.berghahnbooks.com

First published in 2022 by
Berghahn Books
www.berghahnbooks.com

© 2022, 2024 Steven Willemsen and Miklós Kiss
First paperback edition published 2024

All rights reserved. Except for the quotation of short passages
for the purposes of criticism and review, no part of this book
may be reproduced in any form or by any means, electronic or
mechanical, including photocopying, recording, or any information
storage and retrieval system now known or to be invented,
without written permission of the publisher.

Library of Congress Cataloging-in-Publication Data

Names: Willemsen, Steven, editor. | Kiss, Miklós, (College teacher), author.
Title: Puzzling stories : the aesthetic appeal of cognitive challenge in film, television and literature / [edited by] Steven Willemsen and Miklós Kiss.
Description: New York : Berghahn Books, 2022. | Includes bibliographical references and index.
Identifiers: LCCN 2022019397 (print) | LCCN 2022019398 (ebook) | ISBN 9781800735910 (hardback) | ISBN 9781800735927 (ebook)
Subjects: LCSH: Narration (Rhetoric)--Philosophy. | Mass media--Philosophy. | Drama--Technique.
Classification: LCC PN212 .P89 2022 (print) | LCC PN212 (ebook) | DDC 808--dc23/eng/20220512
LC record available at https://lccn.loc.gov/2022019397
LC ebook record available at https://lccn.loc.gov/2022019398

British Library Cataloguing in Publication Data
A catalogue record for this book is available from the British Library

ISBN 978-1-80073-591-0 hardback
ISBN 978-1-80539-314-6 paperback
ISBN 978-1-80539-427-3 epub
ISBN 978-1-80073-592-7 web pdf

https://doi.org/10.3167/9781800735910

Contents

List of Figures and Tables	ix
Introduction *Steven Willemsen and Miklós Kiss*	1

Part I The Attractions of Cognitive Challenge in (Post-)Classical Narratives and Genre Fiction

1 Aesthetics and 'Active Discovery': The Pleasure of Moderate Cognitive Challenge in Mass Art *Todd Berliner*	15
2 Narration, Implicature and the Deceptive Puzzle Film *Warren Buckland*	43
3 Cognitive Challenge in Complex Science Fiction: Knowledge, Reason and Threat in Narratives of Time Travel and Extraterrestrial Contact *Hilary Duffield*	68
4 Strange Loops and Nonhuman Realities: Complex Narrative Faces the Climate Crisis *Marco Caracciolo*	93

Part II Mesmerized Minds and Bodies: Art Cinema and Modernist Aesthetics

5 The Puzzling Film Environments of Fellini's *8½* *Steffen Hven*	115

6 2 or 3 Things? Polyphony, Cognitive Challenge and Aesthetic Pleasure in Godard's (Counter) Cinema   138
   Maria Poulaki

7 Embodying Fragmentation in Film: The Spatio-temporal Logic of Cinematic Modernism   157
   Maarten Coëgnarts

8 The Most Difficult Riddle: Paradoxical Personalities in Puzzle Films   195
   András Bálint Kovács

Part III Novel Pleasures in Contemporary Serial Television: From Complexity to Confusion

9 Multiform Television   217
   Matthew Campora

10 'I Can't Keep Track of Any of It Anymore': Cognitive Challenge and Other Aesthetic Appeals in *Community*   236
    Jason Gendler

11 How Not to Comprehend Television: Notes on Complexity and Confusion   259
    Jason Mittell

Part IV Reading, Viewing, Engaging: Conceptualizing the Pleasures of Being Challenged

12 Challenges of Enjoying Morally Ambiguous Character Drama: The *Dexter* Case   281
    Ed S. Tan, Monique Timmers, Claire M. Segijn, Suzanna J. Opree and Guus Bartholomé

13 The Fascination of Failure: On Predictability, Unpredictability and Postdictability in Art   306
    Marina Grishakova

14 Expressive Challenge and the Metaphoricity of Literary Reading 326
Don Kuiken

15 Who Likes Complex Films? Personality and Preferences for Narrative Complexity 355
Steven Willemsen, Katalin Bálint, Frank Hakemulder, Miklós Kiss, Elly Konijn and Kirill Fayn

Index 384

Figures and Tables

Figures

0.1.	*Twin Peaks* (season 3) © Lynch/Frost Productions, Showtime 2017. Screen capture by authors.	xii
1.1.	Berlyne's graph of the relationship between potentially arousing stimuli and 'pleasingness' (1971: 89). Figure created by Todd Berliner.	22
1.2 and 1.3.	Signs of Tracy's infidelity in *The Philadelphia Story* (1940). Screen captures by Todd Berliner.	29
1.4–1.6.	Katharine Hepburn looking flirtatious, then concerned, then resigned in *The Philadelphia Story* (1940). Screen captures by Todd Berliner.	33
1.7 and 1.8.	Hepburn's performance quickly shifts from sensuality to worry in *The Philadelphia Story* (1940). Screen captures by Todd Berliner.	35
1.9–1.14.	Dynamic changes in Hepburn's performance of Tracy, from theatricality (Figure 1.9) to pouting (Figure 1.10), to combined severity and intimacy (Figure 1.11), to worry (Figure 1.12), to coquettishness (Figure 1.13), to bashfulness (Figure 1.14) in *The Philadelphia Story* (1940). Screen captures by Todd Berliner.	36
2.1–2.4.	*Lost Highway* (David Lynch 1997). © Lost Highway Productions, Three Pictures Production Company, Asymmetrical Productions and CIBY 2000. Screen captures by Warren Buckland.	60
4.1.	The interspecies 'transplant' of a parasitic worm in *Upstream Color* (2013). Screen capture by Marco Caracciolo.	103
4.2.	Jeff embracing Kris in the bathtub in *Upstream Color* (2013). Screen capture by Marco Caracciolo.	105
7.1.	Time-RP conceptual metaphor. © Maarten Coëgnarts.	160
7.2.	The spatio-temporal container logic of a shot. © Maarten Coëgnarts.	162

7.3.	Containment in *The Eclipse*. © Cineriz, Interopa Film, Paris Film 1962. Screen captures by Maarten Coëgnarts.	165
7.4.	Dynamic patterns of containment. © Maarten Coëgnarts.	167
7.5.	Landscapes including the protagonist in *The Eclipse* (A and B) and *The Passenger* (C and D). © Cineriz, Interopa Film, Paris Film 1962, and © MGM 1975. Screen captures by Maarten Coëgnarts.	168
7.6.	Landscape excludes the protagonist in *The Passenger*. © MGM 1975. Screen captures by Maarten Coëgnarts.	170
7.7.	Past and present homogenized in the same container. © Maarten Coëgnarts.	172
7.8.	Including and excluding different times in *Last Year at Marienbad*. © Argos Films, Cineriz 1961. Screen captures by Maarten Coëgnarts.	173
7.9.	Creating spatio-temporal ambiguity. © Maarten Coëgnarts.	177
7.10.	Exchanging the image for off-screen sound. © Maarten Coëgnarts.	180
7.11.	The underlying dynamic structure of *Mouchette*'s ending. © Maarten Coëgnarts.	181
7.12.	The viewer as participant in the character's diegetic world of *Contempt* (A) and *A Woman Is a Woman* (B). © Rome Paris Films, Les Films Concordia, Compagnia Cinematografica Champion 1963; and © Euro International Films, Rome Paris Films 1961. Screen captures by Maarten Coëgnarts.	184
7.13.	The on-screen space forces the viewer to cross the natural spatio-temporal boundary and to become part of the diegetic space. © Maarten Coëgnarts.	185
7.14.	Excluding and including talking characters in *A Woman is a Woman* (A–C) and *Contempt* (D–F). © Euro International Films, Rome Paris Films, 1961; and © Rome Paris Films, Les Films Concordia, Compagnia Cinematografica Champion 1963. Screen captures by Maarten Coëgnarts.	186
8.1.	Proportion of narrative portions representing coherent vs. paradoxical identities in some 'impossible puzzle films'. © András Bálint Kovács.	209
12.1.	Playful exercise in games of fictional make-believe. Diagram by the authors.	284

Tables

15.1.	PNC scale factor loadings for EFA and CFA, factor means, skew and kurtosis.	368
15.2.	Correlations between PNC scale and personality traits.	370
15.3.	Regression models predicting PNC scales with NFC and ToA.	371
15.4.	Correlations between behavioural and emotional engagement and personality.	372
15.5.	Correlations between behavioural and emotional engagement and PNC scales.	373
15.6.	Regression results predicting behavioural and emotional engagement with the PNC scale and the best personality predictor.	374

Introduction

Steven Willemsen and Miklós Kiss

Prologue

Boom! 'Trinity' (codename for the first nuclear weapon) and our minds are blown. The five-minute explosion in the outstanding, and standing out, eighth episode of the third season of David Lynch's *Twin Peaks: The Return*, through its aesthetic qualities and ambiguous narrative affordances, lends itself to an intertextual comparison to Kubrick's Starchild scene from *2001: A Space Odyssey*. But while Kubrick's hovering fetus gleaming in a placental orb emanates a certain optimism about a new beginning for the human race, Lynch's mesmerizing spectacle depicts a dark genesis of the downfall of mankind. It is not only marking the birth of all evil – manifested in the show as Killer BOB (16 July 1945, White Sands, New Mexico) – but also signposting a pivotal moment in the history of televisual seriality (25 June 2017, Showtime).

The 'horrifying, horrifyingly beautiful, thought-provoking and thought-annihilating' (Seitz 2017) episode and its awed detonation scene – 'a mesmerizing rush of pure-cut WTF' (Jensen 2017) – is the sublime apex of a complex show that has been building up to, but did not prepare viewers for, this jaw-dropping segment. At this point in time, eight episodes or 409 minutes deep into the third season, the episode bears an unclear relation to all the storyworld construction that the viewer of the series has been engaged in so far. None of the central characters are involved, and nor do we know anything about the scene's connection to the show's setting, events or backstory. Its black-and-white-shot images, which include strange ghostly woodsmen circling around an abandoned convenience store, and a scene of a young girl swallowing an amphibious or insectoid creature – 'a hideous frog-cockroach hybrid, seemingly hatched from an egg on the nuked salt flats of New Mexico' (Seitz 2017) – increasingly raise the question of what exactly we are witnessing. The bold indeterminacy calls forth a variety of responses from its puzzled viewers: it might represent a specific narrative clue (the birth of the show's ultimate antagonist), or invite a symbolical or allegorical reading (the original sin that conceives of all evil); it might point at experimental surrealism and non-narrative stylistic excess (psychedelic images appealing to a pure perceptual pleasure); or it could be seen as a deliberate disruption of the conventions of seriality (upsetting the rulebook of what television is supposed to be).

This hypnotic, beautiful and utterly bizarre scene, occurring within an already quite unruly series, seems to be illustrative of a wider trend among contemporary narratives. Labyrinthine storytelling, intricate enigmas, and persistent ambiguities that have been central to the effect of various narrative traditions (e.g. modernist and postmodern literature, art-cinema) have now found their way into popular fiction (e.g. the so-called 'puzzle films', 'complex television', or 'new weird fiction'). While some degree of cognitive challenge (e.g. novelty, complexity, uncertainty) has been recognized as an aspect of many art experiences, responses such as confusion, puzzlement and incomprehension have not generally been regarded as conducive to aesthetic liking. After all, high degrees of complexity and persistent confusion seem to upset the organizing and communicative functions usually attributed to narratives; they may even obstruct access to the elementary mimetic levels of action and emotion in which readers or viewers are typically immersed. But then, what are the reasons for audiences' engagement with such mind-bending works of fiction? What could be attractive, or at least engaging, about complex narratives' triggered perplexity – a state of mind that most people in real life would prefer to avoid? Why would anyone be interested in confusingly complex stories or storytelling forms?

The Appeal of Cognitive Challenge in Narrative

Narrative theorists have long understood the importance of knowledge gaps to story engagement. Moderate information gaps and other 'spots of indeterminacy' (Ingarden 1973: 249) can work to raise an audience's interest in a story, stimulating their involvement by inviting mental activities described as 'gap-filling' (Iser 1978: 169), 'naturalization' (Culler 1975: 138), 'mental model building' (van Dijk and Kintsch 1983; McNamara and Magliano 2009) and 'problem-solving' (Tan 1996: 90). The notion that aesthetic appeal is optimal at moderate and manageable levels of complexity recurs in many theories of aesthetic engagement, such as Daniel E. Berlyne's influential model of the inverted U-curve of optimal arousal (Berlyne 1971), or, more recently, Mihaly Csikszentmihalyi's (1990) notion of the 'flow' state. Consequently, confusion may appear as an unwanted result that occurs when the challenge becomes too complex or dominant. This subjective result – a consciously experienced state of cognitive disequilibrium – has not typically been associated with heightened aesthetic appeal. This has at least two reasons.

Firstly, confusion is typically seen as a *negative valence* state – an emotional or cognitive state not associated with reward or enjoyment but rather with disengagement, frustration or avoidance. As Winfried Menninghaus et al. (2019) note in their review of aesthetic emotions, these feelings have proven more resistant to being integrated into accounts of aesthetic enjoyment: '[T]hroughout the entire tradition of aesthetics, aesthetic emotion terms that designate unambiguously negative emotions have been far less nuanced and frequently used than those of the positive spectrum, with boredom and anger as elicited by artworks being the most pronounced exceptions' (ibid.: 181). Although still a minority, recent work in emotion studies and empirical aesthetics has been seeking to nuance this – for instance, by pointing to the role that negative or 'mixed' valence states may play in aesthetic experiences (e.g. Silvia 2009, 2010; Larsen and Green 2013; Menninghaus et al. 2015; Menninghaus et al. 2017).

Secondly, many views of (empirical) aesthetics have been prone to associate aesthetic appeal with *fluent processing* of a stimulus (Reber, Schwarz and Winkielman 2004) and the positive affects that accompany cognitive and perceptual fluency (e.g. Winkielman and Cacioppo 2001; Belke, Leder and Carbon 2015). In the study of narrative, too, findings have pointed to factors like 'ease of comprehension' as a reliable predictor of what makes a text interesting (Wade, Buxton and Kelly 1999; Silvia 2006) and a key determinant of narrative engagement (Buselle and Bilandzic 2009). However, when seeking to explain more challenging aesthetic stimuli, many scholars have pointed out the shortcomings of the processing fluency thesis (e.g. Armstrong and Detweiler-Bedell 2008; Graf and Landwehr 2015; Belke, Leder and Carbon 2015). Moreover, research on the concept of 'foregrounding' (Bálint et al. 2017) indicates that, in some cases, aspects of a story perceived as strange or deviant do not obstruct absorption but rather enhance meaningful engagement with narratives.

In our previous work on complex narratives in contemporary cinema (Kiss and Willemsen 2017), we ran into similar questions concerning the appeal of high degrees of cognitive challenge. In the process, we became aware of the rich diversity of approaches these questions can entail. After all, is the enjoyment of complex and confusing works primarily related to recipients' expertise or 'literacy', or is the attraction to such works more determined by psychological factors, such as one's tolerance of uncertainty and ambiguity? Can we assume that puzzling stories tap into more universal modes of cognitive and aesthetic engagement, as the more widespread popularity of complex narratives in today's mainstream film, television and literature suggests? Or are they best understood in the contexts of shifting conventions, competencies, and culturally situated reception practices?

We felt that both the weight and scope of these questions warranted an anthology: an opportunity to invite a range of specialists to approach and unpack these questions from a variety of angles. The goal of this volume has been to host contributions from leading scholars in narrative theory, literary studies, film and media studies, cognitive psychology, media psychology, and philosophical and empirical aesthetics, seeking to offer the first comprehensive – multidisciplinary and transmedial – approach to questions of audiences' fascination with cognitively challenging narratives.

While common to all contributions is an interest in the notion of complexity, the chapters vary in the exact types of complexity that are being scrutinized: many of these address narrational complexity or complex narrative temporalities, while others focus on moral complexity, the complexity of the interpretive responses that a story can evoke, or ideas of complex systems as developed in the sciences. Unifying all chapters, however, is an ultimate interest in the potentially *engaging effects* of these complexities. Collectively, the theoretical and case-study-driven chapters cover psychological, philosophical, formal-historical and empirical perspectives in their attempt to explore the appeal of cognitive challenge in puzzling stories.

Outline of the Chapters

The various authors' contributions mark out interesting affinities and common ground in their choices of media, approaches, and case studies. Based on these commonalities, we have organized the volume into four parts, which we hope will help our readers to orient themselves through the book's multiple angles and interests.

Part I, *The Attractions of Cognitive Challenge in (Post-)Classical Narratives and Genre Fiction*, examines the status that challenging storytelling forms have enjoyed in popular fictional stories. While cognitive disfluency is often regarded as a staple of avant-garde art and experimental narrative, the contributions in this part all demonstrate how the rewards of challenged comprehension have become integral to some popular genres of storytelling – from classical Hollywood to the contemporary 'puzzle film', and from traditional genres to the 'new weird fiction'.

The opening chapter, *Aesthetics and 'Active Discovery': The Pleasure of Moderate Cognitive Challenge in Mass Art* by Todd Berliner, explores how Hollywood cinema – often regarded as the definitive mass art form – balances the pleasures of cognitive challenge against the pressure of ease of comprehension for a mass audience. The chapter surveys how a number of works in philosophical and psychological aesthetics have recognized both cognitive challenge as a key component of aesthetic value, and when this challenge may produce some amount of confusion and stress. Consequently, Berliner demonstrates how even a celebrated classical Hollywood film such as *The Philadelphia Story* (1940) creates moderate degrees of cognitive challenge through odd narrative structures and inconsistent information, even if such movies appear to be designed to facilitate effortless understanding.

Warren Buckland's chapter *Narration, Implicature and the Deceptive Puzzle Film* examines the role of 'deception' in popular film narration, likening it to magic – the art of deceiving everyday rational understanding. Building on H.P. Grice's influential theory of 'conversational implicature', Buckland defines narrative deception as any violation of communication conventions that problematizes a spectator's cognitive construction of the fictional storyworld. The chapter proposes a hierarchy of four types of filmic narration – cooperative, discrepant, flouted and deceptive – to describe the degrees to which film narration may facilitate or obstruct a spectator's cognitive construction of the storyworld, leading to different viewing pleasures that may be associated with each.

Hilary Duffield's contribution, *Cognitive Challenge in Complex Science Fiction: Knowledge, Reason and Threat in Narratives of Time Travel and Extraterrestrial Contact*, turns the focus to the connection between cognitive challenge and genre appeal. Tracing the lineage and development of the science fiction genre from literature to contemporary cinema, Duffield points out a consistent tradition of 'complex science fiction', structured around knowledge-seeking narrative formats. The tradition includes the story's introduction of a 'novum' (defined by Darko Suvin [1979] as a storyworld departure from real-world possibilities entailing a mode of 'cognitive estrangement') and a 'conceptual breakthrough' that promises an insight or expansion of perception to resolve the narrative incongruities. Duffield shows how contemporary exponents of the genre, such as *Looper*, *Interstellar* and *Arrival*, adopt this logic to provide pleasures related to a distinct kind of cognitive exhilaration in discovering higher-level truths within the narrative world.

Marco Caracciolo's *Strange Loops and Nonhuman Realities: Complex Narrative Faces the Climate Crisis* elevates the stakes of these questions by interrogating the ability of complex fictional narrative forms to mimetically express and channel the complexity of real-world interrelations. A global issue like the current ecological crisis confronts us with complexity on a scale that ranges beyond – yet is deeply enmeshed with – that of human actions. Examining Shane Carruth's 2013 *Upstream Color*, Caracciolo shows how narrative, through complex form and puzzling experiences, can defamiliarize the world of human-scale interactions. The analysis highlights how storytelling strategies can create effects that approximate the qualities of real-world complexity, such as nonlinearity, multiscalarity and self-organization, as well as the enmeshment of the human and nonhuman. The chapter thereby shows how challenging narrative strategies can also work as platforms to (re)shape our thinking and affects about real-world matters characterized by complex interrelations.

Part II, *Mesmerized Minds and Bodies: Art Cinema and Modernist Aesthetics*, focuses on the phenomenon of art-cinema narration, which has historically been the primary mode for experimentation with challenging formal play in audiovisual storytelling. Paying particular attention to the bodily and affective dimensions of cognition, the contributions of this part are unified by their in-depth explorations of how art-cinema narratives challenge their audiences' cognitive routines and embodied dispositions to create distinct aesthetic effects – and of where the limits of this appeal may be.

Steffen Hven's chapter, *The Puzzling Film Environments of Fellini's 8½*, looks into the landmark Italian art film from 1963. While much has been said and written about its intricate formal and narrative design, Hven contends that this descriptive focus on the film as a 'cognitive-analytical puzzle' has sidelined another important set of effects: the film's creation of 'impossible spaces' and 'complex narrative environments' that create a disorienting experience through bodily influenced forms of meaning-making – complexities that need to be experienced to be understood. In his argument, Hven highlights the importance of 'second generation' cognitive-narratological approaches that draw attention to the bodily, affective and enactive strategies of comprehension.

Maria Poulaki's *2 Or 3 Things? Polyphony, Cognitive Challenge and Aesthetic Pleasure in Godard's (Counter) Cinema* scrutinizes the work of another often-discussed cinematic auteur, Jean-Luc Godard. Through an in-depth exploration, Poulaki claims that the challenges in Godard's counter cinema do not just reside on the narrative level of disrupted causality or chronology but are also characterized by complexity on the primary sensory and perceptual level. Her analysis shows how Godard's stylistic innovations create perceptual 'noise' that already affects the film experience at the stage of front-end processing. This, Poulaki argues, not only results in challenged comprehension and heightened medium-awareness but also contributes to modes of heterogeneity and polyphony that entail unique aesthetic pleasures.

Maarten Coëgnarts' *Embodying Fragmentation in Film: The Spatio-temporal Logic of Cinematic Modernism* provides an embodied-cognitive perspective on the aesthetic effects of modernist European art cinema. Building on findings from cognitive linguistics and conceptual metaphor theory, Coëgnarts shows how in film, like in language, abstract concepts such as time are grounded in everyday action patterns and concrete spatial concepts. The chapter then illustrates how various modernist filmmakers – Antonioni, Resnais, Bresson and Godard – have adopted and adapted this logic of embodied cinematic meaning to convey more puzzling and fragmented conceptions of time. Coëgnarts thereby shows how modernist films employ the same preconceptual patterns and sensory-motor experiences that inform our everyday sense-making, but at the same time, challenge the commonly unreflected narrative functioning of these patterns to facilitate a different kind of embodied-cognitive resonance in the spectator.

András Bálint Kovács' *The Most Difficult Riddle: Paradoxical Personalities in Puzzle Films* examines the connection between historical art cinema and contemporary 'puzzle films'. Kovács argues that the transposition of complex and confusing storytelling techniques from art cinema to popular film genres may be explained by cultural habituation, but that the potential for a wider appeal of such techniques also has a natural limit. This limit, according to Kovács, occurs at the coherence of a protagonist's identity: narrative engagement is so intricately tied up with the actions, motivations and intentions of characters that a disruption of these central components means a disruption of narrative coherence altogether. Some films have nonetheless experimented with such disruptions in character identity, and so the chapter examines how avant-garde cases have differed from their more widely viewed counterparts, resulting in different kinds of spectator engagement.

Part III, *Novel Pleasures in Contemporary Serial Television: From Complexity to Confusion*, targets television, the medium that seems to have witnessed the strongest upsurge in novel storytelling approaches recently, delivering unique narrative pleasures by challenging, bewildering, and yet hooking their audience.

Matthew Campora's chapter, *Multiform Television*, surveys how the rise of complex narrative television is rooted in prior storytelling traditions, such as art cinema and the puzzle film. He takes a closer look at *Mr Robot* (2015–19), *Maniac* (2018) and *Russian Doll* (2019–), examining how these shows use multiple ontologies in their storyworlds to create novel and sometimes jolting narrative experiences. They combine the series/serial hybridity (Mittell 2015) with the multiform narrative tradition (Campora 2014) to produce a mode of television that offers the viewing pleasures previously associated with modernist and postmodernist literature or art cinema.

Jason Gendler's *'I Can't Keep Track of Any of It Anymore': Cognitive Challenge and Other Aesthetic Appeals in Community* provides a close examination of a very distinct kind of cognitive challenge – one that functions as a mode of parody. Focusing on a single episode – 'Conspiracy Theories and Interior Design' – from the second season of the cult show *Community* (2009–15), Gendler argues that its hard-to-follow, twist-ridden narrative seems not so much to tempt viewers to resolve its puzzling plot, or to marvel at its clever construction, but rather invites them to identify and then appreciate it as a reflexive parody of the tropes of the conspiracy theory genre, thus catering to a wholly different kind of appeal – namely, that of the *comedy* that can result from incongruity and exaggeration.

Jason Mittell's *How Not to Comprehend Television: Notes on Complexity and Confusion* offers a reflection on a new aesthetic phenomenon that seems to have emerged in serial television after his seminal monograph *Complex TV* (Mittell 2015). Besides noting how the narrative innovations of complex television are still in place and have expanded globally in the twenty-first century, Mittell also observes a new trend: programmes that move into the territory of excessively unpredictable, illogical or incongruous narrative moments in order to bewilder viewers. Mittell proposes that while this phenomenon may be more like a playful rarity, it marks a novel mode, that of 'Batshit TV', which forms a new step in the medium's experiments with complex storytelling, and provokes a new range of affective and puzzled responses.

Our final part, Part IV, *Reading, Viewing, Engaging: Conceptualizing the Pleasures of Being Challenged*, turns the focus predominantly onto questions of reception. These chapters target some of the more general processes and factors that underlie engagement with complexity and cognitive challenge in art and fiction.

The contribution by Ed S. Tan, Monique Timmers, Claire M. Segijn, Suzanna J. Opree and Guus Bartholomé, *Challenges of Enjoying Morally Ambiguous Character Drama: The* Dexter *Case*, draws attention to a particular sort of challenge: the moral and psychological complexity of engaging with ambiguous protagonists who regularly commit immoral acts. Focusing on what they define as the 'Morally Ambiguous Character drama' in television, popularized by shows such a *Breaking Bad, The Wire, House of Cards* and *Dexter*, the authors investigate this phenomenon from a psychological point of view. They characterize its challenges as primarily affective, and propose how such fiction invites viewers to engage in elaborate emotion regulation strategies that may produce their own kind of aesthetic reward.

Marina Grishakova's *The Fascination of Failure: On Predictability, Unpredictability and Postdictability in Art* explores how engagement with cognitively challenging art may be understood from the perspective of the 'predictive processing' framework. Predictive processing has emerged in recent years as a new approach that may bridge the Cartesian gap by positing how the internal and external resources of cognition function together in a continuous predictive-corrective loop, making sense of the environment through the (dis)confirmation of predictions. Grishakova's chapter explores how art's tendency to amplify (rather than minimize) prediction errors may produce perceptual and cognitive challenges that can engage the human ability to tolerate uncertainty and explore alternate meanings, thus providing a new take on long-standing discussions of the aesthetics of defamiliarization.

Don Kuiken's *Expressive Challenge and the Metaphoricity of Literary Reading* offers an in-depth, medium-specific examination of the cognitive challenges unique to literary reading. While many of the other contributors focus on audiovisual media or on concepts assumed to be largely medium-independent, Kuiken zooms in on challenges specific to the comprehension of written text. The chapter explores two forms of challenging deviation that may occur in the reading process: the first resulting from metaphoric cross-domain resemblances, the second involving explanatory relations between temporal intervals. Kuiken argues how these two challenges entail two different modes of absorbed reading – *expressive enactment*, associated with the challenges of constructing metaphoricity, and *integrative comprehension*, predominantly associated with plot assembly – with both modes entailing different forms of aesthetic responses and engagement.

Finally, Steven Willemsen, Katalin Bálint, Frank Hakemulder, Miklós Kiss, Elly Konijn and Kirill Fayn's *Who Likes Complex Films? Personality and Preferences for Narrative Complexity* offers an explorative empirical approach to people's preferences for complexity in storytelling. Complex narratives often produce a particular kind of experience characterized by heightened degrees of uncertainty, ambiguity and sensed incongruity. In everyday life, people vary in their willingness and ability to cope with uncertain, ambiguous or contradictory epistemic states. Could these personality factors also influence one's enjoyment of complexity in fiction? Through an online survey that combined a newly created 'Preference for Narrative Complexity Scale' with existing measures of the 'Big Five' personality traits, 'Tolerance for Ambiguity' and 'Need for Cognition', this final chapter provides evidence for the link between one's personality and one's preference for, or dislike of, complexity, ambiguity and incongruity in storytelling.

The variety of topics, media, disciplinary backgrounds and methodological approaches presented in this anthology inevitably entails some notable differences in tone between chapters. We hope our readers will be willing to not only tolerate but embrace this diversity (which may itself pose some degree of cognitive challenge) and, while joining the contributors in exploring the central questions, ultimately learn as much as we have in the process of editing this volume.

Steven Willemsen is Assistant Professor in Arts, Culture and Media at the University of Groningen, and Senior Researcher at the Max Planck Institute for Empirical Aesthetics in Frankfurt. He is co-author of *Impossible Puzzle Films: A Cognitive Approach to Contemporary Complex Cinema* (with Miklós Kiss, Edinburgh University Press, 2017).

Miklós Kiss is Associate Professor of Audiovisual Arts and Cognition, and Chair of the Arts, Culture and Media department at the University of Groningen, the Netherlands. His research intersects the fields of narrative and cognitive film studies. He is co-author of the books *Film Studies in Motion: From Audiovisual Essay to Academic Research Video* (with Thomas van den Berg, Scalar, 2016) and *Impossible Puzzle Films: A Cognitive Approach to Contemporary Complex Cinema* (with Steven Willemsen, Edinburgh University Press, 2017).

References

Armstrong, Thomas, and Brian Detweiler-Bedell. 2008. 'Beauty as an Emotion: The Exhilarating Prospect of Mastering a Challenging World', *Review of General Psychology* 12: 305–29. https://doi.org/10.1037/a0012558.

Bálint, Katalin, Frank Hakemulder, Moniek Kuijpers, Miruna Doicaru and Ed Tan. 2017. 'Reconceptualizing Foregrounding: Identifying Response Strategies to Deviation in Absorbing Narratives', *Scientific Study of Literature* 6(2): 176–207.

Belke, Benno, Helmut Leder and Claus Christian Carbon. 2015. 'When Challenging Art Gets Liked: Evidences for a Dual Preference Formation Process for Fluent and Non-Fluent Portraits', *PloS one* 10(8): e0131796. https://doi.org/10.1371/journal.pone.0131796.

Berlyne, Daniel E. 1971. *Aesthetics and Psychobiology*. New York: Meredith Corporation.

Busselle, Rick, and Helena Bilandzic. 2009. 'Measuring Narrative Engagement', *Media Psychology* 12(4): 321–47. https://doi.org/10.1080/15213260903287259.

Campora, Matthew. 2014. *Subjective Realist Cinema: From Expressionism to Inception*. New York and Oxford: Berghahn Books.

Csikszentmihalyi, Mihaly. 1990. *Flow: The Psychology of Optimal Experience*. New York: Harper Perennial.

Culler, Jonathan. 1975. *Structuralist Poetics: Structuralism, Linguistics and the Study of Literature*. London: Routledge and Kegan Paul.

Graf, Laura K.M., and Jan R. Landwehr. 2015. 'A Dual-Process Perspective on Fluency-Based Aesthetics: The Pleasure-Interest Model of Aesthetic Liking', *Personality and Social Psychology Review* 19(4): 395–410.

Ingarden, Roman. 1973. *The Literary Work of Art*. Evanston, IL: Northwestern University Press.

Iser, Wolfgang. (1976) 1978. *The Act of Reading: A Theory of Aesthetic Response*. Baltimore, MD: Johns Hopkins University Press.

Jensen, Jeff. 2017. 'Twin Peaks Recap: "The Return: Part 8"', *Entertainment Weekly*. Retrieved 23 March 2021 from https://ew.com/recap/twin-peaks-season-3-episode-8/.

Kiss, Miklós, and Steven Willemsen. 2017. *Impossible Puzzle Films: A Cognitive Approach to Contemporary Complex Cinema*. Edinburgh: Edinburgh University Press.

Larsen, Jeff T., and Jennifer D. Green. 2013. 'Evidence for Mixed Feelings of Happiness and Sadness from Brief Moments in Time', *Cognition and Emotion* 27(8): 1469–77.

McNamara, Danielle S., and Joe Magliano. 2009. 'Toward a Comprehensive Model Comprehension', *Psychology of Learning and Motivation*, vol. 51, pp. 297–384.

Menninghaus, Winfried, Valentin Wagner, Julian Hanich, Eugen Wassiliwizky, Thomas Jacobsen and Stefan Koelsch. 2017. 'The Distancing-Embracing Model of the Enjoyment of Negative Emotions in Art Reception', *Behavioral and Brain Sciences* 40: e347.

Menninghaus, Winfried, Valentin Wagner, Julian Hanich, Eugen Wassiliwizky, Milena Kuehnast and Thomas Jacobsen. 2015. 'Towards a Psychological Construct of Being Moved', *Plos One* 10(6): e0128451.

Menninghaus, Winfried, Valentin Wagner, Eugen Wassiliwizky, Ines Schindler, Julian Hanich, Thomas Jacobsen and Stefan Koelsch. 2019. 'What Are Aesthetic Emotions?', *Psychological Review* 126(2): 171–95.

Mittell, Jason. 2015. *Complex TV: The Poetics of Contemporary Television Storytelling*. New York: New York University Press.

Reber, Rolf, Norbert Schwarz and Piotr Winkielman. 2004. 'Processing Fluency and Aesthetic Pleasure: Is Beauty in the Perceiver's Processing Experience?', *Personality and Social Psychology Review* 8: 364–82.

Seitz, Matt Zoller. 2017. 'The Eighth Episode of *Twin Peaks: The Return* Is Horrifyingly Beautiful', *Vulture*. Retrieved 28 June 2021 from https://www.vulture.com/2017/06/twin-peaks-the-return-part-8-atom-bomb-flashback.html.

Silvia, Paul J. 2006. *Exploring the Psychology of Interest*. Oxford: Oxford University Press.

———. 2009. 'Looking Past Pleasure: Anger, Confusion, Disgust, Pride, Surprise, and Other Unusual Aesthetic Emotions', *Psychology of Aesthetics, Creativity, and the Arts* 3(1): 48–51.

———. 2010. 'Confusion and Interest: The Role of Knowledge Emotions in Aesthetic Experience', *Psychology of Aesthetics, Creativity, and the Arts* 4(2): 75–80.

Suvin, Darko. 1979. *Metamorphoses of Science Fiction: On the Poetics and History of a Literary Genre*. New Haven, CT: Yale University Press.

Tan, Ed. 1996. *Emotion and the Structure of Narrative Film: Film as an Emotion Machine*, trans. B. Fasting. Lawrence Erlbaum Associates, Inc.

Van Dijk, Teun, and Walter Kintsch. 1983. *Strategies of Discourse Comprehension*. New York: Academic Press.

Wade, Suzanne, William Buxton and Michelle Kelly. 1999. 'Using Think-Alouds to Examine Reader-Text Interest', *Reading Research Quarterly* 34: 194–216.

Winkielman, Piotr, and John T. Cacioppo. 2001. 'Mind at Ease Puts a Smile on the Face: Psychophysiological Evidence that Processing Facilitation Leads to Positive Affect', *Journal of Personality and Social Psychology* 81: 989–1000.

PART I
The Attractions of Cognitive Challenge in (Post-)Classical Narratives and Genre Fiction

CHAPTER 1
Aesthetics and 'Active Discovery'
The Pleasure of Moderate Cognitive Challenge in Mass Art

Todd Berliner

Introduction

Some viewers have described *Memento* (2000) as 'exhausting', 'irritating', 'incomprehensible', and 'a headache'. Some have described *Primer* (2004) as 'incoherent', 'pointless', 'unwatchable', and 'a waste of time'. *Donnie Darko* (2001) has been called 'convoluted', 'rubbish', 'bizarre', and 'confuzzled'.[1] Laborious, stressful and bewildering, some 'puzzling stories', it would seem, do not afford pleasure to the average viewer. We might regard them as a curious subset within the narrative arts, designed for a coterie that takes perverse enjoyment in experiences that other viewers find unpleasant. But puzzling stories point us towards a central component of aesthetic experience in general: cognitive challenge. This chapter sets out to explain how artworks create aesthetic pleasure through cognitive challenge. My argument addresses both explicitly puzzling works – like the cult movies noted above – and, in a more elaborate discussion, less challenging artworks designed to please mass audiences.

The argument falls into three parts, which I lay out here. In the subsequent sections, I expound on each part.

First, philosophers and psychologists often regard cognitive challenge as a key factor in aesthetic value, even when the challenge results in confusion and stress. Many valuable artworks create unpleasant experiences, and we cannot separate the value of the works from the negative emotions they instil in us. We can even describe such experiences as 'pleasurable' if we regard pleasure as a broad category of intrinsically rewarding emotional experiences. Emotional rewards vary among different perceivers, however, and artists tailor the intensity of their artworks' challenges to the coping potential of their intended audiences.

Second, although theorists often distinguish mass art by its lack of cognitive challenges, research in cognitive psychology suggests that average perceivers find cognitive challenges stimulating, even exhilarating, and that lack of challenge leads to boredom. Cognitive challenges, I shall argue, generate pleasure by creating opportunities for creative problem solving, incongruity resolution, insight and stress relief. Mass artforms, however, must balance their cognitive challenges against the competing pressure for easy comprehension by mass audiences.

Finally, we can understand how mass artworks negotiate that balance through a case study drawn from the definitive mass artform, Hollywood cinema. Seemingly simple and straightforward, *The Philadelphia Story* (1940) creates moderate challenges through slightly misshapen narrative structures and occasionally inconsistent information, even though the narrative may seem perfectly designed and effortlessly understood.

Aesthetic Pleasure and Cognitive Challenge

Let us talk first about the pleasure of art. Many aesthetic philosophers point to a key relationship between pleasure and artistic value. Jerrold Levinson writes:

> The idea that the value of an artwork is closely related to the pleasure that a perceiver derives from it has surely too much initial plausibility, and is of too long standing, to be wholly without basis. And indeed, there is a substantial core of truth to it. The arts are intended, as much as anything, to give pleasure and are, by and large, well suited to provide it. (Levinson 1996: 11)

Levinson also warns, however, that if we regard pleasure as a gauge of artistic value, the pleasure must be 'actively achieved' (12). Pleasure from art, he says, 'is typically a pleasure in *doing* something – listening, viewing, attending, organizing, projecting, conjecturing, imagining, speculating, hypothesizing, and so on – rather than just allowing things to happen to one on a sensory plane' (13). According to this line of thinking, artworks typically offer pleasure by giving our minds something to work on.

Indeed, although philosophers disagree about the nature of aesthetic pleasure, a common theme runs through much of the literature: modern philosophers typically regard the pleasure of aesthetics and art as a *pleasure of cognitive activity*. Immanuel Kant's conception of beauty involves 'the free play of the cognitive powers' (Kant [1790] 1987: 62). John Dewey emphasizes the cognitive challenges that accompany aesthetic pleasure as the perceiver attempts to unify the different aspects of an artwork: 'That which distinguishes an experience as aesthetic is a conversion of resistance and tensions, of excitations, that in themselves are temptations to diversions, into a movement toward an inclusive and fulfilling close' (Dewey [1934] 1980: 56). Alexander Nehamas also points to the demands that beautiful artworks make of their viewers when he questions the traditional relationship between beauty and attractiveness: 'As long as we continue to identify beauty with attractiveness and attractiveness with the power of pleasing quickly and without much thought or effort, we can't even begin to think of many of the twentieth century's great works as beautiful' (Nehamas 2010: 29–30). Like many aestheticians, Nehamas emphasizes not the ability of the artwork to please but rather the 'thought or effort' that beauty may inspire.

Monroe Beardsley similarly commends art's capacity to create exhilaration through cognitive challenge. He argues that one symptom of aesthetic value is

> *a sense of actively exercising constructive powers of the mind, of being challenged by a variety of potentially conflicting stimuli to try to make them cohere; a keyed-up state amounting to exhilaration in seeing connections between percepts and between meanings, a sense (which may be illusory) of achieved intelligibility. For short:* active discovery. (Beardsley 1979: 741)

Like Dewey, Beardsley locates aesthetic value in the perceiver's effort to master an artwork – a potentially challenging cognitive activity that results in the 'exhilaration' of seeing connections, real or imagined, among the object's features and of attaining (or attempting to attain) understanding of the object. He calls this effort 'active discovery'.

In all of these accounts, aesthetic experience involves mental labour. Indeed, philosophical descriptions of aesthetic experience do not always sound pleasant – on the contrary, the experience sounds stressful. But human beings find pleasure in all sorts of curious places, such as in challenging artworks that would seem to offer predominately unpleasant experiences. Levinson points to this human quality when he writes:

> *Even were we to agree that an artwork is valuable, ultimately, only insofar as experience of it is in some way worthwhile, it does not follow that an artwork is valuable only insofar as experience of it or engagement with it is* pleasant, or straightforwardly enjoyable ... Much art is disturbing, dizzying, despairing, disorienting – and is in fact valuable in virtue of that. (Levinson 1996: 12; emphasis in original)

The value of many artworks results precisely from the manner in which they thwart our desires and resist mastery, at times inducing a feeling of exhilaration unavailable with more straightforwardly pleasing and immediately intelligible artworks. So, Nehamas may be correct in saying that 'beauty is less opposed to ugliness than to the nondescript' (2010: 42). The point may sound unreasonable – given a conception of beauty as that which brings joy – but Levinson and Nehamas remind us not to equate aesthetic pleasure with pleasant emotions. Instead, we should regard aesthetic pleasure as a broad category of intrinsically rewarding emotional experiences that may involve negative emotions, including the stress that comes from an artwork's challenges. Hence, we might gauge an aesthetic experience not by the positive emotions it generates but rather by the behaviour it reinforces. Negative emotions, we could say, afford aesthetic value when they increase the likelihood that someone will seek out the same type of aesthetic experience again.

But how much cognitive challenge can people take before their pleasure diminishes and they give up the search for understanding and satisfaction? When does too much challenge decrease the likelihood that someone will seek out the same type of experience? Is the amount different for different people? Such tricky questions point to the difficulty of charting the relationship between aesthetic pleasure and aesthetic value. Although aesthetic value relies on normative judgements, based on objective reasoning, philosophers also acknowledge the subjective component of aesthetics. Kant argues, oxymoronically, that judgements of taste claim 'subjective universality' because, on the one hand, they depend on subjective experience and, on the other, they claim universal validity. For Noël Carroll, aesthetic properties are 'response dependent' in that they rely on 'human perception' and connect to our 'experience' of an artwork (Carroll 1999: 157–58). Reason alone cannot lead us to conclude that Marvin Gaye's 'What's Going On' is a beautiful song; we must experience it too.

To understand the subjective component of aesthetics, some aesthetic researchers have turned to empirical psychology. Aesthetic experience constitutes an empirical event, and psychology has accumulated stacks of empirical research on the pleasures of art. Such research often addresses the interactions among an artwork's objective properties, the subjective experience of its perceivers, and cognitive challenge, as well as their collective contribution to aesthetic pleasure.

Several empirical studies support the conclusion that pleasure depends on both objective properties (such as an artwork's levels of complexity and novelty) and subjective properties (such as the perceiver's preferences, ability to cope, knowledge, personality and experience). For instance, studies across multiple art forms have shown that art experts prefer more complex art, and novices prefer simpler art (Smith and Melara 1990; Winston and Cupchik 1992; Hekkert and van Wieringen 1996; Axelsson 2007; Silvia and Berg 2011). Keith Millis (2001) found that subjects enjoyed abstract paintings more when given titles that increased understanding. Ronald Heyduk (1975) found that the degree to which subjects liked a musical composition depended on (1) how complex the composition was, (2) each subject's preferred level of complexity, and (3) how often the subject heard the composition. Heyduk exposed subjects repeatedly to compositions at, above, or below their preferred level of complexity. He found that subjects who listened to a composition more complex than their preferred level liked it more the more they heard it, whereas subjects who listened to compositions less complex than their preferred level liked it less the more they heard it.

Psychologists have tested the effect of several personality factors – including intellect, political leaning, and what they call the 'Big Five' dimensions of personality (neuroticism, extroversion, openness to experience, agreeableness, and conscientiousness) – on aesthetic experience. Whereas some studies (Furnham and Avison 1997; Feist and Brady 2004) have shown that factors such as extroversion correlate with preferences for novelty, complexity and abstraction, other studies have found that the only factor that significantly correlates with such preferences is openness to experience (Rentfrow and Gosling 2003; Silvia 2007; Chamorro-Premuzic et al. 2010). Openness to experience is associated with inventiveness, inquisitiveness, unconventionality, flexibility and creativity (John and Srivastava 1999; McCrae 2007) as well as adaptive coping strategies (O'Brien and DeLongis 1996; Watson and Hubbard 1996; Lee-Baggley, Preece and DeLongis 2005). Kirill Fayn et al. (2015) found that those highly open to experience took greater pleasure and interest in artistic novelty. Gregory Feist and Tara Brady conclude: 'There exist some people for whom novelty, complexity, and unusual stimulation are going to be less aversive and perhaps even appealing' (Feist and Brady 2004: 86).

Hence, the pleasures of art and aesthetics depend on interactions among various objective and subjective properties, making it difficult to form general theories explaining the contribution of cognitive challenge to aesthetic value. When it comes to aesthetic pleasure, the particular audience group matters. Some researchers have nonetheless attempted to summarize and model the empirical findings. One compelling theory comes from psychologists Thomas Armstrong and Brian Detweiler-Bedell (2008), who argue (à la Beardsley and Dewey) that exhilaration results from the challenge of trying to unite conflicting stimuli. In their review of the literature in aesthetic psychology, the researchers distinguish beauty from prettiness. Although aesthetic pleasure includes both concepts, Armstrong and Detweiler-Bedell regard 'prettiness' as a calm, passively achieved pleasure. The psychology of aesthetics, they suggest, has mainly studied prettiness – a function of 'processing fluency', which denotes the ease with which the perceiver assimilates information (Reber, Schwarz and Winkielman 2004). For Leder et al. (2004), processing fluency in the arts involves perceiving an object, integrating it into memory, classifying it, and cognitively mastering and evaluating it. Researchers have shown that properties that ease processing also increase pleasure. Numerous studies have found, for instance, that people tend to prefer familiar and easily identified objects (Zajonc 1968); prototypical and average objects (Langlois and Roggman 1990); objects with enhanced clarity (Whittlesea, Jacoby and Girard 1990); and objects that show figure-ground contrast, symmetry and 'figural goodness' – a term that denotes an object's simplicity, clarity and order (Koffka [1935] 2013; Reber 2002). Researchers have argued that each of these objective properties increases the efficiency, speed and ease of processing (Whittlesea 1993) and that easy processing creates subjective feelings of comfort, familiarity and spontaneous pleasure (Roese and Sherman 2014: 101).

'Beautiful' objects, in contrast to pretty ones, excite what Armstrong and Detweiler-Bedell term *exhilarated pleasure*: 'Beauty is the exhilarating feeling that something complex, perhaps to the point of being profound, might yield to understanding' (2008: 312). Beautiful objects, because they resist mastery, arouse more heated mental activity (attentiveness, alertness, excitement) and require more effortful processing as the perceiver investigates the object with the hope of understanding it. The prospect of achieving mastery over a challenging object, they argue, increases positive emotions, including exhilaration, as perceivers attempt to reshape and expand their knowledge (ibid.: 305).

To summarize Armstrong and Detweiler-Bedell's theory: whereas 'pretty' (familiar, simple, easily processed) objects enable the calm pleasure of immediate understanding, 'beautiful' (novel, complex, difficult to process) objects stimulate the exhilarated pleasure of potential understanding. But we do not have to agree with Armstrong and Detweiler-Bedell's characterization of prettiness and beauty to see how their distinction can help us to grasp two inverse pleasures afforded by the arts: the pleasure of easy understanding and the pleasure of cognitive challenge. Artists balance these two forms of pleasure in order to create emotional rewards and reinforcements for their intended audiences.

Mass Art and Cognitive Challenge

Mass artworks are designed to offer emotional rewards and reinforcements to mass audiences, so the balance between easy understanding and cognitive challenge is liable to tip in the direction of easiness. Indeed, some theorists distinguish mass artworks by their *lack* of cognitive challenges. In *A Philosophy of Mass Art*, Noël Carroll writes that 'it is the point of mass art to engage mass audiences, and that mandates an inclination toward structures that will be readily accessible – virtually on contact and with little effort' (1998: 196). Kristin Thompson – discussing the definitive mass artform, Hollywood cinema – argues that the 'ideal' American film 'centers around a well-structured, carefully motivated series of events that the spectator can comprehend relatively easily' (1999: 8). Beyond a handful of outliers – such as *The Big Sleep* (1946), *2001: A Space Odyssey* (1968), *Nashville* (1975) and *Mulholland Drive* (2001) – Hollywood makes what David Bordwell calls 'excessively obvious' movies (Bordwell, Staiger and Thompson 1985: 3).

But the fact that Hollywood typically makes movies that spectators find easy to understand does not mean audiences watch passively. If the movies did not offer any challenges, people would feel bored. Experimental psychology research can help us to understand how moderate challenge can excite pleasure for a mass audience. Indeed, because such research typically deals with average responses, it has particular relevance to mass artforms which, by definition, appeal to the average consumer.

A series of studies on aesthetic judgements, many conducted by Daniel Berlyne (1971) and his colleagues, found that people perceive minimally challenging works as boring, overly challenging works as unpleasant, and moderately challenging works as pleasing. Such studies typically graph the relationship between 'pleasingness' and potentially 'arousing' stimuli as an inverted-U (Figure 1.1). The graph indicates that subjects prefer challenging properties (novelty, complexity, incongruity, etc.) in increasing intensity until some optimal level, at which point subjects start to become overwhelmed, and their pleasure diminishes and eventually turns to displeasure. The findings – which pertain to paintings, music, literature, movies, pictures, and other arts – have held up cross-culturally (Berlyne 1980; Triandis 1980; Imamoglu 2000; van Mulken, le Pair and Forceville 2010) and have come to seem almost inevitable (Chmiel and Schubert 2017).[2]

Berlyne relied on a psychobiological theory that measures responses to potentially arousing objects. The theory does little to explain the pleasures that

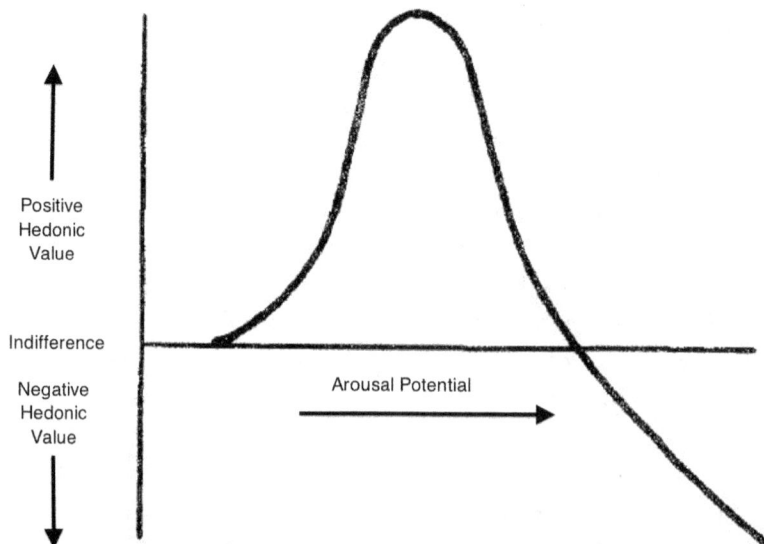

Figure 1.1. Berlyne's graph of the relationship between potentially arousing stimuli and 'pleasingness' (1971: 89). Figure created by Todd Berliner.

result from cognitive engagement. For Berlyne, pleasure is merely a biological response to stimuli. By contrast, aesthetic philosophers typically focus on *pleasures of the mind*, including what Beardsley calls the 'exhilaration' of 'active discovery' (1979: 741). Research in cognitive psychology provides some illumination here. Some research suggests that spectators take pleasure from creative problem solving, incongruity resolution, insight, and stress relief.

Studies of humour help us to understand some of the pleasures of cognitive challenge. According to one theory, humour results when someone meets with an incongruity and feels motivated to resolve it. Consider the Woody Allen joke in which a group of prisoners escape, 'twelve of them chained together at the ankle, getting by the guards posing as an immense charm bracelet'. The incongruity comes from the fact that charm bracelets are never that big. However, a resolution seems possible because prisoners chained at the ankle have an appearance oddly similar to a charm bracelet. Although we do not rationally believe that such a ruse could work, the joke enables a potential resolution the moment we find a connection within the incongruous information.[3]

The Incongruity Theory of humour dates back to Aristotle's *Rhetoric*, and was advanced further by Kant, Beattie, Schopenhauer and others. For humour theorist John Morreall, the value of incongruity rests in the 'drive to seek variety in our cognitive input' (1987: 201). Too much congruity gets boring, whereas incongruity enlivens our cognition. 'Instead of following well-worn mental paths of attention and thought,' Morreall says, 'we switch to new paths, notice things we didn't notice before, and countenance possibilities, and even absurdities, as easily as actualities' (1983: 91).

Incongruity Theory can help us to understand some of the pleasures sparked by challenging narrative artworks. As Morreall observes, '[w]e enjoy incongruity in other ways than by being amused' (1987: 204). Challenging narratives create incongruity by presenting story information that conflicts with expectations or other information. Mystery films, such as *DOA* (1945), *Chinatown* (1974) and *Looper* (2012), regularly traffic in puzzling incongruities. However, every Hollywood film violates expectations through some degree of incongruity, requiring that we adjust our understanding of the story in light of surprising narrative information. Literary theorist Frank Kermode acknowledged the prevalence of surprise in fiction when he said that a 'story that proceeded very simply to its obviously predestined end would be nearer myth than novel or drama' (1967: 18). Like incongruities in jokes, incongruities in narratives exercise our cognitive agility, adding richness and variety to works that would otherwise seem obvious, dull and predictable.

Cognitive research on 'insight' provides additional support for the notion that people enjoy incongruities, provided they can resolve them. 'Insight' refers to the 'aha' moment when someone suddenly grasps a solution to a mental problem (Metcalfe 1986; Kaplan and Simon 1990). Faced with an incongruity in the environment, we endeavour to resolve the problem creatively and restore consistency to our beliefs. With insight, a solution pops into consciousness as we understand relationships among elements in a new way or break free of unwarranted assumptions (Mayer 1992). Abundant scientific evidence supports the existence of this moment of sudden apprehension, and further evidence testifies to the pleasures that accompany it (Seifert et al. 1994; Gick and Lockhart 1995; Gruber 1995; Jung-Beeman et al. 2004). A twist film like *Witness for the Prosecution* (1957), for example, sparks insight when it reveals that a character who we thought loathed our protagonist defendant was actually working to exonerate him the entire time. The revelation resolves incongruities in the plot and enables a series of pleasurable insights as we retrace and reinterpret earlier scenes in light of the twist: 'aha!'

More like free association than crisp reasoning or intellectual scrutiny, insight requires imagination, but it can be prompted. In one classic insight study, Maier (1931) placed subjects in a room with various objects and instructed participants to tie together two strings hanging from the ceiling. The strings, however, fell too far apart to hold at the same time. The solution came to those few participants who spontaneously thought to create a pendulum motion by tying an object to one string. Although most subjects failed to see the solution, researchers found that they could guide participants towards insight by 'accidentally' bumping into one of the strings as they left the room. Movies such as *Witness for the Prosecution* prompt just this sort of insight when they guide us to tie together the strings of the narrative in a new way.

Insight relieves the stress created by cognitive challenge – a tension-release pattern that has intrigued some aesthetic researchers, particularly those who study music. Musicologist Leonard Meyer wrote the seminal work on music psychology, in which he writes: 'The greater the buildup of suspense, of tension, the greater the emotional release upon resolution' (1956: 28). Cognitive musicologist David Huron argues that delaying an expected musical outcome 'creates a longer and more intense period of tension' (2006: 314). Music psychologist Jamshed Bharucha argues that a 'dissonant musical event often has a dynamic quality, inducing an expectation of resolution to a following consonant event' (1994: 485). The interplay between instability and stability adds variety and emotional diversity to an artwork, arousing stress at first and then relieving it.

Psychologist Daniel Kahneman (1999) has conducted studies that suggest that people enjoy moments of emotional stability and satisfaction after a period of emotional intensity. He found that two factors predicted subjects' retrospective evaluation of an episode: (1) the intensity of the peak emotion recorded during the episode (in the case of aversive episodes, the worst moment); and (2) a positive final emotion, recorded just before an episode's end. Michael Kubovy, reviewing psychology research pertaining to 'pleasures of the mind', concludes that 'some distributions of emotions over time are particularly pleasurable, such as episodes in which the peak emotion is strong and the final emotion positive' (1999: 44). Such findings lend further support to the notion that tension-release patterns lead to pleasure.

Together, these theories and empirical findings suggest that average spectators enjoy experiences that involve: (1) an amount of cognitive challenge sufficient to engage perceivers' mental capacities but not so great as to thwart the effort to achieve understanding, insight and incongruity-resolution; (2) a dynamic of emotions, including an intense peak emotion; and (3) a release from tension and a favourable final emotion. These conclusions sound a lot like a Hollywood formula for mass viewer engagement: moderate cognitive labour and intense emotions, followed by a feel-good ending.

Moderate Challenge in *The Philadelphia Story*

We can turn to any number of Hollywood films to illustrate the formula I laid out in the previous paragraph. We could, for instance, look at movies with ambiguous protagonists or anti-heroes – a common narrative device in Hollywood, found in such films as *Red River* (1948), *White Heat* (1949), *Winchester 73* (1950), *Pickup on South Street* (1953), *The Searchers* (1956), *The French Connection* (1971), *The Godfather* (1972) and *Joker* (2019). These and countless other Hollywood films contain moral inconsistencies that require cognitive effort to resolve. We could say something similar about Hollywood's fondness for engaging villains, evidenced in such films as *Angels with Dirty Faces* (1938), *The Maltese Falcon* (1941), *The Third*

Man (1949), *Cape Fear* (1962), *Blade Runner* (1982), *Wall Street* (1987) and *The Dark Knight* (2008). We could examine Hollywood films with narrative convolutions or gaps, which make it difficult, at times, to find causal linkages between story elements, including *The Big Sleep* (1946), *The Killing* (1956), *2001: A Space Odyssey* (1968), *The Godfather, Part II* (1974), *Blade Runner* (1982), *Back to the Future, Part II* (1989) and *Source Code* (2011). Or, we could examine twist films such as *And Then There Were None* (1945), *Planet of the Apes* (1968), *Fight Club* (1999), *A Beautiful Mind* (2001), *The Prestige* (2006) and other films that spur audiences to suddenly revise their understanding of the story and its direction.

These are, for the most part, famously challenging movies, at least by Hollywood standards. But what if we instead turn to a movie that is challenging without ever seeming to be so? *The Philadelphia Story* (1940) is often regarded as an exemplar of classical Hollywood cinema of the studio era. The MGM screwball comedy, directed by George Cukor and closely adapted from Philip Barry's hit stage play, always feels light and straightforward; no one would describe it as a 'puzzle film'. Immensely popular upon its release in 1940, it received rave reviews, earned six Oscar nominations and two wins, and resurrected the film career of Katharine Hepburn. The film has since become a beloved classic and appears on numerous 'best' lists, including AFI's top ten romantic comedies of all time.

The Philadelphia Story, however, poses moderate challenges for spectators trying to make sense of the film. By peppering an otherwise straightforward plot with incidental bits of narrative incongruity, the film illustrates how a mass artform like Hollywood cinema will sometimes insert trivial challenges into a work that would otherwise seem 'excessively obvious'. Because classical Hollywood films are wedded to time-tested principles for generating aesthetic pleasure for mass audiences, films such as *The Philadelphia Story* can risk a handful of inconsistencies and story-logic violations without sacrificing classical Hollywood's formal unity. Indeed, the film is stabilized by all of Hollywood's traditional narrative structures (a goal-oriented protagonist, obstacles to goal attainment, deadlines, a definitive resolution, etc.) and genre conventions typical of screwball (an intelligent female lead character, a battle between the sexes, quick and witty dialogue, a divorce-remarriage plot). Consequently, we never have cause to worry that the film might undermine its solid classical structure.

Elsewhere, I have argued that many Hollywood films that offer exhilarating aesthetic experiences over extended periods demand an unusual amount of cognitive challenge compared to more typical Hollywood films; however, they never sacrifice a mass audience's ability to cope with the challenge. Hollywood films that endure, I argued, often take aesthetic risks, sparking exhilarated pleasure when they seem on the verge of confounding spectators in an unusual way (Berliner 2017: 30). *The Philadelphia Story*, I want to show, takes such risks. Even though the film may seem to be well structured and effortlessly understood, the narrative is more misshapen and challenging than it appears. The film feels perfectly unified and logical, and yet it is not.

The story concerns Tracy Lord (Katharine Hepburn), a Philadelphia socialite who has divorced C.K. Dexter Haven (Cary Grant), tossing him out, we learn, because of his drinking. Two years later, she intends to marry nouveau riche businessman George Kittredge (John Howard), whom no one but Tracy seems to like. The plot primarily concerns the efforts of various characters – including Dexter, writer Mike Connor (James Stewart) and Tracy's younger sister Dinah (Virginia Weidler) – to prevent the impending marriage, scheduled to take place that weekend. Dexter wants not only to thwart Tracy's marriage but also to persuade Tracy to develop tolerance: 'You'll never be a first-class human being or a first-class woman,' he tells her, 'until you've learned to have some regard for human frailty'. Meanwhile, Mike falls for Tracy and ultimately competes with George and Dexter for her affection. By the film's climax, the audience's desire for Tracy to reject George reaches peak intensity, but the question remains whether she should instead marry Dexter or Mike. In the end, she remarries Dexter, restoring order to the storyworld through a happy resolution.

The film closely follows the Hollywood formula I articulated at the end of the previous section: moderate cognitive labour, intense emotions, followed by a feel-good ending. I want to focus on the *moderate cognitive labour* part of the formula because my plot description ignores several narrative incongruities that crop up in the film's last two scenes. Such incongruities threaten the perfect unity of the film's conclusion. Although *The Philadelphia Story* is a comedy, the incongruities are not flagrant enough to generate humour. Yet, they have an effect akin to humour because, like a joke, they prompt us to resolve incongruous story information creatively. Many of the incongruities come right at the end of the film when pressures for closure and audience expectations for harmonious resolution are strongest. *The Philadelphia Story* goes a little haywire right at the moment it is tying everything up. Let me explain.

Tracy rejects George towards the end of the film because he suspects her of having slept with Mike on the eve of her wedding day, demonstrating George's apparently unforgivable lack of faith in her. The fact that Tracy herself thought that she had slept with Mike does not seem to interfere with spectators' willingness to accept her rationale for dumping her fiancé. Indeed, we too suspect that Tracy has slept with Mike, since, as George rightly points out, 'all the evidence was there': a passionate kiss (Figure 1.2), Tracy succumbing to Mike's affection ('put me in your pocket, Mike'), then a dash off to the pool, followed by Mike amorously carting a visibly smitten Tracy, drunk and barely dressed, in what looks like post-coital reverie (Figure 1.3). Dinah also witnesses the proceedings and thinks Mike and Tracy have had an affair, and, if all of that were not evidence enough, Tracy herself admitted to George that they did ('on the very eve of your wedding,' George admonishes, 'an affair with another man!' 'I told you I agree, George, and I'll tell you again good riddance to me'). Still, we blame George for believing what Tracy, Dinah and we ourselves believed until Mike clears up the confusion. Indeed, the only reason Tracy and Mike did not have sex, we learn from Mike, was that he refrained because of her drunkenness; Tracy was willing. Nonetheless, we accept her rebuke of George ('somehow I'd have hoped that you'd think better of me than I did') and support her decision to leave him because he assumed she did what she admitted to doing and would indeed have done had Mike showed less restraint. The story logic here takes a bit of effort and creativity to resolve.[4]

More difficult to resolve is the contradiction that the reason for dumping George now (that he does not think highly enough of Tracy) precisely opposes the reason the movie has previously given for George's unsuitability for her (that he thinks *too* highly of Tracy). 'You're like some marvellous distant queen', George says to her earlier in the film, right after Dexter chastises Tracy for behaving like a 'virgin goddess'. We listened disapprovingly as George told Tracy he 'worships' her, yet I doubt we consciously register the incongruity when, at the climax, the film casts him aside for the opposite reason. Then, a moment after Tracy accuses George of judging her 'guilty straight off', she gives *another* reason for leaving him that cancels out the alibi she had given not a minute before: 'You're too good for me, George,' she says, 'you're a hundred times too good'.

I suspect that we fail to notice that Tracy's reasons utterly oppose one another because we are looking for any excuse for Tracy to reject George. The film had already inspired our antipathy for George, so his description of Tracy as a 'distant queen' merely offered a pretext for the unfavourable impression George made upon

Figures 1.2 and 1.3. Signs of Tracy's infidelity in *The Philadelphia Story* (1940). Screen captures by Todd Berliner.

us with his stiff, abrasive manner, his inability to mount a horse, and his blunder in thinking the horse's name was Bessie when it was Jack. George, moreover, makes an unfavourable impression on characters we like and, set next to either Cary Grant's Dexter or James Stewart's Mike, looks a pompous fool. Since we already consider George a bad mate for Tracy (not for the various reasons the movie offers but because we do not like him), the fact that Tracy's reasons do not logically coordinate with one another does not have enough urgency to gain our attention. Had we liked George, we might have considered her reasons more closely.

Moreover, although Tracy's various reasons do not cohere, the lines of dialogue that present those reasons do sound vaguely similar: 'It's what I first worshipped you for' (George to Tracy); 'Somehow I'd have hoped that you'd think better of me than I did' (Tracy to George); and 'You're too good for me' (Tracy to George). Therefore, in the absence of the kind of scrutiny that I am applying to them, the justifications seem coherent enough to excuse Tracy's rejection of him. In short, the moment when Tracy rejects George makes sense only because we *want* it to make sense and because the demands of romantic comedy insist that the moment must make sense.

I have yet to describe the climax's most illogical moment – the moment of Tracy's maturation into a 'first-class person' (to use Dexter's phrase) or into 'a human being' (to use Tracy's). When Tracy finds herself having to announce to the wedding guests that her marriage to George is off, Dexter says to Tracy, 'You've been got out of jams before ... you always have been'. Tracy then resolves, 'I won't be got out of anything anymore'. The movie induces spectators to understand that Tracy's resolution signals her redemption, and the moment seems to make sense unless one recalls that, far from having to be 'got out of' things, Tracy has had precisely the opposite problem. Have not the terms of Tracy's redemption stipulated, as Dexter says to her early in the film, that she must lose her 'prejudice against weakness' and that her 'own foot [should] slip a little sometime', but her 'sense of inner divinity wouldn't allow that'? Philosopher Stanley Cavell considers those words to be Dexter's chief criticism of Tracy (1981: 148). Spectators probably regard them as the thematic heart of the movie – that is, until the final scene when, to make sense of the story logic, spectators must imagine that they have just witnessed a story about a woman who continually gets into jams from which others must rescue her.

In fact, the *only* scene in the movie in which we see someone get Tracy out of anything is the very scene in which she resolves that she 'won't be got out of anything anymore'. Immediately after the movie invites us to understand that, for once, Tracy is going to take charge of her own life (even though we have seen her run her own life ever since the movie's first scene), she turns to Dexter when she cannot find the words to tell the wedding guests that she and George have cancelled the wedding. Dexter gets her out of the jam by feeding her lines, which she slavishly repeats to the guests, including the announcement that she plans to remarry Dexter.

So, to summarize the story logic at the climax of the movie: the narrative first asks us to understand that Tracy's redemption comes when she resolves to be the autonomous woman that she has been all along, and then it asks us to understand that she is redeemed when, for the first time in the movie, she does not behave autonomously and does precisely the opposite of what she has just resolved to do. There is no way to make that moment make sense; go ahead and try.

How can we justify the aesthetic value of a climax so riddled with violations of story logic? And how can we account for the fact that *The Philadelphia Story* has one of Hollywood's most admired screenplays, earning scriptwriter Donald Ogden Stewart an Oscar in 1941? Moreover, Barry's stage play, which contains the same incongruities, had such a successful Broadway run in 1939 that the play helped to rescue the Shubert theatre from bankruptcy. The writers, furthermore, could easily have constructed the film's climax coherently. They could have found a consistent reason for Tracy to dump George; and if Dexter had said to Tracy, 'For once in your life, forget your composure and follow my lead', then the ending would have avoided its most explicit incongruities and Tracy's redemption would have proceeded logically. An hour more on the script and the story could have made perfect sense.

To explain the aesthetic value of the film's climax, we must rethink common assumptions about story logic. I propose that *The Philadelphia Story*'s logical flaws do not result in aesthetic flaws. On the contrary, I propose that they add aesthetic value to the narration by providing the spectator with enduring opportunities for creative problem solving, insight, and incongruity resolution. At the climax, spectators must attempt to quickly resolve a series of incongruities in order to prevent the narrative from collapsing into disarray. Beardsley calls this effort 'active discovery' (1979: 741). Faced with inconsistencies in the film's plot, spectators can enjoy the exhilaration of active discovery as they try to make sense of the narrative.

How might spectators go about making this incoherent climax intelligible? I suspect methods may differ for different spectators, but it is worth noting that spectators have likely been puzzling over Tracy throughout the movie and may experience the puzzles at the climax as an extension of deep complexities they have already sensed in the character. Indeed, Hepburn's commanding performance unifies a mass of inconsistent character traits: weakness and strength, autonomy and vulnerability, superiority and insecurity, decisiveness and ambivalence, authority and submissiveness, prudishness and sexuality. Tracy changes from scene to scene, often moment to moment, a dynamism within the character enhanced by Hepburn's dynamism as a performer. We must *actively discover* Tracy and piece her together out of inconsistent information.

Take, for example, the complexity of personalities, emotions and attitudes expressed by Hepburn in just one shot in a scene between Tracy and Mike just before they head to the pool. In this long take, which lasts just under two minutes, Hepburn merges her character's inconsistencies into a unified performance. The shot begins with the two actors facing each other, their noses practically touching, her lips parted, her waist bent, eyes turned upward, in an obvious gesture of flirtation (Figure 1.4). 'You can't marry that guy', Mike warns. His statement sparks the slightest sign of surprise in her as she stiffens and her shoulders fall backwards. She looks like she plans to say something, then thinks better of it. The brief moment is followed by expressions of concern and disappointment in Hepburn's face and voice – she turns away from Mike, looking at nothing (Figure 1.5), and stumbles when she asks, 'why – why not?' However, she quickly recovers her confidence ('Then the fault's with *me*'), appearing more resigned (Figure 1.6). Within about ten seconds of screen time, Hepburn has already expressed Tracy's sensuality, surprise, disappointment, concern, doubt, determination and confidence.

In the remainder of the shot, Hepburn finds the slightest cues in the script that enable her to express the complexity of Tracy's character – a combination of desire, flirtation, standoffishness, judgement, vulnerability, uncertainty, theatricality, and a variety of other, often very brief, emotions and character traits, many of them conflicting or ambiguous. As Mike continues to make a case for calling off the wedding, she chastises him, calling him a 'snob', but seems to be flirting with him at the same time. She gives him a contemptuous once-over with her eyes when she says, 'You're the worst kind there is – an intellectual snob',

Figures 1.4–1.6. Katharine Hepburn looking flirtatious, then concerned, then resigned in *The Philadelphia Story* (1940). Screen captures by Todd Berliner.

drawing out the word 'in-te-llectual' and giving 'snaahhb' an exaggerated New England inflection to express her scorn. At the same time, she moves her face towards and away from his in an unmistakably seductive manner. With the line, 'The time to make up your mind about people is never', Hepburn says the first part with sternness, like a teacher scolding her students, but when she reaches 'is never', her voice softens and becomes breathy. Nothing in the words 'is never' suggests flirtation – that is Hepburn's contribution to the line. When she follows up that line with 'Yes, you are', she leaves her lips parted sensuously at the end of 'are', touching her tongue to the roof of her mouth, studying his eyes closely (Figure 1.7). I imagine audiences can find reasons for Tracy's ambivalent behaviour – somewhere in the realm of character psychology – but, again to quote Beardsley's definition of 'active discovery', we are nonetheless 'challenged by a variety of potentially conflicting stimuli to try to make them cohere'.

In the remainder of the shot, Hepburn adds more 'potentially conflicting stimuli' to her characterization of Tracy, as well as greater ambiguity. Again, the script presents Hepburn with only hints of inconsistency, but her nuanced performance enhances them, making the character more complex and intriguing. At this point in the shot, Tracy's oscillation between aloofness and flirtation seems to motivate Mike to resume his lovemaking: 'You're quite a girl, aren't you?' 'I know any number like me', she replies and, for an instant, we see doubt on her face – her upper lip curls, suggesting the slightest bit of shyness and worry (Figure 1.8). Why? Is his praise having the desired effect on her? Might she be losing control of the conversation? When Mike stands and puts distance between them, as the camera pulls back to a medium-long shot, she withdraws from him, and her body language now signals unfriendliness and judgement. 'You're just a mass of prejudice, aren't you?' she says, tossing her head back imperiously and histrionically (Figure 1.9), a theatrical gesture we have seen her perform before. She follows that gesture with a pouty expression (Figure 1.10). Is she disappointed now that their lovemaking might be over? She approaches him, stands proudly, and scolds, 'Your intolerance infuriates me', her voice too loud, given how close she has moved towards him – an inviting gesture performed at the very instant of her rebuke (Figure 1.11). Catching herself, she adopts a false tone: 'Aren't the geraniums pretty, professor?' As she turns away from him, she allows some worry to cross her face the moment it is out of Mike's view (Figure 1.12); we can only guess what's worrying her now. Before the shot ends, she stands like a coquette

AESTHETICS AND 'ACTIVE DISCOVERY' · 35

Figures 1.7 and 1.8. Hepburn's performance quickly shifts from sensuality to worry in *The Philadelphia Story* (1940). Screen captures by Todd Berliner.

against a pillar (Figure 1.13), a posture that Hepburn turns, finally, into one of bashfulness (Figure 1.14).

Moments like these suggest a complex Tracy, a more inconsistent character than the one described in plot summaries of the movie and one that requires some attention and thoughtfulness on the part of the audience to follow and sort out. In this way, the incongruities in the movie's final moments magnify those we have witnessed in the character throughout the film. At the climax, it seems that our main character is changing in potentially meaningful, even profound,

Figures 1.9–1.14. Dynamic changes in Hepburn's performance of Tracy, from theatricality (Figure 1.9) to pouting (Figure 1.10), to combined severity and intimacy (Figure 1.11), to worry (Figure 1.12), to coquettishness (Figure 1.13), to bashfulness (Figure 1.14) in *The Philadelphia Story* (1940). Screen captures by Todd Berliner.

ways – changes so profound that we can hardly understand them. Some of them we do not understand, I argue, because they do not make sense.

Would the climax of *The Philadelphia Story* have been better if it had made better sense? Would it be preferable to have incongruity *and* story logic? I think not. Screenwriters call an incongruity that has a logical resolution a 'reversal': a revelation that suddenly changes narrative direction. Reversals are the defining characteristic of twist films like *Whatever Happened to Baby Jane* (1962), *The Usual Suspects* (1995) and *The Sixth Sense* (1999). But a reversal creates only a moment of surprise when spectators confront a narrative incongruity and use logic to revise their story hypotheses. Hence, although momentarily thrilling, using logic to resolve incongruities ultimately quashes the pleasure of incongruity-resolution by erasing the incongruity once and for all. Resolving incongruity with logic leaves one without incongruity. That is why a twist in a twist film or an incongruity in a joke only really works once. Although one can use logic to understand twists and jokes, the pleasures of twists and jokes come not from understanding them but rather from the flash of insight when, in the face of incongruous information, we suddenly rethink relationships among story elements and break free from our assumptions. It is the transition, not the understanding, that we find pleasurable.

Works that contain 'conflicting stimuli' that logic cannot reconcile provide enduring aesthetic pleasure. *The Philadelphia Story* offers spectators various opportunities for incongruity resolution, and it preserves the flash of insight required to follow the narrative by maintaining both the resolution and the incongruity. Whenever one rewatches the film, one must, once again, rethink relationships among narrative elements and break free from prior assumptions. Hence, the film enables one to enjoy insight and incongruity-resolution without the mastery that would annihilate the incongruity and mar the film's enduring ability to provide pleasure. Imagine a joke so subtle and tenacious that it enabled you to experience incongruity and resolution that were not mutually exclusive; you might never grow tired of it. Like a beloved movie, that is a joke you could enjoy again and again.

Conclusion

The essays in this volume focus on puzzling artworks that perceivers find puzzling, but there are also puzzling works that perceivers do not find puzzling. Perceivers may never realize that they have endeavoured to fix an artwork's story logic, resolve its inconsistencies and make the work intelligible. Perceivers of *The Philadelphia Story*, I hope I have shown, can only make sense of the narrative through 'active discovery'.

I began this chapter by arguing that cognitive challenge is fundamental to aesthetic experience. Mass artforms must balance the aesthetic pleasures of cognitive challenge against the need for easy understanding by mass audiences. Hollywood cinema and other mass artforms rarely create undue challenges for spectators or violate classical narrative principles in a pervasive way. Such principles serve to make the works unified, stable and comprehensible for a mass audience. But some celebrated mass artworks contain slightly misshapen narratives, even though the narratives may come across as flawlessly designed and easy to understand. Compared to explicitly puzzling artworks, *The Philadelphia Story* seems like a breeze, but the narrative blows a few puzzle pieces our way, and 'active discovery' offers us some hope of connecting them.

Todd Berliner, Professor of Film Studies at the University of North Carolina, Wilmington, teaches film aesthetics, narration and style, and American film history. He is the author of *Hollywood Aesthetic: Pleasure in American Cinema* (Oxford University Press, 2017) and *Hollywood Incoherent: Narration in Seventies Cinema* (University of Texas Press, 2010). He was the founding chairman of UNCW's Film Studies Department and the recipient of two Fulbright Scholar awards, including the Laszlo Orszagh Distinguished Chair in American Studies.

Notes

1. Viewer comments on these movies come from Amazon, IMDB and Reddit.
2. In a meta-study that reviewed inverted-U model findings from 115 years of music psychology, Chmiel and Schubert (2017) found that 87.7 per cent of studies comport with the model. Some researchers have reinterpreted Berlyne's results using theories other than Berlyne's psychobiological theory (Martindale, Moore and Borkum 1990; Silvia 2005), but the inverted-U findings themselves remain largely persistent.
3. For a fuller discussion of the pleasure of incongruity-resolution in narrative, see Berliner 2017, pp. 60–64.

4. I use the word 'logic' not in the strict sense employed by logicians but as it is regularly used in narratology to denote the relationship between narrative elements or the relationship between an element and the whole. See Chatman 1978 and Herman 2002.

References

Armstrong, Thomas, and Brian Detweiler-Bedell. 2008. 'Beauty as an Emotion: The Exhilarating Prospect of Mastering a Challenging World', *Review of General Psychology* 12(4): 305–29.

Axelsson, Östen. 2007. 'Individual Differences in Preferences to Photographs', *Psychology of Aesthetics, Creativity, and the Arts* 1(2): 61–72.

Beardsley, Monroe C. 1979. 'In Defense of Aesthetic Value', *Proceedings and Addresses of the American Philosophical Association* 52(6): 723–49.

Berliner, Todd. 2017. *Hollywood Aesthetic: Pleasure in American Cinema*. New York: Oxford University Press.

Berlyne, Daniel E. 1971. *Aesthetics and Psychobiology*. New York: Appleton-Century-Crofts.

———. 1980. 'Psychological Aesthetics', in H.C. Traindis and W.J. Lonner (eds), *Handbook of Cross-Cultural Psychology*, vol. 3. Boston: Allyn and Bacon, pp. 323–61.

Bharucha, Jamshed J. 1994. 'Tonality and Expectation', in R. Aiello and J. Sloboda (eds), *Musical Perceptions*. New York: Oxford University Press, pp. 213–39.

Bordwell, David, Janet Staiger and Kristin Thompson. 1985. *The Classical Hollywood Cinema: Film Style and Mode of Production to 1960*. New York: Columbia University Press.

Carroll, Noël. 1998. *A Philosophy of Mass Art*. Oxford: Clarendon.

———. 1999. *Philosophy of Art: An Introduction*. London: Routledge.

Cavell, Stanley. 1981. *Pursuits of Happiness: The Hollywood Comedy of Remarriage*. Cambridge, MA: Harvard University Press.

Chamorro-Premuzic, Tomas, Charlotte Burke, Anne Hsu and Viren Swami. 2010. 'Personality Predictors of Artistic Preferences as a Function of the Emotional Valence and Perceived Complexity of Paintings', *Psychology of Aesthetics, Creativity, and the Arts* 4(4): 196–204.

Chatman, Seymour. 1978. *Story and Discourse: Narrative Structure in Fiction and Film*. New York: Cornell University Press.

Chmiel, Anthony, and Emily Schubert. 2017. 'Back to the Inverted-U for Music Preference: A Review of the Literature'. *Psychology of Music* 45(6): 886–909.

Dewey, John. (1934) 1980. *Art as Experience*. New York: Putnam.

Fayn, Kirill, Carolyn MacCann, Niko Tiliopoulos and Paul J. Silvia. 2015. 'Aesthetic Emotions and Aesthetic People: Openness Predicts Sensitivity to Novelty in the Experiences of Interest and Pleasure', *Frontiers in Psychology* 6(1877): 1–11.

Feist, Gregory J., and Tara R. Brady. 2004. 'Openness to Experience, Non-Conformity, and the Preference for Abstract Art', *Empirical Studies of the Arts* 22(1): 77–89.

Furnham, Adrian, and Margaret Avison. 1997. 'Personality and Preference for Surreal Paintings', *Personality and Individual Differences* 23(6): 923–35.

Gick, Mary L., and Robert S. Lockhart. 1995. 'Cognitive and Affective Components of Insight', in Robert J. Sternberg and Janet E. Davidson (eds), *The Nature of Insight*. Cambridge, MA: MIT Press, pp. 197–228.

Gruber, Howard. 1995 'Insight and Affect in the History of Science', in Robert J. Sternberg and Janet E. Davidson (eds), *The Nature of Insight*. Cambridge, MA: MIT Press, pp. 397–432.

Hekkert, Paul, and Piet C.W. van Wieringen. 1996. 'Beauty in the Eye of Expert and Nonexpert Beholders: A Study in the Appraisal of Art', *The American Journal of Psychology* 109(3): 389–407.

Herman, David. 2002. *Story Logic: Problems and Possibilities of Narrative*. Lincoln, NE: University of Nebraska Press.

Heyduk, Ronald G. 1975. 'Rated Preference for Musical Compositions as it Relates to Complexity and Exposure Frequency', *Perception & Psychophysics* 17(1): 84–91.

Huron, David. 2006. *Sweet Anticipation: Music and the Psychology of Expectation*. Cambridge, MA: MIT Press.

Imamoglu, Çagri. 2000. 'Complexity, Liking and Familiarity: Architecture and Non-Architecture Turkish Students' Assessments of Traditional and Modern House Facades', *Journal of Environmental Psychology* 20(1): 5–16.

John, Oliver P., and Sanjay Srivastava. 1999. 'The Big Five Trait Taxonomy: History, Measurement, and Theoretical Perspectives', in Lawrence A. Pervin and Oliver P. John (eds), *Handbook of Personality: Theory and Research*, 2nd edn. New York: Guilford Press, pp. 102–39.

Jung-Beeman, Mark, Edward M. Bowden, Jason Haberman, Jennifer L. Frymiare, Stella Arambel-Liu, Richard Greenblatt, Paul J. Reber and John Kounios. 2004. 'Neural Activity when People Solve Verbal Problems with Insight', *Public Library of Science: Biology* 2(4): 500–510.

Kahneman, Daniel. 1999. 'Objective Happiness', in Daniel Kahneman, Ed Diener and Norbert Schwarz (eds), *Well-Being: The Foundations of Hedonic Psychology*. New York: Russell Sage Foundation, pp. 3–25.

Kant, Immanuel. (1790) 1987. *Critique of Judgment*, trans. Werner S. Pluhar. Indianapolis, IN: Hackett.

Kaplan, Craig A., and Herbert A. Simon. 1990. 'In Search of Insight', *Cognitive Psychology* 22(3): 374–419.

Kermode, Frank. 1967. *The Sense of an Ending*. New York: Oxford University Press.

Koffka, Kurt. (1935) 2013. *Principles of Gestalt Psychology*. New York: Routledge.

Kubovy, Michael. 1999. 'On the Pleasures of the Mind', in Daniel Kahneman, Ed Diener and Norbert Schwarz (eds), *Well-Being: The Foundations of Hedonic Psychology*. New York: Russell Sage Foundation, pp. 135–54.

Langlois, Judith H., and Lori A. Roggman. 1990. 'Attractive Faces Are Only Average', *Psychological Science* 1(2): 115–21.

Leder, H., B. Belke, A. Oeberst and D. Augustin. 2004. 'A Model of Aesthetic Appreciation and Aesthetic Judgements', *British Journal of Psychology* 95(4): 489–508.

Lee-Baggley, Dayna, Melady Preece and Anita DeLongis. 2005. 'Coping with Interpersonal Stress: Role of Big Five Traits', *Journal of Personality* 73(5): 1141–80.

Levinson, Jerrold. 1996. *The Pleasures of Aesthetics: Philosophical Essays*. New York: Cornell University Press.

Maier, Norman Raymond Frederick. 1931. 'Reasoning in Humans. II. The Solution of a Problem and Its Appearance in Consciousness', *Journal of Comparative Psychology* 12(2): 181–94.

Martindale, Colin, Kathleen Moore and Jonathan Borkum. 1990. 'Aesthetic Preference: Anomalous Findings for Berlyne's Psychobiological Theory', *American Journal of Psychology* 103(1): 53–80.

Mayer, Richard E. 1992. *Thinking, Problem Solving, Cognition*, 2nd edn. New York: Worth.

McCrae, Robert R. 2007. 'Aesthetic Chills as a Universal Marker of Openness to Experience', *Motivation and Emotion* 31(1): 5–11.

Metcalfe, Janet. 1986. 'Feeling of Knowing in Memory and Problem Solving', *Journal of Experimental Psychology: Learning, Memory, and Cognition* 12(2): 288–94.

Meyer, Leonard B. 1956. *Emotion and Meaning in Music*. Chicago: University of Chicago Press.

Millis, Keith. 2001. 'Making Meaning Brings Pleasure: The Influence of Titles on Aesthetic Experience', *Emotion* 1(3): 320–29.

Morreall, John. 1983. *Taking Laughter Seriously*. Albany: State University of New York Press.

———. 1987. 'Funny Ha-Ha, Funny Strange, and Other Reactions to Incongruity', in John Morreall (ed.), *The Philosophy of Laughter and Humor*. Albany: State University of New York Press, pp. 188–207.

Nehamas, Alexander. 2010. *Only a Promise of Happiness*. Princeton, NJ: Princeton University Press.

O'Brien, Tess B., and Anita DeLongis. 1996. 'The Interactional Context of Problem-, Emotion-, and Relationship-Focused Coping: The Role of the Big Five Personality Factors', *Journal of Personality* 64(4): 775–813.

Reber, Rolf. 2002. 'Reasons for the Preference for Symmetry', *Behavioral and Brain Sciences* 25(3): 415–16.

Reber, Rolf, Norbert Schwarz and Piotr Winkielman. 2004. 'Processing Fluency and Aesthetic Pleasure: Is Beauty in the Perceiver's Processing Experience?' *Personality and Social Psychology Review* 8(4): 364–82.

Rentfrow, Peter J., and Samuel D. Gosling. 2003. 'The Do Re Mi's of Everyday Life: The Structure and Personality Correlates of Music Preferences', *Journal of Personality and Social Psychology* 84(6): 1236–56.

Roese, Neal J., and Jeffrey W. Sherman. 2014. 'Expectancy', in Arie W. Kruglanski and E. Tory Higgins (eds), *Social Psychology: Handbook of Basic Principles*. New York: Guilford Publications, pp. 91–115.

Seifert, Colleen, David E. Meyer, Natalie Davidson, Andrea L. Patalano and Ilan Yaniv. 1994. 'Demystification of Cognitive Insight: Opportunistic Assimilation and the Prepared-Mind Perspective', in Robert J. Sternberg and Janet E. Davidson (eds), *The Nature of Insight*. Cambridge, MA: MIT Press, pp. 65–124.

Silvia, Paul J. 2005. 'Emotional Responses to Art: From Collation and Arousal to Cognition and Emotion'. *Review of General Psychology* 9(4): 342–57.

———. 2007. 'Knowledge-Based Assessment of Expertise in the Arts: Exploring Aesthetic Fluency', *Psychology of Aesthetics, Creativity, and the Arts* 1(4): 247–49.

Silvia, Paul J., and Christopher Berg. 2011. 'Finding Movies Interesting: How Expertise and Appraisals Influence the Aesthetic Experience of Film', *Empirical Studies of the Arts* 29(1): 73–88.

Smith, David J., and Robert J. Melara. 1990. 'Aesthetic Preference and Syntactic Prototypicality in Music: Tis the Gift to be Simple', *Cognition* 34(3): 279–98.

Thompson, Kristin. 1999. *Storytelling in the New Hollywood*. Cambridge, MA: Harvard University Press.

Triandis, Harry C. 1980. 'Reflections on Trends in Cross-Cultural Research', *Journal of Cross-Cultural Psychology* 11(1): 35–58.

van Mulken, Margot, Rob le Pair and Charles Forceville. 2010. 'The Impact of Perceived Complexity, Deviation and Comprehension on the Appreciation of Visual Metaphor in Advertising across Three European Countries', *Journal of Pragmatics* 42(12): 3418–30.

Watson, David, and Brock Hubbard. 1996. 'Adaptational Style and Dispositional Structure: Coping in the Context of the Five-Factor Model', *Journal of Personality* 64(4): 737–74.

Whittlesea, Bruce W.A. 1993. 'Illusions of Familiarity', *Journal of Experimental Psychology: Learning, Memory, and Cognition* 19(6): 1235–53.

Whittlesea, Bruce W.A., Larry L. Jacoby and Krista Girard. 1990. 'Illusions of Immediate Memory: Evidence of an Attributional Basis for Feelings of Familiarity and Perceptual Quality', *Journal of Memory and Language* 29(6): 716–32.

Winston, Andrew S., and Gerald C. Cupchik. 1992. 'The Evaluation of High Art and Popular Art by Naive and Experienced Viewers', *Visual Arts Research* 18(1): 1–14.

Zajonc, Robert B. 1968. 'Attitudinal Effects of Mere Exposure', *Journal of Personality and Social Psychology* 9(2, pt. 2): 1–27.

CHAPTER 2
Narration, Implicature and the Deceptive Puzzle Film
Warren Buckland

The puzzle film is cognitively challenging to the extent that spectators take pleasure in being tested and outwitted as if 'by magic'. Magic is the art of deception that manipulates rational thinking by undermining the everyday understanding of time, space, matter and causality. This type of deception plays a significant role in explaining how the puzzle film's narration challenges spectators. Narration becomes deceptive when it covertly violates the communicative function embedded in the implied author, a violation that hinders the spectator's construction of a coherent fictional storyworld. I interpret what Wayne Booth calls the implied author's norms in terms of H.P. Grice's pragmatic theory of conversational implicature. This pragmatic theory defines the underlying conventions of communication regarding the Cooperative Principle, cognitive categories, maxims of communicative behaviour, and two levels of meaning (direct and inferred).

In this chapter, I adopt Grice's theory in order to construct a hierarchy of four types of filmic narration (cooperative, discrepant, flouted and deceptive), which I define according to the degree to which each facilitates or obstructs the spectator's process of constructing a coherent mental representation of a film's storyworld, and illustrate them with examples from a mainstream classical narrative film (*Rear Window*, 1954) and a puzzle film (*Lost Highway*, 1997). From this hierarchy emerges the idea of the 'deceptive puzzle film', which I define as a puzzle film whose narration is permanently deceptive, in that it perpetually obstructs the spectator's ability to construct a coherent storyworld. It is the permanence of this obstruction that makes the deceptive puzzle film cognitively challenging.

The Implied Author

The implied author embodies the norms of storytelling. It is a useful concept to explain the selection of stylistic and narrational options in a film, and assists in pinpointing discrepancies between what is stated and what is inferred. Each film develops a distinct relation to these norms, choices and discrepancies, with the nature of the puzzle film being to challenge those norms. In previous discussions of the puzzle film, I identified several of its attributes (discussed below), including the concept of unreliable narration, but I did not develop that concept further. Investigating it now has led me to examine deceptive narration and the need to distinguish it from unreliable narration. Both of these developments require the implied author, or, at least, a certain (non-anthropomorphic, non-intentionalist, cognitive pragmatic) conception of the implied author.[1]

For Booth, unreliability is a matter of disconnection or variation of distance between different narrative agents: characters (in the fictional storyworld), the narrator (on the discursive level of narration) and the implied author (norms and standards of communication). Distance is measured in terms of the discrepancy or (non-)alignment of norms between these agents. Booth defines the narrator as '*reliable* when [it] speaks for or acts in accordance with the norms of the work (which is to say, the implied author's norms), *unreliable* when [it] does not' (Booth 1983: 158–59; emphasis in original). For Booth, unreliability names a narrator who has been duped by the implied author and reader, especially evident in deficiencies in communication (such as inconsistencies, contradictions, lies, deception and irony, where the implied meaning differs from the literal meaning).

We need to make two observations in the way Booth's ideas have been appropriated by film scholars. Firstly, as Matthias Brütsch (2014: 60) has made clear, the concept of unreliability in film studies does not refer to the duped narrator, but to a type of narration that dupes the spectator: it is the spectator (not the narrator) who is duped, and the cause of the deception is the narration. Tom Gunning's theory of the narrator system explains why narration is primary in film. Although film can depict a narrator on screen (an internal, explicit narrator), this narrator's presence is purely contingent. The more fundamental issue is whether an implicit or invisible narrator is permanently at work in all filmic storytelling. Gunning identifies this invisible narrator across the whole of film form:

> *The narrator system created an intervening narrator who comments on the action of the film through the form of the film itself. ... This narrator was not located off-screen, but was absorbed into the arrangement of the images themselves. The narrator system seems to 'read' the images to the audience in the very act of presenting them. This narrator is invisible, revealing its presence only by the way images are revealed on the screen. (Gunning 1991: 93)*

The narrator's existence is 'in' the narration in the way images are arranged and presented on screen – and because, in film, the 'narrator' is invisible, absorbed into the very fabric of the narration, narration becomes the primary and permanent feature of film. In film, the concept of unreliability is therefore conferred upon narration.

Secondly, to distinguish between unintended and purposeful unreliable narration, unreliability is understood as an integral part of the film's total design – a design attributable to the narration's distance from the implied author. Purposeful unreliable narration deviates from the implied author's norms of communication but signifies its unreliability, making it recognizable. By contrast, narration becomes deceptive only if it purposely deviates from the implied author's norms of communication *and* does not signify that deviation, making it unrecognizable.[2] For this reason, it is imperative to identify 'deceptive narration' as a category distinct from unreliable narration. But in what sense does narration purposely deviate from the implied author's norms of communication? For an answer, we must look at H.P. Grice's pragmatic theory of meaning and its concept of the 'conversational implicature'.

Conversational Implicatures

Grice's pragmatic theory comprises two levels of meaning (direct and inferred), a process of inference generation, and general conditions and constraints that govern this process. Direct meaning refers to the level of what is said (or literally conveyed), whereas inferred meaning refers to indirect (or speaker) meaning. The distinction separates explicit from implicit communication. Whereas direct meaning is encoded in the literal meaning of words, in the inferential component, the sender conveys an indirect meaning that goes beyond literal meaning. The receiver needs to generate a series of inferences to recover the potential meanings of the message; a speaker purposely creates a message that aims to modify the receiver's mental representation of an event or situation.

For the modification to take place, the receiver needs to become cognitively active by recognizing the message and inferring the sender's purpose or meaning – in other words, the receiver needs to recognize the message as overtly communicative – and once the receiver recognizes the message to be purposeful, they generate a series of inferences (which Grice calls 'implicatures') to recover the potential meanings of the message. Inference works, not because there is a stable channel between sender and receiver who share an identical, fixed system of codes, but because interlocutors try to act rationally by mutually adhering to a pre-existing set of rational standards. Once a piece of behaviour is recognized as communicative, interlocutors assume (although it is not guaranteed) that they have a common rational purpose, and adhere to general standards – the norms of communication.

The process of inference generation, the two levels of meaning, and the norms are general properties of all forms of communication. For example, successful comprehension of a film is not only dependent on the spectator's construction from its narration of basic story events (direct meaning that is explicitly conveyed – shown or denoted in images) but also by inferring from its narration a number of indirect meanings, guided by the norms of communication. These norms, which guide the narration and spectator, are embodied in the implied author.

In Grice's (1975) concept of conversational implicature, the general conditions and constraints that govern communication are defined in terms of default rational capacities: the Cooperative Principle, cognitive categories, and maxims of conversation. A 'conversational implicature' goes beyond direct meaning, for it explains how more can be communicated than what is explicitly said. Grice argues that indirect or implied information is not ad hoc or subjective but is generated by what is explicitly said in conjunction with general cognitive maxims and principles:

> *Our talk exchanges do not normally consist of a succession of disconnected remarks, and would not be rational if they did. They are characteristically, to some degree at least, cooperative efforts; and each participant recognizes in them, to some extent, a common purpose or set of purposes, or at least a mutually accepted direction.* (Grice 1975: 45)

Cooperation is an implicit contract or agreement between interlocutors, and it extends far beyond speech to all forms of communication and behaviour. The Cooperative Principle assumes speakers act rationally and believe what they say. Following Kant's a priori set of general conceptual categories (that make the cognition of reality possible), Grice supplements the Cooperative Principle with a distinct set of cognitive categories (Quantity, Quality, Relation and Manner) that make communication possible, which in turn govern a series of maxims that interlocutors assume and expect will guide communicative behaviour. Under the category of Quantity, Grice lists two maxims of communicative behaviour: 'Make your contribution as informative as required (for the current purposes of the exchange)', and 'Do not make your contribution more informative than is required' (ibid.: 45). These maxims conform to the criterion of optimality, which is weakened by imprecision. The category of Quality contains the supermaxim, 'Try to make your contribution one that is true', and two additional maxims: 'Do not say what you believe to be false' and 'Do not say that for which you lack adequate evidence' (ibid.: 46). The supermaxim is fundamental because it needs to be satisfied first in relation to other maxims.

Under the category of Relation, Grice places the maxim 'Be relevant', and acknowledges that different kinds of relevance exist (1975: 46). Under the category of Manner, he places the supermaxim 'Be perspicuous' and four additional maxims: 'Avoid obscurity', 'Avoid ambiguity', 'Be brief', and 'Be orderly' (ibid.: 46). Grice adds that these maxims are not limited to verbal language: 'At least some of the foregoing maxims have their analogues in the sphere of transactions that are not talk exchanges' (ibid.: 47).

The hearer tacitly assumes the speaker is following the maxims – a rational assumption based on the efficient and effective use of language. In Stephen Levinson's summary, 'these maxims specify what participants have to do in order to converse in a maximally efficient, rational, cooperative way: they should speak sincerely, relevantly and clearly, while providing sufficient information' (Levinson 1983: 102). Levinson points out that the theory acknowledges that communication does not need to follow these maxims explicitly: 'When talk does not proceed according to their specifications, hearers assume that, contrary to appearances, the principles are nevertheless being adhered to [indirectly] at some deeper level' (ibid.). Maxims are followed either directly (on the level of what is said) or indirectly (implicated).

Levinson provides an example of indirect communication (A asks 'Where's Bill?' and B responds 'There's a yellow VW outside Sue's house') and provides an analysis in terms of Grice's maxims:

> B's contribution, taken literally, fails to answer A's question, and thus seems to violate at least the maxims of Quantity and Relevance. We might therefore expect B's utterance as a non-cooperative response, a brushing aside of A's concerns with a change of topic. Yet it is clear that despite apparent *failure of cooperation*, we try to interpret B's utterance at some deeper (non-superficial) level. We do this by assuming that it is in fact cooperative, and then asking ourselves what possible connection there could be between the location of Bill and the location of a yellow VW, and thus arrive at the suggestion (which B effectively conveys) that, if Bill has a yellow VW, he may be in Sue's house. (Levinson 1983: 102; emphasis in original)

Levinson adds that 'in cases of this sort, inferences arise to preserve the assumption of cooperation; it is only by making the assumption contrary to superficial indications that the inferences arise in the first place' (102). In other words, interlocutors infer the implication in order to comprehend the message. He concludes: 'So Grice's point is not that we always adhere to these maxims on a superficial level but rather that, whenever possible, people will interpret what we say as conforming to the maxims on a least some level' (103).

When a maxim is flouted, making the surface meaning unclear, ambiguous or opaque, the receiver assumes the maxims are adhered to on a deeper level; receivers then increase their cognitive processing effort by generating implicatures in order to retrieve a literal meaning from what was said. These implicatures are important because they are 'fundamental to our sense of coherence in discourse' (107). Furthermore, because implicatures (generated from openly flouting the maxims) are not stated directly in the utterance, they are contingent or defeasible, and can be cancelled without creating confusion or contradictions. This revision of implicatures is a normal part of everyday communication, for flouting is overt, openly signifying the breach of the maxims. Irony, indirect communication and metaphor are typical forms of communication that openly flout maxims – it is evident that the surface message is obtuse or false, and the hearer infers that the speaker meant something different.

Overtly flouting (or simply flouting) maxims is different from covertly violating (or simply violating) maxims, for the latter aims to mislead, or deceive: '*Deception is typically understood as intentionally causing the hearer to (continue to) hold a false belief,* i.e. to believe to be true something the speaker *believes to be false*' (Dynel 2011: 139; emphasis in original). One tactic for creating deception is via the omission or withholding of information relevant to the receiver. This act of omission violates the maxim of Quantity, for the omission of relevant information encourages the receiver to generate a false inference or to hold a false belief. Yet, the deception is not stated directly but is indirect; deception is caused by the concealment of relevant information and is located in the receiver's generation of an inference, which they do not realize is untrue.

Lying is different; it is based on the direct assertion of false information. It violates the all-important maxim of Quality, for the deception is located in what is said, not in what is inferred, and there are (obviously) no signs in the message that indicate it is a lie. Deception is not the same as lying; deceptions are half-truths, for they do state the truth, but not the whole truth. As St Augustine said: 'Concealing the truth is not the same as putting forth a lie'. Deception withholds relevant information, which encourages the receiver to generate false inferences.

In sum, either the interlocutors (sender and receiver) adhere to the maxims, or the sender overtly flouts the maxims – that is, signals the flouting in the message so that the receiver can overcome the infringement by generating implicatures – or violates the maxims in order to deceive, or on occasion lie to, the receiver.

Filmic Narration

Translated into the terms of filmic narration, mainstream cinema may flout the maxims embedded in the implied author (leading spectators to generate implicatures to recover meaning) or may, on occasion, deceive by violating the maxims of Quantity, Relation and Manner, but rarely does mainstream cinema lie by violating the maxim of Quality. One of the intrinsic features of mainstream cinema is that any imbalances caused by flouting or deception are temporary – that is, they are eventually resolved. By contrast, puzzle films deceive and lie more frequently than mainstream films, and either their deception and lying are resolved or, more significantly, remain unresolved. The distinguishing feature of the deceptive puzzle film is that its deceptive narration is permanent.

The narration of the deceptive puzzle film covertly violates the implied author's maxims. Whereas a 'standard' puzzle film tries to explain away its unresolvable contradictions and logical inconsistencies by resolving them on an imaginary level, a deceptive puzzle film does not pretend to unravel and decipher contradictions (those that are generated from time travel, time loop paradoxes, multiple versions of the same character, etc.). The deceptive puzzle film's narration creates ambiguity and contradictions but does not confirm any single reading to resolve them. Thus, the idea of a single fixed meaning breaks down, creating confusion, for the deceptive narration undermines the Cooperative Principle and some of its maxims, destabilizing the spectator's belief in the trustworthiness of the narration and even the implied author. The deceptive puzzle film, therefore, permanently problematizes the processes of storyworld construction and comprehension, for these processes are no longer pregiven and assumed but instead become cognitively challenging activities.

In a similar move, Thomas Elsaesser characterized the mind-game film's cognitively challenging nature in terms of a crisis in the traditional film-spectator contract. This contract normally creates a stable subject position and a reliable form of narration from which to view (the impression of) a spatio-temporally unified, enclosed, fixed, autonomous and linear storyworld. In place of this traditional subjective position, mind-game films create a new film-spectator contract via 'unreliable narrators, the multiple time-lines, unusual point of view structures, unmarked flashbacks, problems in focalization and perspectivism, unexpected causal reversals and narrative loops' (Elsaesser 2009: 18) and an 'insistence on temporality as a separate dimension of consciousness and identity, the play on nonlinear sequence or inverted causality, on chance and contingency, on synchronicity and simultaneity and their effects on characters, agency, and human relations' (ibid.: 21). With these features, mind-game films do not present an imaginary resolution of real contradictions but exacerbate those contradictions; the contradictions are not resolved but remain deadlocked. In the following pages, I employ Grice's pragmatics to analyse this new film-spectator contract that the deceptive puzzle film's narration establishes between film and spectator.

Four Types of Narration

We can now employ Grice to develop the category of deceptive filmic narration and distinguish it from Booth's theory of unreliability. Unreliability, as we have seen, is a matter of the variation of distance between the implied author (understood here in terms of Grice's principles of communication), the narration (the discursive level), and characters and events (the fictional story level). Distance, the discrepancy or (non-)alignment between these levels, can be measured according to whether the narration and/or characters adhere to the implied author's general maxims, overtly flout the maxims, or violate them. The default value is that a film follows the maxims until a discrepancy is detected. Combining Grice and Booth, I have identified a hierarchy of four narrational options – cooperative, discrepant, flouted and deceptive:

>(1) *Cooperative.* Characters and the narration adhere to the implied author's Cooperative Principle and maxims of communication. Characters on the story level act as reliable focalizers, and the narration (the discursive level) reliably conveys the characters' experiences to the spectator. There is no distance but a complete alignment among the implied author, narration, characters and spectators.
>(2) *Discrepant.* A character flouts the implied author's maxims, but the narration adheres to them. A film's character may be ironic, deceptive or lie, but their behaviour is framed by a reliable narration. The narration dispels ambiguity and confusion by exposing the character as unreliable (for example, the character may believe a hallucination to be real while the narration presents it as a hallucination). There is no distance, and there is a complete alignment among implied author, narration and spectators, but there is a discrepancy (distance and non-alignment) between the character and the narration. As Suzanne Keen points out, a character perceives but 'does not actually narrate; the character can possess an incomplete or misguided perspective, but he or she cannot narrate unreliably' (2015: 44).
>(3) *Flouted.* The narration flouts the implied author's maxims; the narration is still reliable because it signals its flouting, allowing spectators to recover the communicated meaning and construct the storyworld through the generation and revision of implicatures. The narration, therefore, follows the maxims at a deeper level. The flouting creates a distance and partial non-alignment between the narration and implied author, but the narration remains reliable, for it continues to align with spectators. As Keen points out (discussing prose fiction), the reader is aware that the narrator/narration is unreliable (2015: 44).

(4) *Deceptive*. The narration violates the implied author's maxims. The narration either conveys a character's reliable experiences or story events in an unreliable manner and conceals its own unreliability, or, inversely, it presents a character's unreliable experiences/story events as if they were actual. In each case, the narration is deceptive and ends up creating maximum distance and non-alignment between itself, the implied author, characters and spectators. To paraphrase Booth (1983: 158), the total effect of the work is transformed – specifically, it transforms the spectator's contractual relation to a text. Due to unresolvable ambiguity and contradictions, storyworld construction and meaning-making break down, creating confusion, for the deceptive narration destabilizes the spectator's belief in the trustworthiness of the narration and the implied author.

Within the delimited sphere of fiction film, the narration in options (1) and (2) unequivocally adheres to the implied author's norms (defined here in terms of Grice's Cooperative Principle and maxims); in option (3), the narration flouts the norms but presents the spectator with privileged information in order to construct the storyworld by generating implicatures; however, in option (4), the spectator is not privileged but is the victim of deception. The narration covertly ignores the implied author's norms, leaving the receiver to believe falsely that the narration is still following those norms. The result is a deceptive narration that is ambiguous and confusing, leading to a breakdown in communication because it obstructs the spectator's construction of a coherent storyworld.

Booth disparages the breakdown in communication created by unreliable narration because the text no longer conveys a clear (moral) message. He finds this breakdown throughout the history of fiction, although it is prominent in contemporary fiction due to the demise of the explicit narrator commenting on and evaluating story events for the reader, replaced with impersonal narration and unreliable character narrators. He identifies three specific techniques that create ambiguity and confusion in fiction (Booth 1983: 316–24): firstly, such fiction fails (in Gricean terms) to signify its flouting of communicational maxims (or, as Booth put it, there is a lack of adequate warning that irony is at work); secondly, the implied author's norms are extremely complex, as is the relation between the narration and the implied author's norms, resulting in a work that is indecipherable and inconclusive; and thirdly, such fiction is based on vivid psychological realism, in which the modern novel, in particular, focuses intently on representing the inner perspective of one character to the exclusion of all other perspectives.

Booth laments that many vividly psychological works of contemporary fiction represent the inner worlds of reprehensible characters sympathetically, for such works are without an external narrator to frame and judge these characters. Such fictions, he says, 'bind the reader so tightly to the consciousness of the ambiguously misguided protagonist that nothing will interfere with his delight in inferring the precise though varying degrees of distance that operate from point to point throughout the book' (Booth 1983: 324). Booth argues that each of these three sources of difficulty dominate modern fiction: 'Everyone recognizes that each of these three sources of difficulty is present in some modern fiction, frequently in forms much more deceptive than anything encountered in earlier work. Any one of them alone can give trouble. And in some modern fiction all three are present' (ibid.: 323–24). Booth mentions James's *The Turn of the Screw*, Joyce's *A Portrait of the Artist as a Young Man*, Camus's *The Fall*, and Kafka's *The Castle*.

In the puzzle film, these techniques of narration go even further. It is no longer simply a matter of their presence in a text but, instead, their extreme and relentless dominance in shaping a text's narration. One reason for this trend in cinema is that mainstream film conventions are well known and predictable (they constitute a restricted code). Puzzle films develop new strategies of narration, making storytelling more elaborate and unpredictable by increasing the possibilities of story development and challenging its assumptions (that characters are coherent entities, that the storyworld is stable, etc.). Puzzle films are aesthetically attractive because they add complexity to storytelling by anticipating the spectator's knowledge of mainstream storytelling and subverting its conventions (trying to outwit the spectator, like a magician).

The narration's violation of the implied author's maxims (the fourth narrational option identified above) formulates the operational limits or threshold of reliable narration, in conjunction with Booth's three techniques that create ambiguity and confusion. Narration becomes deceptive when it contributes to the creation of a contradictory, incoherent storyworld whose very existence is brought into question. I shall argue this point through a series of examples, beginning with narration in mainstream narrative film before discussing the narration of a deceptive puzzle film.

Mainstream Filmic Narration: *Rear Window*

The default value for discussing narration is the implied author. We have already established that, from a Gricean perspective, the implied author 'embodies' the Cooperative Principle and maxims – that is, guides and constrains the process of narration, storyworld creation, and generation of implicatures. Events and character experiences that the narration creates and narrates in a novel or film are assumed to follow the implied author's Cooperative Principle and maxims, yielding a coherent and logically consistent fictional storyworld. Like everyday verbal communication, a mainstream narrative film will either follow the maxims (option 1) or openly flout them (options 2 and 3) as a matter of routine. Violation of the maxims (option 4) is rare, for this mode of narration is deceptive and sometimes untruthful.

In *Rear Window* (Hitchcock, 1954), Jeff is confined to his wheelchair, looking out of his window at the neighbours. The film begins with a shot that pans and tracks around the courtyard outside Jeff's window and around his apartment while he sleeps. This shot is non-focalized or objective – it is not tied to the consciousness or awareness of any character in the storyworld. In the following scene, the camera becomes attached to Jeff's awareness (external focalization) and optical–aural experience – internal focalization (surface) – of events in the storyworld. The narration filters and restricts the spectator's access to the storyworld through Jeff's awareness and experience. One night, he hears a scream from an apartment occupied by Thorwald and his wife; he later sees Thorwald leave and return to his apartment several times, carrying a large case. The spectator experiences these events through Jeff. But in the early morning, Jeff falls asleep. The camera then pans slowly from the sleeping Jeff across the courtyard and shows Thorwald and a woman (filmed from the back, at a distance) leaving the apartment; it then slowly pans back to Jeff, still asleep. This is a moment of omniscient narration, which sets up a hierarchy of knowledge between the main character Jeff and the spectator, for the spectator is given more information than the main character. When nurse Stella turns up, Jeff tells her he thinks Thorwald has murdered his wife and has disposed of her body, and provides her with the clues (screams, Thorwald's comings and goings with a large case).

Up until the moment Jeff falls asleep, spectators generate the same implicature, for they share the same information. But when Jeff falls asleep, the narration places the spectator in an omniscient position over him (and the other characters who know as much as he does), for the narration privileges the spectators with additional information: Thorwald leaving the apartment with a woman. The narration, therefore, appears to follow the Cooperative Principle by providing spectators with all the relevant information needed to know what is going on in the storyworld. But as the film unfolds, Jeff's detective friend, Doyle, becomes involved and eventually discovers the same piece of information – Thorwald was seen leaving the apartment with a woman and took her to the train station before returning to the apartment. Doyle then reinterprets the events as a domestic dispute, and the characters and spectators alike assume the woman who left the apartment was Mrs Thorwald. Eventually, however, the characters discover it was not Mrs Thorwald, but another woman – Mr Thorwald's new love interest – and he did, in fact, murder his wife, cut up her body, and carry it out of the apartment in his case.

Is the narration cooperative? Does it flout any maxims? Is it covert and deceptive? Jeff and the spectator hear a scream, but the narration does not cut to inside Thorwald's apartment to show what happened. The narration withholds information, but the spectator knows it withholds it, and it is justified in withholding it because the narration presents a limited range of knowledge by aligning itself to Jeff's consciousness and his physical position in his apartment: if he cannot see into Thorwald's apartment then neither can the spectator. This is the 'contract' restricted narration establishes with the spectator. The restricted access to the storyworld is overtly signalled, acknowledged and motivated. The narration flouts the maxim of Relation by withholding relevant information; it creates a flaunted gap, which the spectator then fills in by drawing upon the canonical story schema and generating a tentative implicature (Mr Thorwald could have murdered his wife).

When Jeff falls asleep, the narration momentarily disengages from him and becomes non-focalized or objective again (just like the film's opening shot). The slow camera movement away from and then back to the sleeping Jeff not only conveys basic information – Mr Thorwald and a woman leaving the apartment (direct meaning, in Grice's terms) – it also conveys additional meaning about this information. Firstly, spectators need to recognize that the narration is overtly placing them in an omniscient position over Jeff because they receive additional information – a woman leaving Thorwald's apartment – that Jeff does not receive. In other words, spectators not only receive this additional information, but they also need to recognize that the narration is providing them with this additional information.

Secondly, spectators need to figure out why they received this additional information. Like all forms of indirect information, it is designed to encourage spectators to generate an implicature that will modify their construction of the film's storyworld. In showing Mr Thorwald and a woman leaving the apartment, spectators are encouraged to generate the implicature that the woman is Mrs Thorwald and that, consequently, she was not murdered but has gone travelling (for Thorwald later returns to the apartment alone). This implicature is not encoded in the film, but this does not mean it is generated by chance; instead, spectators follow the maxim of Relation by generating the most relevant implicature based on the overtly signalled information provided by the narration.

In the morning, Jeff generates the most relevant implicature based on the knowledge he possesses: that Thorwald murdered his wife. Spectators believe that his knowledge of the situation is incomplete, which leads them to generate another (the most relevant) implicature – that Mrs Thorwald has left her husband – which cancels out Jeff's implicature. However, the film eventually presents a twist, for the additional information is misleading and the resulting implicature that spectators generate from it is incorrect. Nonetheless, this twist is not a complete shock due to the presupposition that the film would lack tellability if no crime took place and Jeff's investigation was futile.

The narration, therefore, encourages spectators to generate the most relevant implicature by presenting them with more information than Jeff; yet, Jeff's implicature is eventually established to be correct and the spectator's implicature incorrect. We need to pause and consider in more detail the discrepancy between Jeff and the spectator. What has happened is that the narration is deceptive because it has, temporarily at least, violated the implied author's maxims of Quantity and Relation. The narration provides additional and at the same time insufficient information: additional in that it privileges the spectator with the information that a woman left the apartment; insufficient in that it does not show this woman entering the apartment, and when she leaves she is filmed from a distance with her back to the camera. In the latter case the narration is not informative because it does not provide all relevant information to the spectator – it covertly suppresses the moment the woman entered the apartment and, because of this, the spectator is led to generate a false implicature and assume wrongly that the woman leaving the apartment is Mrs Thorwald.

Nonetheless, the narration does not lie to the spectator. Unlike Hitchcock's earlier film *Stage Fright* (1950), the narration of *Rear Window* does not violate the maxim of Quality (it does not provide false information); at best, it presents a half-truth by omitting information.[3] After all, the event shown on screen is true – a woman did leave the Thorwald apartment – but it leads the spectator to generate a false implicature (this woman is Mrs Thorwald, she has not been murdered) because it violates the maxim of Relation (suppression of relevant information – the narration did not show the woman entering the apartment). The narration strategically deceives, not by presenting false information, but by overtly providing the spectator with more information than Jeff *and* by covertly withholding information relevant to understanding that additional information. It purposefully performs an act of deception via the omission of information. Furthermore, this deception is only temporary because the narration eventually communicates to the spectator that the woman was not Mrs Thorwald.

The false implicature the narration led the spectator to generate is, like all implicatures, defeasible and is therefore simply cancelled. Because the spectator generated the false implicature, they revise or cancel it. The spectator takes responsibility for its generation, even though it was the narration that concealed relevant story information. This is one reason the narration of *Rear Window* is successful: it momentarily deceives by encouraging spectators to generate wrong implicatures before correcting their inferential error by directly stating the correct implicature at the end of the film.

The Puzzle Film's Deceptive Narration: *Lost Highway*

In the Introduction to *Puzzle Films* (Buckland 2009), I defined the puzzle film in terms of several shared features, ranging over three distinct categories: order; different levels of reality; and character psychology:

> *Puzzle films embrace nonlinearity, time loops, and fragmented spatio-temporal reality. These films blur the boundaries between different levels of reality, are riddled with gaps, deception, labyrinthine structures, ambiguity, and overt coincidences. They are populated with characters who are schizophrenic, lose their memory, are unreliable narrators, or are dead (but without us – or them – realizing).* (Ibid.: 6)

The puzzle plot is not the same as Aristotle's complex plot, which remains classical and mimetic. In *Poetics*, Aristotle provided a definition of the complex plot to complement his simple plot. In the Introduction to *Puzzle Films*, I argued that puzzle films go beyond Aristotle's understanding of complex plot, whereby the hero's plotline is interwoven and integrated with a second plotline, which comprises recognition and reversal. Such an interweaving of two narrative plots is not sufficient to characterize contemporary puzzle films. Instead, 'A puzzle plot is intricate in the sense that the arrangement of events is not just complex, but complicated and perplexing; the events are not simply interwoven, but *entangled*' (Buckland 2009: 3; emphasis in original). 'Complicated', 'perplexing' and 'entangled' all imply a higher level of disorganization and confusion than the more straightforward term 'complex'. In *Hollywood Puzzle Films*, I developed this earlier formulation that puzzle plots are complicated, perplexing and entangled by introducing into the discussion the concepts of 'ontological pluralism' and 'cognitive dissonance' (Buckland 2014). However, I downplayed some narrational dimensions when defining the puzzle film, including the roles of the implied author, unreliable narration and deceptive narration – an omission I rectify here.

Like mainstream films and art cinema, the puzzle film temporarily flouts the implied author's maxims by withholding significant story information. But, crucially, the deceptive puzzle film's narration – while also violating some of the implied author's maxims by covertly withholding significant information (in Booth's terms, a lack of adequate warning that irony or deception is at work) – never reveals its violation by employing the permanently suppressed gap or restricted narration (limited to the vivid psychological realism of one character only, who may be schizophrenic, suffering from memory loss, or dead), complex norms, or may deceptively juxtapose unrelated events to imply an indirect causal connection. Like an uncooperative witness in a trial, the puzzle film's narration may violate the maxims associated with Manner by not wanting to be understood, or by being difficult just for its own sake, or may present irrelevant information (in order to conceal relevant information), or deliberately present a clash of maxims (i.e. present an abundance of information, only some of which is true). In extreme cases, it may either opt out of following the maxims altogether (by not communicating or remaining silent), or it can be said to lie if it violates the all-important maxims associated with Quality.

In the following discussion of *Lost Highway* (David Lynch, 1997), I analyse the scene of Fred's murder of Renee in terms of maxims, unreliability, deception and implicatures. Whereas the narration of a mainstream film such as *Rear Window* is constructed in a way that encourages spectators to generate one or two strongly evidenced implicatures (Thorwald murdered/did not murder his wife; the woman leaving the apartment is Thorwald's wife, etc.), *Lost Highway* encourages spectators to generate an array of weakly evidenced implicatures.

The Murder Scene

The murder scene (35 minutes into the film) demonstrates the fundamental flouting of maxims. Fred and Renee return from Andy's party. The first half of the scene shows Renee going into the bathroom to remove her make-up, and Fred seeing her in the bathroom before he takes off his jacket. The second half of the scene shows Fred walking down a dark corridor, where he looks at himself in a mirror. Renee exits the bathroom and calls out to him, but he does not reply. She returns to the bedroom, and Fred re-emerges out of the dark corridor.

The couple are briefly seen together in the bathroom mirror. Fred walks from the warm-lit bedroom into the bright, cold-lit, en suite bathroom, and sees Renee in there; the shot shows Renee with her back to the camera, her reflection oriented towards the camera but looking at Fred; while, in the background, Fred's reflection is seen entering the frame – however, his head is out of shot (Figure 2.1). This mirror shot is initially objective or non-focalized (the shot begins and ends with Fred absent) before Fred 'claims' it as his visual experience. That is, for those moments when he appears in the reflection, the shot becomes an externally focalized (or over-the-shoulder) shot representing his visual awareness (if it were his optical point of view, representing his own visual experience, Renee's reflection would be looking into the camera lens). An objective shot is indifferent to the way a character experiences the filmed events; yet, when Fred steps into this objective shot, he momentarily claims it as the representation of his own experience. (Of course, the camera is carefully positioned in the bathroom to enable him to claim it.) The scene then cuts to the bedroom and shows Fred looking off-screen into the bathroom (Figure 2.2), and then cuts back to the bathroom's interior as Fred walks out of the shot.

The cutting then alternates between Fred and Renee in their own spaces. As Fred takes off his jacket, the scene cuts to Renee in the bathroom;[4] just before he enters the dark corridor (Figure 2.3), the scene cuts back to Renee once again; and after Fred disappears into the darkness, the scene cuts back to Renee a third time.

Figures 2.1–2.4. *Lost Highway* (David Lynch 1997). © Lost Highway Productions, Three Pictures Production Company, Asymmetrical Productions and CIBY 2000. Screen captures by Warren Buckland.

Figures 2.1–2.4. (continued)

The editing creates omniscient narration (omniscient over Renee) to the extent that it sets up a hierarchy of knowledge (both Fred and the spectator know where Renee is, whereas Renee does not know where Fred is), and at the end of the dark corridor is another mirror, where Fred looks intently at himself. (From the spatial layout of the house, the spectator can discern that the mirror in the dark corridor is behind the bathroom mirror.) The shot is framed to show only his reflection, but a few seconds later, Fred steps forward and enters the shot with his reflection (Figure 2.4).

The framing of Fred in the bathroom mirror (Figure 2.1) is unusual. The spectator only sees his reflection (whereas Renee and her reflection are visible), and he is cut off at the neck. It is as if his reflected face cannot appear in the same mirror as Renee's reflection – they cannot be framed together in the same space. Fred needs his own mirror, which he finds at the end of the dark corridor. The shot of Fred just before he enters the dark corridor is framed as an over-the-shoulder (externally focalized) shot: the camera is positioned over Fred's shoulder as he stares into the corridor (Figure 2.3). He then walks slowly into the darkness. As he walks forward, the camera remains fixed, whereby the narration changes from externally focalized to non-focalized.

As Fred disappears, Renee (still in the bathroom) looks up and off-screen as if something is wrong. The scene then cuts to Fred and the mirror. Cut back to Renee, who enters the bedroom and is surprised to discover Fred is not there. She then walks to the edge of the dark corridor, framed in the same way: an externally focalized shot with the camera positioned over her shoulder as she stares into the corridor. But she does not walk into it; instead, she calls out, motivating a reverse cut, showing her face before cutting back to the over-the-shoulder shot. She receives no response and walks out of the frame back into the bedroom. The camera remains fixed on the dark corridor, whereby the narration changes from externally focalized to non-focalized. The next shot shows the living room with two shadows moving along the wall. The restricted framing does not reveal who creates the shadows. The next shot returns to the dark corridor, and, in reverse of a previous shot, Fred emerges out of the dark, walking towards the camera until his head fills the entire frame and the image goes black. The scene ends with a shot of a closed door.

This scene's narration combines brief moments of omniscience with the film's extremely narrow and restricted narration, offering very limited access to the story. It, therefore, flouts a series of interconnected maxims: the maxims of Quantity (by being uninformative), Relation (by not providing relevant information), and Manner (by being obscure and ambiguous).

The omniscient narration aligns spectators with Fred at the beginning of this scene (it gives the spectator privileged access to his location in the dark corridor), but that privilege is soon eroded when the spectator sees the two shadows in the living room (the restricted framing does not reveal who created the shadows) and when Fred obstructs the camera entirely with his head as he walks out of the dark corridor. (In the bathroom mirror, Fred's head is absent, but in the shot of him walking out of the dark corridor, his head fills the whole frame.) The black screen and the following shot of the closed door create the impression of the camera and spectator being shut out of the storyworld. The next scene fades up and begins in the living room with Fred watching a videotape (the third one) that was left on the doorstep. The first videotape had shown the outside of the house, and the second one the inside of the house with Fred and Renee sleeping in bed; the third tape shows Fred murdering and dismembering Renee in the bedroom (he looks at and acknowledges the video camera filming him).

Although the scene employs techniques of continuity editing – match-on-action cuts, directional continuity, alternating editing between Fred and Renee – the deceptive narration overrides any cohesion these techniques create, for the second part of the scene remains fragmented and restricted. Indeed, in the last two shots (Fred's head obstructing the camera, and the closed door), story information is withheld entirely, giving the impression that the narration at this point is not simply flouting the maxims to create an underlying implicit thematic meaning (the doppelganger theme); rather, the narration momentarily signals to the spectator that it is *opting out* of following the maxims entirely. It is refusing to be communicative or cooperative by not presenting sufficiently relevant story information or the links between the fragments that are presented, thereby preventing spectators from generating implicatures that could lead to a coherent storyworld. What is evident is that Fred walks into a dark corridor, looks at himself in a mirror, and walks out of the dark corridor again. But the narration's obscure and ambiguous presentation of these events renders them almost unintelligible. These shots of Fred are mixed with shots of Renee looking for him (thereby maintaining the alternation Renee/Fred from the first part of the scene), plus the shot of two shadows on the wall. To which side of the alternation does the shot of the shadows belong? They appear to belong to Fred's part of the story. Grouping together his shots in the second part of the scene yields the sequence: (a) Fred walks into a dark corridor; (b) Fred looks at his mirror image; (c) two shadows on the wall; and (d) Fred emerges alone from the dark corridor.

In particular, the movement of the two shadows walking across the living room wall matches the movement of Fred walking out of the dark corridor towards the camera – the movement links the shadows to Fred. However, he is alone. The narration's lack of information regarding the second shadow creates an anomaly, for it does not provide a reverse shot to reveal who caused the second shadow.

The lack of story information and the anomaly are flouted, but the narration only offers a few sparse cues to enable spectators to generate implicatures to organize them into a coherent storyworld. That is, spectators need to expend cognitive effort to generate an array of weak implicatures that try to make sense of this fragmented information. Firstly, within the scene, Fred looks at himself in the mirror, the spectator sees him and his reflection on-screen – there are two of him. And there are two shadows. One weak implicature is that his doppelganger has materialized as a physical entity, and it is Fred and his mirror image/doppelganger creating the two shadows (the doppelganger becomes a shadow, which has a similar ontological status to a reflection). But even this non-obvious implicature needs to be modified almost immediately because Fred exits the dark corridor alone. One further implicature is that his doppelganger has merged into him and taken possession of him. Fred/the doppelganger then completely obstructs the spectator's access to the storyworld.

The spectator can also draw upon (sparse) cues in previous scenes. Earlier in the film, Fred recounts a dream to Renee. In the dream, Fred looks around the dark house at night, hears Renee calling out to him (in an identical way to how she did in the murder scene), followed by a shot of Renee in bed being frightened by a rapidly approaching off-screen agent. The mystery man's face is briefly superimposed upon Renee's face. After seeing the content of the third videotape – of Fred murdering Renee – the spectator can infer that the dream was a premonition of this future murder.

This mystery man also appears at Andy's party, which takes place just before the murder scene. The mystery man says to Fred that they have met before (although Fred does not remember) and then defies Newtonian space-time physics by suggesting that he is in Fred's house at that very moment (that is, in two places at once). The mystery man 'confirms' this by persuading Fred to phone his home, where, indeed, the mystery man also answers. The most relevant implicature the spectator can generate is that the mystery man is also Fred's doppelganger, and that it was he who had created the second shadow.

The narration of *Lost Highway* is careful not to lie openly. Still, it is deceptive, for it undermines the maxims of Quantity, Relation and Manner by withholding a significant amount of relevant story events on screen, and presenting the remaining small fragments of events in an obscure and ambiguous manner. Collectively, these uncommunicative narrational techniques undermine the spectator's ability to generate implicatures to create a coherent storyworld, rendering the narration deceptive. Most importantly, *Lost Highway* is a deceptive puzzle film because these (and many other) indeterminate events remain permanently unresolved.

Conclusions

To the puzzle film's main features, organized into its three categories – order, different levels of reality, and character psychology – I have added *deceptive narration* and promoted it to the status of a dominant and permanent feature within a small group of puzzle films I am calling the 'deceptive puzzle film'. By focusing on narration, I have not denied the significance of the story level, but have instead shifted focus to the activity of narration in the creation of the deceptive puzzle film's logically inconsistent fictional storyworld. I have then considered how deceptively narrating undermines the spectator's belief and trust in both the implied author's norms and the activity of narration.

I have defined the implied author's norms and values in terms of Grice's Cooperative Principle, cognitive categories, maxims of communicative behaviour, and direct and inferred meaning. Deceptive narration does not follow the Cooperative Principle and maxims, and it does not indicate that it does not follow them, whereas flouted narration does signify that it does not follow them. Deceptive narration, therefore, manipulates spectators by violating the Cooperative Principle and maxims, creating misunderstanding and a breakdown in communication.

The deceptive puzzle film employs the techniques of deceptive narration without resolution, resulting in a permanent breakdown in communication. Spectators may find this breakdown frustrating and unpleasant, or they may discover its attractiveness and appreciate the new possibilities of storytelling and skilful techniques employed to achieve the sleight of hand, like a magic trick. Magic invisibly manipulates rational thinking by challenging its boundaries. For example, the murder scene is one of many challenging and deceptive scenes in *Lost Highway* designed to delight by manipulating rational thinking. Thomas Elsaesser speculates as to why such moments may appeal to spectators – their disorienting effects are a form of liberation:

> *Some of the pleasure of the mind-game film comes from this sense of light disorientation, the levity of having the realist rug pulled from under you – the sort of disorientation you experience when the punchline of a joke shows how you've been mistaken about where this story was going, or the feeling of being freed from gravity on a roller coaster. So a moment of vertigo, but also of weightlessness, can be one of the trick or twist effects of mind-game films.* (Elsaesser 2021: 299)

Spectators who are willing to accept the deceit do so because, within the aesthetic realm, real-world fears (of being 'freed from gravity' – that is, the fear of falling from a great height, for example, or of losing one's reasoning faculties) are switched off or are 'off-line' (to use Kendall Walton's term). In this off-line state, deception becomes a form of liberation, where spectators are eased out of their habitual subject-centred individualism, and their minds are freed from rigid, linear causal thinking.

Lost Highway successfully challenges cognitive thinking limited to linear cause-effect logic that searches for a singular, fixed, permanent meaning. Of course, some spectators may not want their search for a definitive single meaning or their habitual way of thinking to be challenged (just like some people do not like roller coaster rides, for their fear of falling cannot be switched offline), but for spectators who accept cinema's ability to challenge their rational and habitual ways of thinking, Grice's pragmatic theory of conversational implicature is invaluable for outlining the boundaries of rational thinking. Grice's theory explains the way the deceptive puzzle film's narration is designed to creatively manipulate and transcend the boundaries of that rational thinking in an attempt to delight spectators.

Warren Buckland is Reader in Film Studies at Oxford Brookes University. He is the author or editor of a number of books, including *Puzzle Films: Complex Storytelling in Contemporary Cinema* (ed., 2009), *Hollywood Puzzle Films* (ed., 2014), *Film Theory: Rational Reconstructions* (2012) and *Wes Anderson's Symbolic Storyworld* (2019).

Notes

With thanks to Paul Cobley, Ruggero Eugeni, Agnieszka Piotrowska, Paolo Russo, Eleftheria Thanouli and Yannis Tzioumakis for their comments on an earlier draft of this chapter.

1. 'Non-anthropomorphic' and 'non-intentionalist' in the sense that meaning in a novel or film is not produced by figuring out the maker's intention, but is generated from general pragmatic principles of communication.
2. My definition of the deceptive puzzle film cuts across Kiss and Willemsen's (2017) categories of 'deceptively unreliable' and 'impossible' puzzle films, in which 'deceptively unreliable' refers to a momentary surprise, such as a twist ending, and 'impossible' puzzle films, like mind-game films, create unresolvable contradictions or ontological incongruities on the story level that cannot be attributed to a character. The cognitive dissonance in the impossible puzzle film that Kiss and Willemsen attribute to the story level is readily explainable via the more straightforward narrational concept of permanent deception.
3. In the opening scene of *Stage Fright* (1950), the narration aurally, as well as visually, represents a character's lie in a flashback, but initially conceals the fact that the flashback is representing a lie. The narration therefore violates the Cooperative Principle and the maxim of Quality, for the lie is initially presented deceptively, as if it were true. Because the lie was visually and aurally presented on screen (that is, stated directly rather than inferred or implied), it cannot be dismissed or cancelled as easily as a false implicature. In this example, the responsibility for the veracity of the flashback lies with the narration rather than the spectator. The narration's

act of showing the spectator the images in a flashback is a cooperative informative gesture, which later turns out to be uncooperative. *Stage Fright*'s narration violates the implied author's maxims by conveying the character's unreliable experiences/story events as if they were actual. However, at the end of the film, the narration replaces the lie with a truthful account of events, making the deception temporary.

4. As Fred closes the door to the wardrobe, the sound of the closing door is coordinated with the sound of a low boom – which is likely to be nondiegetic, although it could be an internally focalized (depth) sound from inside Fred's head.

References

Booth, Wayne. 1983. *The Rhetoric of Fiction*. Second Edition. Chicago: University of Chicago Press.
Brütsch, Matthias. 2014. 'From Ironic Distance to Unexpected Plot Twists: Unreliable Narration in Literature and Film', in Jan Alber and Per Krogh Hansen (eds), *Beyond Classical Narration: Transmedial and Unnatural Challenges*. Berlin: De Gruyter, pp. 57–79.
Buckland, Warren. 2009. 'Introduction: Puzzle Plots', in Warren Buckland (ed.), *Puzzle Films: Complex Storytelling in Contemporary Cinema*. Chichester, UK: Wiley-Blackwell, pp. 3–12.
———. 2014. 'Introduction: Ambiguity, Ontological Pluralism, and Cognitive Dissonance in the Hollywood Puzzle Film', in Warren Buckland (Ed.), *Hollywood Puzzle Films*. New York: Routledge, pp. 1–14.
Dynel, Marta. 2011. 'A Web of Deceit: A Neo-Gricean View on Types of Verbal Deception'. *International Review of Pragmatics* 3: 139–67.
Elsaesser, Thomas. 2009. 'The Mind-Game Film', in Warren Buckland (ed.), *Puzzle Films: Complex Storytelling in Contemporary Cinema*. Chichester, UK: Wiley-Blackwell, pp. 13–41.
———. 2021. *The Mind-Game Film: Distributed Agency, Time Travel, and Productive Pathology*. Edited by Warren Buckland, Dana Polan and Seung-hoon Jeong. New York: Routledge.
Grice, H.P. 1975. 'Logic and Conversation', in Peter Cole and Jerry L. Morgan (eds), *Syntax and Semantics. Vol. 3, Speech Acts*. New York: Academic Press, pp. 41–58.
Gunning, Tom. 1991. *D.W. Griffith and the Origins of American Narrative Film: The Early Years at Biograph*. Chicago: University of Illinois Press.
Keen, Suzanne. 2015. *Narrative Form*. Second Edition. Basingstoke: Palgrave Macmillan.
Kiss, Miklós, and Steven Willemsen. 2017. *Impossible Puzzle Films*. Edinburgh: Edinburgh University Press.
Levinson, Stephen. 1983. *Pragmatics*. Cambridge: Cambridge University Press.

CHAPTER 3

Cognitive Challenge in Complex Science Fiction

Knowledge, Reason and Threat in Narratives of Time Travel and Extraterrestrial Contact

Hilary Duffield

Introduction: Cognitive Challenge and Complexity in Science Fiction

Science fiction (SF) is a substantial field of narrative, ranging from the pure adventure stories of pulp space opera through to highly complex thought experiments. SF thought experiments are multifaceted constructions involving fictional space, time, interacting life forms and future history. Although they are not always constructed as puzzles that prompt the recipient to desire an answer or explanation for an enigma, paradox or incongruity, the texts belonging to what I shall refer to in this chapter as 'complex science fiction' do frequently operate like this. However, most complex SF texts do not aim for complete impossibility (i.e. 'more radical and disconcerting narrative structures' – Kiss and Willemsen 2017: 27) but construct narrative worlds with higher levels of coherence than fully anarchic cognitive dissonance. As I will show in this chapter, the narrative dynamics of complex science fiction are structured around a quest for knowledge that can range from logical puzzle solving to scenarios of cosmic epiphany and revelation. The central shared pattern is of some form of journey to a higher level of knowledge – and thus of *science* in its fundamental meaning rather than its equation with technology – as opposed to the endless frustration of insight practised by enduring enigma. The chapter will thus demonstrate how the aesthetic appeal of complex science fiction moves far beyond the repetition of previously successful genre formulas, and instead offers readerly pleasure through the prospect of the experience of the cognitive exhilaration attained in the discovery of higher-level 'truths' revealed within the narrative configuration of time, space and identity in the fictional world.

Moreover, precisely because science fiction is a genre of thought experiment, it is in a constant process of building upon and moving beyond the limits of its own conventions. Interesting new SF narratives thus perform thought experiments that challenge or revise previous conventions and archetypes of the genre, seeking new ways of imagining scenarios that transcend those of previous narratives. In doing so, science fiction can be cognitively challenging by prompting the recipient to imagine a configuration of existence not only beyond their own reality but also outside the norms of previous SF models. In this way, complex science fiction – rather than repeating a successful formula – builds on its own complexity to create further innovative thought experiments.

The chapter will explore the various forms of cognitive challenge in science fiction, and show how its specific forms of complexity can be understood using the interlinked concepts of *conceptual breakthrough* and *expansion of perception*. Furthermore, it will highlight how the multifaceted historical-cultural genealogy of science fiction has created a cognitive aesthetic of complexity involving the (often conflicting) interaction of worldviews shaped by (a) a belief in the primacy of rational mental operations, and (b) forms of predominantly emotional stimuli relating to threat and danger. Thus, complex science fiction is configured not only via the narrative pattern of enigma followed by revelation but is based in a field of tension between two separate historical-cultural cognitive traditions.

The chapter will reference a range of texts in print and film, ultimately giving special attention to three recent films that use various configurations of the time travel and extraterrestrial contact subgenres. *Looper* (2012), *Interstellar* (2014) and *Arrival* (2016) form an interesting sequence of recent films through which different narrative strategies of complex science fiction can be highlighted. The first sections of this chapter will set up three successive conceptual frameworks to discuss these films and other relevant texts: the first relates to the SF concepts of the novum and conceptual breakthrough; the second concerns the stimulation of rational vs emotional threat-based cognitive responses in science fiction; the third concerns one specific subgenre of science fiction that is often constructed around the threat response but that also provides interesting examples of variations in cognitively challenging SF storytelling through its depiction of the extraterrestrial Other.[1]

Conceptual Breakthrough, the Novum and Expanded Perception in Science Fiction

Science fiction narratives construct scenarios that, in contrast to the contemporaneous world of the author, contain at least one new element: the novum, 'a novelty [that] is "totalizing" in the sense that it entails a change of the whole universe of the tale, or at least of crucially important aspects thereof' (Suvin 2016: 80). Not all SF thought experiments, however, involve the same level of complexity: the interplanetary adventure narratives that developed, in particular, in the pulp SF of the early twentieth century (for example, the *Buck Rogers* stories) are forms of war narrative relocated to a different environment, and here the novum of space flight is closely allied to the machines used in real-world military conflict. In the overall history of SF, there is a gradual onset of complexity. In the British context, the ground-breaking narratives of H.G. Wells in the late Victorian period single-handedly established key SF genres such as time travel and extraterrestrial invasion. However, not many of Wells's narratives can be designated as complex or cognitively challenging; *The Time Machine* (1895), for example, does not complexify its story of time travel to the future and back with the concept of time paradoxes. On the other hand, the less-well-known story *The Man Who Could Work Miracles* (1898) narrates two contradictory versions of events and erases the first version, indicating that Wells was also moving towards new ground (Dannenberg 2008: 247).

Historically, however, what can be seen as the postmodernization of SF in terms of effects, such as time loops, paradoxes and multiple bifurcating timelines, occurs in a cluster of innovative and experimental texts in US science fiction in the 1930s and early 1940s. Narratives such as Murray Leinster's *Sidewise in Time* (1934), L. Sprague de Camp's *The Wheels of If* (1940) and Robert Heinlein's *By His Bootstraps* (1941) create complex and enigmatic maps of history and time.[2] Such innovations in late modernism are also an indication that print SF was a significant forerunner of postmodernist narrative complexity, which was only later expanded in postmodernist experimental narrative. Science fiction is, therefore, not only the sister genre of postmodernism as proposed by McHale (1987), but a forerunner of postmodernist narrative complexity.

During the twentieth century, science fiction moved from being a genre viewed from the outside as a lightweight narrative of pure entertainment to a theorized narrative genre. Key terms proposed for its analysis confirmed it as a fundamentally cognitive genre. Accordingly, Suvin (2016) defines SF as the genre of 'cognitive estrangement', while for Philip K. Dick (1990: 9–10) science fiction involves a 'conceptual dislocation' that causes a '*shock of dysrecognition*'[3] in the reader. For Suvin, the thought experiments of science fiction are structured around at least one novum or key innovation (such as time travel) in the setup of the narrative world that necessitates a cognitive reconceptualization on the part of the reader. However, the novum in itself does not make for a challenging or puzzling narrative scenario, only an innovative one.

In the context of this chapter, a more significant term in SF theory is that of *conceptual breakthrough*. A conceptual breakthrough can take a number of forms: it can involve an 'altered perception of the world' (scenarios in which 'the world is not what it seems') or scenarios 'where information about the world is not complete' (Nicholls 1993: 255). Conceptual breakthrough is therefore a particularly narratively effective form of the novum because it involves the discovery of a hidden truth or the revelation of a paradigm shift in the course of the narrative, as opposed to simply being an a priori plot device to initiate the story. It is thus crucial to the understanding of science fiction as a genre, driven not so much by science in its technological sense but by 'the quest for knowledge' (254): 'All the most exciting scientific revolutions have taken the form of breaking down a paradigm and substituting another' (255). While Suvin's concept of the novum has a wider currency in SF theory, for the purposes of discussing the aesthetics of complex science fiction and the modelling of its narrative structure, conceptual breakthrough is crucial. It has presumably received less attention because of it being less applicable to all forms of SF; still, it goes to the heart of the attraction of science fiction: readers of SF, like those of puzzle narratives, enter the narrative experience with the hope of engaging with experimental or innovative ideas. They thus approach SF, not with the prospect of attaining hard scientific knowledge (as SF primarily offers imagined science rather than the real thing), but an expansion of perception involving the *simulation* of the attainment of higher knowledge.

Indeed, Nicholls sees conceptual breakthrough in SF as 'springing from a deep-rooted human need: to reach out, escape mental traps, prefer movement to stasis; to understand. Sf [sic] is preeminently the literature of the intellectually discontented' (Nicholls 1993: 256). Conceptual breakthrough is also connected to a further term in SF aesthetics, the *sense of wonder*: 'the peculiar power of science fiction to generate a feeling of awe and perhaps a slightly elevated state of awareness in the reader or viewer' (Wolfe 1979: 23). Yet, a sense of wonder can be triggered by any breathtaking SF scenario (indeed, as Wolfe shows, it can be invoked just by a description at the beginning of a science fiction narrative). By contrast, conceptual breakthrough can only be attained after a narrative process of enigma or mystification.

A crucial distinction from more experimental puzzle narratives now becomes evident: readers of an SF text approach it with the genre-based expectation of attaining this higher plateau of expanded perception. However, the larger corpus of narratively complex texts also includes texts like *Memento* (2000), which ultimately frustrate any upwards movement to greater clarity of vision, and leave the recipient facing incongruous or contradictory fragments rather than 'zooming out' to offer an elevated mode of vision. Some forms of SF – like the film *2001: A Space Odyssey* (1968), which made SF film history by being seriously enigmatic – can be seen as the SF equivalent of the narratively complex *Memento*, in that they frustrate the attainment of a higher vision by leaving too many lacunae. However, it is significant that, in contrast to the non-SF reader who accepts the epistemic disappointment of the impossible puzzle text as an experimental norm, recipients of Kubrick's film, who were viewing it as science fiction, tended to feel short-changed by the lack of coherent explanation, particularly in the final phase of the narrative.

The position of conceptual breakthrough in a science fiction narrative is crucial. If it is introduced in an expositional position, it is simply a novum – the new aspect that creates a significantly different version of the world in which the narrative then unfolds. For example, in Christopher Nolan's *Inception* (2010), the idea of dream theft and its technology is introduced in a matter-of-fact, informative way in the initial stages of the film; it is not subjected to any mystification or equivocation that would turn it into a puzzle that needs solving by attaining a higher level of knowledge. The journeys through the complex dream levels are therefore more akin to an adventure narrative than a quest for knowledge, particularly as the quest is actually to bestow fake knowledge rather than gain access to a higher truth, and Mal Cobb actually dies as a result of believing in false knowledge. *Inception* thus shows that narrative complexity and conceptual breakthrough are distinct processes. By contrast, Nolan's *Interstellar* is a good example of conceptual breakthrough used in an enigmatic fashion: when the fourth dimension, the tesseract, and the enigmatic time loop that underlies them are revealed in the final sections of the film, the viewer feels that they have worked hard to reach them because they have hitherto been given much puzzling input (notably, regarding the role of the 'ghost' in Murphy's bedroom). Moreover, the viewer's processing of the complexity is further intensified by a crucial play-off between a cluster of elements involving science, reason and emotions. This interaction will be considered further below.

The positioning of conceptual breakthrough in the narrative is crucial for the level of complexity and the *cognitive pleasure* of the reader experiencing the discovery or revelation. The discovery, or reveal, towards the point of closure is a cognitive reward that gives the recipient a sense of expanded perception and new insight into life and the universe; this feature can be posited as one of the crucial attractions for engaging with this kind of configuration of narrative complexity. Yet, granting the recipient an expanded vision or insight into the larger workings of a (fictionally) expanded version of the universe is not the same as setting up a truly impossible puzzle narrative (see Kiss and Willemsen 2017): a fully impossible puzzle narrative withholds access to the upper plateau of knowledge or perception that conceptual breakthrough offers.

To summarize, it is thus possible to distinguish between (at least) the following four types of narrative configuration of the novum and conceptual breakthrough:

- *Expositional novum + linearity + subsequent small conceptual breakthroughs.* A novum at the beginning initiates a linear narrative that progresses towards a conceptual breakthrough. For example, in Wells's *The Time Machine* (1895), time travel is the novum, and it is the time traveller's experience of Earth's future, culminating in the demise of the planet itself, that constitutes the conceptual breakthroughs.
- *Expositional novum + complexity.* The narrative introduces a novum near the beginning, and uses it to fashion an unfolding complex narrative scenario, as in *Inception* (2010) or *Looper* (2012).
- *Expositional novum + complexity + late-stage revelatory conceptual breakthroughs.* The narrative may introduce some form of novum in the initial scene-setting, but a further puzzling or incongruous scenario constitutes the enigma that drives the narrative. Here, the impact of the final conceptual breakthrough is powered and built up during the course of the narrative; this pattern is followed by *Interstellar* (2014) and a variety of novels by Philip K. Dick in which the world offers itself as a seemingly impossible puzzle to the protagonist until a conceptual breakthrough ushers in a major discovery through which his

understanding of reality is transformed: for example, *Flow My Tears, the Policemen Said* (1974) and *Eye in the Sky* (1957).

- *Novum + complexity + enduring enigma.* This involves narratives that are so puzzling that they never fully emerge onto the higher plateau of conceptual breakthrough. For example, *2001: A Space Odyssey* (1968) contains various novums and visually offers an expansion of perception, particularly in the cosmic journey undertaken by astronaut David Bowman. However, the enigmatic extraterrestrials, their nature and intentions, and ultimately the point of the creation of the star child, mean that while providing a *visual* expansion of perception, the film does not offer a conceptual breakthrough with *heightened understanding*.

Thus, for a theorization of cognitive challenge from an SF perspective, conceptual breakthroughs can be seen as the reward for the viewer's imaginative cognitive engagement with a challenging narrative world. At the same time, seen from the reverse perspective of the impossible puzzle, conceptual breakthroughs provide clarity – which, ultimately, is the killer of the truly and permanently mind-breaking puzzle. If we posit two fundamental types of puzzle reader – one who hopes the puzzle will provide a gateway to higher knowledge, and one who enjoys the mental work or ambivalence of the enigma itself – then science fiction largely speaks to the former.

Science Fiction as Variations in the Interplay of Knowledge and Threat

As seen thus far, a desire for knowledge and an expansion of perception underlies the readerly attraction of science fiction; the novum supplies the new element for the construction of the SF world, but it is conceptual breakthrough that is the vehicle for the promise of a higher level of knowledge or perception to the reader. However, there is a different and equally significant tradition of science fiction that, cognitively, runs entirely contrary to the dynamics of a positive cognitive journey towards conceptual breakthrough. We can nevertheless see this other tradition interacting within the narrative dynamics of cognitive challenge in science fiction, which is why this section will first introduce this alternative tradition before showing how it plays a role in three examples of complex science fiction.

Cognitively, as a genre, SF exists within a field of tension constructed around the interplay of two fundamental elements: that of knowledge (comprising rational thought, science, and also the process of conceptual breakthrough) and a completely different set of cognitive states involving the stimulation of a sense of threat and fear. Historically, this is because – rather like a complex puzzle narrative – science fiction does not have one linear history but multiple starting points, trajectories, and entangled strands. These different strands involve fundamental contradictions in attitudes towards science and scientific rationality, while the two traditions are connected to two very different mental operations that take place in completely different areas of the brain: rational thought and the threat response. It is these divergent cognitive phenomena that also fuel the dynamics of narrative complexity in science fiction.[4]

Historically, these contradictory impulses are connected to the intellectual forces that have shaped culture in recent centuries: the Enlightenment and Romanticism. Thus, Mary Shelley's *Frankenstein* – seen by many as a founding text of SF (e.g. Aldiss 1973) – clearly occupies the Romantic/threat domain, articulating a deep unquiet about the quest for knowledge, of scientific knowledge in the hands of scientists, and its power to transform society with negative consequences. Cognitively, such narratives are based on the *identification of threat*: they identify science and scientists as a danger to society, and their thought experiments produce horror and admonition. Their cognitive-narrative structure is thus disconnected from that of the puzzle narrative or the desire for the expansion of perspective, because the quest for knowledge itself is framed as potentially damaging: Victor Frankenstein provides a grotesque depiction of the human ego so negatively consumed by the desire to push the novum forward to conceptual breakthrough that he disregards life itself. The cognitive focus on threat within this SF tradition extends to other narrative scenarios, notably to sources of threat from outer space in the disaster tradition of the asteroid collision narrative and, most notably, to the alien invasion narrative, which can be seen as the threat-based variant of the extraterrestrial contact narrative to which *Arrival* also belongs.

What unites these different forms of the SF tradition focused on sources of threat is that the threatening figure is depicted as an 'Other' in contrast to the 'we-identity' of the threatened community: scientists are depicted as Others who pose a threat to society, while, in one of the most extreme imaginations of the Other, extraterrestrials take the form of hostile aliens, their Otherness defined via their physical appearance and often their *lack of emotions*, which is another indication of the inherently Romantic cognitive-cultural position underlying this representational mode.

If the threat tradition in science fiction can be seen as allied to the dystopian narrative tradition that developed fully in the twentieth century, then the pro-science Enlightenment tradition – in which science is a source of fascination, and where rational thought processes and knowledge are largely a source of optimism – can clearly be seen as allied to utopian tendencies. In particular, the pulp science fiction of the mid-twentieth century was grounded in popular aesthetics, which combined the imagination of futuristic scenarios with a publishing strategy that targeted the reader's desire for concrete scientific knowledge, as is indicated by the frequency of additional articles and teasers in the SF pulp journals of the period with titles like 'The Science of Science Fiction' and 'What is Your Science I.Q.?'

The implications for cognitive challenge and complex SF narratives for this dual tradition are numerous. In the most extreme cases of threat-based SF narrative, the sheer force of the threat response they trigger – both on the fictional story level as well as in the recipient, who enjoys the narrative exhilaration of the vicarious threat response – means that there is hardly room for the logical-rational operation of puzzle solving. Indeed, contemporary cognitive science has demonstrated that rational cognition and the processing of threat run on two completely separate systems of the brain: the frontal cortex and the limbic system. The latter is a 'quick and dirty processing system' (LeDoux 1998: 163) that, in order to function properly in dangerous situations, activates the fight, flight or freeze response immediately, and without rational/analytical input from the cortex: 'Emotional responses can occur without the involvement of the higher processing systems of the brain' (ibid.: 161). The threat response is thus so cognitively consuming that recipients of scenes within SF narratives with a strong depiction of threat are far less likely to devote attention to problem-solving issues.

However, observed in the larger context of narrative dynamics, we can see the interplay of rational and threat-based forms of science fiction interacting in the construction of complexity in three different ways. First, we can analyse science fiction for the relative weighting of threat vs rationality/pro-science attitudes to see which is the dominant impulse. Second, in some narratives, threat indicators can be used rhetorically to create a more effective suspense trajectory to ultimately give the conceptual breakthrough more narrative impact when it finally comes. Third, in the tradition of the extraterrestrial contact/invasion narrative, we can see some very interesting variants of cognitive challenge and narrative complexity that use various combinations of threat, knowledge and paradox. Thus, even if the different systems of the human brain cannot efficiently run both responses at the same time, the narrative systems of science fiction run them together in a number of interesting ways. Below, I will give an account of the first and second forms, before concluding with a more extensive discussion of the extraterrestrial contact/invasion narrative.

Two very different examples illustrate how science fiction narratives are based on a field of tension between rationality and emotion, in which the ultimate dominant can fall either way. Both of these examples are structured as puzzles or enigmas, and both contain a sharp contrast not simply between emotion and reason but between scientific knowledge and the strong emotional reaction of hysteria. Nevertheless, they are diametrically opposed in their positioning with regard to the rational and the emotional.

One of the most renowned short stories from the 'Golden Age' of SF, Isaac Asimov's 'Nightfall' (1941), is a puzzle narrative that constructs an enigma concerning why the human civilization on the planet Lagash collapses every 2,050 years. The solution to this puzzle, fully revealed at the end of the narrative, asks the reader to imagine the effects of a complex cosmological scenario on the human mind. Lagash is located in a multiple-sun system that gives it permanent daylight. Something like night only occurs once every 2,050 years, when darkness finally descends due to a rare constellation in which four of the five suns have set and there is an extended eclipse of the remaining sun (the size–distance relations of this fictional sun/moon constellation mean that the moon covers the sun for much longer than in solar eclipses on Earth). The story thus offers the reader an interesting cosmic conceptual breakthrough as well as inviting them to imagine a society suddenly engulfed by darkness when its citizens are habituated to constant light.

The emphasis on the hysterical response of the human characters is strong: even characters who rationally know the scientific reason for the sudden disappearance of light find themselves succumbing to the mass hysteria engulfing the planet as darkness descends. The solution to the puzzle thus hinges on a pivotal distinction between reasoned observation and fear on two levels: the reader is given the rational explanation and can feel enlightened by the interesting cosmic solution to the puzzle, and cognitively superior to the hysterical humans of Lagash, while in the story, civilization descends into madness. The story is thus a literal as well as figural discourse on light and darkness, enlightenment and madness, which clearly comes down on the side of enlightenment: while a small group of scientists try to warn the public of Lagash in vain, the destructive forces of mass hysteria are unleashed when both light and enlightenment are absent.

By contrast, a very different science fiction configuration of the dynamics of emotion and rationality occurs in the seminal invasion narrative, *Invasion of the Body Snatchers* (1956).[5] The film's underlying scenario, only revealed halfway through, is that the people of the Californian town of Santa Mira are gradually and subtly being replaced by duplicate humans born from extraterrestrial seedpods. However, in contrast to the conventional invasion narrative where the threat is evident at the outset, the film's initial discourse is constructed around the enigma of human hysteria in response to an as yet unknown phenomenon, so that the existence of threat is subject to substantial equivocation for the first half of the film. This equivocation is built on a contrastive dialogue between emotion and scientific rationality.

Here, however, rationality is depicted as inferior because it is incapable of detecting the threat due to its implausibility and the lack of evidence: as a lack of emotion is the only distinction that can be observed between a human original and their copy, it is the more sensitive members of society – in the film, represented by women and children – who perceive that their relatives and loved ones are no longer their genuine selves, and who, propelled by the deep fear stimulated by the discovery, try to seek help. Conversely, the scientist figures are the characters who are depicted as being sceptical about the perceived threat until it is too late. Ultimately, however, the two main scientist figures function contrastively in the film's science-emotion continuum: the protagonist and local doctor Miles Bennell is the sceptical every(rational)man at the outset of the story, but has become hysterical and deeply damaged by terror and loss by the end of the story; conversely, the psychiatrist Mannie Kaufman, the film's core example of dangerous rationality, who writes the phenomenon off as 'mass hysteria' is revealed to have been transformed into an emotionless 'pod person' at an unknown point in the narrative. Indeed, it is never made clear exactly when Kaufman is replaced by his pod version, and therefore whether the hyper-rational figure that is introduced near the film's beginning is already an alien life form or simply an ultra-rational scientist incapable of understanding the nature of the threat that is perceived by others with more intuitive minds.

The dual narrative dynamics of *Invasion of the Body Snatchers* and 'Nightfall' reveal how the aesthetics of science fiction can work either way in eliciting and stimulating the recipient's response to the dynamics of emotion vs reason. In 'Nightfall', the reader is given an *expansion of perception* through a dynamic in which reason and science are depicted as superior to the emotional-hysterical human response to the perceived threat of darkness. By contrast, on an interhuman level, *Invasion of the Body Snatchers* depicts more intuitive *emotional perception* as a core survival strategy not possessed by the purely rational. Indeed, *Invasion of the Body Snatchers* is an interesting literalization of cognitive science's findings that the brain's threat response in the limbic system must work independently of the rational cortex in order to function as an effective defence in dangerous situations (LeDoux 1998).

The Interplay of Reason and Threat in Two Recent Complex SF Films: *Looper* and *Interstellar*

Two notable SF puzzle films of recent years show the interaction of threat and reason on a heightened level. As in the contrasting examples of the previous section, a combined dynamic of 'science and knowledge vs threat and emotion' powering the narrative renders it cognitively challenging and stimulating for the viewer within a narrative trajectory that also ultimately leads to a form of conceptual breakthrough at the close.

Recent science fiction puzzle films frequently hinge on elements of time travel, exploiting the potential for disruptions in causal-linear plotting to create cognitive dissonance: i.e. 'puzzling conflicts in narrative comprehension' (Kiss and Willemsen 2017: 67). Despite its tremendous complexity (ibid.: 140–41), *Primer* (2004) is a more literal and grounded configuration of time travel that asks the recipient to try to imagine the inscrutable convolutions of scientists experimenting with low-range time travel over short periods, such as six hours. Relatively speaking, while it does use time travel as a novum, it does not have such a significant component of conceptual breakthrough despite setting up a considerable cognitive challenge for the viewer within its smaller-scope time-travel thought experiment due to the complex and entangled personal timelines and causalities with multiple versions of characters influencing events. By contrast, both *Looper* and *Interstellar* construct more epic temporal networks; however, a distinction between these two films also highlights how substantially different configurations of the dynamic of threat levels vs science and reason can be.

Interstellar (2014) offers the most visionary rendering of the rational-cognitive treatment of time travel; it takes the viewer on what is ultimately a journey of exhilarating expanded perception. It does this by using a covert and defamiliarized time-travel plot to construct a deeply puzzling enigma concerning the mystery of the ghost in Murphy's bedroom. This is then further complicated by the temporal and personal relations, as well as the shared or hidden knowledge between different groups of characters during Cooper's mission to find a new habitable planet for humanity. Not all of these complexities and complications can be discussed within the scope of this chapter, but I would like to highlight the main ones in the overall dynamic of the narrative.

The rational-scientific complexity that the film sets up is composed of two different aspects that are less and more cognitively challenging respectively, and are also presented in different story-discourse relations within the text. One level is not truly a puzzle, although it may be a cognitive challenge for the viewer: the unequal time relations between various character groups located on Earth and in separate locations on the space mission may be confusing or slightly inscrutable, but are based on Albert Einstein's 1905 theory of relativity (Hawking and Mlodinow 2005: 33–35). By contrast, the narrative's visionary denouement of Cooper's journey through space and time is based on a more imaginative configuration of a wormhole idea originally mooted in 1935 by Einstein and Nathan Rosen (ibid.: 110). However, instead of being offered as a priori information, the narrative's underlying complex envisioning of a fourth dimension of space–time is granted to the viewer, not only as a cognitive reward in answer to the enigma of the ghost in the bedroom but also as a positive resolution to Cooper and Murphy's conflicted father–daughter relationship, which spans the narrative. The *deus ex machina* of human wormhole engineering allows Cooper to travel back in time and be the ghost in the bedroom that creates the paradoxical loop that provides his daughter Murphy and an earlier version of himself with the necessary information to trigger Cooper and Murphy's whole involvement with Professor Brand's space project. The construction of a fourth dimension beyond linear time thus becomes the resolution to both the personal and existential dilemmas that the film creates.

However, while *Interstellar* in its entirety is thus firmly founded on Enlightenment traditions of scientific optimism and the unrestricted potential of human endeavour that ultimately eclipses the adverse human-induced environmental scenario on Earth with which the narrative begins, interestingly it does still use the scientist-as-threat trope to construct a more complex narrative experience for the viewer. The crucial scene here is Professor Brand's death scene on Earth in which he confesses that he 'lied' and that there are no viable plans for the astronauts' return, meaning that the Earth is doomed and only the astronauts on the space mission can start a new human civilization beyond Earth. This reversal dramatically remodels him as a manipulative and obsessive scientist, prepared to lie to his family and closest colleagues in order to ensure the success of his project. At the same time, when it comes to the plotting of transtemporal character relations – which provides the narrative interest of the film beyond the enigmatic physics – this revelation seems to ensure the prospect that Murphy will never see her father again, thereby not only cutting Earth off from salvation, but also ensuring that Cooper will break the promise he had made to his daughter that he would return.

However, the construction of Brand as the obsessive scientist prepared to lie to further his scientific project is ultimately a complexifying illusion created to fashion a narrative experience for the recipient in which the trajectory of the viewing experience is more finely balanced between hope and fear so that the interplay of negative and positive anticipation creates narrative suspense. This strategy is a science fiction variant of Kiss and Willemsen's (2017: 164) hypothesis that 'impossible puzzle films achieve their effects by countering their disruptive narrative tactics with classical narration strategies'. This example also shows how, in the aesthetics of suspense, it is sometimes necessary for a narrative to invoke the opposite of its fundamental values (in this case, suggesting that the core scientist figure is a seriously flawed individual) in order to weave an interesting narrative. Ultimately, the film again wholeheartedly embraces science in its brief celebration of the scientific life achievements of the now much older Murphy as well as of the whole human scientific endeavour established in orbit around Saturn. In this narrative world, the fear of the scientist turns out to have been misplaced after all.

In contrast to *Interstellar*, another film constructed around the concept of time travel – *Looper* (2012) – is completely structured around the narrative evocation of threat, with very little invocation of the science aspect of time travel or of rational thought processes right up until the concluding scenes of the narrative. In the film's future scenario of mob assassinations via backwards time travel, the fundamental scenario that provides a form of cognitive challenge consists of the character Joe (one of the protagonists) as a divided self: shifting configurations of the self and Other occur within a fundamentally paradoxical threat scenario in which the younger self is the assassin of the older self. The narrative creates a cognitively highly original scenario that is only achievable by the imaginative potential of time travel, splitting the protagonist's identity into an endangered older self and a threatening younger self as the Other. Moreover, the threat scenario is given far greater complexity by the introduction of multiple perspectives and additional complicating timelines so that, most significantly for the narrative complexity of the film, the self-Other threat relations are reversed through the course of the narrative.

In the first stages of the film, the viewer is introduced to the younger Joe as a threat to his older self. The sense that young Joe is a threat is intensified as the narrative shows him betray his friend Seth (who is on the run after failing to kill his older self), and then depicts the negated existence (a rather cognitively challenging event) of the older Seth as a result of killing younger Seth. These complex causal chains, which set up young Joe as the threatening Other to old Joe's endangered self further down his timeline, characterize the film's narrative strategy and make the ultimate denouement even more narratively effective. The appearance that older Joe is the endangered self – that is, the version of the protagonist that the recipient is supposed to sympathize with – is reinforced in the central sections, where we see older Joe's life thirty years hence from young Joe's existence, culminating in the day on which his wife is murdered and he is sent back thirty years in time to be assassinated.

However, from the point where the young Joe, on the run after losing sight of the escaped older Joe, seeks shelter at the farm of Sara and her son Cid, the locus of threat subtly changes and shifts to older Joe. The latter now embarks on a quest to prevent the emergence of the Rainmaker – the all-powerful criminal boss responsible for his wife's death in the future – by killing all the boys, including Cid, born on a particular date and at a particular location that makes them potentially the Rainmaker. The dynamic is further transformed as young Joe takes on a new role as a substitute father figure for (fatherless) Cid.

The surprising and highly clever ending comes when young Joe identifies the negative patterns underlying the whole cause-and-effect entanglement of timelines, and decides to destroy its emergence by killing himself. He thereby prevents older Joe from attempting to kill Cid as a child and, most significantly, prevents Cid from losing his mother, because, at the moment when young Joe shoots himself, older Joe is about to kill Sara as she stands protectively in front of Cid. By terminating his own life, young Joe thus prevents Cid from embarking on the path that leads to him becoming the Rainmaker. This ending is elegant in its complex cutting-through of the causal trajectories of the character timelines, because it neatly destroys all sources of threat. Cognitively, it also represents a form of subjective conceptual breakthrough for young Joe, as he mentally cuts through all the layers of threat and fear by perceiving the logical and rational solution to the cause-and-effect network in which he is entangled, and then administers the solution without hesitation.

Therefore, in this film, while the novum is provided by the time travel concept, in terms of the narrative trajectory, the conceptual breakthrough comes with young Joe's insight into his own key position in the causal network of influences, and his realization that the only way to provide an effective solution to the problem is by cutting his life short. This particular conceptual breakthrough is a moment of insight across the timelines shared briefly by character and recipient which is, paradoxically, destroyed at the very moment of expanded perception because young Joe's suicide negates all the timelines of the film's narrative. The viewer experiences the expansion of perception in terms of young Joe's incisive and hyper-rational vision of the negative chains of cause-and-effect, creating a new world in which all the sources of threat that the narrative has set up never even existed.

The Threat of the Other and Its Deconstruction in the Extraterrestrial Contact Narrative

This final section will explore variations of a narrative that is one of the most substantial embodiments of the cognitive pattern of threat in science fiction: the alien invasion narrative. This tradition, which Sontag (1965: 209) characterizes as a five-phase formulaic narrative commencing with '[t]he arrival of the thing', has little cognitive subtlety or complexity in its basic form beyond the invocation of a supremely threatening Other, but has been subject to substantial revision by more complex counternarratives of extraterrestrial contact.

The alien invasion tradition was established by H.G. Wells in *The War of the Worlds* (1897) and subsequently expanded and diversified, particularly by key works of science fiction cinema in the 1950s (see Dannenberg 2010). More recent films like *Independence Day* (1996) have resurrected the simplistic pattern highlighted by Sontag, stimulating a form of nostalgia for narratives of raw threat in which the extraterrestrial is a purely hostile force and a singular threat to humanity. Cognitively, these narratives are the opposite of complex in that they tap into and stimulate the default response towards a threatening Other with which humans and other life forms are programmed to respond (LeDoux 1998), thereby creating a very simple but exhilarating aesthetic of vicarious fear in the viewer. As part of this narrative pattern, the alien is intensively othered via unpleasant physical or mental distinguishing features involving the lack of emotion or other noble attributes used to idealize humans in the binary hierarchy of human self vs alien Other.

In this basic form of the alien invasion narrative, there are rarely any puzzles because the threat is all too evident: the overt and powerful othering of the alien presents a clear justification for action rather than thought. Such narrative scenarios of extreme threat are primarily powered by emotions and the triggering of the recipient's mental map of 'we' vs 'they' identities (Hall 1996) – a basic feature of human experience and behaviour linked to the othering of cultural outsiders (Said 1995), which is here applied in a 'safe' fictional scenario where the recipient can emotionally side with characters defending their homeland from outside invaders. This cognitive model is one of the most fundamental historical-existential patterns of both human and non-human terrestrial existence.

However, in the heyday of alien invasion narratives in the 1950s, filmmakers were swift to develop more thoughtful counternarratives to the adrenalin-powered exhilaration of extraterrestrial threat and simple othering. These presented a cognitively more complex configuration of self and Other in which the extraterrestrial visitors are ultimately revealed as not hostile, and the human threat response is often represented as misjudged. However, the confirmation of the extraterrestrials' peaceful intentions is delayed in order to create a suspense arc in which the viewer *may* be given an insight into the aliens' minds and motivations before the characters more fully understand their true nature – e.g. *The Day the Earth Stood Still* (1951) – or they may not – e.g. *It Came from Outer Space* (1953). Most importantly, such narratives perform a more complex cognitive pattern of othering that challenges the simple binary hierarchy of 'humans good'/'aliens bad', and reconfigures it into a less familiar mental map that undermines the anthropocentric idealization of humans.

The developing cognitive challenge to the prioritization and celebration of humans in relation to other life forms, which is staged by these counternarratives to the traditional alien invasion narrative, is environmentally and culturally significant because it highlights a gradual shift in human self-perception that began in the first half of the twentieth century and reaches a significant apex in *Arrival* (2016). Thus, in *It Came from Outer Space*, instead of being technologically superior while also aggressive (the standard alien invasion combination), the extraterrestrial species is technologically *as well as* cognitively, ethically and culturally superior, while the human figures are represented as ethically inferior due to their automatically hostile response to the extraterrestrials. As the departing extraterrestrial says: 'We are not yet ready to meet in friendship' (0:57.37). Human misjudgements and erroneous responses are thus part of the *reverse-othering* pattern of such narratives: they invite the recipient to perform a cognitive operation that goes against the grain of the normal threat response. The recipient has to identify fellow (fictional) humans as fallible, and is invited to identify and empathize with the extraterrestrial rather than the human.

Such science-fiction thought experiments involving reverse-othering are cognitively interesting narrative operations that challenge conventional human attitudes and behaviour patterns regarding self-Other identity configurations. This narrative practice, which goes against the standard accounts of patterns of othering in real-world human culture (Spivak 1985; Said 1995; Hall 1996 – and also against some popular perceptions in these times of heightened nationalism and populism), has not yet been adequately acknowledged; significantly, it challenges the predominant schema of anthropocentric hierarchy by casting the hegemonic 'we' group as inferior to the outsider-Other. The emergence of such narrative texts that practise the reverse-othering of humans in relation to fictional extraterrestrial Others thus suggests that, during the twentieth century, the unchallenged celebration of not only nationalism but of the innate superiority of humanity was slowly being challenged.

In *Invasion of the Body Snatchers*, the narrative configuration of the Other fashions a cognitively even more complex form of the self-Other configuration. Here, as discussed above, the invasion involves the replacement of humans by imposters born from giant seed pods, after which the original human self ceases to exist. The replaced version of the self, who has all the memories of the original, only differs from the genuine human through their lack of emotion. This narrative, therefore, sets up an intricate but ultimately paradoxical thought experiment in which the self *becomes* the Other but, at the same time, can hardly be perceived as such. The film is thus a fascinating rendering of the paradox contained in Freud's concept of the Uncanny, in which striking narrative effects are achieved through the incorporation of the familiar, the unfamiliar and the secret. Freud's theory explains how, in The Uncanny, the sense of threat is intensified through a cognitively challenging paradox that blends the familiar and the unfamiliar. In *Invasion of the Body Snatchers*, the threat is posed by figures who resemble a familiar and beloved person, which is all the more unsettling because the threat is paradoxically posed by both the Other and the non-Other. The pod people are ultimately a chilling puzzle created out of a nightmarish imagination: they are Others who are versions of the self but who destroy the self in order to secure their own existence.

In summary, the examples above show how complex SF narratives of extraterrestrial contact do not follow a simple formula of alien-as-threatening-Other in a binary hierarchy. Rather, they produce a variety of thought experiments, often with cognitively challenging self-Other relations that invite the recipient to vicariously perform mental configurations of identity that extend well beyond the standard response of simplistic narratives depicting threatening Others. We will now see how *Arrival* continues in the same tradition of 'writing back' to the alien invasion narrative by producing a counternarrative of the cognitive model of the threatening Other. The narrative does so while also laying on the cognitive complexity even further, so that it can be seen as the contemporary state of the art in extraterrestrial narrative modelling, and a consummate realization of Larry Niven's idea that 'the only universal message in science fiction is as follows: There are minds that think as well as you do, or better, but differently' (Niven 1987: 3).

Arrival weaves many of the elements already discussed in this chapter into an intricate configuration of science fiction complexity. It combines an extraterrestrial contact narrative with a novel representation of time involving subjective time travel and a substantial conceptual breakthrough. As part of its deconstruction of the alien as Other, in terms of the extraterrestrial contact aspect of the film, *Arrival* performs a fascinating dialogue with previous alien invasion narratives: the shape and positioning of the extraterrestrials' spaceships as vertical pods visually instate them as different from the standard flying saucer shape associated with threat that is familiar from films like *Independence Day*. And yet, at a strategic point in the film's suspense structure, and to signal a possibility that the Heptapods might be moving to aggression after all, the spaceships turn on their side to take the more traditional form. In its visual representation as well as in its story, the film stands in intertextual dialogue with the alien invasion narrative: it follows a similar trajectory to earlier films by setting up an equivocal framework regarding the extraterrestrials' intentions and whether they pose a threat; but, ultimately, due to the film's complex plotting, this layer of enigma is a subterfuge for a more complex conceptual breakthrough.

The film's structure consists of three distinct but interrelated levels of enigma or puzzle:

1. On the level of the discourse, the narrative plays a series of rhetorical-intertextual games with the viewer, already alluded to above: it plays with the viewer's expectations regarding whether the extraterrestrials are a threat or not, and (similar to *Looper*) the narrative goes through several stages of this complicating pattern of possible victim-threat relations. The Heptapods are threatened by the rogue soldiers who take things into their own hands by planting a bomb in the spaceship, while, later, the Heptapods' actions seem to be moving towards aggression (complicated by the mistranslation of one of their logograms as 'weapon' in response to a key question about their intentions).
2. On another level, the central enigma is not only the extraterrestrials' intentions but also actual communication. The degree of the narrative's complexity in the range of extraterrestrial narrative variants can be gauged on this factor alone; in the majority of basic alien invasion films, narrative communication between human and alien is (highly unrealistically) automatically assumed. Here, language and intercultural communication assume a more realistic and highly challenging complexity, with the logograms representing the ultimate visual puzzle. Thus, while the standard narrative of alien invasion automatically configures Otherness as a threat, in this narrative, the extraterrestrials, represented by their complex form of written language, are an enigma that needs decoding. In this rendering of extraterrestrial contact, the alien Other is first the enigma but also ultimately provides the solution.
3. The third level of enigma is linked to the second one, but this does not become clear until the closing sections of the narrative: the sequences where (for a first-time viewer) Dr Banks seems to be *recalling* her dead daughter, take on an increasingly powerful resonance because of their relevance to and interaction with her life in the narrative present. The viewer does not understand their significance, and only gradually comes to realize that

Dr Banks does not either – that is, that they are not flashbacks at all but mysterious visions. The big reveal comes when, in dialogue with the Heptapod Costello, Banks asks, 'Who is this child?' (1:31.14). From this point on, all the puzzles are gradually unravelled, and the viewer receives confirmation that the Heptapods are not hostile but would like to trade cooperation. Their side of the deal is the gift of their language, which gives the user a complexity of vision that collapses the linearity of time. As a result, Banks (and also the viewer) now realizes that her visions hitherto have been of her future child and the story of her future life. One of the most fascinating things about the storytelling complexity of *Arrival* is how it tells the story of Banks, her husband Ian and their child, without actually depicting it.

Arrival, like *Looper*, constructs a narrative scenario in which the conceptual breakthrough is linked to a character's individual experience and perspective across time. However, unlike *Looper* and more like *Interstellar*, this breakthrough involves a positive expansion of perception that takes the character to a higher plateau of knowledge and vision, breaking down Banks's conventional perception of time so that 'there is no time' (1:23.21). For her, time becomes 'non-linear' (1:38.10) and she is no longer 'bound by time' (0:01.55). Moreover, the film renegotiates the narrative of the utterly hostile, othered alien in many ways. It chooses to render the Other as non-humanoid in form: it defines the extraterrestrial in terms of strong physical difference, which in SF convention is often used as a marker of negativity. However, the film combines this physical difference with intellectual complexity, highly advanced conceptual abilities, and a positive attitude towards the humans of Earth in bringing the gift of nonlinear temporal perception. However, all these ultimate 'truths' are wrapped up in the three-level puzzle described above, so that they feature as multiple conceptual breakthroughs shared by the viewer and protagonist by the end of the narrative.

Moreover, the level of expanded perception experienced by Dr Banks involves a sense of acceptance of life: at the close of the narrative, she undertakes steps that she knows will lead to the conception and death of her child, and to her husband leaving her. This implies that the conceptual breakthrough of a reconfigured vision of time that the heptapods' language has given her has led to a complete acceptance of her life trajectory, especially as she no longer views it from one temporal standpoint. What is notable about this conclusion, when we compare it with young Joe's final insight in *Looper* and Cooper's journey to the tesseract in *Interstellar*, is that each resolution of the previous enigma and narrative complexity concludes with a higher vision of timelines facilitated by a conceptual breakthrough that breaks the puzzle and gives clarity. Thus, all three of these films indicate that complex science fiction is intrinsically built on the solving of puzzles to reach the higher imaginative level of conceptual breakthrough, which brings an expansion of perception, as opposed to creating permanent enigmas.

Conclusion

All narratives are thought experiments, but science fiction narratives are thought experimens that take place in a universe with at least one deviation from the real world (the novum). Complex SF narratives offer at least one further *cognitively complex novum* in the form of a conceptual breakthrough, which almost invariably occurs towards the end of the narrative and provides a crucial *expansion of perception*. This expansion of perception may be the revelation of a whole new system of physics, as in *Interstellar*, or it may be experienced by a character on a more personal level, as in *Arrival* and *Looper*. Crucially, readers and viewers of complex SF texts (as opposed to pure adventure SF) enjoy and expect SF to offer them this expansion of perception. As such, a truly (i.e. permanently) enigmatic puzzle narrative is not the norm in complex SF narratives. Rather, the cognitive challenge takes the form of leading the recipient through conceptually complex realizations or cognitively complex scenarios of self and Other (*Looper, Arrival*), which challenge the popular schemata of the self and Other encountered both in everyday life and in simpler science fiction narratives. In the case of narratives using time travel, the dissolution or overwriting of linear structures of time is a frequent point of closure: *Looper, Arrival* and *Interstellar* all, in some way, destroy linear perceptions, narrative flow or hitherto established character timelines. *Arrival* is a particularly notable film in this context because it merges the dissolution of linear time with a groundbreaking depiction of the extraterrestrial Other, in which the latter is first the enigmatic Other but, in the process of the solving of the enigma, also provides the solution to the puzzle through the revolutionary cognitive power of their language to reconfigure the perception of time.

Moreover, while it is a given that complex puzzle narratives are intrinsically based on rational thought that stimulates the recipient's frontal cortex, emotions – particularly emotions in response to the depiction of threatening Others, from scientist to extraterrestrial – are a substantial element of the SF tradition that also feed into complex SF in various ways. Each SF text can therefore be analysed for its unique blend of the rational and the threatening, ranging from the use of threat as a strategy to create suspense in the build towards the conceptual breakthrough (*Interstellar*) to narratives that involve a more radical revision of the extraterrestrial as an archetype of threat, and thus challenge the popular and cognitively lazy tendency across human societies to see Others as potential threats. SF narratives of reverse-othering, such as *Arrival*, challenge this mode of thought and suggest an idea that may be cognitively challenging for many: that Others can bring gifts and lasting enrichment to society.

This chapter has also identified the science fiction genre as straddling two separate intellectual traditions: that of the Enlightenment and scientific reasoning and that of Romanticism and scepticism towards science. Both of these traditions also feed into the aspect of conceptual breakthrough but differ in how the narrative is plotted in relation to the discovery of the higher-level knowledge that comes with the breakthrough. In the Enlightenment SF tradition, conceptual breakthrough implies the potential for breaking through scientific boundaries that limit human knowledge. *Interstellar* is a notable contemporary text in this tradition, but many other SF narratives exist in the same optimistic line of moving on to the next, more complex level of human existence. The cultural scepticism of Romanticism towards the Enlightenment, which, as we have seen, involves a caution towards the pursuit of technological knowledge, nevertheless contains a fundamental desire to transcend the material surfaces and cognitive restrictions of human existence to reach a higher level of perception; this aspect is also partly embodied in the experience and spirit of conceptual breakthrough in science fiction. In this respect, *Arrival* contains more of the Romantic spirit of conceptual breakthrough than *Interstellar*, in that the vision attained by Louise Banks brings a higher awareness, vision and emotional acceptance of life than pure scientific discovery. The fact that we can see both the cultural and intellectual legacy of the Enlightenment and Romanticism manifested in the heightened perception offered to the reader/viewer in complex science fiction narratives shows that narrative complexity is a product of their long-standing interaction in the history of the genre. As this chapter has hopefully shown, such interaction has produced some notable new narratives in the present.

Hilary Duffield is Professor of English Literature at the University of Trier, Germany. As well as having a long-standing interest in science fiction, her current research interests include cognitive approaches to narrative, invasion narratives, and narratives of environmental crisis. She has published articles in journals such as *Poetics Today, Narrative, Current Writing, Journal for the Study of British Cultures, Journal of Postcolonial Writing, Interventions* and *Sprachkunst*. Her book *Coincidence and Counterfactuality: Plotting Time and Space in Narrative Fiction* (published as Hilary Dannenberg) won the George and Barbara Perkins award for the most significant contribution to the study of narrative in 2010.

Notes

1. This chapter's early development greatly benefited from some lively online discussions with Steven Willemsen and the participants of the seminar 'Humanity and Society Transformed: The Worlds of Science Fiction'.
2. See the discussion of this 'advent of ontological pluralisation' in Dannenberg 2008: 202–7.
3. Italics in original.
4. In addition to science fiction's lack of a set story formula (Rose 1981: 2), this innate cognitive-historical complexity is a key reason why there is no consensual definition of science fiction.
5. *Invasion of the Body Snatchers* was adapted from the equally interesting serialized print narrative by Jack Finney, *The Body Snatchers* (1955). The print version's scenario is similar but not as dark, and the representation of the emotional dimension is more intense in the film, both due to the alterations to the story made for the screen version and the heightened emotional effects created by the film discourse. These aspects, unfortunately, cannot be elaborated on in the scope of this chapter, but are under investigation in a separate project on invasion narratives in print and cinematic narrative.

References

Aldiss, Brian W. 1973. *Billion Year Spree: The True History of Science Fiction*. London: Weidenfeld & Nicolson.

Dannenberg, Hilary P. 2008. *Coincidence and Counterfactuality: Plotting Time and Space in Narrative Fiction*. Frontiers of Narrative. Lincoln: University of Nebraska Press.

———. 2010. 'Invasion Narratives and the Cold War in the 1950s American Science-Fiction Film', in Kathleen Starck (ed.), *Between Fear and Freedom: Cultural Representations of the Cold War*. Newcastle upon Tyne: Cambridge Scholars, pp. 39–52.

Dick, Philip K. (1981) 1990. 'Preface', in *Beyond Lies the Wub: The Collected Stories of Philip K Dick*, vol. 1. London: Grafton, pp. 9–11.

Freud, Sigmund. (1919) 2003. *The Uncanny*. David McLintock (trans). London: Penguin.

Hall, Stuart. 1996. 'Introduction: Who Needs 'Identity'?', in Stuart Hall and Paul du Gay (eds), *Questions of Cultural Identity*. London: Sage, pp. 1–17.

Hawking, Stephen, with Leonard Mlodinow. 2005. *A Briefer History of Time*. London: Bantam Press.

Kiss, Miklós, and Steven Willemsen. 2017. *Impossible Puzzle Films: A Cognitive Approach to Contemporary Complex Cinema*. Edinburgh: Edinburgh University Press.

LeDoux, Joseph. 1998. *The Emotional Brain: The Mysterious Underpinnings of Emotional Life*. London: Phoenix.

McHale, Brian. 1987. *Postmodernist Fiction*. London: Methuen.

Nicholls, Peter. 1993. 'Conceptual Breakthrough', in John Clute and Peter Nicholls (eds), *The Encyclopedia of Science Fiction*. London: Orbit, pp. 254–57.

Niven, Larry. 1987. 'The Alien in Our Minds', in George E. Slusser and Eric S. Rabkin (eds), *Aliens: The Anthropology of Science Fiction*. Carbondale: Southern Illinois University Press, pp. 3–12.

Rose, Mark. 1981. *Alien Encounters: Anatomy of Science Fiction*. Cambridge, MA: Harvard University Press.

Said, Edward. (1978) 1995. *Orientalism*. Harmondsworth, UK: Penguin.

Sontag, Susan. 1965. 'The Imagination of Disaster', in *Against Interpretation and Other Essays*. New York: Picador, pp. 209–25.

Spivak, Gayatri Chakravorty. 1985. 'The Rani of Sirmur: An Essay in Reading the Archives', *History and Theory* 24(3): 247–72.

Suvin, Darko. (1979) 2016. *Metamorphoses of Science Fiction: On the Poetics and History of a Literary Genre*, edited by Gerry Canavan. Oxford: Lang.

Wolfe, Gary K. 1979. *The Known and the Unknown: The Iconography of Science Fiction*. Kent, OH: The Kent State University Press.

CHAPTER 4
Strange Loops and Nonhuman Realities
Complex Narrative Faces the Climate Crisis

Marco Caracciolo

Introduction

'You can force your story's shape but the colour will always bloom upstream', announces the trailer of Shane Carruth's 2013 film *Upstream Color*, the words appearing one by one against a backdrop of felt-like fabric. The film does succeed in forcing the story's shape; perhaps more accurately, it bends the linearity of narrative progression into a number of looping structures. Viewers familiar with Carruth's debut – the widely acclaimed time-travel film *Primer* (2004) – will undoubtedly expect confusing, paradoxical and largely inexplicable twists. Despite the meagre budget, *Primer* delivered one of the best cinematic renditions of the puzzles of time travel, and one that has not gone unnoticed by theorists of complex narrative in film (see Kiss and Willemsen 2017: 140–42). *Upstream Color* proves more difficult to categorize and interpret, even if it remains grounded in the genre of science fiction.

'To describe the plot of *Upstream Color* is an exercise in comical futility', explains Scott Tobias (2013) in an online review, echoing what has almost become a trope in critical commentary on complex film. Essentially, the film centres on the relationship between two characters, Kris (Amy Seimetz) and Jeff (Carruth himself), who gradually discover that they have both gone through the same harrowing experience of abduction. The perpetrator – and here is where the plot synopsis waxes trippy – is a character known as the Thief (Thiago Martins), who kidnaps Kris and uses a larva harvested from blue orchids to control her mind. Kris wakes up at home, without any recollection of the recent events but with worms crawling under her skin – one of the film's most memorable moments of body horror. Another character, the Sampler (Andrew Sensenig), enters the scene: he appears to run a pig farm, but he also collects sounds that, when played through large speakers, have the effect of summoning the Thief's victims. Kris thus turns up at the Sampler's farm, where she undergoes a surgical operation that purges her of the parasites. The process involves linking up Kris's body with one of the Sampler's pigs. When she recovers consciousness, Kris seems to have forgotten both the abduction and the Sampler's operation. It is only through her growing intimacy with Jeff that dim memories of those events start surfacing. Eventually, Kris and Jeff kill the Sampler and put an end to the Thief's operations. Together with the Thief's previous victims (known as the 'Sampled', according to the end credits), the protagonists storm the Sampler's farm and liberate the pigs.

As both a love story and an exploration of the uneasy link between consciousness and the material world, *Upstream Color* resonates strongly with contemporary arguments on the interrelation of human subjectivity and nonhuman realities.[1] This chapter examines how the film's complex narrative form, combined with cinematic style and theme, evokes a vivid image of human societies' material and cultural entanglement with the nonhuman. The prospect of gaining this kind of insight may well be one of the reasons why certain audience members take an interest in complex narrative, and are willing to work through its difficulties and paradoxes. When read as an ecological parable, *Upstream Color* explores and exposes the traumas of contemporary society's instrumentalization of the natural world (symbolically hinted at here by the Sampler's pig farm and the Thief's parasites). We will see that the film deploys a number of what I call 'material anchors' for human–nonhuman interconnectedness in an order that suggests a conceptual movement from a dystopian beginning to a utopian ending. Material anchors are visual images or diegetic objects that stand in for abstract ideas such as human–nonhuman linkage: they serve to 'anchor' the thematic and conceptual dimension of the film to concrete formal devices.[2] I argue that these anchors guide our understanding of the complexity of the film's storytelling, inflecting the viewer's meaning-making, and steering it towards ecological issues.

The aesthetic appeal of *Upstream Color* (and critics have been virtually unanimous in praising the film's boldness) thus sheds light on our position vis-à-vis an environment that, in times of climate change, is being dramatically reshaped by human activities. Understood in this way, the formal complexity of *Upstream Color* is satisfying because it mirrors the material and cultural complexity of humanity's reliance on the natural world. Narrative complexity is thus resolved, or at least addressed, by bringing it to bear on extratextual issues that appear equally puzzling or disconcerting. Of course, arriving at this conclusion requires interpretive effort, which may in itself be perceived as rewarding by certain audiences. There may be a larger pay-off, too (although arguing this point lies beyond the scope of this chapter): learning to engage with and appreciate the formal complexity of narrative may train audiences' ability to better coexist with the complexity of real-world concerns.

In the next section, I start by building on recent work that has attempted to establish a common ground between narrative (theory) and complex systems theory. The assumption that guides my argument – which I share with Miklós Kiss and Steven Willemsen's (2017) cognitive approach to formal complexity – is that complex narrative puzzles call for interpretation to overcome or at least reduce the audience's disorientation. I focus here on a particularly significant but largely underexplored interpretive pathway: mapping complex narrative form onto the extrinsic complexity of humanity's capture in biological, climatological and geological processes. We will see that the form of that capture is a distinctively strange 'loop' involving three features: nonlinearity, multiscalarity and self-organization. Strange loops abound in Carruth's *Upstream Color* and underlie the film's engagement with ecological themes, as I detail in the final section of this chapter.

Varieties of Complexity

Work on narrative complexity tends to fall into three, partly overlapping strands of research. First, there has been a great deal of interest in complexity as a *formal* phenomenon involving strategies that complicate and challenge conventional storytelling techniques: for example, those of 'the classical, unified mimetic plot' in film (Buckland 2009: 5). Complexity is thus defined as a deviation from the expectations surrounding various aspects of narrative, particularly the construction of a coherent plot. Second, work by Kiss and Willemsen (2017) as well as Maria Poulaki (2019) has explored the psychological underpinnings of narrative complexity – that is, how audiences go about addressing the cognitive and interpretive difficulties raised by stories rich in formally complex devices. Finally, scholars like John Pier (2017), Marie-Laure Ryan (2019), and Richard Walsh and Susan Stepney (2018) have discussed the possibilities of narrative vis-à-vis a scientific – as opposed to a predominantly formal – understanding of complexity.

This view of complexity is grounded in debates on complex systems. In this section, I will take my cue from this third approach to narrative complexity, though I will return to the formal and cognitive dimensions of complex narrative in my account of *Upstream Color*.

Much ink has been spilled on the definition of complex systems in physics and related sciences. For my purposes, a phenomenon can be said to be complex when it displays three features: nonlinearity, multiscalarity and self-organization (see Baranger 2000). For a simple illustration of the first two concepts, consider surface tension in fluids such as water – here, I follow Terrence Deacon's discussion (Deacon 2006: 127–29). Surface tension is not a property of individual water molecules; it emerges from interactions between a certain number of water molecules as a function of the *shape* that these molecules tend to take when grouped together. Surface tension does not increase linearly, with one water molecule displaying a certain amount of surface tension, two molecules double the amount, and so on. Rather, it is a property that springs up 'suddenly' (i.e. nonlinearly) after a certain critical mass has been reached. Likewise, surface tension operates differently depending on spatial scale: on the scale of a single water molecule, it does not exist; on the scale of a group of molecules, it creates a cohesive force that is responsible for the distinctive shape of a droplet; but on the scale of, for example, a pond, it is what enables the insects commonly known as 'water striders' to skip across the water. These features of nonlinearity and multiscalarity are typical of complex systems. To understand complexity more fully, we need to bring in the third concept, that of self-organization. The molecular interactions producing surface tension remain relatively predictable, as are the physical arrangements they give rise to (a flat surface, a drop or bead of liquid). In a truly complex system, the overall shape of the system changes dynamically and unpredictably over time, but the system does not dissolve or break down: it keeps adjusting to external and internal circumstances. This is what is meant by self-organization.

Complexity exists at multiple levels of reality, from snow crystals to the evolutionary pressures that drive natural selection, to patterns in the development of urban areas (see West 2017: 21–22). Nonlinearity, multiscalarity and self-organization are evidently abstract principles with profoundly different manifestations in the physical and social world. Crucially for my argument, these three concepts also shed light on the complexity of the human impact on the planet in times of ecological crisis.

The Ecological Crisis and Its Narrative Challenges

The 'Anthropocene' is the proposed name for the current geological epoch (Crutzen and Stoermer 2000): it suggests that humanity has become a planetary agent capable of dramatically reshaping the Earth's ecosystems through, for example, the burning of fossil fuels and the release of polluting substances that leave a physical mark on the planet's crust (think about the tremendous amounts of plastic piling up in landfills and clogging the oceans). While the term 'Anthropocene' remains, in some respects, controversial (see Simon 2018) and has not been officially adopted in scientific terminology, it drives home the main difference between the current climate crisis and the many fluctuations in the planet's climate that preceded it: only the former can be linked to the activities of a single species over a short period of time (geologically speaking).

More accurately, the ecological crisis is the result of specific technologies and forms of social organization such as advanced capitalism and large-scale industrialization, which have spread from a handful of Western countries to the rest of the world. Thus, famously, historian Dipesh Chakrabarty argues that anthropogenic climate change

> *brings into view the collision – or the running up against one another – of three histories that, from the point of view of human history, are normally assumed to be working at such different and distinct paces that they are treated as processes separate from one another for all practical purposes: the history of the earth system, the history of life, including that of human evolution on the planet, and the more recent history of industrial civilization (for many, capitalism).* (Chakrabarty 2014: 1)

I bring up Chakrabarty's 'collision' metaphor in this context because it encapsulates with remarkable precision the nonlinear, multiscalar and self-organizing nature – and therefore the complexity – of humanity's entanglement with the climate.

Effectively, the ecological crisis reveals that, when they become ingrained in the day-to-day routine of millions of people, simple actions such as driving a car to work can have an enormous impact on the planet's climate. The nonlinearity of this process has to do with the experienced gap between a quotidian and seemingly inconsequential gesture and its dramatic results on a planetary scale (e.g. rising sea levels, increased average temperatures, frequent extreme weather events). If we look closely at the effects of individual choices on the climate, we find a dizzying number of factors that shape, for example, our decision to drive to work in a truly multiscalar way: the availability of certain technologies and infrastructure, policies that incentivize the car industry and, last but not least, a vast set of cultural assumptions and biases. Moreover, climate change is the result of self-organizing behaviour as the Earth's climate and ecosystems adapt to the multiple effects of human activities, with devastating consequences for both animal and plant species and, increasingly, vulnerable human communities around the globe. In short, the ecological crisis bears all the hallmarks of complex systems, even as this complexity tends to elude everyday experience (which explains, at least in part, why it is so politically and culturally difficult to develop comprehensive measures against climate change).

What can narrative do with this astounding complexity? Although this question has rarely been framed in relation to climate change as such, narrative theorists hold varying views on storytelling's capacity to capture nonlinear, multiscalar and self-organizing processes. In discussing mathematician John Conway's famous 'Game of Life' (a cellular automaton displaying a remarkable degree of self-organization), Richard Walsh argues pessimistically that any 'conceivable narrative of the higher-level behavior [of the system] would … misrepresent what is happening in the system, while any description of the system itself, with its multiple simultaneous recursive operations, necessarily defies narrative form' (Walsh 2011: 75). At the opposite end of the spectrum, John Pier contends that a degree of nonlinearity is necessarily bound up with narrative sequence, so that narrative 'is self-organizing to the extent that, through its exchanges with the outside world, the system itself evolves irreversibly' (Pier 2017: 558). In this chapter, I seek a compromise between these positions: while I agree with Walsh that complex systems (including human–nonhuman interdependency as it is revealed by climate change) cannot be narrativized as such, individual stories can approximate more or less effectively the triad of nonlinearity, multiscalarity and self-organization that defines complex systems. In this way, I shift the emphasis from an ontological question ('is narrative an intrinsically complex system?') to the possibilities and effects of storytelling ('can specific narratives channel the features that underlie complex systems?'). In the next section, I explain why formal experiments are central to the narrative remediation of complexity.

The Form of Ecological Awareness

The collision of histories envisaged by Chakrabarty (2014) resonates with Timothy Morton's concept of 'the mesh', which evokes 'the interconnectedness of all living and non-living things' (2010: 28) – an interconnectedness brought to the fore by climate change. Not only are human societies shaped by the geological and climatological setup of their environment, but they have gained the power to reshape it in fundamental ways. In itself, the idea of interconnectedness is nothing new; notions of human–nonhuman interdependency already had wide circulation within the deep ecology movement from the 1970s onwards (see Fox 1995). What distinguishes Morton's brand of 'ecological thought' is its insight into the *strangeness* of this interrelation:

> The mesh is vast yet intimate: there is no here or there, so everything is brought within our awareness. The more we analyze, the more ambiguous things become. We can't really know who is at the junctions of the mesh before we meet them. Even when we meet them, they are liable to change before our eyes, and our view of them is also labile. These beings are the strange stranger. (Morton 2010: 40; emphasis in original)

Morton's statements are characteristically ambiguous; one way to understand them is to think about our uneasy intimacy with plastic – a human-made polymer that is ubiquitous in the modern world and that will survive us by hundreds of years due to its slow rate of decay. By seeing plastic in this light, we defamiliarize it and reveal its inherent strangeness.

Crucially, this strange interrelation between human culture and the material world takes a specific form in Morton's oeuvre. The spatial form of human–nonhuman entanglement is the loop, which already appears in one of the environmentalist movement's most characteristic images, the symbol for recycling. Talk about 'feedback loops' is also common in the science of complexity; the loop is one of the ways in which self-organization manifests itself, and it is plainly a nonlinear figure.

In *Dark Ecology*, Morton explores the strange loop-like quality of ecological awareness, which is humanity's growing awareness of being entangled with nonhuman realities: 'Ecological awareness is weird: it has a twisted, looping form. Since there is no limit to the scope of ecological beings (biosphere, solar system), we can infer that all things have a loop form. Ecological awareness is a loop because human interference has a loop form, because ecological and biological systems are loops' (Morton 2016: 6). A loop is different from a circle because it is dynamic; it bends around itself in a puzzling fashion. Hence, the 'strange loops' famously theorized by Douglas Hofstadter (1999), a concept also referenced by Morton (2016: 178). Why does ecological awareness trace a weird loop? Because we realize (if, of course, we ever come to that realization) that our actions produce effects well beyond our intentions, feeding the climate crisis and at the same time being fed by a whole cultural system that supports consumption and (reckless faith in) unlimited growth. Through that loop formed by culture and the material ramifications of our actions, each of us is implicated in climate change in deeply multiscalar and nonlinear terms.

It is significant that one of Morton's concrete examples of the weird loop is 'Terry Gilliam's ecological apocalyptic time-loop movie, *Twelve Monkeys*, [in which] the lunatic who releases the virus that wipes out almost all humans doesn't even open the vial of deadly pathogens himself' (2010: 122). The 'time-loop movie' maps the abstract loop of human–nonhuman entanglement onto a narrative strategy that breaks with conventions of chronological linearity and clear-cut teleology (as would be the case if the lunatic *did* open the vial himself in order to achieve his destructive goal). This observation points to the bridge between formal complexity and the abstract features of complex systems I discussed above: by experimenting with established conventions, narrative can convey the nonlinear, multiscalar and self-organizing quality of complex systems, including the ecological crisis itself. The question of whether narrative is an inherently complex system is thus rendered moot; what matters is that story can evoke, formally and also (as my discussion of *Upstream Color* will reveal) affectively, the main characteristics of complex systems.

The need for such innovative narrative strategies has been highlighted by many commentators on the climate crisis. Indian writer Amitav Ghosh (2016), for instance, has drawn attention to the limitations of the realist novel as a genre geared towards a fundamentally bourgeois notion of 'probability' that does not sit well with the inherent weirdness of climate change. Literary realism, as the modern novel has practised it, is starting to show its limits. Hence, earlier forms of narrative – stories that 'delighted in the unheard-of and the unlikely', in Ghosh's words (ibid.: 16) – are making a comeback or entering the mainstream with increasingly intense traffic between genre fiction (e.g. science fiction or fantasy) and literary writing. Examples of this traffic are Jeff VanderMeer's novels – typically discussed under the heading of 'New Weird fiction' (Ulstein 2017) – or works by established literary writers such as Cormac McCarthy (*The Road*), Jeanette Winterson (*The Stone Gods*) and Colson Whitehead (*Zone One*) that draw inspiration from science fiction.

As Ian Watt (1957) argued in his seminal *The Rise of the Novel*, literary realism emerged in conjunction with the industrial revolution and Western modernity – historical processes that are causally implicated in climate change. In light of this complicity between realism and the causes of the ecological crisis, it is unsurprising that doing justice to the current predicament, with its strange loops discussed by Morton, requires stepping outside of a realist framework. *Upstream Color* attempts a similar operation within the medium of film by combining loop-like formal devices with an ecological subject matter. It builds on science fiction motifs to convey a deeply perplexing view of human–nonhuman entanglement, and it does so by disrupting, at the formal level, the illusory chronological sequentiality and teleological coherence of realism (here embodied not by the realist novel but by classical Hollywood narration). This is perhaps part of what the film's trailer means by 'forcing the story's shape': as the conventions of realist representation are distorted, the viewer's puzzlement channels deep insight into the nonlinear, multiscalar and self-organizing nature of human–nonhuman relations in times of climate crisis. Formal complexity is thus put at the service of the more intangible complexity of humanity's entanglement with the nonhuman world.[3] Now that these conceptual tools have been introduced, it is time to turn to a close analysis of Carruth's film.

Looping Upstream

The challenge of piecing together the plot of *Upstream Color* depends primarily on Carruth's unwillingness to engage in any sort of exposition; the most important causal links have to be inferred from the characters' actions. The plot unfolds in fits and starts, with characters disappearing and then making a sudden reappearance later in the story. Jeff, for example, is seen for the first time four minutes into the movie: the editing flips back and forth between images of him running and two boys playing, while the character known as the Thief watches them. Jeff only re-enters the scene half an hour later, after a sequence focusing on

Kris's abduction at the hands of the Thief, who drugs her using worms collected from the petals of blue orchids – a detail the importance of which only emerges much later. The Thief appears to be in control of Kris's mind and he forces her to sign over to him her house and savings. He is not seen again until the very end of the film. These gaps and ellipses contribute to the viewer's disorientation so that – as is typical in 'puzzle films' – the full story can only be reconstructed after multiple viewings, and provided that the audience is willing to put in the necessary 'forensic' work.[4]

Despite the difficulty of inferring the plot, the film does tell a reasonably coherent (if perplexing) story. The starting point is the symbiotic relationship between the Sampler and the Thief. These characters participate in a cycle, which begins with the Sampler, who runs a pig farm, drowning some of the piglets in a river. A series of close-up shots reminiscent of medical imagery show a blue substance seeping from the animals' decomposing bodies and coursing through the water (a scene that is the clearest diegetic justification for the titular 'upstream colour'). The orchids that grow on the riverbank absorb this colour; the flowers turn blue, attracting worms that the Thief harvests and uses to drug his victims and strip them of all their possessions. The Sampler then tracks down the Thief's victims and proceeds to transfer the worms they have ingested (and which are taking control of their bodies) into one of his pigs, whose offspring are thrown into the river. When the protagonists (Kris and Jeff) kill the Sampler at the end of the film, we see that the orchids by the river have white, not blue, petals. The Thief examines them and shakes his head upon failing to find any worms. The protagonists have thus managed to end the partnership between the Sampler and the Thief.

This cycle involving the Sampler and the Thief is only shown once and is interspersed with Kris and Jeff's love story – a juxtaposition that, of course, greatly increases the viewers' cognitive workload as they attempt to piece together the plot. The film clearly suggests that this sequence (pigs are killed, the orchids turn blue, the worms are collected, etc.) is not a one-off occurrence but has taken place multiple times before. It is comparable to a self-organizing feedback loop, with the idea of self-organization being strongly implied by the fact that both the Thief and the Sampler never meet and seem unaware of their reliance on each other's activities. In this way, the cycle at the heart of the film's plot is triggered by human interference in natural processes but remains uncoupled from human intentions: both the Thief and the Sampler exploit a dynamic they do not fully understand, just as climate change is shaped, nonlinearly, by minor, unconscious gestures and decisions rather than by a deliberate intention to harm the environment.

The Thief and the Sampler's inadvertent symbiosis thus evokes a deep sense of enmeshment between various domains and scales of reality – the vegetal (orchids), the animals (worms and pigs), and the microscopic (when the blue substance migrates from the decomposing pigs to the flowers) – all of which are revealed to be closely intertwined with human life. This is the first strange loop brought into focus by the film. Perhaps the most forceful image of human–nonhuman interconnectedness offered by *Upstream Color* is the sequence in which Kris's body is linked up with a pig's, and we see a long worm, at the centre of the shot, being transplanted from the woman to the unconscious animal (see Figure 4.1). The worm is a vivid and deeply disturbing material anchor for the chain of connection that inspires the film's plot. As I am using the term, a 'material anchor' is a concrete diegetic manifestation of an abstract idea that helps viewers to navigate the thematic and formal complexity of certain narratives.[5] In this case, the worm image stands in for the human–nonhuman loop created by the relationship between the Thief and the Sampler.

I am not the only critic to see the loop as the most significant shape traced by the film. Developing a parallel between Carruth's film and Terrence Malick's works, Manohla Dargis notes in a *New York Times* review:

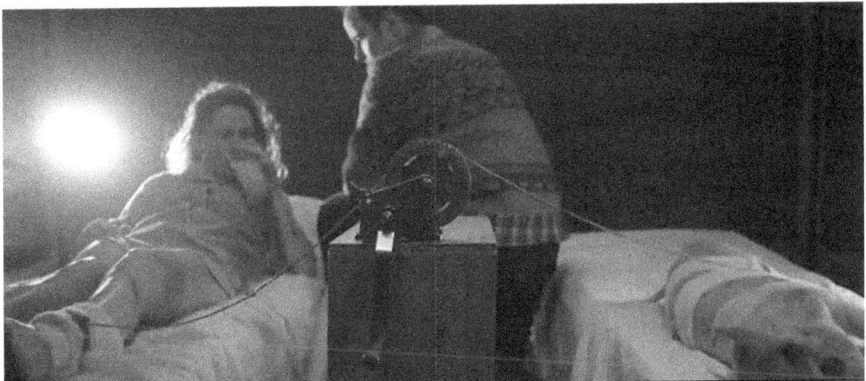

Figure 4.1. The interspecies 'transplant' of a parasitic worm in *Upstream Color* (2013). Screen capture by Marco Caracciolo.

> Mr. Malick's influence also extends to shots of Kris and Jeff walking, whispering and touching that are not moored in a specific time but could be from the past, present or future. In these Malick moments, time becomes as circular as the rising and setting of the sun. ... Mr. Carruth also expresses this circularity through the editing, skipping through time to create narrative ellipses. (Dargis 2013: n.p.)

Importantly, however, the significance of the loop evolves through the course of the film: when the Thief–Sampler cycle is halted by the protagonists, who liberate the pig farm together with several other victims of the Thief, the film's complex circularity comes to suggest positive affective entanglement and moral responsibility towards the nonhuman. To understand that development, we need to factor in another salient loop that can be encountered at the level of the story. It points suggestively to the father of American nature writing, Henry David Thoreau.

While Kris's mind is under the Thief's control, he keeps her busy by asking her to transcribe Thoreau's *Walden* onto slips of paper. These slips are then folded into rings to form a long chain. It is difficult to overstate the influence of Thoreau's works on both the environmental movement and the American imagination of natural landscapes.[6] In this part of *Upstream Color*, however, Thoreau's appreciation of the physical and moral rewards of deepening one's relationship with nature is completely overturned. Kris's mindless transcription is not a gesture of liberation from the shackles of human civilization but one of submission to the Thief's all-too-human schemes. The paper chain, then, may be loop-like in visible form, but it functions antithetically to the other looping images offered by the film. It is not a figure of interconnectivity across the human–nonhuman divide but a symbol of Kris's bondage and traumatic exclusion from the nonhuman world. It is not a coincidence that Kris recovers the memory of her abduction by reciting, together with Jeff, the lines she had memorized while transcribing Thoreau's work. This gesture involves a reappropriation of Thoreau's thinking on the emancipating value of our connection with the nonhuman.

The ending of the film translates this insight into an embodied reality by evoking two convergent gestures of affectionate entanglement that counter the oppressive Thief–Sampler cycle. The first is the image of Kris and Jeff embracing in the bathtub after barricading in their home's bathroom to keep an unknown evil force (perhaps the Sampler himself) at bay. The two overlapping bodies (see Figure 4.2) are presented as a looping structure rich in positive affect, versus the

Figure 4.2. Jeff embracing Kris in the bathtub in *Upstream Color* (2013). Screen capture by Marco Caracciolo.

Thief's and the Sampler's horrific exploitations. This circle of tender affectivity is then extended to the nonhuman in the film's very last shot, where Kris embraces a piglet after killing the Sampler and liberating his animals, much as she had been embraced by Jeff in the bathtub scene. Physical contact translates the abstract insight of the strange human–nonhuman loop into a concrete and emotionally powerful image. This embodied link reaches towards the nonhuman, and negates the mindless bondage encapsulated by the paper chain while Kris was under the Thief's control.

To sum up the discussion so far, the film's plot offers three material anchors for the abstract idea of linkage, which appear in the following order: the paper chain, the worm connecting the bodies of Kris and the pig, and Kris's embrace of both Jeff and the piglet. While the paper chain unambiguously channels human violence, the embrace is a gesture of affective empowerment – a connection that creates a level playing field for human and nonhuman realities (the pigs are freed, just as the Thief's victims are made aware of the abduction they had experienced and then forgotten). The intermediate anchor, the worm, is a more ambivalent image – at the same time repulsive and suggestive of a visceral connection. The material anchors are thus positioned in a sequence that evokes a gradual transition from what can be seen as the dystopian loop of the beginning (involving the Thief and the Sampler) to a utopian and deeply affective vision of human–nonhuman interconnectedness (conveyed by the ending, with the protagonists freeing the pigs from the Sampler's farm).

This conceptual trajectory sheds new light on narrative complexity in *Upstream Color*. As Dargis suggests in the review quoted above, the film's editing tends to juxtapose sequences that the viewer understands to have taken place at different points in the story's chronology, with run-on dialogue tying them together. For instance, roughly an hour into the film, Kris and Jeff discover that many of their childhood memories coincide (possibly because the Thief had implanted these memories during the abduction of the two characters). However, this twist is not delivered in a single, spatio-temporally coherent scene, but through rapid back-and-forths between conversations that have taken place (going by the setting and the characters' clothing) at different moments. The effect is that the characters' lives hover in an indistinct time, which is a complexifying strategy that mirrors Kris and Jeff's own disorientation upon finding out that their most cherished memories might be fabricated. Similarly, a number of lines are repeated (Kris remarks twice 'We should go on a trip', for example) for no apparent reason other than disrupting the viewer's expectation of linear progression. Self-organization in this film means that the presentation of the story tends to take a circular or loop-like form that partly obfuscates the sequentiality of the narrated events. *Upstream Color* also evokes multiscalarity, with microscopic images (the parasites spreading through Kris's body, the blue fluid seeping into the orchids) being repeatedly interspersed with shots of the characters' human-scale world.

These temporal indeterminacies and scalar shifts contribute to the narrative complexity of Carruth's film (at the formal level) and the viewer's puzzlement (at the experiential level). Complexity, as argued by Kiss and Willemsen (2017), calls for interpretive strategies aimed at reducing the viewer's puzzlement. More specifically, the film's complex form can be justified by bringing the audience's thematic interests into dialogue with it.[7] The film's difficulty is thus overcome – and its form interpreted – by drawing connections with extratextual realities that appear equally complex and disorienting, such as human–nonhuman relations in times of climate crisis.

This mirroring of internal (formal) complexity and extrinsic (ecological) complexity is what makes the interpretive effort worthwhile for certain audiences. My own engagement with *Upstream Color* has explored this possibility by focusing on how the film stages and critiques humanity's painful separation from the nonhuman world. The Thief and the Sampler violently instrumentalize both the nonhuman (the pigs, the worms) and the human (their victims) without fully understanding the vicious cycle they create through their actions. By contrast, the love story between Kris and Jeff moves towards the utopian reintegration of the nonhuman, as is suggested by the pig farm's eventual liberation and by the material anchor of Kris's embrace of a piglet in the final scene.[8] The film thus works through a series of strange loops but ends with a 'virtuous' (if still, in some sense, weird) loop of affective intimacy with animals, which involves both an awareness of interconnection with the nonhuman and a deep sense of ethical responsibility towards it.

The film's ending enacts a form of ecological awareness that is clearly indebted to the work of many nature writers, including Thoreau, a towering figure for the environmental movement and an explicit source of inspiration for Carruth's characters. Material anchors play a key role in this dynamic that brings together the formal and the conceptual, the complexity of narrative strategies and the larger complexity of human–nonhuman relations. The evocation of nonlinear, multiscalar and self-organizing patterns through narrative form and theme mediates between these meanings of complexity.

Conclusion

Having completed my reading of *Upstream Color*, I would like to circle back to my starting point, the sentence from the trailer: 'You can force your story's shape but the color will always bloom upstream'. We know that Carruth tends to shape his story circularly, but how should we read the second half of that line? I suggest that, here, 'upstream' means something like 'against the grain'; 'color' is a synecdoche for conscious experience, with its perceptual and affective textures so admirably probed by Carruth's cinematography. Repeatedly in the film, we see the characters collecting and admiring the sensory patterns of the material world: Jeff stroking the fabric of an armchair, for instance, or the Sampler recording the sound of stones scraping against a concrete surface. These patterns resist the logic of narrative justification ('your story's shape') and point to the unruliness of Carruth's storytelling – how it toys with circular forms without ever settling on a single, diegetically grounded structure. In that sense, *Upstream Color* remains essentially distinct from classic time-loop narratives, whose loop-like patterns tend to be more straightforward and diegetically justified.

If, as we have seen above, Morton's discussion of the strange, loopy quality of ecological awareness draws inspiration from Terry Gilliam's time-loop film *Twelve Monkeys*, the multiplicity and instability of Carruth's loops go much further in translating today's ecological crisis into narrative form. While the time loop remains a relatively conventional narrative device, Carruth's vision is both more challenging and more adequate for rendering the complexity of our predicament. Of course, what counts as an 'adequate' form vis-à-vis the climate crisis is in itself a matter of interpretation – of connecting texts to extratextual concerns.

My commentary on *Upstream Color* has argued that, in contemporary narrative practices, complex forms can hold up a mirror to the complexity of humanity's capture in nonhuman processes. This complexity can be understood as the result of nonlinear, multiscalar and self-organizing processes – the main features of complex systems, which can be evoked in narrative by way of formal choices. Carruth's *Upstream Color* is an excellent example of that formal operation, but many other instances can be found in contemporary fiction (see Caracciolo 2021). That is my main contribution to debates on narrative complexity, including those staged by this volume: the appeal of complexity is sometimes an extrinsic one, and narrative strategies can function as a platform for (re)shaping the ways in which we think and feel about real-world issues. By exposing ourselves to the complexity of narrative form, and learning to appreciate it, we take significant steps towards developing what political scientist Jens Kersten has called a new 'Anthropocene culture that enjoys complexity' (2013: 52). This kind of cultural training involves, of course, a specific *framing* of complexity, which pushes away from the mere entertainment value of complex narrative – or, rather, capitalizes on the cognitive pleasure it generates – to steer the audience's meaning-making towards real-world issues.

Innovative narrative strategies can evoke humanity's enmeshment with climatological, geological and biological processes – the 'strange loop' theorized by Morton and probed so forcefully by Carruth's film. In narrative (and again, this is an insight that can be extrapolated from *Upstream Color* to many other instances of narrative complexity), the translation of abstract ideas into a story's concrete characters and situations is typically mediated by what I call, here and elsewhere (Caracciolo 2020), *material anchors* for human–nonhuman interconnectivity. Thus, I hope to have demonstrated that scholarship on complex stories and their effects is well positioned to come to terms with the opening up of narrative form to the challenges of the present.

Marco Caracciolo is an Associate Professor of English and Literary Theory at Ghent University in Belgium. His work explores the phenomenology of narrative or the structure of the experiences afforded by literary fiction and other narrative media. He is the author of six books, including, most recently, *Narrating the Mesh: Form and Story in the Anthropocene* (University of Virginia Press, 2021) and *With Bodies: Narrative Theory and Embodied Cognition* (co-authored with Karin Kukkonen; Ohio State University Press, 2021).

Notes

While working on this chapter, the author received funding from the European Research Council (ERC) under the European Union's Horizon 2020 research and innovation programme (grant agreement no. 714166).

1. For a number of insightful perspectives on the nonhuman, see Richard Grusin's landmark edited collection *The Nonhuman Turn* (2015).
2. Linkage is also an 'image schema' in the sense of cognitive linguistics (Hampe and Grady 2005). Image schemata fall halfway between an abstract idea (such as 'connection' or 'cycle') and the concreteness of what I call 'material anchors'. For more on image schemata, embodiment, and film narrative, see a seminal article by Maarten Coëgnarts and Peter Kravanja (2012).
3. For an extended discussion of the link between ecological form and narrative, see Caracciolo 2019 and the introduction and the first chapter of *Narrating the Mesh* (Caracciolo 2021).
4. For more on 'forensic' viewership and complex narrative, see Mittell 2015. Based on the user reviews available on the IMDb database, it seems clear that many viewers are *not* willing to engage in this forensic activity, and dismiss the film as confusing after a cursory viewing.
5. I discuss the concept of material anchors in more detail in Caracciolo 2020. The term comes from Edwin Hutchins's 1995 account of distributed cognition.
6. See also Buell (1995) on Thoreau's multifaceted relationship with the natural world.
7. See Caracciolo 2016 (pp. 188–89) for a more comprehensive account of this interpretive process.
8. In Hubert Zapf's (2001) terminology, the film thus shifts from 'cultural-critical metadiscourse' on the violence embodied by the Thief and the Sampler to a form of utopian 'imaginative counterdiscourse', with the farm's liberation in the ending.

References

Baranger, Michel. 2000. 'Chaos, Complexity, and Entropy: A Physics Talk for Non-Physicists'. Retrieved 4 April 2020 from http://necsi.edu/projects/baranger/cce.pdf.

Buckland, Warren. 2009. 'Introduction: Puzzle Plots', in Warren Buckland (ed.), *Puzzle Films: Complex Storytelling in Contemporary Cinema*. Chichester: Wiley-Blackwell, pp. 1–12.

Buell, Lawrence. 1995. 'Thoreau and the Natural Environment', in Joel Myerson (ed.), *The Cambridge Companion to Henry David Thoreau*. Cambridge: Cambridge University Press, pp. 171–93.
Caracciolo, Marco. 2016. 'Cognitive Literary Studies and the Status of Interpretation: An Attempt at Conceptual Mapping', *New Literary History* 47(3): 187–208.
———. 2019. 'Form, Science, and Narrative in the Anthropocene', *Narrative* 27(3): 270–89.
———. 2020. 'Object-Oriented Plotting and Nonhuman Realities in DeLillo's *Underworld* and Iñárritu's *Babel*', in Erin James and Eric Morel (eds), *Environment and Narrative: New Directions in Econarratology*. Columbus: Ohio State University Press, pp. 45–64.
———. 2021. *Narrating the Mesh: Form and Story in the Anthropocene*. Charlottesville: University of Virginia Press.
Chakrabarty, Dipesh. 2014. 'Climate and Capital: On Conjoined Histories', *Critical Inquiry* 41(1): 1–23.
Coëgnarts, Maarten, and Peter Kravanja. 2012. 'Embodied Visual Meaning: Image Schemas in Film', *Projections* 6(2): 84–101.
Crutzen, Paul J., and Eugene F. Stoermer. 2000. 'The Anthropocene', *Global Change Newsletter* 41: 17–8.
Dargis, Manohla. 2013. 'Worms, a Botanist and Pigs: Sounds Like a Love Story', *The New York Times*, 4 April.
Deacon, Terrence W. 2006. 'Emergence: The Hole at the Wheel's Hub', in Philip Clayton and Paul Davies (eds), *The Re-Emergence of Emergence: The Emergentist Hypothesis from Science to Religion*. Oxford: Oxford University Press, pp. 111–50.
Fox, Warwick. 1995. *Toward a Transpersonal Ecology: Developing New Foundations for Environmentalism*. Albany: State University of New York Press.
Ghosh, Amitav. 2016. *The Great Derangement: Climate Change and the Unthinkable*. Chicago: University of Chicago Press.
Grusin, Richard (ed.). 2015. *The Nonhuman Turn*. Minneapolis: University of Minnesota Press.
Hampe, Beate, and Joseph E. Grady. 2005. *From Perception to Meaning: Image Schemas in Cognitive Linguistics*. Berlin: Walter de Gruyter.
Hofstadter, Douglas R. 1999. *Gödel, Escher, Bach: An Eternal Golden Braid*. New York: Basic Books.
Hutchins, Edwin. 1995. *Cognition in the Wild*. Cambridge, MA: MIT Press.
Kersten, Jens. 2013. 'The Enjoyment of Complexity: A New Political Anthropology for the Anthropocene?', *RCC Perspectives* 3: 39–56.
Kiss, Miklós, and Steven Willemsen. 2017. *Impossible Puzzle Films: A Cognitive Approach to Contemporary Complex Cinema*. Edinburgh: Edinburgh University Press.
Mittell, Jason. 2015. *Complex TV: The Poetics of Contemporary Television Storytelling*. New York: New York University Press.
Morton, Timothy. 2010. *The Ecological Thought*. Cambridge, MA: Harvard University Press.
———. 2016. *Dark Ecology: For a Logic of Future Coexistence*. New York: Columbia University Press.
Pier, John. 2017. 'Complexity: A Paradigm for Narrative?', in Per Krogh Hansen et al. (eds), *Emerging Vectors of Narratology*. New York: Walter de Gruyter, pp. 534–65.
Poulaki, Maria. 2019. 'Between Distancing and Immersion: Embodiment in Complex Narrative', in Marina Grishakova and Maria Poulaki (eds), *Narrative Complexity: Cognition, Embodiment, Evolution*. Lincoln: University of Nebraska Press, pp. 291–313.
Ryan, Marie-Laure. 2019. 'Narrative as/and Complex System/s', in Marina Grishakova and Maria Poulaki (eds), *Narrative Complexity: Cognition, Embodiment, Evolution*. Lincoln: University of Nebraska Press, pp. 29–55.

Simon, Zoltán Boldizsár. 2018. 'The Limits of Anthropocene Narratives', *European Journal of Social Theory* 20(1): 146–63.
Tobias, Scott. 2013. 'Upstream Color', *The A.V. Club*. Retrieved 4 April 2020 from https://film.avclub.com/upstream-color-1798176362.
Ulstein, Gry. 2017. 'Brave New Weird: Anthropocene Monsters in Jeff VanderMeer's "The Southern Reach"', *Concentric: Literary and Cultural Studies* 43(1): 71–96.
Walsh, Richard. 2011. 'Emergent Narrative in Interactive Media', *Narrative* 19(1): 72–85.
Walsh, Richard, and Susan Stepney (eds). 2018. *Narrating Complexity*. New York: Springer.
Watt, Ian. 1957. *The Rise of the Novel*. Berkeley: University of California Press.
West, Geoffrey. 2017. *Scale: The Universal Laws of Growth, Innovation, Sustainability, and the Pace of Life in Organisms, Cities, Economies, and Companies*. London: Penguin.
Zapf, Hubert. 2001. 'Literature as Cultural Ecology: Notes Towards a Functional Theory of Imaginative Texts, with Examples from American Literature', *REAL – Yearbook of Research in English and American Literature* 17: 85–100.

PART II
Mesmerized Minds and Bodies
Art Cinema and Modernist Aesthetics

CHAPTER 5
The Puzzling Film Environments of Fellini's 8½

Steffen Hven

Introduction

A car is slowly moving forward in a crammed tunnel. Guido Anselmi (Marcello Mastroianni), the alter-ego film director in Federico Fellini's heralded 8½ (1963), is filmed from behind, his face concealed. In the car in front of him, a passenger turns around and stares apathetically at him. For a brief moment, the moving image turns into still photography. A camera track evidences the immensity of the traffic jam. Another apathetic stare. Guido's expirations become frantic. Asphyxiating smoke leaps out of the car's interior. After failed attempts to break out of the car, Guido's expirations are nearing a state of panic. A shot to a bus with headless passengers hanging their limbs out of the window, the camera tracks to another unaffected stare. Squeaking, creaking, banging on the windows. More frantic expirations. A man caresses his lover in an adjacent car. Another series of numb, staring faces. The moment of release. Guido climbs out of the sunroof of his car and hovers above the traffic jam. His ascent into the heavens is halted by a rope tied around his ankle, making him appear more like a helium balloon than a Christ-like figure. His producers tow him down to earth but his descent becomes a free fall. Just before crashing to the ground, Guido is awakened.

Wherein lies the puzzlement of films like 8½, whose famous opening scene continues to fascinate cinephiles? And how do we explain the unremitting attraction of this storytelling modality to media audiences? A part of the attraction is, undeniably, to be found in the cognitive, interpretative and analytical challenges that these films present due to their intricate plot structures and the sometimes 'impossible' task of establishing their narrative 'texts' – the how, what, why and when of the narrative actions (e.g. Buckland 2009b, 2014; Cameron 2008; Kiss and

Willemsen 2017). Consequently, the study of puzzle films has been theoretically oriented towards textual film analysis (for an overview, see Bateman and Wildfeuer 2017), structuralist narratology (e.g. Genette 1983, 1988) and cognitive formalism (e.g. Bordwell 1985, 2008). Yet, the intricate textual, formal and narratological designs of these films offer more than cognitive-analytical puzzles to be solved; they also produce 'narrative filmic environments' (atmospheric narrative spaces that make a direct impression on our felt bodies) that are in many ways 'impossible', too.

This chapter aims to counterbalance the disproportional attention granted to plot structure and narrative ordering in the study of complex film by examining the complex narrative environments of Fellini's 1963 landmark: the most important precursor of the contemporary 'complex narrative' (Simmons 2008; Poulaki 2014; Hven 2017; Kiss and Willemsen 2017; Grishakova and Poulaki 2019), 'puzzle film' (Panek 2006; Buckland 2009a, 2014) and 'mind-game' film (Hesselberth and Schuster 2008; Elsaesser 2009).[1]

From Texts to Environments: An Embodied Approach to Complex Film

The opening scene of *8½* not only communicates to its audience that Guido is undergoing a condition related to claustrophobia, panic attack and anxiety but also creates a narrative *environment*. Through the dream sequence of the traffic jam, the cacophonic stares and his ascent to the sky, the narrative environment produces an affective state that resonates with (yet by no means pretends to be equal to) the suffering of the main protagonist of the film. This chapter argues that the impossible worlds of complex narratives might not only shed light on cognitive functions related to problem solving, attention, narrative comprehension, inference making, hypothesis testing and the reordering of narrative events but might also offer insights into how affective and cognitive-embodied processes contribute to the transformation of the filmic material into a meaningful environment. Of interest to this chapter is less the complex 'puzzle plot' (Buckland 2009b) of *8½* (related to its interwoven, nonlinear and unconventional plot arrangements) but more its puzzling narrative environments (related to the mysterious, atmospheric, aesthetic and expressive spaces and worlds of the film) and how these environments rely upon the bodily investments of the film's spectator to 'come alive'.

Shifting attention from the textual to the environmental takes the cognitive study of the puzzle film into a 'second-generation mode of cognitive inquiry' (Lakoff and Johnson 1999), which foregrounds 'the embodiment of mental processes and their extension into the world through material artefacts and socio-cultural practices' (Kukkonen and Caracciolo 2014: 261). The second-generation approach is thus interchangeable with the recent recasting of cognitive processes in enactive, embodied, extended, embedded, experiential, emotional, relational and affective terms.[2] Regardless of their individual emphasis, these new approaches reject the commitment of the first-generation approach to a representational and disembodied theory of cognition and the mind (see Johnson 2017, 2018).

Against the neglect of the body in first-generation cognitive science, analytical philosophy and structuralist semiotics, the second-generation approach maintains that 'an embodied account of syntax, semantics, pragmatics, and value is absolutely necessary for an adequate understanding of human cognition and language' (Johnson and Lakoff 2002: 1). Rather than grounding filmic meaning in internal semantic structures that disregard the actualization of the 'text' by the embodied spectator, a second-generation cognitive approach to cinema is relational in its proposition that 'organism–environment interactions generate meaningful experience' (Johnson 2017: 1).

Where cognitive film studies, structural linguistics and film semiotics have mainly focused on how the spectator understands a film through 'disembodied' mental activities, Adriano D'Aloia and Ruggero Eugeni (2014) have argued that an embodied, enactive, embedded and affective theory of the film spectator needs to move beyond this spectatorial paradigm of the 'viewer-as-mind'.[3] Elaborating on the film-phenomenological exploration of the 'viewer-as-body', the authors suggest the 'enactive' model of the 'viewer-as-organism', which is irreducibly both mind *and* body, intellect *and* passion, emotional *and* rational, cognitive *and* affective.[4] By this account, the viewer-as-organism 'handles simultaneously many processes of different nature (sensory, perceptual, cognitive, emotional, motor, active, mnemonic), within different time windows; they are constantly striving to coordinate the first and synchronize the latter' (ibid.: 19–20).

If we apply this spectatorial paradigm shift to the (impossible) puzzle film, it corresponds to a substitution of the cognitive-analytical, yet affectively disengaged, 'puzzle solver' with the 'puzzled viewer', who is ecologically, viscerally, cognitive affectively invested in disorienting and perplexing narrative cinematic environments. Of crucial importance is that the puzzled viewer cannot occupy the objective, distanced, observational or analytical position of the puzzle solver but is herself constituted in the puzzle, in the 'very experience, in complex, dynamical and provisional forms' (D'Aloia and Eugeni 2014: 19).[5] Moving from the puzzle solver to the puzzled viewer thus implies for the complex narrative film what second-generation cognitive philosopher Mark Johnson (2017) has called for on a larger philosophical ground, namely a readdressing of 'the entire hermeneutic (interpretive) process of understanding, not merely as an intellectual and linguistic act, but rather as constituting our whole embodied way of being in, and making sense of, our world' (12).

However, if the spectator and the narrative environment mutually constitute each other, the dominant textual conception of the diegesis must also be revised. As a 'temporal gestalt' (Merleau-Ponty 1991: 54), the film weaves several scenarios into a 'world' larger than the sum of its parts. Thus, the narrative environments combine into a filmic world: its *diegesis* (Souriau 1951, 1953). Although the term originated with filmology, the dominant model of diegesis today is rooted in film semiotics and cognitive formalism. In this textual conception, diegesis is understood in disembodied terms as the place of the film's denotation, its signified instance or its literal meanings (see Genette 1988: 17; Metz 1990: 98). This 'diegesis-as-text' is assumed to exist independently of its material vehicles of communication as well as the affective and emotional responses pertaining to it. Moreover, in line with structural linguistic narratology, the relation between the specific cinematic means of expression (e.g. a high or a low camera angle) is considered to be arbitrary to its signified content.[6]

By contrast, the alternative model of the 'diegesis-as-environment' conceives the cinematic diegesis as an *Umwelt* (Uexküll 2001; see also Pollmann 2013).[7] Thus, the cinematic diegesis can neither be abstracted from its material means of expression nor from our affective-emotional, kinaesthetic or sensorimotor engagement with these. The diegesis-as-environment thus emerges from the interaction between the meaning-making embodied activities of the spectator and the artistically crafted cinematic spaces designed to enhance, amplify, disorient, complement or otherwise modulate or guide human embodied perception.[8] Integral to the diegesis is our perception of the cinematic environment as well as our proprioception of it; the diegesis comprises not only the movements of the film but also the movements that it instantiates on our felt bodies. The film thus communicates by literally *moving* its spectator, which means the diegesis-as-environment is necessarily both materially and affectively anchored.

Consequently, the film's diegesis is relational and pragmatic as its 'meaning always emerges from a feedback loop between the human mind-body and its natural and cultural environments' (Kukkonen and Caracciolo 2014: 266). This, in turn, 'inverts the view of the relation between perceiver and film, and thereby highlights how film itself engages and requires the viewer's body, as well as how both together constitute a reality and body of their own' (Fingerhut and Heiman 2017: 359).

In its appeal to bodily forms of meaning-making, the film creates environments that quite literally move its spectators; simultaneously, the film's diegesis becomes a lived space only by being induced with the affective investments of its spectator. Edgar Morin ([1946] 2005) referred to this as a cinematic symbiosis that 'integrates the spectator into the flow of the film' and 'the flow of the film into the psychic flow of the spectator' (102, emphasis omitted). Consider the impossible narrative environment created in the opening scene of *8½*. Devoid of verbal communication, the scene enacts Guido's personal crisis kinaesthetically – that is, through the fluid orchestration of an impossible environment that, in no logical manner, variously affords suffocation, alienation, alleviation/liberation, before finally culminating in downfall/submission.[9]

Asa Nisi Masa and the New Criteria for the Complex Film

Along these lines, the second-generation approach allows for a possible redirection of the study of puzzle films. The focal point of analysis is no longer the establishment of the film's text, but rather an examination of how films (or other narrative media) employ complex narrative structures to embed the audience in narrative environments – environments that afford enigmatic, puzzling, unsettling, disorienting or atmospheric experiences, which differ significantly from those proffered by both traditional forms of filmmaking as well as real-world experiences. In relation to *8½*, I would suggest that the famous magical phrase, 'asa nisi masa', a form of Italian 'pig Latin' for a-ni-ma (soul), performs the role of inducing an atmosphere of mystery and enigma to the film. The phrase presents itself as referring to an underlying, deeper 'hidden' textual meaning.[10] And while 'asa nisi masa' certainly evokes Fellini's fascination with the psychoanalytical writings of

Carl Gustav Jung, the phrase is neither given a precise technical definition nor does it obtain a clear propositional function within the framework of the film. Its main function, I suggest, is affective – namely, to bathe the film in the sentiment of enigma, puzzlement and mystery.

The phrase runs parallel with the film's tendency to move through dreams, imaginings, fantasies and hallucinations to transcend time and place. 'Asa nisi masa' thus evokes the dwelling in various forms of subjective spaces (dream-spaces, fantasy-spaces, memory-spaces, etc.) that, from a strictly objective point of view, are in many ways 'impossible', in the sense of not needing or desiring a propositional predicate to be understood. In this sense, the phrase takes us from the terrain of the puzzle film into that of the *puzzling* film. The puzzles of the film thus function more to provoke novel experiences than they are to be deciphered in clear propositional terms. Fellini (1976) has often relinquished his apathy 'against things that try to define themselves too precisely, and against people who do the same' (151). In fact, the very idea of regarding the film as a text – a series of propositional meanings, whose enigmas can be solved on a purely rational basis – is foreign to the affective locus of *8½*.

Responding to the demand that films need to be grounded in rational logic and referential, fixed meanings, Fellini declared that we need 'new criteria of judgment to appreciate [*8½*]' (Fellini, in Kael 1966: 237). In reference to the second-generation cognitive approach outlined above, I propose three new criteria of judgement that will guide the following examination of *8½*. These new criteria concern: (1) the irreducibility of the film to a text, whose meanings depend solely on 'disembodied' cognitive processes that are grounded in a conceptual/propositional comprehension of the content in disregard from our corporeal affective and emotional engagement with the film; (2) the recognition that films are not primarily invested in delivering 'meanings' or 'messages' but experiences; and (3) a renewed emphasis on the affordances of the cinematic medium in producing affectively charged spaces that transform into meaningful narrative environments based on resonances with our meaning-seeking embodied organisms.

These new criteria help us to address the aesthetic appeal of the puzzle film in a manner that departs from just solving the narrative puzzles themselves. Instead, they locate the main attraction of these films in the enigmatic and puzzling environments that are enabled by the complex narrative form in its audiovisual expression and the embodied experiences that our interaction with them generates. Thereby, the aesthetic employment of cinematic techniques (whether colouration and lighting, sound effects and soundscapes, or camera framings, positionings and movements) no longer need to be regarded as relatively 'arbitrary' to the 'messages', 'information' or 'significations' of the film. While expressive filmmaking techniques might not always aid the teleological drive of the plot, they inevitably contribute to the specific material-affective feel of the mediated environment (as, for example, the turning of the image into a still image in the opening scene of 8½). In foregrounding the environmental capacities of cinematic techniques, we further distance ourselves from the focus of first-generation perspectives on the cognitive-analytical establishment of the 'text' – the 'objective' reality of the film – as abstracted from affective and material concerns.

Narrative Complexity and Decomplexification

Immediately following the opening scene, Guido awakens in the spa where the doctors at the resort are treating him. This suggests that the opening scene was a nightmare, and we are now in the 'real' world of the spa. What follows is an example of a subtle and refined blurring of the imaginary and objective spaces at play in 8½. When Guido gets out of bed and enters his bathroom, the lights begin to glare as if they were studio arc lamps, the sound of Wagner's 'Ride of the Valkyries' plays on the soundtrack with its grandeur and valour, and the buzzing of a sound stage transforms the now brightly lit bathroom into a performance space. In a trademark Mastroianni gesture, Guido inaugurates this space with a performative 'dance' move signalling 'a physical fatigue alluding to an even deeper moral ennui' (Dewey 1993: 47).

This scene then smoothly transitions into the 'real world' of the spa, where Guido has taken refuge to relax and concentrate while reconnecting with his artistic inspiration. However, in a surreal reversion of the apathetic gazes of the opening scene, a series of smiling faces gesture at the camera as it passes by. All those who constantly demand something from Guido – his producers, the actors, the production crew, his mistress, his wife, journalists – are somehow present at his retreat in the spa, thereby making its status as 'objective reality' ambiguous. In addition, as the renowned Fellini scholar Peter Bondanella (2002) has observed, at the spa there is a curious mixture of fashion styles from the 1930s (the time of Guido/Fellini's childhood) and the 1960s (the 'present' time) – a subtle play with the filmic environment that further adds to the difficulty of pinning down an exact time frame for the spa and of determining its reality status (101).

Textual film analysis, however, is posited on reconstructing the 'reality' of the text despite the difficulties surrounding its discursive presentation. From this perspective, the viewer's primary task in comprehending the narrative becomes to resolve the intermingling of the ontological layers of the text. The entanglement of the temporal layers of the film thus becomes a *problem* that needs epistemological fixing according to a clear propositional logic. An example is Edward Branigan's (1984) cognitive-formalist analysis of *8½*. Here, the author argues that the 'film becomes, crucially, a working out of the precise status of author with respect to reality, imagination, text, subject (consciousness), and the other terms' (161). A thorough textual reading of the film, like the one provided by Branigan, is thus devoted to determining how these are not given a priori in the text 'but are placed in a set of relations by the semantic system, or argument, of the text' (161). According to Branigan, even though the film is focalized through the subjective viewpoint of Guido, *8½* never succumbs to pure subjective nonsense: 'The viewer never stops trying to make sense, and the text never stops making sense with respect to a "reality"' (152). Branigan can thus conclude his analysis by arguing that the film actually 're-enacts the presuppositions and logic of classical discourse in its placement of author, text, art, and reality' (162).

Branigan's analysis of *8½* illustrates how first-generation cognitive approaches assume that the spectator's primary task is the cognitive-analytical re-establishing of a coherent and logical film text beyond the potential difficulties of its narrative presentation. It is, therefore, the task of the spectator to pick up the cues of the film and reassemble the text (see Bordwell 2008: 149). Crucially, this procedure of narrative sense-making can operate in isolation from affective or emotional responses. The main problem is that it effectively leads to a methodological exclusion, if only announced as temporarily, of affection: 'Up to a point, setting emotion aside is a useful methodological idealization. In principle, you can understand a film without discernibly having an emotional reaction to it' (Bordwell 2008: 150). The idea is that the complex narrative structure of the 'puzzle film' conceals a coherent and logical text, and that the attraction of these films lies in the spectator's efforts to disentangle, decomplexify or otherwise restore it to rational discourse. From such a perspective, puzzle films are not actually 'complex' but 'complicated' (Bordwell 2013: 53).[11]

From a first-generation perspective, the cognitive-affective state of uncertainty, perplexion or disorientation once confronted with the complex environments of the puzzle film must be resolved by the cognitive-analytical individual, who is rewarded with the pleasure that human beings take 'in solving puzzles and riddles' (Mulvey 2006: 191). Although a part of the attraction of the puzzle film can undoubtedly be found in the satisfaction related to problem solving and the restoring of order, this perspective assumes the 'text' to be unanchored from material and embodied experience. Thereby, a gap emerges between the analytical study of the film (in which the film is turned into a semiotic construct, a text) and the experience it gives rise to (see Sobchack 2004: 53), which obscures the embodied, aesthetic appeal.

As Hava Aldouby (2020) has argued, Fellini's films seek 'modes of engagement anchored in sensorimotor arousal' (223) that 'appeal to viewers' tactile and motor sensibilities, demanding bodily attention and feedback to deal with environments that are sensed as disturbing, disorienting, or just exaggerated with respect to more familiar reality' (228). For Fellini, cinematic 'meaning' does not necessarily take on a propositional form but could equally rest upon the ability of the medium to defamiliarize the perception of going beyond quotidian reality and of transcending the mundane and ordinary, and thus opening the experience up to the unknown: 'The deepest meaning of film is its magic, ironic, mysterious meaning. When you take it away, you take away from film its obscure fascination' (Fellini, in Stubbs 2006: 3). Demonstrating that a film's organization of affect is not dislocated from the narrative blurring of its ontological layers or the meta-cinematic reflections afforded by its mise en abyme structure allows for a readdressing of the aesthetic appeal of the puzzle film, not just in cognitive but also affective terms.

Rather than a problem to be solved, the smooth transitions between fantasy and reality, the intermingling of memory spaces and real spaces, and the blurring of the temporal layers of the film should be studied as part of the film's narrative organization of affect, and related to its construction of spaces that defy the logic of 'objective' reality. As Bondanella (2002) has observed, '[t]he irrational, the dream state, the magical – as opposed to the rational, "reality," and the mundane – constitute the territory staked out by Fellini in his presentation of how Guido attempts to create' (101).

8½ thus carves out a cinematic space of coexistence. We are here reminded of the poetic Fellini quote provided by Gilles Deleuze (2005) within the framework of his film philosophy: 'We are constructed in memory; we are *simultaneously* childhood, adolescence, old age and maturity' (99, emphasis in original). More than merely blurring the lines between the real and the imaginary to satisfy our cognitive pleasure in straightening out the text, 8½ offers a cinematic experience defined by the coexistence of various temporal and ontological layers of existence that questions the very legitimacy and validity of any strict dichotomy of 'real vs imaginary', 'objective vs subjective' or 'cognitive vs affective'. Fellini both denies us the illusion of inhabiting a pure 'objective' space as well as of entertaining the film's imaginations as unanchored from real-world experience. As Fellini once stated, 'there is no objective reality in my films, any more than there is in real life' (Fellini, in Waller 2002: 3).

Emotional Landscapes

Having crossed a blizzard to buy presents, the adult Guido enters his childhood home, now turned into a harem run by his wife Luisa (Anouk Aimée), from whom he has been estranged since she met his mistress at the spa. The snow continues to fall inside, clearly marking this as a fantasy space. The women of the harem bathe Guido in wine vats, just as the women did in an earlier childhood memory. The (in)famous harem gives us access to a comforting fantasy – an 'affective niche' (see Hven 2019) – in which all Guido's worries, anxieties, and failed romantic relations are turned into the 'ultimate fantasy for an Italian male' (Bondanella 2002: 105). Yet, just as memories, fantasies and imaginations continue to intrude upon 'reality', the fantasy world of the harem cannot shield Guido from his affective distress. Once again, the 'Ride of the Valkyries' dominates the soundtrack, and the harem women begin to revolt against the male tyranny imposed by Guido. In an attempt to regain control of his fantasy, Guido brings out a bullwhip. However, even in the intimate sphere of his fantasy, Guido's 'desire to control reality is a fundamental limitation' (Burke 1989: 40).

Regardless of their reality status, the narrative environments of 8½ leave an affective imprint that precedes all definite recognition. Our immediate bodily apprehension of the qualities of a space is thus pre-reflective and atmospheric. The architect Juhani Pallasmaa (2014) observed that the 'immediate judgement of the character of space calls upon our entire embodied and existential sense, and it is perceived in a diffuse and peripheral manner, rather than through precise and conscious observation' (231). Similarly, narrative comprehension does not proceed from already discriminated and categorized facts but relies, in the first instance, on our ability to be affected by an environment. Cognitive operations such as the inferential elaborations of cues are secondary to and dependent on a prior affective apprehension that allows elements of the film to stand out as 'cues' in the first place (for a discussion of affective appraisal, see Colombetti 2014). Whereas our cognitive activities in relation to complex narrative forms have been studied broadly (e.g. Bordwell 2002; Newman 2006; Buckland 2009a, 2014; Ghislotti 2009; Kiss and Willemsen 2017), the ability to affectively apprehend the complex narrative environments as mysterious, perplexing, atmospheric, affectively charged, intriguing, spectacular and/or irrational aesthetic experiences without necessarily 'resolving' them has yet to be adequately theoretically addressed.

Thus, if narrative complexity can be a pretext for the cognitive pleasure related to puzzle solving, it can also be such for the construction of spaces liberated from the laws of non-contradiction, physics, quotidian embodied perception and the rational discourse of classical filmmaking – in brief, 'impossible' narrative environments. Concerning *8½*, it could be argued that the mise en abyme structure affords the construction of narrative spaces that smoothly transport us from distant moments of the past to the world of dreams, fantasies, memories and magic. In this 'stream-of-consciousness' dramaturgy, the plot is no longer the Archimedean point from which the film's meanings can be fixed. As Fellini declares, 'the story illustrates the environment, rather than the other way around' (Fellini, in Perry 1972: 85). The environments of the film are thus infused with the sentiments of its main protagonist and, as such, act as 'signifiers for the feelings of the scenes; or, to use Fellini's term, they are emotional landscapes for the action' (ibid.; see also, Bachmann 1967: 202).

The Death of the Auteur on Film

A convoy of cars is heading towards the spaceship launchpad, the magnificent structure Guido ordered to build for his science fiction film. Like a prisoner, Guido is transported in the back of the car, crammed in between his producers, who, despite the director's comic and unsuccessful attempts to escape, escort him from the car to the press table where a crowd of journalists eagerly await him.

Nino Rota's hectic, circus-themed music dominates the soundtrack. An orchestra is playing, but its instrumentation is not that of the music we hear. A frenetic series of intense, interrogative faces confront Guido: 'Don't you take yourself a little too serious, Mr Anselmi?'; 'Are you for or against eroticism?'; 'Well, are you afraid of the atomic bomb?' The camera moves erratically, the journalists continue their bombardment, but their voices are no longer heard. 'Do you really think your life is of interest to others?' a woman is heard screaming, while a man enquires, 'Can you really admit that you have nothing to say?' An American lady laughs hysterically and agitatedly in the direction of the camera: 'Ha! He has nothing to say!' A tracking shot of the roused journalists. The producer threatens to end Guido's career if he abandons the film now. Luisa appears as a mirror image at the press conference table. She informs Guido that she wants a divorce. Armed with a pistol handed to him by his loyal assistant Bruno (Bruno Agostini), Guido crawls under the table. The shouting from the crowd continues: 'Buffoon!'; 'Lunatic!'; 'Get out here, you coward'. Abrupt cut to a windy beach. Guido's late mother, dressed in funeral clothing, yells, 'Guido, Guido, where are you running off to, you naughty boy?' as the camera moves rapidly away from her. Cut back to under the table; a shot is heard. Guido's head falls to the ground. The director has committed suicide. It is the death of the great auteur on film.

Today, Fellini is an established part of cinema's hall of fame, and 8½ remains 'the most influential film of the 1960s, liberating filmmakers everywhere from the conventions of time, place, and mode of experience that had prevailed in cinema for decades' (Sesonske 2010). Fellini scholars have argued that the director's critical acclaim is tied to the rise and fall of 'auteur theory' (Bondanella 2002: 1–2; Burke 1989: 36–7). Regardless of the accuracy of this claim,[12] 8½ plays directly into the proclamation of the film director as *auteur*, which enabled the 'virtual canonization of Fellini as the archetypal genius, the auteur of auteurs, the undisputed king of what is today, in retrospect, referred to as the European "art" film' (Bondanella 2002: 26). Yet, by displaying the machinery behind the production of a film, 8½ critically reflects upon the notion of the auteur as an essentially 'literary and Romantic conception of the artist as the central, even the sole source of meaning in a text' (Stoddart 1995: 39).

Although today Fellini is emblematic of the 'film auteur', Albert Sbragia (2015) argued that not all of his contemporaries were pleased with the director's eschewal of 'readable referential meaningfulness', an aspect of his films that 'continued to provoke strong negative reactions in auteurist-oriented critics' (673).[13] It has been maintained that from 8½ onwards, Fellini completely eradicated the auteur-subject (an argument recuperating his oeuvre within the poststructuralist proclamation of the 'death of the author'; see Burke 1989). However, it is perhaps more exact to say that Fellini deconstructed the auteur and offered a self-reflective examination of the artist as an anxiety-driven, morally depraved, self-loathing individual who is completely incapable of having an original idea. As Christian Metz (1990) observed in his brilliant analysis of the formal-structural complexity of 8½, the paradoxical and startling thing about the film is that it is 'a powerfully creative mediation on the inability to create' (234).

In the context of 1950s–1960s film criticism, 8½ self-reflectively inscribes the 'auteur' into the very fabric of the film, which makes Fellini the 'master ironist of auteurism' (Sbragia 2015: 661), a meta-auteur, but also of a modernist, self-reflective style of filmmaking. Likewise, the narrative environments of 8½ are not just 'Felliniesque' but 'meta-Felliniesque' – reflecting and problematizing their very status as spaces in a Fellini film.[14] Yet, the film not only reflects its own act of creation but also anticipates its critical reception.[15]

The Rebirth of the Auteur and the Demise of the Critic

Immediately after his (imaginary) suicide, Guido is congratulated by Carini Daumier (Jean Rougeul) – the acclaimed writer and critic, who Guido has hired to assist on the script – for having decided to abandon the film:

> You did the right thing. Believe me, today is a good day for you. These are tough decisions, I know. But we intellectuals – and I say 'we' because I consider you one – must remain clear-headed right to the end. There are so many superfluous things in the world already. No need to add chaos to chaos. ... No need for nostalgia or remorse. Destroying is better than creating when we are not creating those few truly necessary things ... We're smothered by words, images, and sounds that have no right to exist, that come from the void and return to the void. Of any artist truly deserving of the name we should ask nothing but this act of faith: to learn silence.

Daumier, representing a modernist art conception, continues his tirade, but Guido's attention is caught by Maurice (Ian Dallas) – the magician who works with the telepath that read from Guido's mind the words 'asa nisi masa' – who informs him that 'we're ready to begin'. Several characters now appear in stylized portrait shots, dressed all in white and brightly lit. Over the images, we hear Daumier continue his modernist monologue: 'If we can't have everything, nothingness is true perfection. Forgive me for making all these references, but we critics do what we can'. We see a shot of the star actress Claudia (Claudia Cardinale), then of Guido lost in thought. Daumier continues his monologue:

> *Our true mission is to sweep away the thousands of miscarriages that try every day, obscenely, to come into this world ... What monstrous presumption to think that others could benefit from your squalid catalogue of mistakes. What do you gain by stringing together the tattered pieces of your life, your vague memories, the faces of those you could never love?*

As Daumier delivers this rejection of what is effectively the film we have been watching, all of the representatives of Guido/Fellini's past and present gather as if summoned by a magic force. For the first time in the film, Guido is struck by a moment of creative instigation to act. He whispers to himself: 'Now everything is all confused once again, like it was before. But this confusion is me as I am, not as I like to be. I am no longer afraid of telling the truth about what I don't know, what I'm looking for, and what I haven't found. Only this way do I feel alive'.[16] At the end of his monologue – reality and fiction by this point no longer separate ontological categories – Guido is talking to his wife Luisa, who agrees to reconsolidate their marriage and accept him for what he truly is, confused and incomplete. At the abandoned set of the magnificent and eerie launchpad, a circus orchestra is playing. Guido grabs a megaphone and, for the first time in the film, starts to direct all the characters that have come to join the circle dance.[17]

In her review of the film, Pauline Kael (1966), a known adversary of Fellini's films, complains that self-absorption is now mistakenly taken for artistic creativity, and mockingly asserts that those 'who owned their wits interpreting what inspired *Last Year at Marienbad* [Resnais, 1959] now go to work on *8½* separating "memories" and fantasies from "reality"' (238). Echoing Daumier, Kael declares: 'Fellini throws in his disorganized ideas, and lets the audiences sort out the meanings for themselves' (237). However, Kael's predictable – if also somewhat justified – criticism of the film's lack of an inexorable logic is anticipated and thus disarmed by the film itself.

The self-reflective mise en abyme structure allows for not only the interrogation and problematization of the act of filmmaking but also that of its critical reception. As Metz (1990) observes, 'it is the mirror construction alone that has allowed Fellini to integrate into his film a whole series of ambiguous reflections on whatever his own film might be accused of' (229). In this context it is worth noticing that, as Bondanella (2002) observes, Fellini 'had long been accused by his critics of being a *bozzettista*, a character-sketch artist stringing along episodes with little connection' (98). And as Metz further points out, we never see Guido's film, not even extracts, and thus 'any distance between the film Guido dreamt of making and the film Fellini made is abolished' (231). As has often been pointed out, even though Guido is supposed to make a science fiction film, Daumier's criticism is not directed at Guido's film but at the one he is planning on doing, the one we are watching: Fellini's film.[18]

Using a complex narrative mise en abyme structure, Fellini anticipates and confronts his critics in advance by showing that Guido is only able to create once he frees himself from Daumier's insistence upon 'logic, rationality, ideology, and intellectual consistency' (Bondanella 2002: 109). Guido accepts that his life is a 'great confusion' and commits himself to the magical world of Maurice, a world of dreams, fantasies, childhood memories, Baroque spaces, extravagant costumes, performers and circus artists – all the 'stuff' that makes up the soul of Fellini's cinematic worlds: its 'asa nisi masa'.[19]

Thus, where Guido has sought redemption in the solace of his mistress – in the healing waters of the spa, the Catholic church, the affective niches of his fantasies, or through reinventing/reliving his childhood memories – it is by transforming his personal and professional failures into aesthetic performance spaces (i.e. impossible narrative environments) that he eventually finds a sort of redemption. As Joshua Landy argues:

> Thanks to the magic of art, then, suffering has been transfigured into aesthetic bliss. Guido's painful mess of a life turns out to have a beautiful shape to it; and each of its inhabitants turns out to have a necessary place within that shape, like tiles within a mosaic, or daubs of paint on a canvas. It is not that all conflicts can actually be resolved; it is just that all conflicts can be seen as vital contributors to a thing of beauty, and hence given a justification, and hence, in a special sense, redeemed. (Landy 2015: 563)

8½ does not simply contain a story narrated via a complex puzzle structure; it is the story of how that narrative structure came into being. However, its 'story' cannot be extrapolated by a rational discourse but must be 'understood' through embodied experience. Herein lies a largely neglected aesthetic and pleasurable attraction of the puzzle film. The self-reflective puzzle structure allows the film a mandate to create filmic worlds that are to be understood affectively. I believe a significant aesthetic appeal of the contemporary puzzle film lies precisely in how the puzzle structure justifies the construction of 'impossible' narrative environments that never cease to mystify, complexify, captivate, enchant, and move their audiences. Thus, *8½* is a reminder that film puzzles are not first and foremost to be uncracked by cognitive rehearsals of problem solving, but are to be experienced. As Bondanella (2002) argues, *8½* 'can be seen and embodied on the screen but not easily explained by rational discourse' (115).

Conclusions

8½ not only renders problematic a clear outlining of its 'text' but also embeds its audience in 'impossible' narrative environments that do not abide by the rule of non-contradiction; that defy or leave unexplained their intrinsic laws; that blur the boundaries between reality, hallucination, dream and imagination; that are defined by non-generic atmospheres; that retain the audience in a sustained affective state of uncertainty; and that rely on creative use of highly expressive cinematic techniques. Importantly, these filmic spaces are self-reflective meta-cinematic spaces that portray not only the world of a struggling film director but are also themselves reflections on the creative and receptive acts of filmmaking – more precisely, reflections on the particular act of *this film* being made and seen (see Metz 1990: 230).

8½ is both a satiric negation of auteur theory and one of its most powerful manifestations. The divide between the work and its author is blurred, eradicated or impurified, creating an 'impossible' diegetic space that constantly reflects back upon its own creation. However, the mise en abyme structure not only weaves the act of creation into the fabric of the film but also reflects upon its recipients' engagement with the mise en abyme structure as oscillating between attempts to 'control' the film through analytical recognition and the sustained affective feeling of disorientation resulting from the film's resistance towards a coherent, rational logic.

Thus, whilst we 'feel the vertigo of the mise en abyme of story within story within story' (Vanelli 2020: 208), the lines between the filmic 'text' and our cognitive-embodied investments begin to blur. We no longer entertain the illusion of the filmic diegesis as an independently existing cinematic world that we look upon as if through a window frame.[20] Instead, we are caught up in the infinite regress of the meta-cinematic mirroring of the film's 'impossible' narrative environments. In a manner typical of the puzzle film, 8½ thereby 'unsettles the textual boundaries of the film itself, collapsing inside and outside into a fluid significatory space' (Isaacs 2014: 203). In shifting to a second-generation cognitive approach, this chapter has argued that an important part of the cognitive, aesthetic and affective attraction of puzzle films is to be found in their construction of 'impossible', 'fluid significatory spaces' that need not to be resolved but to be experienced in order to be 'understood'.

Steffen Hven is currently a Fellow at the Cinepoetics Research Group at the Freie University in Berlin, where he is also an independent lecturer in Film Studies. Prior to that, he was a Visiting Postdoctoral Fellow at the University of Chicago and an Associate Postdoc at the Bauhaus-Universität Weimar, where he also obtained his doctoral degree. Hven is the author of two books – *Cinema and Narrative Complexity* (Amsterdam UP, 2017) and *Enacting the Worlds of Cinema* (Oxford UP, 2022) – as well as numerous articles.

Notes

I would like to express my gratitude to the German Research Foundation (DFG, HV 8/2-1) for financial support. I would also like to thank the editors of this volume and two anonymous reviewers for their very constructive criticisms and helpful feedback on an earlier version of this chapter.

1. Although 8½ is not technically a 'puzzle film' but rather inscribes itself into the category of 'modernist art cinema' or the 'puzzling art film' (see Holland 1964), it has been formative for the emergence of the contemporary complex film. For a discussion of the intersection of modernist art cinema and puzzle films, see Kiss and Willemsen 2017: 140–82. For a characterization of the art cinema in terms reminiscent of the current discourse on the 'puzzle film', see Holland 1964. Like Holland, I prefer to speak of the 'puzzling' effect of these films rather than their 'puzzle'. In both cases, this serves to underline the affective focal point of the 'puzzling art films'. Kiss and Willemsen (2017), addressing the contemporary 'impossible puzzle film', argue, however, that 'today's narrative complexification seems to aim at eliciting cognitive puzzles, primarily for

the puzzle's sake' (19). I do not intend to disregard the cognitive puzzle that these films pose; but in focusing on the often-ignored puzzling narrative environments that complex storytelling affords, it becomes possible to examine an aspect of the puzzle film that deserves more critical attention, namely, the media environments and their bodily effects that this narrative form entails. While this oscillation between a rational discourse trying to set the film straight, and an affective but illogical force driving the film, is particularly pronounced and self-reflectively discussed in *8½*, it is also formative of the complex puzzle film – for example, in a film such as Spike Jonze and Charlie Kaufman's *Adaptation* (2002), which carries the legacy of *8½* into the era of complex narrative cinema. For an approach that accentuates the embodied effects of complex storytelling, see Hven 2017.

2. What was first summarized as '4E approaches' (Menary 2010) (enactive, embodied, extended, embedded) has now expanded to also include affective (4EA) (Protevi 2009) and experiential and relational '5EAR' (D'Aloia and Eugeni 2014) processes.
3. Although film studies has experienced a 'turn to the body', much of its conceptual and theoretical heritage remains rooted in the 'disembodied' paradigms that conceived the 'film as text'. For an extended elaboration of this claim, see Hven (2022). A series of cognitive-oriented theories have recently emerged that challenge this 'disembodied' scheme. These include, from the perspective of embodied cognitive linguistics, Coëgnaarts and Kravanja 2012 and 2015, Coëgnarts 2019, and Fahlenbrach 2016, and from the standpoint of multimodal semiotics, Bateman 2019. For embodied cognitive approaches to complex narratives, see Kiss and Willemsen 2017, Hven 2017, and Grishakova and Poulaki 2019; and for a neurology-based theory of 'embodied simulation' in the cinema, see Gallese and Guerra 2020.
4. The term enactive is here used in the technical sense first given to it within the embodied cognitive philosophy of Varela, Thompson and Rosch (1992). Here, the term 'enactive' is used to 'emphasize the growing conviction that cognition is not the representation of a pregiven world by a pregiven mind but is rather the enactment of a world and a mind on the basis of a history of the variety of actions that a being in the world performs' (ibid.: 9). For an enactive approach to literary narratology, see Caracciolo 2014.
5. For an exploration of how this works in *Memento* (Nolan, 2000) – a film that employs a reverse-chronological narrative structure to impose a sense of difficulty in constructing a causal-linear fabula, which creates a sensation of memory defunction on the part of the viewer that is analogous to the condition of anterograde amnesia suffered by the main character of the film – see Hven 2017: 175–204.
6. This approach is rooted in Ferdinand de Saussure's ([1916] 1998) structural linguistic assertations that the signifier relates arbitrarily to the signified. This has led to the narratological separation of the 'message' of a text from its material vehicles of communication, an idea that has not only been formative of structuralist narratology (see Brémond 1964) but also of cognitive-formalist film theory (see Thompson 1977).
7. For an exploration of the 'diegesis-as-text' and its replacement with the 'diegesis-as-environment', see Hven 2022.
8. Thus, as Inga Pollmann (2013) has convincingly argued, we cannot simply equate the perception of a cinematic environment to the perception of a real-world environment, because the former has been techno-perceptively shaped, such that 'we perceive film images as embodied spectators, yet these images themselves present a perception of the world that is not dependent on our body' (783).

9. The creation of impossible environments with a high degree of kinesthetic involvement is a trademark of complex storytelling, and is thus also to be found in more contemporary examples, such as the opening title sequence of *Fight Club* (Fincher, 1999).
10. As Bondanella (2002) clarifies, '[t]he magic words are a form of Italian "pig Latin" that has transformed the Italian word anima (soul, spirit, conscience, even consciousness) by adding letters to the different syllables: a + sa, ni + si, ma + sa' (103). As has often been pointed out, the anima refers specifically to the use of this term within Carl Gustav Jung's psychoanalysis. On the influence of Jung on Fellini, see Bondanella 2002: 27–29, 93–94 (see also Conti 1972; Fredericksen 2014; Surliuga 2020).
11. For a discussion on puzzle films being 'complex' vs 'complicated', see Kiss and Willemsen 2017: 19ff.; for a study of the relation between complexity theory and complex narratives, see Grishakova and Poulaki 2019.
12. For a discussion of the relation of Fellini's critical acclaim to auteur theory, see Sbragia 2015.
13. It is worth noticing, however, that it was exactly this lack of readability and its foregrounding of breaches in narrative causality that caused the auteur-oriented theories of André Bazin and Gilles Deleuze to reserve a special place for Fellini in the history of cinema.
14. In his study of Fellini's 'style of excess', John C. Stubbs (1993) argues, 'The most important aspect of Fellini's visual style is the sense viewers have that they are receiving images of life that are highly charged with movements, contrasts, textures, colors, and, above all, surprises' (55; see also Stubbs 2006: 1–36).
15. As Marco Vanelli (2020) has described this, 'Fellini not only makes use of the artificial scenery, the make-up, the narrative distortion, to stretch the limits of figurative meaning, but also wants the viewer to realize what he is doing, to take note of it, to enter and become familiar with another dimension that is no longer the simple realm of being told a story, but the experience of putting oneself in the shoes of the storyteller (or in the position of one who no longer knows how to tell the story, or no longer wants to tell it)' (208).
16. Note here the working title of the film: *La Bella Confusione* [The beautiful confusion] (see Bondanella 2002: 109).
17. As Christian Metz (1990) has observed, in this perplexing final scene of the film Guido ends up joining the celebratory circle dance, thereby abandoning the place of the director-in-the-film and leaving it open for the film's real auteur, Fellini (234). Due to its self-reflective negation of the auteur, it has been argued that Fellini takes upon himself the role of the auteur only to reject it: 'Nowhere is Fellini the auteur more dead than in his own work' (Burke 1989: 37). In Fellini's 'impossible' Schrödinger universe, the auteur Guido is both dead and alive.
18. Thus, it is effectively *8½* that is accused by Daumier of its 'lack of a central idea that establishes the problematic of the film'; of becoming a series of 'absolutely gratuitous episodes'; of its 'ambiguous realism'; of not making it clear 'what the authors really intend'; of displaying an 'impoverished poetic inspiration'; of demonstrating that the 'cinema is irremediably fifty years behind all the other arts'; of not even being worthy of an avant-garde film, 'even though it has all the weaknesses of that genre'; and finally, of being 'absent of a higher degree of culture, as well as, of course, inexorable logic and clarity'.
19. For an examination of the role of the circus in the cinema of Fellini, see Stoddart 2002.
20. On the cinema as window and frame, see Elsaesser and Hagener 2009.

References

Aldouby, Hava. 2020. 'Fellini's Visual Style(s): A Phenomenological Account', in F. Burke et al. (eds), *A Companion to Federico Fellini*. Hoboken, NJ: Wiley-Blackwell, pp. 223–36.
Bachmann, Gideon. 1967. 'How I Make Films: An Interview with Federico Fellini', *U.S. Camera World Annual*.
Bateman, John Arnold. 2019. 'Multimodality and Materiality: The Interplay of Textuality and Texturality in the Aesthetics of Film', *Poetics Today* 40(2): 235–68.
Bateman, John Arnold, and Janina Wildfeuer. 2017. 'Introduction: Bringing Together New Perspectives of Film Text Analysis', in J.A. Bateman and J. Wildfeuer (eds), *Film Text Analysis: New Perspectives on the Analysis of Filmic Meaning*. London: Routledge, pp. 1–23.
Bondanella, Peter. 2002. *The Films of Federico Fellini*, Cambridge Film Classics. Cambridge: Cambridge University Press.
Bordwell, David. 1985. *Narration in the Fiction Film*. Madison: University of Wisconsin Press.
———. 2002. 'Film Futures', *SubStance* 31(1): 88–104.
———. 2008. *Poetics of Cinema*. New York: Routledge.
———. 2013. *Christopher Nolan: A Labyrinth of Linkages*. Madison: Irvington Way Institute Press.
Branigan, Edward. 1984. *Point of View: A Theory of Narration and Subjectivity in Classical Film*. Amsterdam: Mouton Publishers.
Brémond, Claude. 1964. 'Le message narratif', *Communications* 4 (special issue: 'Recherches sémiologiques'): 4–32.
Buckland, Warren (ed.). 2009a. *Puzzle Films: Complex Storytelling in Contemporary Cinema*. Malden, MA: Blackwell-Wiley.
———. 2009b. 'Introduction: Puzzle Plots', in W. Buckland (ed.), *Puzzle Films: Complex Storytelling in Contemporary Cinema*. Malden, MA: Blackwell-Wiley, pp. 1–12.
———. (ed.). 2014. *Hollywood Puzzle Films*, AFI Film Readers. New York: Routledge.
Burke, Frank. 1989. 'Fellini: Changing the Subject', *Film Quarterly* 43(1): 36–48.
Cameron, Alan. 2008. *Modular Narratives in Contemporary Cinema*. Basingstoke: Palgrave Macmillan.
Caracciolo, Marco. 2014. *The Experientiality of Narrative: An Enactivist Approach*. Boston, MA: De Gruyter.
Coëgnarts, Maarten. 2019. *Film as Embodied Art: Bodily Meaning in the Cinema of Stanley Kubrick*. Boston, MA: Academic Studies Press.
Coëgnarts, Maarten, and Peter Kravanja. 2012. 'Embodied Visual Meaning: Image Schemas in Film', *Projections* 6(2): 84–101.
———. (eds). 2015. *Embodied Cognition and Cinema*. Leuven: Leuven University Press.
Colombetti, Giovanna. 2014. *The Feeling Body: Affective Science Meets the Enactive Mind*. Cambridge, MA: MIT Press.
Conti, Isabella. 1972. 'Fellini 8 1/2 (A Jungian Analysis)', *Ikon* 23(82–83): 123–70.
D'Aloia, Adriano, and Ruggero Eugeni. 2014. 'Neurofilmology: An Introduction', *Cinéma & Cie* XIV(22–23): 9–26.
Deleuze, Gilles. 2005. *Cinema 2: The Time-Image*, trans. H. Tomlinson and B. Habberjam. London: Continuum.
Dewey, Donald. 1993. *Marcello Mastroianni: His Life and Art*. Secaucus, NJ: Carol Publishing.
Elsaesser, Thomas. 2009. 'The Mind-Game Film', in W. Buckland (ed.), *Puzzle Films: Complex Storytelling in Contemporary Cinema*. Malden, MA: Blackwell-Wiley, pp. 13–41.

Elsaesser, Thomas, and Malte Hagener. 2009. 'Cinema as Window and Frame', in T. Elsaesser and Hagener (eds), *Film Theory: An Introduction through the Senses* (1st edition.). New York: Routledge, pp. 14–38.

Fahlenbrach, Katrin. 2016. *Embodied Metaphors in Film, Television, and Video Games: Cognitive Approaches*, Routledge Research in Cultural and Media Studies. New York: Routledge.

Fellini, Federico. 1976. *Fellini on Fellini*, trans. I. Quingley. London: Eyre Methuen Ltd.

Fingerhut, Joerg, and Kathrin Heiman. 2017. 'Movies and the Mind: On Our Filmic Body', in C. Durt et al. (eds), *Embodiment, Enaction, and Culture: Investigating the Constitution of the Shared World*. Cambridge, MA: MIT Press, pp. 353–77.

Fredericksen, Don. 2014. 'Fellini's 8½ and Jung: Narcissism and Creativity in Midlife', *International Journal of Jungian Studies* 6(2): 133–42.

Gallese, Vittorio, and Michele Guerra. 2020. *The Empathic Screen: Cinema and Neuroscience*, trans. F. Anderson. Oxford: Oxford University Press.

Genette, Gérard. 1983. *Narrative Discourse: An Essay in Method*, trans. J.E. Lewin (1st edition). Ithaca, NY: Cornell University Press.

———. 1988. *Narrative Discourse Revisited*, trans. J.E. Lewin. Ithaca, NY: Cornell University Press.

Ghislotti, Stefano. 2009. 'Narrative Comprehension Made Difficult: Film Form and Mnemonic Devices in Memento', in W. Buckland (ed.), *Puzzle Films: Complex Storytelling in Contemporary Cinema*. Malden, MA: Wiley-Blackwell, pp. 87–106.

Grishakova, Marina, and Maria Poulaki. 2019. *Narrative Complexity: Cognition, Embodiment, Evolution*. Lincoln: University of Nebraska Press.

Hesselberth, Pepita, and Laura Schuster. 2008. 'Into the Mind and Out to the World: Memory Anxiety in the Mind-Game Film', in J. Kooijman et al. (eds), *Mind the Screen: Media Concepts According to Thomas Elsaesser*. Amsterdam: Amsterdam University Press, pp. 96–111.

Holland, Norman Norwood. 1964. 'The Puzzling Film: Three Analyses and a Guess at their Appeal', *Journal of Social Issues* 20: 71–96.

Hven, Steffen. 2017. *Cinema and Narrative Complexity: Embodying the Fabula*, Film Culture in Transition. Amsterdam: Amsterdam University Press.

———. 2019. 'The Affective Niches of Media', *NECSUS: European Journal of Media Studies* (Special Issue: Emotions).

———. 2022. *Enacting the Worlds of Cinema*. New York: Oxford University Press.

Isaacs, Bruce. 2014. 'The Image of Time in Post-Classical Hollywood', in W. Buckland (ed.), *Hollywood Puzzle Films*, AFI Film Readers. London: Routledge, pp. 198–213.

Johnson, Mark. 2017. *Embodied Mind, Meaning, and Reason: How Our Bodies Give Rise to Understanding*. Chicago: Chicago University Press.

———. 2018. 'The Embodiment of Language', in A. Newen et al. (eds), *The Oxford Handbook of 4E Cognition*. Oxford: Oxford University Press, pp. 623–40.

Johnson, Mark, and George Lakoff. 2002. 'Why Cognitive Linguistics Requires Embodied Realism', *Cognitive Linguistics* 13(3): 245–63.

Kael, Pauline. 1966. '8½: Confessions of a Movie Director', in P. Kael, *I Lost It at the Movies*. New York: Bantam Books, pp. 235–39.

Kiss, Miklós, and Steven Willemsen. 2017. *Impossible Puzzles: A Cognitive Approach to Contemporary Complex Cinema*. Edinburgh: Edinburgh University Press.

Kukkonen, Karin, and Marco Caracciolo. 2014. 'Introduction: What Is the "Second Generation?"', *Style* 48 (No. 3, Cognitive Literary Study: Second Generation Approaches): 261–74.

Lakoff, George, and Mark Johnson. 1999. *Philosophy in the Flesh: The Embodied Mind and Its Challenge to Western Thought*. New York: Basic Books.

Landy, Joshua. 2015. 'Mental Calisthenics and Self-Reflexive Fiction', in L. Zunshine (ed.), *The Oxford Handbook of Cognitive Literary Studies*. Oxford: Oxford University Press, pp. 559–80.

Menary, Richard. 2010. 'Introduction to the Special Issue on 4E Cognition', *Phenomenology and the Cognitive Sciences* 9(4): 459–63.

Merleau-Ponty, Maurice. 1991. 'The Film and the New Psychology', in H.L. Dreyfus and P.A. Dreyfus (trans.), *Sense and Non-Sense*. Evanston, IL: Northwestern University Press, pp. 48–59.

Metz, Christian. 1990. *Film Language: A Semiotics of the Cinema*, trans. M. Taylor. Chicago: University of Chicago Press.

Morin, Edgar. (1946) 2005. *Cinema, or the Imaginary Man*, trans. L. Mortimer. Minneapolis: University of Minnesota Press.

Mulvey, Laura. 2006. *Death 24x a Second: Stillness and the Moving Image*. London: Reaktion Books.

Newman, Michael. 2006. 'Character and Complexity in American Independent Cinema: 21 Grams and Passion Fish', *Film Criticism* 31(1–2): 89–106.

Pallasmaa, Juhani. 2014. 'Space, Place, and Atmosphere: Peripheral Perception in Existential Experience', in C. Borch (ed.), *Architectural Atmospheres: On the Experience and Politics of Architecture*. Basel: Birkhäuser, pp. 18–41.

Panek, Elliott. 2006. 'The Poet and the Detective: Defining the Psychological Puzzle Film', *Film Criticism* 31(1–2): 62–88. Special Double Issue on Complex Narratives.

Perry, Ted. 1972. 'Signifiers in Fellini's 8 1/2', *Forum Italicum* 6(1): 79–86.

Pollmann, Inga. 2013. 'Invisible Worlds, Visible: Uexküll's *Umwelt*, Film, and Film Theory', *Critical Inquiry* 39(4): 777–816.

Poulaki, Maria. 2014. 'Puzzled Hollywood and the Return of Complex Films', in W. Buckland (ed.), *Hollywood Puzzle Films*, AFI Film Readers. London: Routledge, pp. 35–53.

Protevi, John. 2009. *Political Affect: Connecting the Social and the Somatic*. Minneapolis: University of Minnesota Press.

Saussure, Ferdinand de. (1916) 1998. *Course in General Linguistics*, trans. R. Harris (Reprint edition). Chicago: Open Court.

Sbragia, Albert. 2015. 'Fellini and the Auteurists', *Italica* 92(3) (Fall): 660–79.

Sesonske, Alexander. 2010. '8½: A Film with Itself as Its Subject', *The Criterion Collection*. Retrieved 29 July 2020 from https://www.criterion.com/current/posts/173-8-1-2-a-film-with-itself-as-its-subject.

Simons, Jan. 2008. 'Complex Narratives', *New Review of Film and Television Studies* 6(2): 111–26.

Sobchack, Vivian. 2004. *Carnal Thought: Embodiment and Moving Image Culture*. Berkeley: University of California Press.

Souriau, Étienne. 1951. 'La structure de l'univers filmique et le vocabulaire de la filmologie', *Revue internationale de filmologie* 2(7–8): 231–40.

———. 1953. *L'univers filmique*. Paris: Flammarion.

Stoddart, Helen. 1995. 'Auteurism and Film Authorship', in J. Hollows and M. Jancovich (eds), *Approaches to Popular Film*. Manchester: Manchester University Press, pp. 37–58.

———. 2002. 'Subtle Wasted Traces: Fellini and the Circus', in F. Burke and M. Waller (eds), *Federico Fellini: Contemporary Perspectives*. Toronto: University of Toronto Press, pp. 47–64.

Stubbs, John Caldwell. 1993. 'The Fellini Manner: Open Form and Visual Excess', *Cinema Journal* 32(4): 49–64.

———. 2006. *Federico Fellini as Auteur: Seven Aspects of His Films*. Carbondale: Southern Illinois University Press.
Surliuga, Victoria. 2020. 'Masina and Mastroianni: Reconfiguring C.G. Jung's Animus and Anima', in F. Burke et al. (eds), *A Companion to Federico Fellini*. Hoboken, NJ: Wiley-Blackwell, pp. 191–204.
Thompson, Kristin. 1977. 'The Concept of Cinematic Excess', *Ciné-Tracts* 1(2): 54–63.
Uexküll, Jakob Johann von. 2001. 'An Introduction to Umwelt' (trans. G. Brunow), *Semiotica* 134(1/4): 107–10.
Vanelli, Marco. 2020. '"Io Non Me Ne Intendo": Fellini's Relationship to Film Language', in F. Burke et al. (eds), *A Companion to Federico Fellini*. Hoboken, NJ: Wiley-Blackwell, pp. 207–21.
Varela, Francisco Javier, Evan Thompson and Eleanor Rosch. 1992. *The Embodied Mind: Cognitive Science and Human Experience*. Cambridge, MA: MIT Press.
Waller, Marguerite. 2002. 'Introduction', in F. Burke and M. Waller (eds), *Federico Fellini: Contemporary Perspectives*. Toronto: University of Toronto Press, pp. 3–25.

CHAPTER 6

2 or 3 Things?
Polyphony, Cognitive Challenge and Aesthetic Pleasure in Godard's (Counter) Cinema

Maria Poulaki

Introduction

In this chapter, I propose to examine, in a new light, the cognitive challenge and aesthetic appeal of a film derived from Jean-Luc Godard's filmography – a filmography in which the incongruities between film as text and film as image, between sound, dialogue and image, and between pleasure and displeasure, still compose a unique narrative experience. As I will argue, Godard's films offer exemplary cases of the negotiation between complexity, cognitive challenge, and the (possibility of) aesthetic pleasure.

The cognitive challenge is not just narrative-based in the classical sense, coming from broken cause-and-effect links and disrupted chronology in the narrated story. Beyond cognitive dissonance, which focuses on 'cognitions (elements of narrative or real-world knowledge) that are in irresolvable conflict' (Kiss and Willemsen 2017: 66), the 'conflict' discussed here also involves the primary sensory and perceptual level. It not only affects higher cognitive processes and larger chunks of narrative meaning – what Magliano, Higgs and Clinton (2019) have called 'back-end processing' – but it happens at the 'front end' as well, creating 'noise' and affecting the film experience on multiple levels. The consequence of such disruption is, I argue, not incomprehension or just self-reflexive medium awareness and estrangement; before and beyond incongruence, what can be observed in Godard's films is heterogeneity and polyphony, which lie at the heart of both cognitive challenge and (aesthetic) pleasure.

It is not just the complexity of the narration itself or its 'intransitivity' (mainly concerning broken continuity, according to Wollen 1972) or the discontinuity of the style through, for example, editing, that challenge the viewer, but a complex layering of elements, all of which seem to be standing separate from one another without assimilating into a coherent whole. The challenge consists of the need to attend to these separate and heterogeneous elements simultaneously, to 'compose' such polyphony, and to inhabit nonetheless the world they are making. Although based on Godard's filmography, this observation may be applied to other films as well.

In Search of Connection

Deux ou Trois Choses Que Je Sais d'Elle ['2 or 3 Things I Know about Her'], released in 1967, is one of the most self-reflexive films of Godard. A reference to one of the most significant influences on him, Bertolt Brecht, is already embedded in the first scene of the film, where the protagonist, actress Marina Vlady and her character Juliette Janson, is doubly introduced to the audience both as her real self and as her role in the film by the whispering voice of the unseen director. This introduction sets up a *motif* that runs throughout the film, a constant address of the conflict between truth and appearance, and a constant commentary on the impossibility of language, including the visual language of cinema, to express the causes of things – to do something more than just describe appearances. This is indeed what the film does in most of its runtime: describe.

Characters, including the protagonist – apparently cued by Godard with her lines via a speaker during the shooting (Ford 2013) – describe, mostly in an indifferent, detached fashion, their everyday lives, feelings, relationships, and thoughts about life, politics and death. Part of this questioning of appearances in the film has, of course, to do with Godard's own relationship to politics and his desire to connect with it more actively, rather than as a passive bystander, and many scenes in the film criticize exactly this passivity. News from the Vietnam War, political announcements, and sounds of shooting and bombing are weaved into the film as distractions from its main narrative line (although there is hardly such a thing) in the same way that such news was reaching Europeans at the time: as distractions within an everyday life indulged in consumerism. In these terms, the film stands as a powerful documentation of the conditions (and 'Zeitgeist') that led to the May 1968 uprising in France a little later.

In his famous essay on Godard's counter cinema, Peter Wollen (1972) criticizes the auteur for his dismissal of fantasy and the 'pleasure principle', something that became particularly apparent in his explicitly political work post-1968, when he co-founded (with Jean-Pierre Gorin) the Dziga Vertov collective. Pleasure, according to Wollen, is political, as the start of any revolution is desire. The imagination of social change is based on desire and a promise of pleasure – a combination of reality with the pleasure principle, in psychoanalytical terms.

I will not expand very much here on the political potential of pleasure, but I will trace its presence in some of Godard's 1960s work prior to the filmmaker's renunciation of pleasure, according to Wollen. Clearly, in '2 or 3 Things' and earlier titles, Godard has not yet renounced pleasure or imagination, if he ever did. The particular film strikes, in my view, a perfect balance between pleasure and reality, aesthetic modernism and political commitment. There is special reference to the importance of imagination: 'the limits of language are the limits of the world', says the narrator – thus, the act of speaking inevitably confines the world. Godard seems to be in search of a filmic language that releases imagination, which makes '2 or 3 Things' a deeply optimistic film in its fundamental desire to connect with the world and give it new expression.

Cognitive Challenge

A usual criticism against cognitive approaches to film is that they bracket out, if not ignore, the social and political ramifications of films in order to focus on aspects of individual and intra-personal reception. Apart from the fact that a film (such as the one discussed here) can invite the viewer to think about politics – through images, text and sounds explicitly referring to political events – it can also train the spectator to a form of response that is radically political, as it is alert and open to new associations and new ways of thinking about what is present or missing from the current situation. The cognitive is also political on many levels, and any informed 'cognitive' approach ought to take this into account.

With this in mind, instances of incongruence and rupture (or indeed montage) in Godard's cinema could be thought of as posing a cognitive challenge to the viewer. Starting from describing some of these instances, Ruth Perlmutter notes techniques used in *Le Gai Savoir* [The joy of learning] (1969), which can also be found in other films by Godard, such as '2 or 3 Things'. For example, what she calls 'word and image montage' refers to the detachment of words from their meanings and associations with images. She also notes how Godard uses sound in an analytical fashion, 'as a separate entity and as it functions in relation to the image, to silence, to the speaking voice and to the spatiotemporal location in which it is heard' (Perlmutter 1975). In a montage sequence of '2 or 3 Things', the main character Juliette's speaking voice, contemplating on the possibility of thinking of what is not there (such as the victims of war), is overlaid by sounds of shooting, the voice of another character heard repeating 'America über alles', as well as images of the Vietnam War. Each element of sound and voice is treated separately and in conjunction with the image, exploring the (im)possibility of their connection.

Even sounds and images belonging to the same spatio-temporal location are treated separately and juxtaposed or combined so that a whole cannot properly be assimilated or becomes uncertain. In '2 or 3 Things', two men sitting at a desk with piles of books around them randomly pick up books and open them at a random page, reading a few lines out loud before closing them and picking up the next book, leading to the next random quotation. The place where they are siting is undefined, yet the loud sound of a pinball machine, and the image of some posters behind them, connects it to the location of a bar where previously seen conversations were taking place. Despite being unpleasant, as it disrupts rather than just accompanies the different conversations taking place in separate corners of the cafe, the sound of the pinball game is constructive as it literally composes the setting, providing a sense of spatio-temporal continuity to the otherwise disjointed events. A bit later, the setting of the two men's desk is disambiguated through a gesture of parody (a counter cinema element as well, according to Wollen) when a waiter comes to take a food order from them. Ambient sound, spoken word (quotations), and image (with *mise en scène* characterized by a mismatch between figure and ground – the desk with the books and the ambiguous setting) are all treated as heterogeneous elements of an absurd puzzle, the relations between its pieces being transient and contingent.

The prominent role of language in Godard's films, itself in a certain antagonism with the medium, introduces a first and fundamental layer of distinction between seen and heard, where oral and/or written language (in titles, for example) distract from the image. Such layering is often complemented by additional and constant counterpoints of image and sound, as well as incongruent music (see Willemsen and Kiss 2013).

When it comes to the contrast or disjunction between seen and heard, often serving the multiplicity of diegesis that Wollen (1972) notes in Godard, the counter-cinematic practice involves a divergence in the narration from what is seen, or at least it casts some doubt on it. For example, in Godard's earlier film *Pierrot le Fou* [Pierrot the fool] (1965), the (here much stronger) narrative line about a runaway couple is interrupted in a scene where the protagonists, Marianne and Ferdinand, are shown talking to the extras on set, and, as the voiceover informs us, narrating their stories (of William of Orange's nephew Vivien, and Guynemer, respectively). The fact that we can only see and not hear what they say, in the absence of diegetic sound, casts further doubt on the unlikely subject of these narrational inserts. After all, as the film narrator explains, one 'should never ask what comes first, the words or the things, and what comes next'.

The correspondence between language, image and reality – a continuous preoccupation for Godard – is negotiated yet another time. Even though images and words do not support each other and exist in an uncertain indexical relationship, the images themselves are just as powerful as the words (if not more so), both in 'Pierrot' and '2 or 3 Things'. In the latter, the narrator (Juliette) rushes to correct 'certainly' (*certainment*) to 'maybe' (*peut-être*) almost as soon as she articulates the word. Yet, in contrast to the words heard, the images shine throughout the film, in what Hamish Ford characterizes as 'intense, never-ending work on the importance of the image itself, both its wonder and absolute violence. Both when it comes to images, which here survive substantively – indeed at the expense of seemingly everything else – and words, which while used extensively, are also almost immediately doubted' (Ford 2013).

In his counter cinema essay, mainly focusing on *Le Vent d'Est* [Wind from the East] (1970) but also looking back on other parts of Godard's filmography prior to the Dziga Vertov group, Wollen uses the term 'rupture' to point at such montage elements. He notes, for example, a 'rupture between the soundtrack and the images' as well as 'between different worlds and different channels', corresponding to his categories of 'multiple versus single diegesis', and 'aperture' versus closure (1972). Apart from rupture, however, he also notes multiplicity and coexistence, which create plurality and 'a genuine polyphony' (Wollen 1972). In what follows, I will emphasize this aspect of polyphony and its role in both cognitive challenge and aesthetic pleasure.

The multiplicity and heterogeneity of elements often coexisting in the same shot or scene in Godard's films may induce a feeling of something constantly escaping perception and interpretation; a sense of something simultaneously present and elusive as it cannot be fully grasped due to perceptual limitations. Alluding to the Kantian mathematical sublime, as long as we focus on the quantitative dimension, this excessive experience brings an awareness of the limited 'bandwidth' of perception and our poor equipment to combat this 'sensory overload'. But, more than mere multiplicity, it is relations and (multimodal) layering that make Godard's filmmaking complex and challenging in cognitive terms.

The cognitive challenge that Godard's method poses could primarily be considered a challenge for attention. Wollen makes special mention of the function of attention in 'Le Vent d' Est', associated with the element of 'intransitivity': as he notes, the spectator is forced to reconcentrate and refocus their attention, but 'of course, his attention might get lost altogether' (1972). For example, in a scene where the protagonist of '2 or 3 Things', Juliette, lies back in the chair of a beauty salon, her dialogue with the manicurist is constantly interrupted by her pronounced words, objectively describing her thoughts and sensations as she becomes aware of them: for example, 'silence', 'blue spiral notebooks', 'phone ringing'. From a narratological perspective, the scene could be considered a case of multiple diegesis or narrative intransitivity, but from a cognitive perspective we can see it as a method of attentional diffusion. While Wollen discusses how breaks in the causal-linear narrative sequence cause attentional refocusing, he does not address cases where attentional focus is impeded through the simultaneity of heterogeneous elements rather than through (nonlinear) narrative succession. For such cases, we could speak of a technique of widening attentional focus rather than just shifting focus and reorienting attention. In the beauty salon scene, the viewer is required to parallelly follow both the lines of the conversation as well as the thought trail of Juliette, and to make meaning of each, both separately and in their interconnection. Moreover, we are required to (cross-modally) check Juliette's description of her senses in relation to the objective (diegetic) images and sounds, such as that of the phone ringing.

In recent psychological research on scene perception and narrative comprehension in different (visual) media, Loschky et al. (2015) have coined the term 'the tyranny of film' for the phenomenon they observed in which, regardless of prior knowledge and narrative expectations, films dictate attentional selection. The medium achieves this through montage, cinematography, *mise en scène* and mere image motion and change, as time is limited for viewers to make a selection or to readjust focus. Loschky et al. associate attentional selection with the 'front-end processes', which feed into the construction of narrative event models happening at the 'back end': 'Attentional selection determines what information to process during single fixations, and where the eyes will be sent for the next fixation' (Loschky et al. 2020).

But what happens when films purposefully diffuse attention and inhibit attentional selection, as with Godard's '2 or 3 Things'? Eye fixations are certainly not the primary means of understanding here, as meaning is as much dependent on the images as it is on sound and their complex intertwining, both intra- and extra-diegetic.

Aesthetic Pleasure

The other main question that this chapter has set out to explore is wherein lies the aesthetic appeal of such strange (if not estranged) film experience – if anywhere? Is there a kind of aesthetic pleasure compatible with such cognitive challenge that seems to run counter to the immersion and enjoyment typically associated with narrative film? Or is Godard heading towards denouncing all pleasure, as Wollen notes in his essay on counter cinema?

There are certainly many sources of aesthetic pleasure in Godard's 1960s films, so, 'just looking at the pictures' as Andy Warhol would say – their beautiful colours, famous stars, landscapes and fashion, especially in films such as Le Mépris [Contempt] (1963) and Pierrot le Fou – could alone provide enough pleasure to the hypothetical viewer. The viewer could isolate certain perceptual channels and manage to attune to those particular elements only, surrendering to the power of the images, as already noted in Ford's observation. But, as I will argue, another level of pleasure comes from practising how to inhabit such strange and rich cinematic worlds, and engaging with, instead of avoiding, the complex interweaving of their elements.

Cognitive challenge and aesthetic pleasure have not been incompatible in the theory and history of arts, including cinema; on the contrary, the complexity of an artwork has often been associated with pleasure. From Shklovsky's definition of art in terms of difficulty and de-automatization in his 'Art as Technique' ([1917] 2017) to William Empson's praise of ambiguity in poetry ([1930] 2004) and Yuri Lotman's association of entropy with artistic creation (see Grishakova and Poulaki 2019), the creation and experience of art are intertwined with a certain degree of cognitive challenge, even though the particular degree of challenge demanded, as well as pleasure associated with it, might differ between lay and expert audiences, as many have suggested.[1] Two concepts, distinct yet relevant to one another, can be useful here: ambiguity and incongruence. When applied to artistic objects, both refer to multiplicities that do not assimilate easily, and demand perceptual and/or cognitive effort to be grasped and resolved – an effort that can still be aesthetically and affectively rewarding.

Starting with ambiguity, Otty and Roberts discuss how ambiguity in the arts, associated with an inherent multiplicity of an artwork inviting alternative meanings, has been linked to cognitive dissonance, puzzlement, and hence to a temporal dimension of delay in processing and interpretation. Referring to Empson's famous work 'Seven Types of Ambiguity', they remark: 'The application of the term "ambiguity" is then justified in terms of the experience of the analytical process: the multiple meanings are too complex to be grasped simultaneously, or "remembered together" ... so a temporal process of working through an experience of puzzlement is necessary' (Otty and Roberts 2013).

While 'default' cognitive processing reduces ambiguity as it has to impose limits to the constant bombardment by stimuli (an opinion put forth by Reuven Tsur's cognitive poetics and shared by other writers as well, as Otty and Roberts remark), ambiguous art follows the opposite direction: through the induction of ambiguity, it can go against this natural tendency, delaying the imposition of 'natural categories', approximating what John Keats called 'negative capability' as the capability to tolerate uncertainty and doubt (Otty and Roberts 2013). Even though ambiguity refers to alternative perceptions and interpretations of the same stimulus (think, for example, of ambiguous figures studied in perceptual psychology), it can also apply to more complex stimuli such as film scenes. These can also be thought to prolong both front- and back-end processes of perception, attention and interpretation when their complexity and ambiguity is increased, as is the case with scenes in Godard's films, such as '2 or 3 Things'. The previously mentioned scene of Juliette in the beauty salon, but also the whole motif that runs throughout the film of doubting appearances, could be considered a tactic of increasing ambiguity by constructing a complex layering of internal and external reality, and disrupting any straightforward attempts at signification.

Incongruence, the coexistence of antithetical tendencies in an artwork, was described by Russian psychologist Lev Vygotsky in his 'Psychology of Art' ([1925] 1972) as a source of aesthetic pleasure. Based on Hegelian dialectics, Vygotsky praised contradictions in art's content and form as conveying the interweaving of politics and aesthetics also expressed by the Russian formalists at the time. Vygotsky, for example, described how 'affective contradiction' – the coexistence of antithetical emotions in Shakespeare's *Hamlet* – leads to catharsis.

The coexistence of antithetical moods – and, indeed, affective contradictions – can also be found in Godard, in cases where events (life stories, personal emotions, etc.) are shown or narrated in a cold, documentary-like fashion. Here, incongruence serves Brechtian distancing rather than catharsis: for example, in cases of tension between the emotional tone of the events depicted and that of their narration, which is usually objective and unemotional. An example from '2 or 3 Things' is the scene where children are left playing in the brothel's living room, under the brothel master's supervision, while their mothers do their part-time prostitution job. The events depicted here would normally elicit negative emotions to the viewer, but the narration style, which creates a neutral if not jolly atmosphere, gives the scene a positive emotional tone. Hence, a coexistence of opposite emotional tendencies creates a balance that serves to distance the viewer emotionally.

Incongruence in art does not necessarily preclude aesthetic pleasure. Adrián et al. note how Vygotsky relates artistic complexity, which he found in contradiction, as already noted, to aesthetic pleasure:

> *Vygotski suggests a relationship between contradictions and level of complexity, and aesthetic pleasure. More complex works of art are more able to induce different emotions and provoke a deeper aesthetic feeling. Research on experimental aesthetics partially confirms this idea: a positive link between phenomenic complexity and aesthetic pleasure is a consistent empirical result.* (Adrián, Páez and Álvarez 1996: 110)

Even in scenes with intense incongruences, such as those employing the types of montage that Perlmutter describes in Godard, comprehension of events might be inhibited but aesthetic pleasure may still be enhanced. Recent research in narrative comprehension seems to suggest the same: for example, Zacks and Magliano (2011) remark that films with techniques such as jump cuts, temporal reordering and 'deviation from perfect audiovisual synchrony' might disrupt perception, memory and comprehension, but still afford 'a richer but stranger experience'. Even though they do not offer further specifications, they link contradiction and incongruence to an aesthetically rewarding experience.

From Conflict to Relation

However, thinking only in terms of conflict and incongruence would not do justice to Godard's motivation, which has been to combine and unite through juxtaposition, rather than only to oppose and alienate – the latter being, like it was for his predecessor Brecht, a means to an end rather than the final purpose.

Making manifest of another major influence on Godard's work, that of French philosopher Jean-Paul Sartre, '2 or 3 Things' is self-reflexive about negation, a central concept in Sartre's philosophy referring to what is not there in a given situation but still is, as the possibility of its own transcendence (Sartre uses the term 'being-for-itself' for the latter, as opposed to 'being-in-itself' for the former). In these terms, '2 or 3 Things' marked Godard's perhaps most strenuous attempt so far (in 1967) to practise negation by contemplating on, addressing, and in a way 'letting in' what is not, which results in a diegesis that does not assimilate into a smooth whole, but has its own (critical, as I will discuss) dynamics nevertheless, as ambiguities and incongruities bring forth the 'being-for-itself'. In these terms, '2 or 3 Things' is a mixture of radical film aesthetics, existentialist philosophy, and political thought and commitment.

The idea of a co-presence of elements that do not assimilate, and even sometimes stand in direct contrast to one another, is not Godard's cinematic invention, as it draws on film aesthetics with Marxist roots dating back to the 1920s, particularly the Soviet Montage movement.[2] Godard was a big admirer of Dziga Vertov, as became apparent from the eponymous film collective he established with Jean-Pierre Gorin in 1968. However, Eisenstein's influence on Soviet Montage as well as on Godard cannot be doubted, as also noted by Wollen (1972) when he remarked on how Godard shares the 'image-building' method of Eisenstein. The latter was a pioneer in his use of juxtaposition and conflict in order to create dialectical tension through graphics, motion, editing rhythm, and so on. Godard's use of conflict might not be as systematic as Eisenstein's, but it still shares some of its ideological background, aiming at a certain 'awakening' of viewers' political consciousness. As Perlmutter writes:

> In contrast with Eisenstein's logical argument pattern, by which logically deduced relations between shots create new associations, Godard tends to emphasize the paradoxical irresolution of the artistic consciousness and human action. ... Godard's motives, however, are precisely those of Eisenstein's. The

> range of semiotic significances involved in the inherence and confrontation of the subjective self with its objective reality and its formal constructs of language and culture must be recombined to produce a change of thought. (Perlmutter 1975)

In Godard – more than a direct and frontal antithesis between filmic elements – it is the coexistence in heterogeneity, which can form new constellations and allow new cognitive associations to emerge, that prevails. Indeed, the characteristic of 'polyphony', emphasized by Wollen and others, can go beyond the literal sense of multiple voices heard in the film, including those of the actors, characters and extras, as well as the filmmaker's own – as in '2 or 3 Things'.

Giving a wider sense and function to polyphony, David Brancaleone notes how Godard follows a

> dialogical approach, such that any useful scrap of citation is thrown into a huge collection of texts, a macrocosm of microcosms that refuse to be called to order, which, in their new quality of fragments, portions of content extracted from an original context, begin to relate to the new neighbours as a polyphony of voices, forming a new whole made of extraneous multiplicities. (Brancaleone 2012)

Such quotes allude to a complex systemic perspective on Godard's 'polyphonic' method – a perspective that has also been applied to Eisenstein's method (see Tikka 2008). Combining the narratological and cognitive frameworks with a complex systems perspective allows one to approach polyphony as complexity: interconnectivity between elements that stay heterogeneous but form transient and emergent wholes. In these terms, the corresponding cognitive experience is not simply one of difficulty and 'dissonance'. The latter connotes a negative emotional valence of stress and discomfort. But an alternative approach, also applied to the precognitive level, could perhaps enable a different way of thinking about cognitive challenge in response to film polyphony and 'incongruence'.

Cognitive Challenge, Entropy and Criticality

In art, a degenerative force can also be a creative one, and the same could be argued for the brain processes corresponding to the experience of a complex (difficult, dissonant, or even chaotic) artwork. As already broached, a thread in art theory, represented by the likes of Lotman and Arnheim (1974), links artistic complexity to the notion of entropy. Recent research in cognitive science inspired by complexity theory, especially dynamic systems theory (DST), can refresh the link between artistic complexity and entropy, and shed light on the neurocognitive aspects of (complex) film reception. In the research I am about to discuss, entropy characterizes the mind-brain dynamics in states of 'criticality'.

In particular, Carhart-Harris et al. (2014) call the brain 'entropic' when it is 'poised at a "critical" point in a transition zone between order and disorder'. Such transition happens when the mind shifts from the 'normal' state of consciousness (what is called 'the secondary state'), which is dynamic but slightly subcritical, to the state of primary consciousness, characterized by increased criticality and higher entropy. Carhart-Harris et al. use the vocabulary of dynamic systems theory to describe the state of the brain found in such a transition zone – a zone where stable configurations, known as 'attractors' (they could be thought of as solid perceptions and thoughts) become shallower, and the system can easily shift to new directions, exerting the property of 'metastability' (ibid.). Thus, a multiplicity of potential states rises, and the system can effortlessly and unpredictably switch to different directions and 'transient states'. In a critical state, the brain is more sensitive to fluctuations (noise) and destabilization (see also Kornmeier and Bach 2012). If we were to search for neurodynamic terms to express the process of negation mentioned earlier, perhaps we could indeed use such vocabulary.

A properly 'supercritical' state would be that of an altered state of consciousness, and the research by Carhart-Harris et al. focuses on such altered states as the psychedelic state (mainly induced through clinical administration of substances such as psilocybin). However, their theory of brain criticality has a wider application: cinema, and especially montage, has often been associated with altered states, and spectatorship historically paralleled to dreaming or hypnosis – not just through psychoanalysis, but since the invention of cinema (see Bellour's interview with Bergstrom 1979; Trifonova 2014: 120–21).

Carhart-Harris et al. mention that, in a critical state, there is an increased tendency for 'disorganization' of brain function, akin to an increase in entropy, which, in information theory, is a measure of uncertainty. In terms of the phenomenology of criticality, according to them, such a state is accompanied by 'increased subjective uncertainty or puzzlement' (2014). When there is a multiplicity of heterogeneous and sometimes incongruent stimuli, as in the filmic cases discussed here, the co-presence of many elements simultaneously competing for the viewer's attention increases noise and uncertainty. In the viewer's neurocognitive response (according to dynamic systems perspectives, as already noted), noise is a factor contributing to the rise of entropy. In his counter cinema essay, Wollen notes that Godard does not render images into pure noise because he does not completely deprive them of signification (like American avant-garde artists did in the 1960s, according to Wollen); rather, he notes that Godard's main purpose was to express and signify negation. Here, my use of the term 'noise' exceeds its role in the Shannon-Weaver communication theory, which seems to be the one to which Wollen refers. I use the term more in line with recent dynamic systems approaches, which, influenced by thermodynamics and the conception of entropy therein, see noise as a destabilizing factor to existing schemata of signification (as already described), and, therefore, as a means to render meaning-making processes uncertain and the film's neurocognitive experience more critical by being open to new and transient formations of meaning. While, in the classical theory of communication, noise is considered a disturbing factor that needs to be eliminated, in a dynamic systems perspective, noise acquires the potential to drive the system out of equilibrium and into new emergent formations.

Without drawing direct correlations, it would not be far-fetched to suggest a model of mind-brain criticality that corresponds to film-induced stimulation, especially when noise and ambiguity are increased and attention is diffused. Here, noise would not be a factor of disturbance or dissonance but a dynamic force that enriches the filmic experience and the pleasure derived from it. This could, after all, be compatible with Godard's intention, as he states in '2 or 3 Things', to liberate the imagination by circumventing the confines of language, as well as those of secondary (waking) consciousness, which is more rigid (in terms of neural connectivity), and more closely associated with symbolic thinking than primary consciousness (see Fromm 1978; Montare 2019).

Primary consciousness adheres to the pleasure principle in Freudian psychoanalytical terms. It is associated with a type of thinking that responds to uncertain situations and induces positive affect: 'There is some enjoyment in uncertainty, perhaps because it promotes imaginative and creative thinking – and ... this is associated with positive affect' (Carhart-Harris et al. 2014). The polyphonic and multiplicious character of the film scenes discussed here, we could say, increases criticality, and this elicits aesthetic reactions that could be pleasurable.

Aesthetic Pleasure and Synaesthesia

While cognitive challenge in Godard can be thought of in terms of entropy and mental criticality, aesthetic pleasure could be further associated with synaesthesia. The affective appeal of '2 or 3 Things' and other films by Godard is related to front-end diffusion of attention as well as perception due to the coexistence of heterogeneous modalities and percepts, all presented with their own intensities, composing a polyphony of stimuli and favouring cross-modal connections akin to a synaesthetic effect. A gestalt of senses emerges from the combination of intense colour (some of the 1960s titles shot in Eastmancolor and Technicolor – see Barry 2012), sound, words (written or spoken), all presented together, sometimes in the same frame or shot, or in close proximity. In line with the suggestion that simultaneity in an artwork 'redoubles and multiplies its sensory contents and amplifies them' (La Chance 2010: 226), the simultaneous, or almost simultaneous (in quick succession or grouping together in the same, albeit uneven, spatio-temporal whole, as in the bar scene discussed earlier), presence of heterogeneous and sometimes incongruent stimuli amplifies sensation.

A connection between attentional diffusion (through polyphony and simultaneity of stimuli) and synaesthesia has been suggested by Kharkhurin, who discusses how a 'synaesthetic-like experience' can be induced by diffusing attention: 'The defocus of attention can be achieved by dividing one's attentional capacity among multiple tasks' (2016: 67). This diffusion and weakening of attention, according to the writer, enhances cross-modal connections, as inhibition mechanisms are set back. Kharkhurin notes that according to a 'decreased inhibition model of synaesthesia', one can induce a synaesthetic-like experience, even in non-synaesthetes, by relaxing the functioning of inhibition mechanisms that suppress cross-modal connections (and thus facilitate those). One of the methods to achieve such relaxation is by defocusing attention:

> The faulty inhibition may result in synaesthetic-like experience, which can also be reached during meditative practice, deep absorption, while falling asleep,

drug use (e.g., LSD use ...), or as a result of a psychological disorder ... The weakening of the inhibition mechanism can be accomplished by the involvement of non-synaesthetes in implicit processing requiring no focus of attention. This processing can enrich cross-modal connectivity. (Kharkhurin 2016: 67)

Approaching Godardian polyphony in its synaesthetic character may shed further light on its potential to evoke pleasure. Indeed, synaesthesia has been associated with aesthetic pleasure and beauty. Steve Odin refers to Stephen Pepper's 'contextualist' theory of beauty according to which the primary aesthetic quality is 'fusion':

An event of immediate experience is permeated by 'aesthetic quality' when, through artistic intuition, one apprehends the 'fusion' of its multitude of details into a felt whole of intrinsic beauty. When we increase fusion, intuition and quality, and decrease discrimination, analysis and relations, all details merge into the felt wholeness of an event, such that aesthetic quality becomes extremely intense, culminating in the experience of seizure and ecstasy. (Odin 1986: 270)

Odin further discusses the embodied aspects of synaesthesia as an experience of the whole body felt at once, akin to what Merleau-Ponty called 'operative intentionality', a pre-reflective contact with the world through a 'sensorium commune' – a Gestalt awareness of the body in the world – with individual senses being 'modalities of a more primitive and generic form of sentient awareness' (Odin 1986: 271). Merleau-Ponty found such wholeness of the sensorium present in the 'temporal gestalt' of film, while film-related synaesthesia has been discussed in the context of 1960s and 1970s expanded cinema (see Youngblood 1970) and given a 'revolutionary significance' (Odin 1986: 273).

While Godard's work has not been discussed through the aspect of synaesthesia, it would be worthwhile to consider his films gesturing at a synaesthetic reception through heterogeneity in multiplicity, like Eisenstein's films have been. Odin notes how Eisenstein pioneered the thinking of cinema in terms of synaesthesia, inspired by the Japanese aesthetics of the Kabuki theatre, which he praised for its 'monism of ensemble' (Odin 1986: 274). This 'monism of ensemble', Odin explains, is at the core of Eisenstein's conception of montage, where shots are juxtaposed to create a total impression – not just accompanying each other but, as Eisenstein himself stated, functioning as 'elements of equal significance' (ibid.). Odin explains Eisenstein's approach that 'in a movie the separate "film shots" (or "cells") must be juxtaposed to produce an "organism" of colour-sound *montage*' (ibid.: 276, emphasis in original). 'Polyphonic' and 'overtonal' montage, in particular, reflect this organic synthesis/wholeness of the sensorium ('intersensory ensemble'), achieved through juxtaposition (ibid.).

This again testifies to Eisenstein's systemic thinking and the relevance of complex systems theory, not only for his own filmmaking but for film and cinema theory as a whole. In light of the previously mentioned parallelism between Eisenstein and Godard, I would argue that the latter's juxtaposition of elements within the shot, as well as between shots/film 'cells' through montage – the polyphony characterizing his filmmaking practice – forms an aesthetics of fusion and synaesthesia where the monism of ensemble finds a new and (at that time, at least) revolutionary expression.

Arguably, the aesthetic pleasure and cognitive challenge in Godard's works lie with the evocation of this intersensory awareness – of an undifferentiated pre-reflective sensorium that exists in the ensemble rather than the individual, and only in superficially incongruent sensations and stimuli. Even though films such as '2 or 3 Things' express, first and foremost, the desire for connecting in an ensemble and pre-individual whole, this desire is constantly commented on and foregrounded but never quite achieved, as a constant reflection on the process does not entirely let go of the individuality of people or things,[3] or auteurism for that matter. Still, Godard's 1960s filmmaking stands as a great case of such negotiation between the individual and the pre-individual, separation and connection, distance and participation. '2 or 3 Things' could be called an 'essay film' that contemplates on, as well as embeds itself into, such complexity.

Epilogue

'Two or Three Things I Know about Her' stands as Godard's most obvious declaration of his rejection to present one sole thing as true and finite; there is always more, two or three things, all occurring at the same time, and without necessarily being compatible. On the contrary, most of the time, they are in tension, never assimilating smoothly in order to retain their heterogeneity, but at the same time dynamically acquiring an organic wholeness. Perhaps the moment where such assemblage is most harmoniously formed in the film is the well-known scene of a close-up of a coffee cup, accompanied by Godard's whispering voice talking about the need to overcome the subjective and the objective and to connect with the other, his 'twin and brother' (Godard here quotes Baudelaire from *Les Fleurs du Mal*: 'mon semblable, mon frère!'). The bubbles of the coffee harmonically and organically gather around one another while the film techniques (for example, the lens focus) are used to accompany, illustrate and accentuate – rather than undermine or render ambiguous – the meaning of the words (e.g. the lens focus becomes crisper to accentuate the meaning of the word 'clarify'). Godard concludes with his wish for a new world and a new cinema 'where people and things will be in harmonious relationships with one another', a goal of his that was both political and poetic, ideological and artistic at the same time. As he stated in an interview in 1967, the same year as the film's release: 'We too should provoke two or three Vietnams in the bosom of the vast Hollywood-Cinecittà-Mosfilm-Pinewood-etc. empire, and, economically and aesthetically, struggling on two fronts as it were, create cinemas [that] are national, free, brotherly, comradely and bonded in friendship' (quoted in Brancaleone 2012).

As no one single image, word or consciousness is to be trusted (after all, a crisis in signification and the relationship between the signifier and signified, word and referent, was at the core of the academic discourse of the time), it is the collective that Godard places his hopes on: the two or three or more that need to coexist and collaborate. When revisiting his films, it is thus vital to take into account the political, ideological and philosophical ramifications of their polyphony, which ultimately shape the cognitive challenge and aesthetic pleasure they offer, and, more importantly, the way these two are intertwined.

Maria Poulaki is the author of various articles and book chapters on cinema, narrative and aesthetics, and co-editor of the volumes *Compact Cinematics* (Bloomsbury 2017) and *Narrative Complexity: Cognition, Embodiment, Evolution* (University of Nebraska Press 2019). Since 2011, she has worked as Lecturer in Film and Media Studies in the Netherlands and the UK. Her current research is focused on psychological aspects of moving image experience.

Notes

1. For recent use of this argument in relation to cinema, see Berliner 2017.
2. For an exploration of Marxism in Godard and Eisenstein, see Kiernan 1990.
3. The distinction between objects and subjects is abolished in '2 or 3 Things', as people and objects blend in 'the attempt to describe a complex (people and things), since no distinction is made between them and, in order to simplify, people are spoken of as things, and things as people' (Godard, quoted in Perlmutter 1975).

References

Adrián, José A., Darío Páez and Javier Álvarez. 1996. 'Art, Emotion and Cognition: Vygotskian and Current Approaches to Musical Induction and Changes in Mood, and Cognitive Complexization'. *Psicothema* 8(1): 107–18.

Arnheim, Rudolf. 1974. *Entropy and Art: An Essay on Disorder and Order*. Berkeley: University of California Press.

Barry, Robert. 2012. 'It's Not Blood, It's Red: Colour(s) of Jean-Luc Godard', *Vertigo* 30: 1–4.

Bergstrom, Janet. 1979. 'Alternation, Segmentation, Hypnosis: Interview with Raymond Bellour', *Camera Obscura* 3(4): 71–103.

Berliner, Todd. 2017. *Hollywood Aesthetic: Pleasure in American Cinema*. New York: Oxford University Press.

Brancaleone, David. 2012. 'The Interventions of Jean-Luc Godard and Chris Marker into Contemporary Visual Art', *Vertigo* 30.

Carhart-Harris, Robin L., et al. 2014. 'The Entropic Brain: A Theory of Conscious States Informed by Neuroimaging Research with Psychedelic Drugs', *Frontiers in Human Neuroscience* 8(1): 20.

Empson, William. (1930) 2004. *Seven Types of Ambiguity*. London: Random House.

Ford, Hamish. 2013. 'Two or Three Things I Know About Her', *Senses of Cinema* 66.

Fromm, Erika. 1978. 'Primary and Secondary Process in Waking and in Altered States of Consciousness', *Journal of Altered States of Consciousness* 4(2): 115–28.

Grishakova, Marina, and Maria Poulaki (eds). 2019. *Narrative Complexity: Cognition, Embodiment, Evolution*. Lincoln: University of Nebraska Press.

Kharkhurin, Anatoliy V. 2016. 'Cognitive Poetry: Theoretical Framework for the Application of Cognitive Psychology Techniques to Poetic Text', *Creativity. Theories – Research – Applications* 3(1): 59–83.

Kiernan, Maureen. 1990. 'Making Films Politically: Marxism in Eisenstein and Godard', *Alif: Journal of Comparative Poetics* 10(1:) 93–113.

Kiss, Miklós, and Steven Willemsen (eds). 2017. *Impossible Puzzle Films: A Cognitive Approach to Contemporary Complex Cinema*. Edinburgh: Edinburgh University Press.

Kornmeier, Jürgen, and Michael Bach. 2012. 'Ambiguous Figures: What Happens in the Brain when Perception Changes but Not the Stimulus', *Frontiers in Human Neuroscience* 6: 51.

La Chance, Michaël. 2010. 'Split-Screen and Synaesthesia in "Timecode": A Quadraesthetic Device', in Marcin Sobieszczanski and Céline Masoni Lacroix (eds), *Du Split-Screen Au Multi-Screen: La Narration Vidéo-filmique Spatialement Distribuée / From Split-Screen to Multi-Screen: Spatially Distributed Video-cinematic Narration*. Berlin: Peter Lang, pp. 225–43.

Loschky, Lester C., et al. 2015. 'What Would Jaws Do? The Tyranny of Film and the Relationship between Gaze and Higher-level Narrative Film Comprehension', *PloS one* 10(11): e0142474.

———. 2020. 'The Scene Perception & Event Comprehension Theory (SPECT) Applied to Visual Narratives', *Topics in Cognitive Science* 12(1): 311–51.

Magliano, Joseph P., Karen Higgs and James Clinton. 2019. 'Sources of Complexity in Narrative Comprehension across Media', in Marina Grishakova and Maria Poulaki (eds), *Narrative Complexity: Cognition, Embodiment, Evolution*. Lincoln: University of Nebraska Press, pp. 149–73.

Montare, Alberto. 2019. *On the Psychology of Primary and Secondary Consciousness: Part 1*. William Paterson University repository. Retrieved 21 November 2020 from https://repository.wpunj.edu/handle/20.500.12164/3072.

Odin, Steve. 1986. 'Blossom Scents Take Up the Ringing: Synaesthesia in Japanese and Western Aesthetics', *Soundings* 69(3): 256–81.

Otty, Lisa, and Andrew Michael Roberts. 2013. '"Dim-conceived Glories of the Brain": On Ambiguity in Literature and Science', *Culture, Theory and Critique* 54(1): 37–55.

Perlmutter, Ruth. 1975. '*Le Gai Saviour*: Godard and Eisenstein-Notions of Intellectual Cinema', *Jump Cut* 7(7): 17–19.

Shklovsky, Viktor. (1917) 2017. 'Art as Technique', in Julie Rivkin and Michael Ryan (eds), *Literary Theory: An Anthology*, 3rd edn. Chichester: John Wiley & Sons, pp. 8–14.

Tikka, Pia. 2008. *Enactive Cinema: Simulatorium Eisensteinense*. Helsinki: University of Art and Design.

Trifonova, Temenuga. 2014. *Warped Minds: Cinema and Psychopathology*. Amsterdam: Amsterdam University Press.

Vygotsky, Lev S. (1925) 1972. 'The Psychology of Art', *Journal of Aesthetics and Art Criticism* 30(4): 564–66.

Willemsen, Steven, and Miklós Kiss. 2013. 'Unsettling Melodies: A Cognitive Approach to Incongruent Film Music', *Acta Universitatis Sapientiae, Film and Media Studies* 7: 169–83.

Wollen, Peter. 1972. 'Godard and Counter Cinema: *Vent d'Est*', *Afterimage* 4: 6–17.

Youngblood, Gene. 1970. *Expanded Cinema*. New York: P. Dutton & Co.

Zacks, Jeffrey, and Joseph M. Magliano. 2011. 'Film, Narrative, and Cognitive Neuroscience', in Francesca Bacci and David Melcher (eds), *Art and the Senses*. Oxford: Oxford University Press, pp. 435–53.

CHAPTER 7

Embodying Fragmentation in Film
The Spatio-temporal Logic of Cinematic Modernism

Maarten Coëgnarts

Introduction

Since at least the 1990s, the research programme of embodied cognition has been redefining our understanding of mind, brain, perception, action and cognition (e.g. Varela, Thompson and Rosch 1991; Lakoff and Johnson 1999; Gibbs 2005; Barsalou 2008; Tversky 2019). The idea that cognition is deeply dependent upon the sensory-motor capacities of an agent situated in a cultural environment, rather than upon formal symbolic manipulation, has gained a strong foothold in the cognitive sciences, while its implications are increasingly being felt across the field of the humanities. In film studies, this change of attitude has been reflected in an increase in the number of studies exhibiting an embodied approach (e.g. Buckland 2000; Branigan 2006; Grodal 2009; Coëgnarts and Kravanja 2012, 2015a; Gallese and Guerra 2012, 2019; Fahlenbrach 2016; Fingerhut and Heimann 2017; Hven 2017; Kiss and Willemsen 2017; Pearlman 2017; Coëgnarts 2019). These studies have incorporated various fields of embodied research to shed new light on many aspects of film aesthetics and film spectatorship. Some scholars have drawn heavily on cognitive linguistics to reframe our understanding of cinematic meaning, while others have used phenomenological and neuroscientific resources to reshape our bodily engagement with films.

This chapter aims to expand on this line of embodied research by exploring its implications for our understanding of postwar European art cinema's aesthetic and cognitive appeal. This cinematic practice gained prominence from the 1950s to the 1980s through the works of such film authors as Michelangelo Antonioni, Alain Resnais, Robert Bresson and Jean-Luc Godard, and is typically experienced as cognitively more demanding than classical Hollywood cinema. It is suggested that the origin of this distinctive feature lies in the very abstract principles of composition that it uses to reconstruct the coherence of reality. As Kovács (2007: 121) points out, 'modern art forms always contain an abstract conception that is meant to mediate between the form and the reality'. Rather than referring to an underlying continuous process of development, as is the case in classical narrative, the surface images of modern art cinema refer to a reality that is fragmented ('the continuous flow of images is not the manifestation of a teleological process') and static ('motion has no direction, it is self-contained or circular'). While the filmmakers cited above propose various stylistic ways to foreground this conception of reality, as this chapter will illustrate, the result is nevertheless the same: the liberation of time, as Gilles Deleuze (1989) formulated it, from the logic of storytelling (see also Kovács 2007: 40–44).

This fundamental essence of modern art cinema poses us an interesting ontological challenge: if, in modern cinema, time plays a significant role, then there must be some way in which this abstract dimension is foregrounded to the viewer, for otherwise, they would not be able to experience the modern art film as significantly different from classical cinema. But how, then, can time be liberated from the traditional logic of dramatic action, given that time as an abstract concept is neither perceivable nor spatially constrained? Addressing this crucial question first requires looking into the cognitive circumstances under which people ordinarily make sense of time. It is only when we have an understanding of the rationale behind this process and the way it operates in cinema that we can begin to outline, in a subsequent step, the various cognitively and aesthetically rich ways in which filmmakers have adopted this logic (and have, in some ways, altered it) for the purpose of fleshing out modernism's fragmented character.

It is precisely in the systemic efforts of cognitive linguists to grasp this logic that the theme of embodiment comes into play. Many cognitive scholars have argued that abstract concepts such as time are fundamentally metaphorical and embodied (e.g. Lakoff and Johnson 1980, 1999; Gibbs 1994; Kövecses 2000; Tversky 2019). The larger theoretical framework that supports this claim is Conceptual Metaphor Theory (CMT). First set forth by Lakoff and Johnson (1980), this theory introduced the idea that people make sense of reality by structuring abstract concepts metaphorically in terms of concrete concepts that are grounded in patterns of our sensorimotor experiences – so-called 'image schemas' (Johnson 1987; Lakoff 1987; Hampe 2005). Not surprisingly, the concept of time is one of the key philosophical concepts that cognitive linguists have examined over the years. As several studies demonstrate, people tend to think and talk about this concept in terms of spatial knowledge (e.g. Lakoff and Johnson 1980, 1999: 137–69; Boroditsky 2000, 2001; Gentner 2001; Gentner, Imai and Boroditsky 2002; Evans 2003; Núñez, Motz and Teuscher 2006; Núñez and Sweetser 2006; Casasanto and Boroditsky 2008). This is most evident in the language we use to reason about time (e.g. 'time *flies* by', 'Christmas is *approaching*', 'Wednesday *follows* Tuesday'). Similarly, one may assume – as Coëgnarts and Kravanja (2015b) have done – that these time metaphors are also pervasive in cinema. After all, if metaphor is conceptual and, in this sense, modality-independent, then there is no reason to assert that these spatio-temporal metaphors, like any other conceptual metaphors, are limited to language.

Consequently, laying bare the spatial foundation of temporal reasoning will be the first aim of this chapter. Having further explored how this spatio-temporal logic is inherent to the art of filmmaking will allow us to explore and illustrate, in the subsequent sections, the various rich stylistic ways in which filmmakers such as Antonioni, Bresson, Godard and Resnais have applied and rearranged this spatio-temporal logic to convey a more ambiguous view of reality. A more thorough understanding of the embodied patterns underlying some of the signature modernist film techniques will eventually lead us to hypothesize, in the concluding section, about the cognitive appeal of modern European art cinema. The various case studies of our analysis will encourage us to situate this appeal at two levels: one is the embodiedness of the modernist film techniques, which, as we shall demonstrate, touch upon aspects of the spectator's own lived existence and their own embodied being-in-the-world; the other is the profound sense of ambiguity and loss of narrative control, which is foregrounded by these modernist techniques, and leads to stronger subjective feelings in the viewer.

Spatio-temporal Reasoning and Cinema

How do we conceptualize time? Cognitive linguists usually provide a twofold answer to this question: either people tend to talk about time in terms of locations that are relative to the presence of a canonical observer (or ego) in the source domain of space, or they tend to conceive times as locations not relative to such an observer's point of view (Núñez and Sweetser 2006). The former model is usually referred to as 'deictic' or 'ego-based', and is exemplified by such ordinary expressions as 'we are *approaching* the end of the year' or 'leave those sad days *behind*'. The second model, by contrast, is also called 'non-deictic' or 'time-based', and considers such examples as 'Christmas *follows* Thanksgiving', 'February *comes before* March', and 'it is now 20 minutes *ahead of* 1 PM'. In this model, the chronological order of times is conceived as a one-dimensional or linear sequence of bounded regions with earlier times (locations) being *in front of* latter times (locations). In the absence of an observer, this conceptualization does not require a compulsory specification of the present or now. Following Núñez, Motz and Teuscher (2006: 136), we may present this model, which the authors coin, 'the Time-Reference-Point (Time-RP) conceptual metaphor', schematically, as in Figure 7.1.

As bounded regions, times also share the spatial logic built into them. Lakoff and Johnson (1999: 31–32) refer to this logic as the CONTAINER schema logic. This logic follows directly from the gestalt structure of a container, which entails an inside, a boundary, and an outside. It is a gestalt structure because the parts make no sense without the whole. As the authors explain: 'There is no inside without a boundary and an outside, no outside without a boundary and an inside, and no boundary without sides'. This structure gives rise to a particular spatial logic which the authors describe as follows: 'Given two containers, A and B, and an object, X, if A is in B and X is in A, then X is in B'. Hence, given that containers map onto times, it reasonably follows that time X and time A occur simultaneously with time B.

Given that cinema is a temporal medium, it should not come as a surprise – as some film scholars (e.g. Buckland 2000; Branigan 2006; Coëgnarts 2019) have already pointed out – that the CONTAINER schema logic is also foundational to our understanding of film. It is inherent to its core concept of a shot in which the CONTAINER schema is instantiated in the boundary of the frame (Coëgnarts 2019:

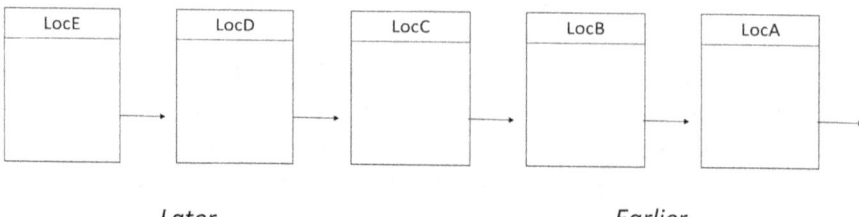

Later   *Earlier*

Figure 7.1. Time-RP conceptual metaphor. © Maarten Coëgnarts.

75–76). A location is inside the shot (i.e. on-screen) if it lies within the four edges of the frame, and vice versa, a location is outside the shot (i.e. off-screen) if it lies beyond these edges. Hence, it follows that the time sphere of any visual object located inside the boundary of the frame collocates with the time sphere of the location: if object X is in location A, then, via the mapping, X shares the same time sphere as A. The same logic also extends to 'aural objects' or 'diegetic sounds'. Although we cannot literally perceive diegetic sounds in the same way as we perceive physical objects, people nevertheless have the tendency to treat them as such, as is evident in such expressions as 'I can hear his voice *in* the film'. As Christian Metz (1985: 156) observes: 'Sounds are more often classified according to the objects [that] transmit them than by their own characteristics'.

Herbert Zettl (2017: 312) refers to these sounds as 'literal sounds' because they refer to a sound-producing source. When, for example, you see the character of Travis Bickle (Robert De Niro) talking to himself in Martin Scorsese's *Taxi Driver* (1975), you obviously associate the sound of his voice with his screen image (as if the sound is *in* the image), even if he should move temporarily into off-screen space. Sometimes, we can even construe a good image of the location merely based on the sound off-screen. This is because literal sounds, as Zettl (ibid.: 318) further points out, have an important outer orientation function: they help us to reveal and define the location of an event, its spatial environment and even off-screen space. If, for example, you accompany the close-up of a young man with such literal outdoor sounds as bombs exploding, guns firing and men screaming, we assume that he is somewhere in a battle. You have no need, as Zettl (ibid.: 319) writes, 'for a cumbersome establishing shot, [as] the sound effects will take over this orientation function'. As we shall see later on, this function of sound plays a crucial role in defining the film style of Robert Bresson. Schematically, we may summarize the spatio-temporal container logic of the shot as in Figure 7.2.

This logic also regulates our understanding of a scene. We speak of the latter insofar as a series of shots (or a single shot) take(s) place in a single location and deal with a single action. In that case, the spatio-temporal logic informs us that all the shots (locations) belonging to the same spatial region also take place in the same time frame. This logic also regulates the use of the shot-reverse-shot in conversation scenes. This editing technique shifts between various sub-locations within the same location, most typically focusing on the character who is doing the talking. By contrast, a single shot may also depict various locations. Such is the case with a dynamic long-take or a sequence shot. Rather than decomposing

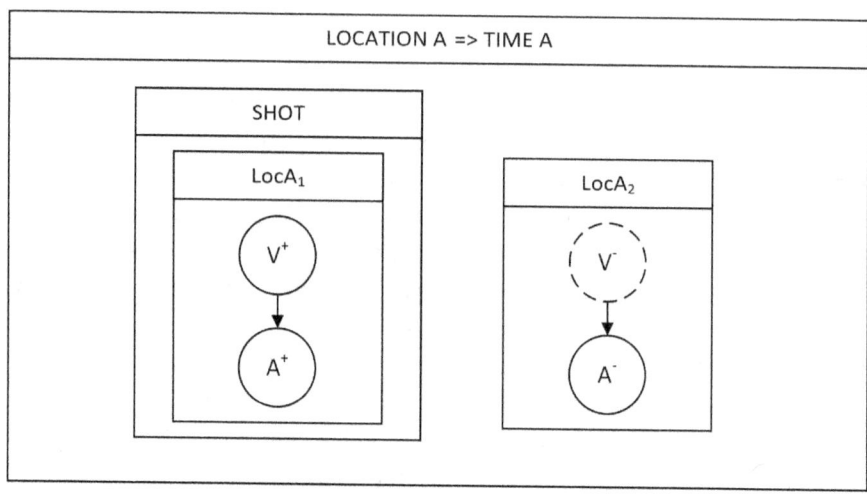

V^+: On-screen sound producing visual source
A^+: On-screen source-connected literal sound
V^-: Off-screen sound producing visual source
A^-: Off-screen source-disconnected literal sound

⊂⊃ : Excluded from audio-visual perception
◯ : Included in audio-visual perception

Figure 7.2. The spatio-temporal container logic of a shot. © Maarten Coëgnarts.

space into a sequence of shots (locations), this device continues for an unusually long time before the transition to the next shot, thus allowing the camera, as opposed to montage, to reveal the sequence of locations (and thus time events). The camera moves uninterruptedly through space, including new locations, while simultaneously discarding them for new ones (see also Coëgnarts 2019: 99–101). Likewise, the spatio-temporal logic built into the long-take prevents us, at least from a naturalistic point of view, from attributing a different time sphere to each of the locations depicted in the shot. Later, we shall see how a filmmaker, such as Alain Resnais, can radically challenge this logic.

While classical narrative cinema often changes the chronological order of time by altering the sequence of locations, as shown in Figure 7.1, it rarely alters the natural spatio-temporal logic of the individual shots.[1] If it does so – for instance, when a single shot depicts different times – it is usually well motivated by the plot. This is because a significant deviation from it would no longer serve the purpose of classical storytelling, which is to convey a traditional conception of reality that is continuous and goal-oriented.

Film, however, would be a far less aesthetically rich medium if it should use this logic for this purpose alone. As we started this chapter, much of the appeal of modern art cinema lies precisely in its ability to defy our conventional capacities for sense-making by freeing the concept of time from the constraints of the plot. The crucial question, then, is as follows: how can the spatio-temporal logic discussed above be employed and reformed in such a way as to create a more ambiguous view of reality? As the next section will show, modern European filmmakers have provided several embodied answers to achieve this.

The Spatio-temporal Logic of Modern Form

In his book *Screening Modernism* (2007), film scholar András Bálint Kovács makes a distinction between two generic stylistic forms in which modernism's fragmented and static view of reality comes to life: 'radical continuity' and 'radical discontinuity'. The former, the author points out, takes the 'exterior' (unarticulated and empty flow of time with no direction) and turns it into the 'interior', while the latter takes the interior (disconnected and fragmented vision of the world) and turns it into the 'exterior'. There are four directors at the beginning of late modern cinema whose works Kovács considers to be foundational in terms of developing the fundamental alternative versions of both types. They are Michelangelo Antonioni and Alain Resnais for the dimension of radical continuity, and Robert Bresson and Jean-Luc Godard with respect to the dimension of radical discontinuity. We start by exploring the spatio-temporal underpinnings of the first formal dimension, and continue by discussing the embodied cognitive foundation of the second one.

Embodying Radical Continuity

While Kovács considers the works of Antonioni and Resnais to be exemplary of the dimension of radical continuity – both directors aim for a form where accentuated continuity creates a dimension of time for the film – the author is also keen to stress the fundamental difference in the way that both filmmakers treat narrative time. This gives rise to two basic original forms of radical continuity in modern cinema. In the first form, rooted in the tradition of neorealism and exemplified by the early cinema of Antonioni, imagination and reality are generally still well discernible, and the plot, despite its often slow development, largely follows a classical linear structure. By contrast, in the second form, influenced by the literary movement of the nouveau roman, the main narrative technique consists precisely of merging different mental and temporal dimensions to blur the transition from one to the other. This form can be illustrated through the work of Alain Resnais. In what follows, we will discuss the aesthetic attractiveness of both forms by showing how the stylistic distinction between the two directors results from an embodied conceptual difference in application and rearrangement of the spatio-temporal logic, as discussed in the previous section.

The Antonioni Style. Together with the film style of Robert Bresson, which will be discussed later on in this chapter, Antonioni's style can be considered part of a tendency within modern cinema known as 'minimalism'. In its broadest sense, minimalism refers to a 'systematic reduction of expressive elements in a given form' (Kovács 2007: 140). At the core of Antonioni's minimalism, which Kovács coins 'analytical', lies the character's alienated relationship with the environment. This alienation is articulated either through the character's imprisonment in the landscape they wander, or through their separation from it. In both cases, the alien landscape protests its traditional allegiance to the character and the plot. In the first, the landscape holds the character in a grip, depriving them of the freedom to determine the outcome of the events. In the second, by contrast, the landscape isolates itself from the character's psychology, taking up a life on its own, independent from the plot.[2] This gives the impression that an Antonioni film is as much about architectural anthropology as it is about characters.

The CONTAINER schema assumes a crucial role in fleshing out both strategic principles. One way in which the first 'containment' principle can be realized is by establishing additional boundaries within the principal boundary of the filmic frame. As Antonioni's work vividly demonstrates, this can be achieved through the device of geometrical framing, in which the filmmaker highlights certain configurational lines within the frame to create the impression that the character is contained. Figure 7.3 shows a selection of such images taken from *The Eclipse* (1962). As can be seen, this geometrical order can be made up entirely of boundaries within the frame (e.g. door, window) or only partly, as when the container is a composite of the edge(s) of the filmic frame and edge(s) of the scenery (e.g. a wall splitting the frame into two halves). Either way, the landscape exerts pressure on the character by reducing their 'breathing room' and prohibiting them from exercising control over the landscape.[3]

EMBODYING FRAGMENTATION IN FILM · 165

Figure 7.3. Containment in *The Eclipse*. © Cineriz, Interopa Film, Paris Film 1962. Screen captures by Maarten Coëgnarts.

Figure 7.3. (continued)

Another, more dynamic way to provoke the containment effect would be by having the environment *include* the character rather than the other way around. As I have discussed elsewhere (Coëgnarts 2019: 95), INCLUSION and its counterpart EXCLUSION can be regarded as two instances of what Dewell (2005) coins 'dynamic patterns of containment'. In the former, the container takes hold of an object, while in the latter, the container moves itself away from its content. If the object rather than the container were to be the central moving entity, then the two corresponding patterns would be ENTRY and EXIT, respectively (Coëgnarts 2019: 85). Schematically, we may diagram these patterns as in Figure 7.4.

The patterns of INCLUSION and EXCLUSION can be turned most naturally into cinematic form by the device of camera movement (see also Coëgnarts 2020). For instance, Antonioni's work contains many occasions in which the central character is only introduced in second-order by virtue of a random figure moving in the landscape, whether it be, as Figure 7.5 shows, a nameless horseman such as in *The Eclipse* (A and B) or an accidental family member in the terminal of an airport, such as in *The Passenger* (1975) (C and D). The camera first follows these unidentified figures, after which it discovers (includes), as it were by coincidence, the main protagonist – here, Pietro (Alain Delon) and John Locke (Jack Nicholson), respectively. Thus, the character is not privileged to initiate their own inclusion; rather, the character is reduced to being the object contained by the camera.

In a way, this strategy radically reverses the narrative purposes commonly associated with the POV shot, a device most typically used in classical narrative

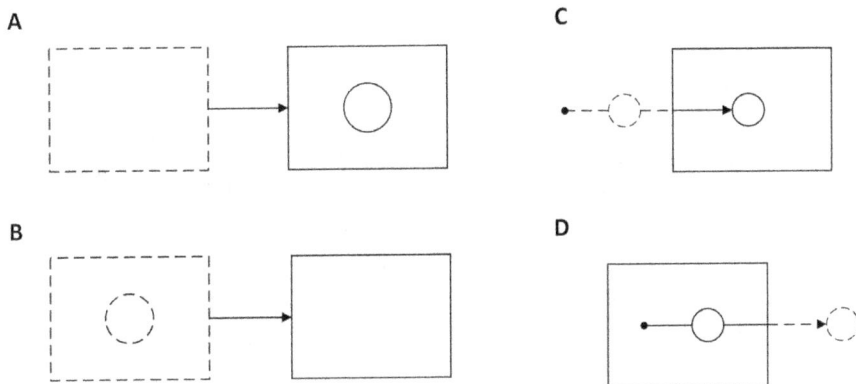

Figure 7.4. Dynamic patterns of containment. © Maarten Coëgnarts.

cinema in which the character, not the landscape, takes control by *including* the landscape into his or her visual field.

The spatial logic of the CONTAINER schema not only serves the purpose of expressing a sense of containment of the character; it also plays a fundamental role in giving form to the character's disconnectedness from the background world. In this case, it is the pattern of EXCLUSION that turns out to be the best fit for the job (see Figure 7.4B). Also here, the most natural way of provoking this pattern is through mobile framing; by moving the camera, the filmmaker is able to *exclude* the central protagonist, the locus of the plot, from the on-screen space in favour of the *inclusion* of environmental objects that, from the plot's point-of-view, are irrelevant.

Cinematic manifestations of this dynamic principle can be found in many of Antonioni's films, including, for example, the notable scene at the beginning of *The Passenger* (1975) in which the central protagonist David Locke (Jack Nicholson) winds up in the Sahara Desert. Locke is a television journalist making a documentary film on postcolonial Africa. Lost with his Land Rover in the midst of the desert, he sees, in the far distance, a man slowly approaching on a camel (see Figure 7.6). Locke stands up to greet him (A), but his waved greeting is left unanswered as the man simply rides past him and his jeep as if they do not exist (B). Most interestingly, the camera, which is placed behind Locke, follows the camel, thus *excluding* Locke from the frame (C). As Martin Walsh (1975) adds: 'So tentatively fixed is the direction of the narrative at this movement that we feel we

Figure 7.5. Landscapes including the protagonist in *The Eclipse* (A and B) and *The Passenger* (C and D). © Cineriz, Interopa Film, Paris Film 1962, and © MGM 1975. Screen captures by Maarten Coëgnarts.

Figure 7.5. (continued)

could easily leave Locke behind forever (except, of course, Nicholson can't be dumped this soon in the movie)'. The latter is to be taken literally, as Locke reclaims his rightful place as the film's central character by re-entering the frame that had abandoned him (D).

On other occasions in the film, it is the wandering camera itself that includes the character again, as if by coincidence. This creates movement in which the character's location serves as both the source and the goal of the camera's pathway. Motion in this way is derived from any direction; it is self-contained or circular. Despite the fact that Antonioni makes use of the spatial logic of the CONTAINER schema to convey a view of reality that is fragmented, his style nevertheless preserves the spatio-temporal order of the shot. For one, there is no succession of contradictory time frames (past, present and future) in one and the same shot (container). As the camera excludes and includes, we are not simultaneously moving from one time frame to another significantly different one.[4] The same loyalty towards the natural temporal order of things cannot, however, be said of director Alain Resnais, whose cinematic practice was aimed precisely at deconstructing this order.

The Resnais Style. In the work of Alain Resnais, in contrast to Antonioni, the continuous flow of narration allows linkages between fragmented layers of time without dissolving the contradictions that naturally exist between them. In other words, boundaries that were usually conceived as intransgressible (a general rule to which the post-realist cinema of Antonioni largely adheres) are now being

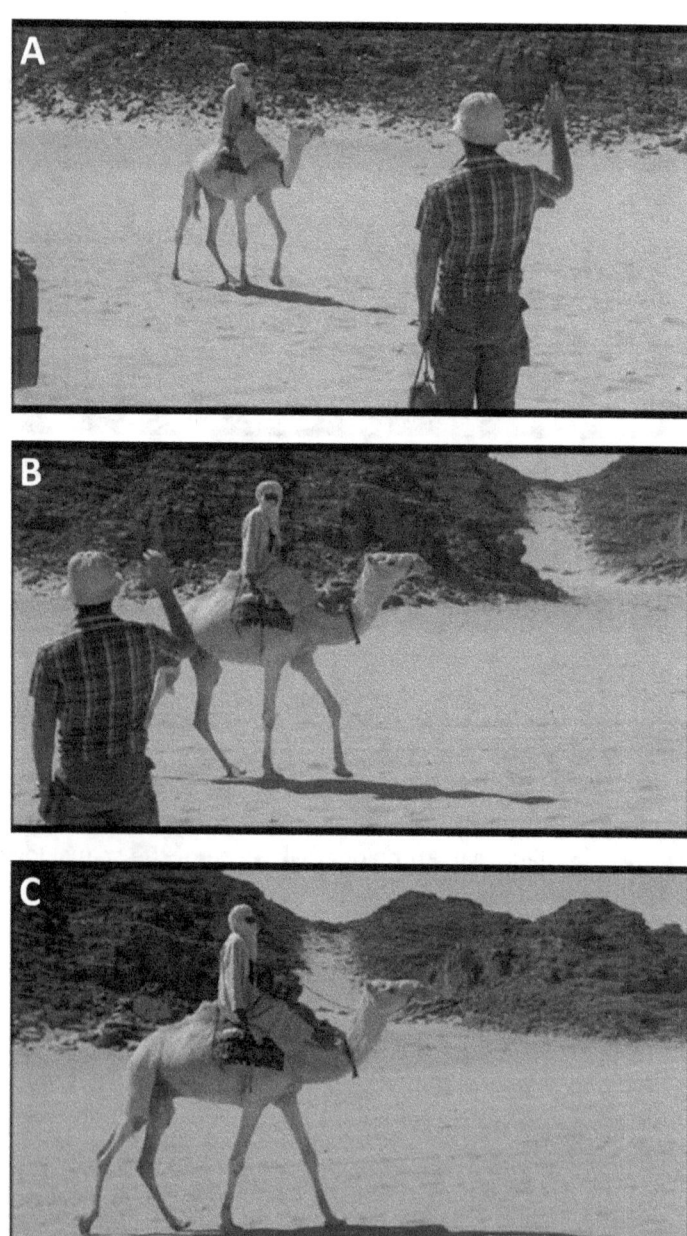

Figure 7.6. Landscape excludes the protagonist in *The Passenger*. © MGM 1975. Screen captures by Maarten Coëgnarts.

Figure 7.6. (continued)

transgressed. As a result, the viewer is no longer presented with a traditional conception of time but with a dreamlike, mental, subjective version of it, in which the natural distinctions between past, present and future have ceased to exist. Rather than conceptualizing times as bounded regions that are separated from each other on a one-dimensional line, with earlier times in front of later times, the various times are now being homogenized by a continuity of thought that turns them into sub-containers of the same spatial region. Locations do not only belong to the present; they are also heavily laden, as Resnais' work illustrates, with decor from the past. Diagrammatically, this new logic, which deviates from the logic represented in figures 7.1 and 7.2, may be rendered as Figure 7.7.

This radical new embodied conception of time, and the viewer's feeling of puzzlement that results from it, has perhaps never been rendered more tangible than in his two most famous films: *Hiroshima Mon Amour* (1959) and *Last Year at Marienbad* (1961). In this respect, it is interesting to compare the style of these films with Antonioni's earlier-discussed film style. Above, we have seen how this Italian director turned to the dynamic patterns of mobile framing (i.e. EXCLUSION and INCLUSION) to embody the character's disentangled relationship with the environment. Resnais now also appeals to these patterns, but he uses them for a different purpose, that of creating a new spatio-temporal order.[5] To illustrate this, let us consider two instances of the many wandering camera movements in *Last Year at Marienbad* (as above, the dynamic patterns are italicized in the text). The first movement, as shown in Figure 7.8 A–C, starts showing one of the two central men of the film in the middle of the frame. Cold and stationary like a statue, the

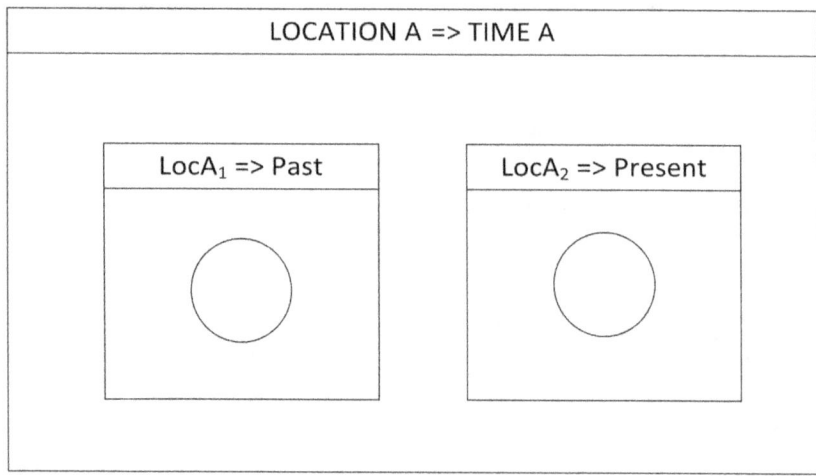

Figure 7.7. Past and present homogenized in the same container. © Maarten Coëgnarts.

man does not give the impression that he will leave his place soon (A). In the right-hand corner, we can see the enigmatic central woman of the film, played by Delphine Seyrig. The camera then passes by, *excluding* them (B), by moving into another room where it *includes* the other male protagonist sitting at a gaming table. This is when the viewer becomes confused about the spatio-temporal order. As the camera stops, we see how the same stationary man from just a few seconds before now *enters* the frame from the right (C). The film thus conveys the temporal passage from one time frame to a significantly different one within a single spatial camera movement.[6]

Another cinematic articulation of the same embodied cognitive strategy (i.e. a shift of time within the same container) appears soon after (see Figure 7.8 D–F). The camera first shows the couple, after which it continues to move on, passing by several other men and women (D). This horizontal movement continues until the camera *includes* the same man again from the beginning (E). As before, the film has shifted towards another temporal dimension in the same container. As the man starts to move, he looks up – a gesture imitated by the camera, which follows the direction of his eye movement by panning up (thus, *excluding* him) and *including* the woman who appears on a balcony, thus *entering* the frame (F).

One may find similar examples in classical narrative cinema, where a passage of time is conveyed within a single shot. However, the crucial difference is that, in

EMBODYING FRAGMENTATION IN FILM · 173

Figure 7.8. Including and excluding different times in *Last Year at Marienbad*. © Argos Films, Cineriz 1961. Screen captures by Maarten Coëgnarts.

Figure 7.8. (continued)

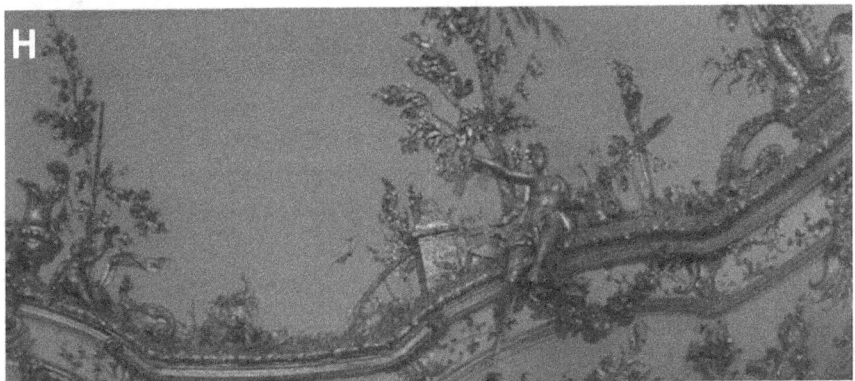

Figure 7.8. (continued)

classical cinema, the temporal boundary is usually signalled as clearly as possible to the viewer for the sake of narrative continuity. To do so, they can rely on such tools as verbal time makers or cues within the sound design and setting. Here, however, the filmmaker's creative choices are precisely aimed at leaving these cues behind in order to blur the natural boundary between past and present.[7]

At other times, the same logic is provoked through the way the images are edited. In another scene, the film shows the woman in an establishing shot as she walks alone through the empty corridor of the impressive baroque hotel (see Figure 7.8 G–I). As with the man earlier, she looks up (G), thus suggesting that she is observing the (off-screen) baroque ceiling of the palace. However, instead of *including* the object of her perception with mobile framing, such as in Figure 7.8 E–F, the film immediately cuts to a lower-angle shot of the ceiling (H). As the camera gradually moves its angle back to ground level and, thus, *includes* new space, an entirely different scene unfolds before our eyes (I). We see the same woman, but now in a different outfit – and no longer in solitude but accompanied by the man. Thus, the film challenges our natural conception of a scene, as it ceases to follow the general rule that all successive shots (locations) that belong to the same location also take place at one and the same time.

This tying of different times in the same container can also be established through combining visuals and literal sounds. We have already seen in the previous section how the latter are linked to visual sources. Depending on the location of these sources, literal sounds can be either connected (on-screen sounds) or disconnected (off-screen sounds). Given these elements, a filmmaker might opt, for example, to disconnect present sounds from its visual sources by using them over the depiction of past images. This is what Resnais does in *Hiroshima Mon Amour*.

In one scene, the two leading characters – a French actress (Emmanuelle Riva) and a Japanese architect (Eiji Okada) – are shown together at a table in a Japanese bar. The woman, referred to as Elle (or Her) in the film, recalls her past experience in the French city of Nevers. During the Second World War, she was locked in her parents' cellar as punishment for having a love affair with a German soldier. As we 'see' the city of her youth and her memories, and we 'see' her as a young woman, a prisoner in her home, we continue to hear the present sounds of their voices, of frogs croaking in the evening dark and of traditional Japanese music playing in the background. The connected literal sounds (the voices) of the present are turned into the off-screen sounds of past images, while the past literal sounds are muted.

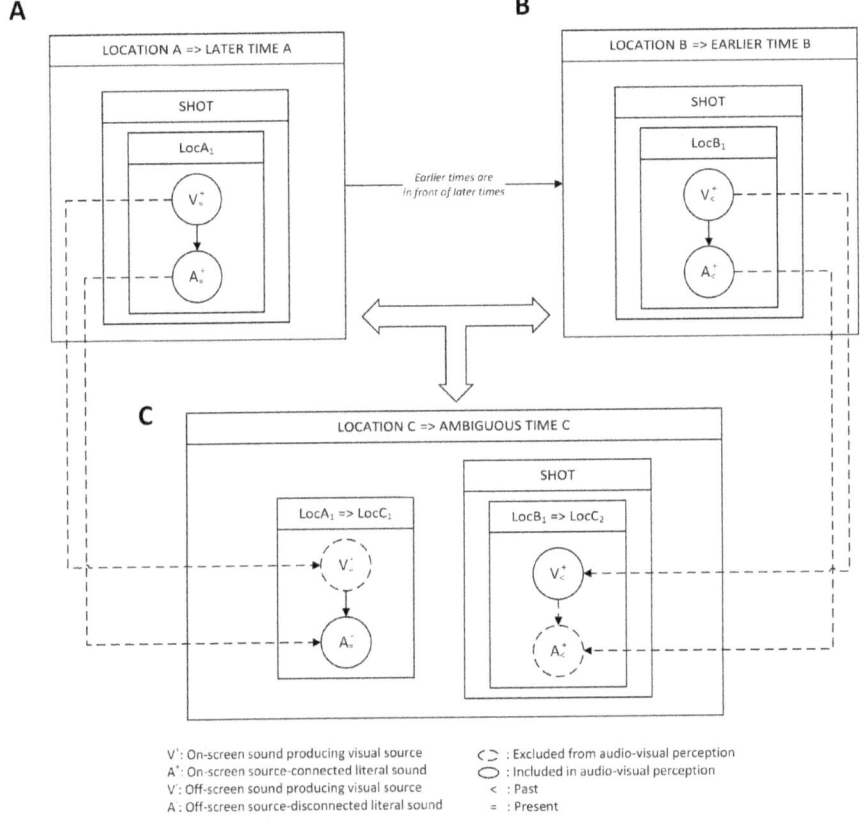

Figure 7.9. Creating spatio-temporal ambiguity. © Maarten Coëgnarts.

The disconnected literal sounds of the present (music, frogs) remain off-screen but have now become the disconnected literal sounds of the past visuals.

Figure 7.9 shows the complex embodied cognitive dynamics behind these actions. Parts A and B of this figure adhere to a 'natural' conceptualization of time. Past and present are linear, rendered as separated containers, with earlier times in front of later times. Part C is the new 'mental' container that results from combining elements from both containers. In this container, the distinction between past and present has become blurred. However, it should be noted that while this kind of radical continuity (i.e. extending present sounds over past images) betrays a highly complex structure, the scene is still relatively easy to grasp. The viewer is still able to pinpoint the visual sources of the off-screen sounds because they have perceived the visual sources in the shots prior to the flashback images. Because the representation of the present is already part of the viewer's working memory, they do not have much difficulty making sense of the temporal ambiguity embodied by the new container. At the same time, it might be misleading to attribute the ease of understanding the scene to a purely mental affair (our working memory 'computing' these different layers of meaning). It is also intuitively appealing and easy to understand, because people often experience the world in the very same sense – for instance, when we are physically experiencing one time and place while simultaneously remembering another one.

Embodying Radical Discontinuity

Having discussed and illustrated how the fragmented view of reality comes to life through two alternative versions of radical continuity, we can move on to discuss its counterpart: radical discontinuity, as epitomized in the works of Robert Bresson and Jean-Luc Godard. As with Antonioni and Resnais, there is a fundamental stylistic difference between these directors, despite their categorical similarities. The latter is strongly rooted in *cinéma vérité* and genre narratives (especially film noir) and tends to employ mosaic or collage-style compositions, while the former is more anchored on a highly elliptical narrative style with visual compositions that, due to their extensive use of off-screen sounds, are predominantly metonymic in nature. As above, let us try to see how this formal difference translates itself to the embodied conceptual level of spatio-temporal reasoning.

The Bresson Style. We have already seen above how Antonioni's cinema represented one trend of modern minimalist form within the dimension of radical continuity known as analytical minimalism. The filmmaker who is to be taken as the leading representative of minimalism within the dimension of radical discontinuity is the Frenchman Robert Bresson. He developed a trend of modern minimalist form that Kovács (2007: 141–42) appropriately calls 'metonymic minimalism'. The author's use of the term 'metonymic' is inspired by the filmmaker's extensive use of off-screen space. As he explains, 'a considerable amount of narrative information is provided, especially by sound effects, from off-screen space that extends just beyond what is visible on-screen. In other words, much of the plot is taking place in spaces not seen but contiguously attached to on-screen space'. From the perspective of spatio-temporal reasoning, this metonymic effect is largely achieved by keeping the on-screen sound-producing visual sources to their narrative minimum, and making the best use of source-disconnected literal sounds. In Bresson's (1975: 34) own words: 'When a sound can replace an image, cut the image or neutralize it'. As we will exemplify below, one way the filmmaker draws attention to the ear is to take away, as Figure 7.10 schematically shows, the sound-producing visual source from the on-screen space, and add its sound to the off-screen container. This creates a listening situation that film sound theorist Michel Chion (2019) refers to as an 'acousmatic' situation: the viewer hears a sound without seeing its originating cause. This situation, however, does not defy the spatio-temporal logic of a shot. Bresson does not create, as Resnais does, a new container in which both past and present are blended together. The dynamics that are going on in the shot are not intended to break with reality but rather to intensify it.

Bresson's depiction of the actual escape of Fontaine (François Leterrier) in *A Man Escaped* (1956) provides us with a striking example of how to put this general conceptual template to use for creating suspense. At one moment, we see how Fontaine climbs over a wall and awaits the right moment to kill the German guard who is patrolling just around the wall's corner, only a metre away from him. Bresson renders this moment by maintaining a long, steady, head-on shot of Fontaine, his back pressed against the wall as he, together with the viewer, tries to mentally visualize the movement of the German soldier by listening carefully to the literal sounds he causes. These sounds consist of the jingle of the soldier's belt buckle and the gravelly crunch of his boots on the courtyard ground, which, together, provoke a pattern that alternates between near and far as the guard walks back and forth. Notice that these sounds trigger a profound metonymic effect. We infer the visual image of the whole soldier solely on the basis of the separate acousmatic sounds, or as Bresson (1975: 67) put it, 'accustom the public to divining the whole of which they are given only a part'. The soldier's presence is further suggested by the black open space on the right side of the frame. In accordance with the diagram above and with his own theory, Bresson subsequently makes good use of this empty space to further neutralize the visual presence of Fontaine. When a train passes by off-screen and its literal disconnected sound increases in volume, Fontaine grasps the chance to disappear into the dark empty space in an attempt to murder the soldier. Because the camera does not follow Fontaine (i.e. it concerns a dynamic pattern of exit into the scenery), the viewer is left with an empty screen. Moreover, they are kept in suspense about the event's outcome, as

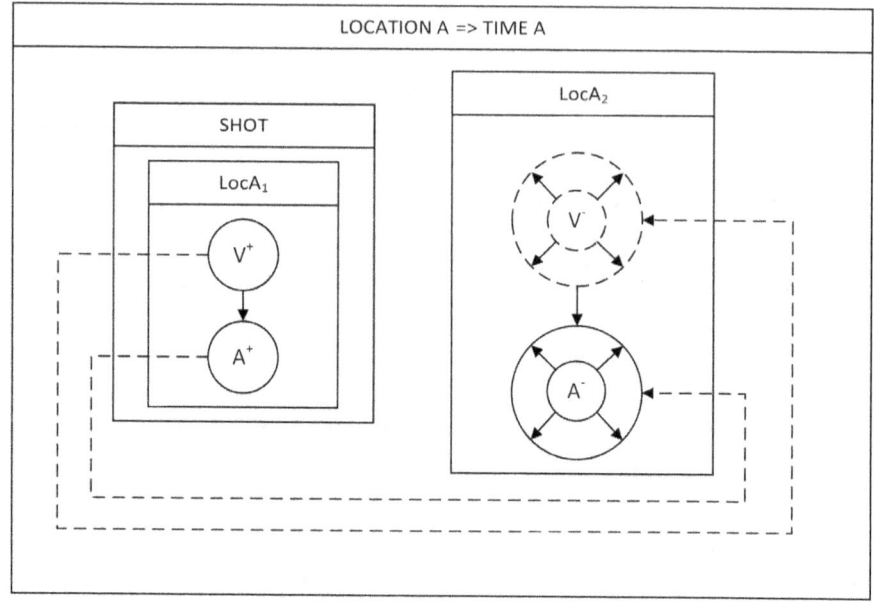

V⁺: On-screen sound producing visual source
A⁺: On-screen source-connected literal sound
V⁻: Off-screen sound producing visual source
A⁻: Off-screen source-disconnected literal sound

⊂⊃ : Excluded from audio-visual perception
◯ : Included in audio-visual perception

Figure 7.10. Exchanging the image for off-screen sound. © Maarten Coëgnarts.

the locomotive engine noise and the noise of the wheels turning on the railway track overpower the sounds of the actual murder.

This empty screen, and the withholding of visual information, is brought to transcendental purity in the last scene of *Mouchette* (1967). After picking up a package of clothes for her mother's funeral, the title protagonist decides to sit down on the banks of a river to open it. When she stands up again with one of the dresses in her hands, she accidentally tears it – the culmination of a series of miserable events in her life. She turns her gaze away from the dress to the river. Bresson makes use of the twofoldness of the POV structure to stress the significance of this perceptual act. Because the first shot shows her in the act of looking off-screen, a metonymy known in the Conceptual Metaphor Theory literature as EYES STAND FOR SEEING, the next shot (container), which depicts the river, is conceived metaphorically as her visual field.[8] In this way, the viewer is instructed to see the river the same way as Mouchette does: as a potential means of escape. Subsequently, she makes three attempts to roll into the water to drown herself. In her first attempt, she halts before she makes it. When a random farmer passes by, there is a sudden spark of hope that she will cease her plan. This hope, however, is short-lived as her attempt to call him is met with indifference. Further strengthened in her intention, she makes a second attempt but fails again. At her third attempt, she finally succeeds and falls into the water. These three attempts are rendered cinematically, as shown in Figure 7.11, as a game-like succession of the dynamic ENTRY and EXIT patterns in three separate series of shots.

The first two series are rendered alike. We see Mouchette rolling into and out of the relative stationary shots. In both cases, the concluding image is strongly visual; we see her body as it fills in an empty frame. This, however, changes with the last attempt. The girl's exit from the first shot and her entrance into the second one are still akin to the previous series, but when she *exits* the second shot from the frame's right edge, the film does not immediately cut to her *entrance* of the

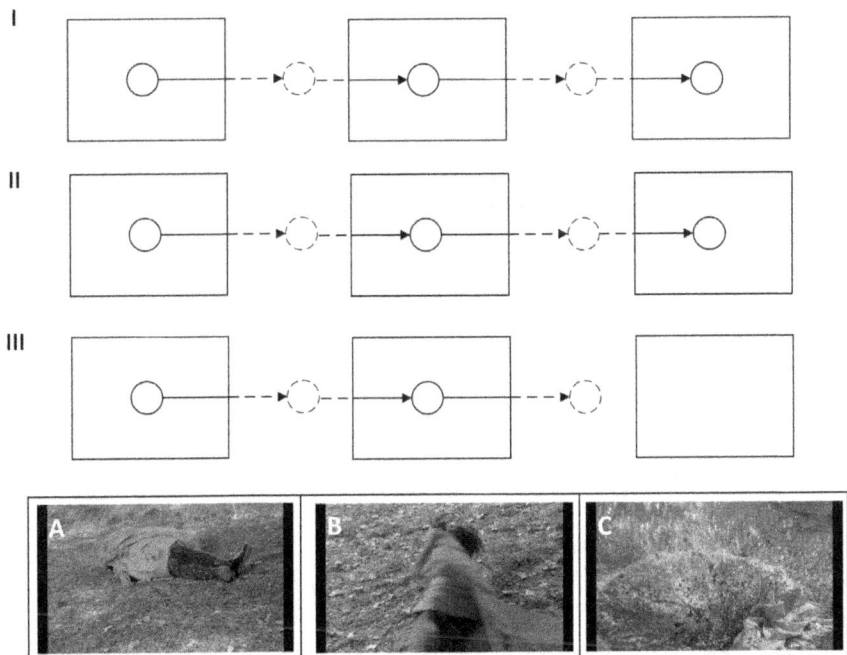

Figure 7.11. The underlying dynamic structure of *Mouchette*'s ending. © Maarten Coëgnarts.

third shot. Rather, the camera stays focused on the empty frame of the second shot as we hear the crucial event, Mouchette falling into the water, off-screen. Sound replaces the image. It is only after hearing the sound of water splashing that the film cuts to the final shot, showing the splash still in progress. Gradually the river restores a flat surface, thus becoming the peaceful image that we had seen earlier through the girl's eyes, except now the roles are reversed: she is in the river as opposed to the river being in her visual field. The spiritual epiphany of this moment is signalled musically by Monteverdi's *Magnificat*, which lifts her death to transcendental heights. As with Antonioni, Bresson does not defy the natural use of the spatio-temporal logic of the CONTAINER schema. He does not create, as Resnais does, an ambiguous conception of time by blending past and present together in one unified container. The dynamics that are going on in Bresson's films (e.g. entries of sounds and exits of visual sources) do not cross the natural boundaries that separate times and places. The same cannot be said of the work of another French director who, while also working within the paradigm of radical discontinuity, nevertheless sought to challenge these boundaries. This director is Jean-Luc Godard.

The Godard Style. As noted earlier, Godard's style was strongly influenced by cinéma vérité. This style of documentary filmmaking, pioneered by (among others) Jean Rouch, differs from neorealism in that it does not so much focus on a particular social environment, but emphasises the subject, who reflects on it (Kovács 2007: 170–71). We have already seen, while discussing Antonioni's style, how the environment, rather than the subject, takes up a very active role by *including* and *excluding* characters. In doing so, Antonioni manages to express his character's alienation. In a sense, one can say that Godard aims for the same goal but by the opposite means, ascribing a much more active role to the unique individual subjectivity of the character. The camera is no longer employed as an objective recording device that exists independently from the character's mental life. Rather, it is used in a participative and collaborative way for the purpose of developing a shared understanding of the character's subjective experiences. By the mediation of the camera, the filmmaker aims to make the viewer a conscious, critical observer of it. The camera becomes the participant as well as the collaborator. To this aim, Godard, like all the other modernist directors considered so far, sought and used various techniques.

Perhaps one of his most celebrated and controversial film techniques, in this regard, is the device of the 'distancing effect'. First presented to the stage by

German playwright Bertolt Brecht, this technique breaks the barrier or 'fourth wall' that naturally exists between the audience and the characters. Exemplary in this regard is the famous opening shot of *Contempt* (1963): in the background of the frame, at the far end of a receding line of dolly tracks, a camera crew slowly tracks an actress in a yellow shirt as she moves closer to the screen and uninterruptedly reads a book. She approaches the screen diagonally and eventually exits the frame from its bottom-left corner. The camera operator is now left behind in the centre of the image. He carefully adjusts his lens until it is no longer aimed at the off-screen space to the right side of the frame but at us, the audience, who are sitting in front of the screen (see Figure 7.12 A).

Another, more widely used way in which Godard breaks the fourth wall is by letting the actors talk directly to the camera. The clearest examples of this distancing effect can be found in *Breathless* (1960) and *A Woman Is a Woman* (1961). Within seconds of the opening of the latter film, the protagonist, Angela (Anna Karina), stares directly into the camera and gives the viewer a coy wink, inviting us to become an active participant in her experiential world (see Figure 7.12 B).

Likewise, the distancing effect can be seen as a radical alteration of the natural use of the spatio-temporal logic of the shot. This use traditionally situates the viewer outside the diegetic space of the film. It is a rule to which the majority of modernist films (including the ones cited so far) generally adhere.[9] Godard, by contrast, breaks this rule by giving the impression, through the actor's behaviour on-screen, that the viewer, who is usually residing in a location both spatially and temporally different from the character's location, is occupying a place within the diegetic world. Diagrammatically, we may represent this crossing of borders as in Figure 7.13.

Another distinctive strategy that Godard resorts to, to make the viewer conscious about his participating role in the diegetic world, is his rejection of shot-reverse-shot in conversation scenes. As Bordwell (2008: 57) pointed out, this technique conventionally alternates between two separate shots, one showing the character in the act of looking (often off-screen) at another character, and then another shot in which the other character is shown looking back at the first character (and responding to the other person): 'Since the characters are shown facing in opposite directions, the viewer unconsciously assumes that they are looking at each other' (ibid.). As his work illustrates, Godard deviates from this technique in two fundamental ways. First, he often favours rendering a dialogue

Figure 7.12. The viewer as participant in the character's diegetic world of *Contempt* (A) and *A Woman Is a Woman* (B). © Rome Paris Films, Les Films Concordia, Compagnia Cinematografica Champion 1963; and © Euro International Films, Rome Paris Films 1961. Screen captures by Maarten Coëgnarts.

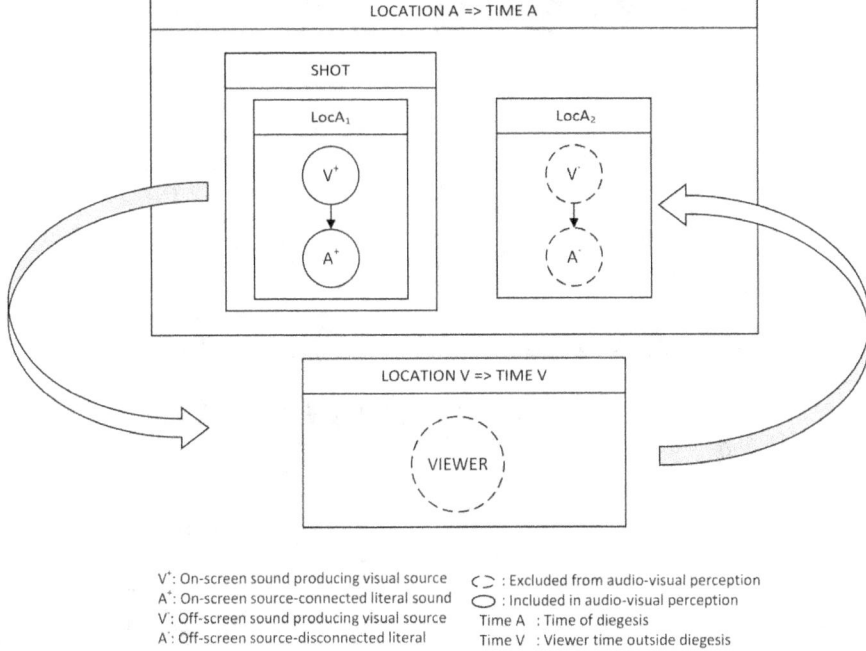

V⁺: On-screen sound producing visual source ⊂⊃ : Excluded from audio-visual perception
A⁺: On-screen source-connected literal sound ◯ : Included in audio-visual perception
V⁻: Off-screen sound producing visual source Time A : Time of diegesis
A⁻: Off-screen source-disconnected literal Time V : Viewer time outside diegesis

Figure 7.13. The on-screen space forces the viewer to cross the natural spatio-temporal boundary and to become part of the diegetic space. © Maarten Coëgnarts.

scene through panning between characters rather than cutting between them. Like a game of ping-pong, the camera moves horizontally from left to right, imitating the viewer's head movement as it follows the dialogue from one character to another. Thus, Godard makes conscious what the shot-reverse-shot reveals (i.e. the location of the viewer).

Through the way the filmmaker moves the camera, we can see yet another conceptual extension of the dynamic patterns of INCLUSION and EXCLUSION. As we saw earlier, Antonioni used mobile framing as a means of suggesting isolation or imprisonment. Resnais used it to connect past and present in one and the same shot. Godard, in his own distinctive way, uses it to attribute the viewer a presence within the diegetic world. Two notable scenes that illustrate this principle are shown in Figure 7.14. It concerns two dialogues, one between Angela and Émile (Jean-Claude Brialy) from *A Woman Is a Woman* (A–C), and another between Camille and Paul from *Contempt* (D–F).

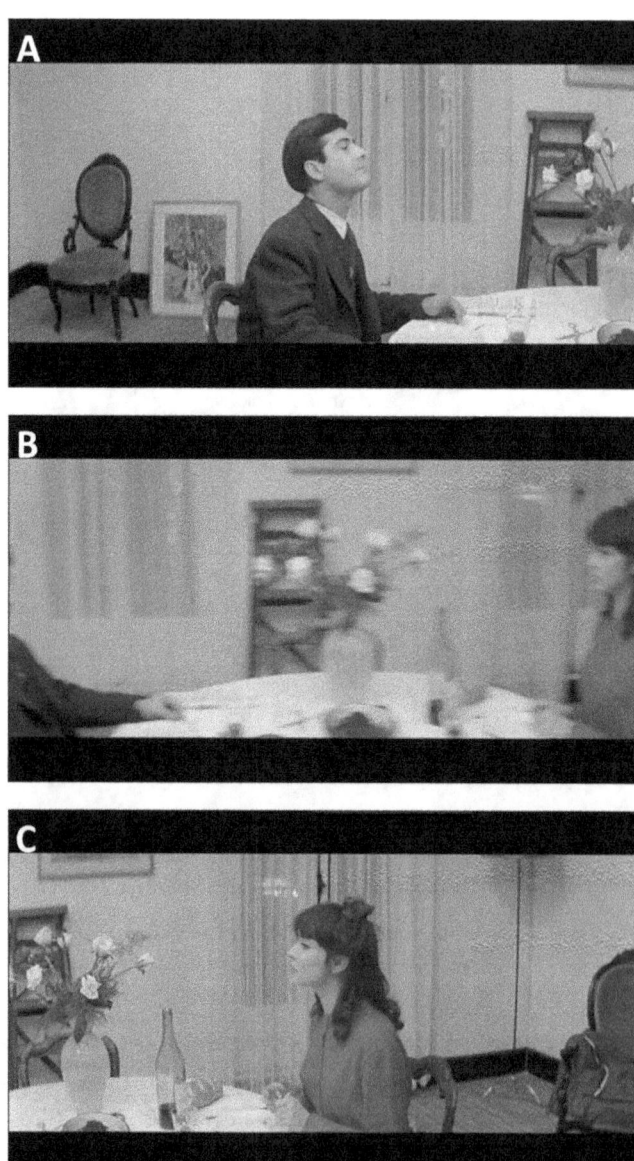

Figure 7.14. Excluding and including talking characters in *A Woman Is a Woman* (A–C) and *Contempt* (D–F). © Euro International Films, Rome Paris Films, 1961; and © Rome Paris Films, Les Films Concordia, Compagnia Cinematografica Champion 1963. Screen captures by Maarten Coëgnarts.

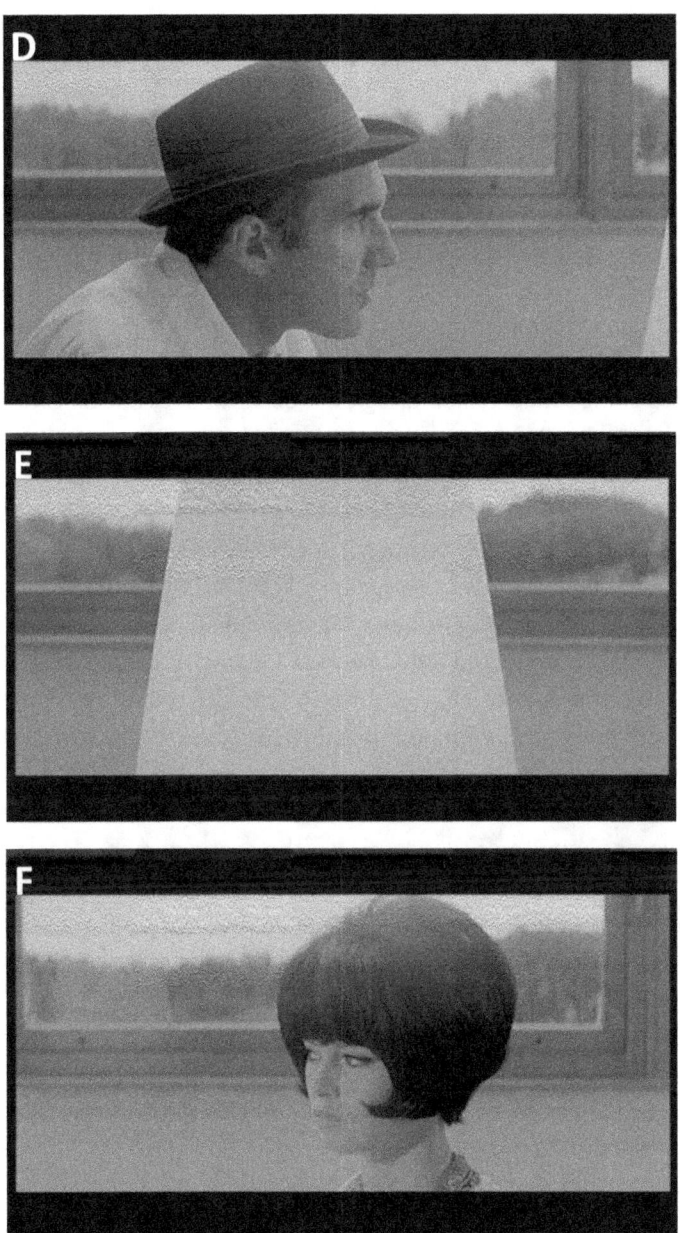

Figure 7.14. (continued)

The second way that Godard defies the convention of the shot-reverse-shot is by moving the focus of the camera away from the character who, in the shot-reverse-shot, is usually the centre of attention (the talking character) to the character who is silently and attentively residing off-screen and who is often the subject of the conversation. In this way, Godard allows the audience to see their initial reactions to the often very personal dialogue. Without breaking away from the character in question, we can see the character in great depth through wordless action and expression. As such, the universal conceptual metonymy 'facial expressions stand for emotions' gets the chance to fully unfold inside the viewer's mind. Contrary to the prior strategy, this visual tactic does not cross the traditional boundaries of the spatio-temporal logic of a scene. It does not allocate a location to the viewer in the diegetic space; rather, it switches attention within the existing locations of the diegetic space by favouring what, in traditional classical cinema, is often located in the off-screen space.

Godard also uses sound to blur the line between film and reality. As noted earlier, when watching movies, we usually make a clear spatial distinction between two types of literal sounds: on-screen source-connected literal sounds, and off-screen source-disconnected literal sounds. Godard now blurs this distinction by treating them interchangeably. A radical manifestation of this aesthetic principle can be found in his *Band of Outsiders* (1964). At one point in the film, the three 'outsiders', Franz, Arthur and Odile, are sitting and talking in a crowded and noisy cafe. When they are running out of ideas, they decide to observe one minute of silence. Given the spatio-temporal logic of Figure 7.2, one would expect that only the on-screen source-connected literal sound (the sound of their voices) would go silent while we are still able to hear, off-screen, the background noise of the cafe. Surprisingly, however, when the actors go silent, not only do their voices become silent but also the entire film. As such, the film becomes as quiet as the theatre in which the spectator is experiencing the film.

In the next scene, when the trio famously dances the Madison, sound is used in a most unconventional way. At first, the on-screen literal sounds bear a most natural relationship with the off-screen literal sounds: the actors are dancing and clapping their hands and stamping their feet to the music. However, when Godard's voice-over interrupts the scene, only the former sound is made silent, not the latter, thus giving the impression that the trio is dancing in complete silence.

In sum, we may conclude that Godard provides yet another creative formulation of the modernist theme of fragmentation. His films share a strong preference for discontinuity with Bresson's style, but whereas discontinuity in Bresson's work overall preserves the spatio-temporal boundary between viewer and film, discontinuity in Godard's work is aimed at further challenging this boundary.

Conclusion

Considering the insights above, we may speculate why modernist films are often experienced as aesthetically and cognitively engaging. The findings suggest a twofold answer. On the one hand, there is the embodied tie that connects the signature techniques of modernist cinema with the spectator's own experiential world. As this chapter shows, modernist filmmakers convey their fragmented view of reality not through structures that are disembodied but through structures that are informed by the same preconceptual patterns of sensorimotor experience that people use to make sense of the world. This common bodily basis may also explain why a lot of the complex spatio-temporal mappings of modernist cinema, as elucidated in this chapter, can be grasped intuitively by many film viewers. This is how, for instance, the viewer was psychologically well prepared to understand the various environmental sounds in the films of Bresson, despite never seeing the sources from which these literal sounds emanated. On the other hand, a shared embodied rootedness may not be sufficient to fully understand modernist cinema's distinctive, engaging quality. After all, the same claim of embodiment holds even truer for the continuity editing system of classical cinema, where techniques such as the POV shot and the shot-reverse-shot are strongly tied to the embodied expectations of the viewer.

In what sense, then, does the embodied film style of modernist cinema differ from the embodied film style of classical cinema? The answer lies in the fundamental difference in their aims and purposes. In classical cinema, the embodied patterns are there to preserve the narrative flow and optimize the flow of information – for instance, when the POV shot maps the container schema onto a character's visual field to convey information essential to the viewer's understanding of the story. In modernist cinema, by contrast, the embodied patterns are mostly stripped away from this classical communication function. As a result, the patterns and techniques through which they originate draw more attention to themselves; they are no longer cued in a direction that helps the viewer to figure out what is happening on screen. As Grodal (2009: 241) has pointed out, this lack of control, in turn, 'elicits strong subjective feelings, which also reflect that the experience is disembodied' (see also Gallese and Guerra 2012: 202).

What gives modernist cinema its secret appeal is precisely this contradictive nature. On the one hand, its techniques have a strong embodied resonance that intuitively appeals to the viewer, but on the other hand, this resonance remains undirected and without clear narrative context. This is possibly why the works of Antonioni, Resnais, Bresson and Godard continue to fascinate us even after multiple viewings: they attract us at a pre-reflective level of embodied understanding but, at the same time, they keep us in the dark at a more conceptual level of narrative understanding.

The findings of this chapter, however, are not without their limitations. First, we should be careful not to make overgeneralizations. Classifications are useful insofar as they allow us to delineate differences and similarities between phenomena, but they rarely capture the many nuances and grey areas that transcend them. For one, the different strategies of this study should not be seen as being tied exclusively to modernist cinema. Today, many of the strategies cited have become popular aesthetic practices that are widely used, often in varied and interchangeable ways, in both narrative cinema and television genres. Secondly, this chapter, despite its many case studies, remains largely hypothetical. In line with my previous work, it mainly draws upon empirical and theoretical work in the field of cognitive linguistics to draw comparable conclusions about meaning-making operations in cinema by predicting and offering a possible explanatory framework for the cognitive and aesthetic attractiveness of modern cinema. However, it does not demonstrate nor explain how viewers experience these different embodied film styles of modern European art cinema in reality. As I have noted elsewhere (Coëgnarts 2017, 2019, 2020), the latter would require the deeper knowledge of neuroscientists and cognitive psychologists, who are better equipped to turn the predicaments of this chapter into empirical statements. In this regard, a critical collaboration with Vittorio Gallese's Embodied Simulation Theory (EST) might provide an interesting and promising neurological framework for testing some of the chapter's claims (see also Coëgnarts 2017).[10]

Despite being largely theoretical, I nevertheless hope to have provided a convincing argument for studying film styles, not only in terms of their formal features but also of their underlying embodied patterns, which, as we have seen, serve as perceptual carriers for a film's abstract themes. In that sense, these patterns provide perhaps the most clear-cut evidence for what film essentially is – namely, an art form capable of expressing meaning and of adding something new to the merely reproductive act of recording reality. Through them, perception and cognition are joined under the same blanket, and in that sense, it is perhaps right to give the last word to the great non-dualist theorist of art, Rudolf Arnheim, who once stated: 'Perceptual dynamics is the very basis of expression, expression is the manifestation of life, and life is what art is all about' (Arnheim 1988: 585).

Maarten Coëgnarts is an assistant professor at the University of Antwerp, where he teaches film studies. Since 2010 he has researched the interplay between embodied cognition, metaphor and cinema. The results have been published in, among others, *Image [&] Narrative, Projections, Cinéma & Cie, Metaphor and Symbol, New Review of Film and Television Studies* and *Art & Perception*. He is co-editor of the book *Embodied Cognition and Cinema* (Leuven University Press, 2015) and author of the book *Film as Embodied Art: Bodily Meaning in the Cinema of Stanley Kubrick* (Academic Studies Press, 2019).

Notes

1. Given the sequence of locations shown in Figure 7.1, filmmakers may impose at least three major possibilities for spatio-temporal manipulation: omitting locations, replacing locations and repeating locations. These operations adhere to the three categories of temporal relations (duration, order and frequency, respectively) as they were first established by Genette (1972) and later adapted by Bordwell (1985: 51) (see also Bordwell and Thompson 2004: 74–76, 326–33).
2. This view, shared by Kovács, contradicts the more common and popular belief that the landscape in Antonioni's work serves as an extension of the character's psyche. In this view, the solitude of the landscape is seen as standing for the character's depressed state of mind. Although it is tempting to draw such a parallel, it would be too easy to say this of all of the landscapes in his films, especially when one considers (as this section hopes to make clear) the embodied logic behind the various stylistic ways that Antonioni renders these landscapes cinematically.

3. This strategy is most typical of the melodrama genre, and can also be found in the films of Douglas Sirk, among others. For a discussion on this, see Coëgnarts and Kravanja 2016.
4. This statement mainly applies to Antonioni's early work. Exceptions can be found in his later work, including the famous flashback scene from *The Passenger* in which both present and past are homogenized in one sequence shot. For a discussion, see Coëgnarts and Kravanja 2015b.
5. For a discussion of how two other film directors, Stanley Kubrick and Éric Rohmer, have used these dynamic patterns of containment in their works, see Coëgnarts 2019 and 2020, respectively.
6. We may refer to this film technique as a 'temporal montage within a shot'. This technique fuses the two basic techniques of editing that Lev Manovich (2001: xvii) labels 'temporal montage' and 'montage within a shot', respectively. In the first, more common technique, 'realities form consecutive moments in time', whereas in the second, more rare technique, 'realities form contingent parts of a single image'.
7. Examples of temporal montage within a shot, with a clear indication of a temporal boundary, can be found, for instance, in *Miss Julie* (Alf Sjöberg, 1957), *Les Girls* (George Cukor, 1957), *Come Back to the 5 & Dime Jimmy Dean, Jimmy Dean* (Robert Altman, 1982) and *Lone Star* (John Sayles, 1996). For a discussion, see Coëgnarts 2022 and Coëgnarts and Kravanja 2015b.
8. The VISUAL FIELD IS A CONTAINER metaphor is a core metaphor in the field of cognitive linguistics (e.g. Lakoff and Johnson 1980: 30). It is licensed by many daily expressions such as 'the ship *is coming into* view' or 'I have him *in* sight'. For a discussion of this metaphor in film, see Coëgnarts 2019: 129–35.
9. This is evidenced in the fact that, until now, the viewer did not play a substantial role in the visual diagrams of this chapter.
10. In cognitive-linguistic literature, EST has been suggested to provide image schemas with a neural and empirical grounding. For a discussion, see, among others, Dodge and Lakoff 2005 and Gallese and Lakoff 2005.

References

Arnheim, Rudolf. 1988. 'Visual Dynamics', *American Scientist* 76(6): 585–91.
Barsalou, Lawrence W. 2008. 'Grounded Cognition', *Annual Review of Psychology* 59: 617–45.
Bordwell, David. 1985. *Narration in the Fiction Film*. Madison: University of Wisconsin Press.
———. 2008. *The Poetics of Cinema*. New York: Routledge.
Bordwell, David, and Kristin Thompson. 2004. *Film Art: An Introduction*, 7th edn. New York: McGraw-Hill.
Boroditsky, Lera. 2000. 'Metaphoric Structuring: Understanding Time through Spatial Metaphors', *Cognition* 75(1): 1–28.
———. 2001. 'Does Language Shape Thought? Mandarin and English Speakers' Conceptions of Time', *Cognitive Psychology* 43(1): 1–22.
Branigan, Edward. 2006. *Projecting a Camera: Language-Games in Film Theory*. New York: Routledge.
Bresson, Robert. 1975. *Notes on the Cinematograph*. New York: New York Review of Books.
Buckland, Warren. 2000. *The Cognitive Semiotics of Film*. Cambridge: Cambridge University Press.

Casasanto, Daniel, and Lera Boroditsky. 2008. 'Time in the Mind: Using Space to Think about Time', *Cognition* 106: 579–93.

Chion, Michel. 2019. *Audio-Vision: Sound on Screen*, 2nd edn, trans. C. Gorbman. New York: Colombia University Press.

Coëgnarts, Maarten. 2017. 'Cinema and the Embodied Mind: Metaphor and Simulation in Understanding Meaning in Films'. *Palgrave Communications* 3: 1–15.

———. 2019. *Film as Embodied Art: Bodily Meaning in the Cinema of Stanley Kubrick*. Boston, MA: Academic Studies Press.

———. 2020. 'How Motion Shapes Thought in Cinema: The Embodied Film Style of Éric Rohmer', *Projections: The Journal for Movies and Mind* 14(2): 26–47.

———. 2022. 'Time-Creation in Film: An Embodied Cognitive Perspective', in Anna Piata, Daniel Alcaraz and Adriana Gordejuela (eds), *On the Edges of Time: Time Representations in the Perspective of Human Creativity*. Amsterdam: John Benjamins.

Coëgnarts, Maarten, and Peter Kravanja. 2012. 'Embodied Visual Meaning: Image Schemas in Film', *Projections: The Journal for Movies and Mind* 6(2): 84–101.

———. (eds). 2015a. *Embodied Cognition and Cinema*. Leuven: Leuven University Press.

———. 2015b. 'With the Past in Front of the Character: Evidence for Spatial-Temporal Metaphors in Cinema', *Metaphor and Symbol* 30(3): 218–39.

———. 2016. 'Perceiving Emotional Causality in Film: A Conceptual and Formal Analysis', *New Review of Film and Television Studies* 14(4): 440–66.

Deleuze, Gilles. 1989. *Cinema 2: The Time Image*, trans. H. Tomlison and R. Galeta. London: Athlone Press.

Dewell, Robert. 2005. 'Dynamic Patterns of Containment', in Beate Hampe (ed.), *From Perception to Meaning: Image Schemas in Cognitive Linguistics*. Chicago: University of Chicago Press, pp. 369–94.

Dodge, Ellen, and George Lakoff. 2005. 'Image Schemas: From Linguistic Analysis to Neural Grounding', in Beate Hampe (ed.), *From Perception to Meaning: Image Schemas in Cognitive Linguistics*. Chicago: University of Chicago Press, pp. 57–91.

Evans, Vyvyan. 2003. *The Structure of Time: Language, Meaning and Temporal Cognition*. Amsterdam: John Benjamins.

Fahlenbrach, Kathrin (ed.). 2016. *Embodied Metaphors in Film, Television, and Video Games: Cognitive Approaches*. New York: Routledge.

Fingerhut, Joerg, and Katrin Heimann. 2017. 'Movies and the Mind: On Our Filmic Body', in Christoph Durt, Thomas Fuchs and Christian Tewes (eds), *Investigating the Constitution of the Shared World*. Cambridge, MA: MIT Press, pp. 353–77.

Gallese, Vittorio, and Michele Guerra. 2012. 'Embodying Movies: Embodied Simulation and Film Studies', *Cinema: Journal of Philosophy and the Moving Image* 3: 183–210.

———. 2019. *The Empathic Screen: Cinema and Neuroscience*. Oxford: Oxford University Press.

Gallese, Vittorio, and George Lakoff. 2005. 'The Brain's Concepts: The Role of the Sensory-Motor System in Conceptual Knowledge', *Cognitive Neuropsychology* 22(3–4): 455–79.

Genette, Gérard. 1972. *Figures III*. Paris: Éditions du Seuil.

Gentner, Dedre. 2001. 'Spatial Metaphors in Temporal Reasoning', in Merideth Gattis (ed.), *Spatial Schemas and Abstract Thought*. Cambridge: Cambridge University Press, pp. 203–22.

Gentner, Dedre, Mutsumi Imai and Lera Boroditsky. 2002. 'As Time Goes By: Evidence for Two Systems in Processing Space > Time Metaphors', *Language and Cognitive Processes* 17(5): 537–65.

Gibbs Jr., Raymond W. 1994. *The Poetics of Mind: Figurative Thought, Language, and Understanding.* Cambridge: Cambridge University Press.
———. 2005. *Embodiment and Cognitive Science.* Cambridge: Cambridge University Press.
Grodal, Torben. 2009. *Embodied Visions: Evolution, Emotion, Culture and Film.* New York: Oxford University Press.
Hampe, Beate (ed.). 2005. *From Perception to Meaning: Image Schemas in Cognitive Linguistics.* Chicago: University of Chicago Press.
Hven, Steffen. 2017. *Cinema and Narrative Complexity: Embodying the Fabula.* Amsterdam: Amsterdam University Press.
Johnson, Mark. 1987. *The Body in the Mind: The Bodily Basis of Meaning, Imagination and Reason.* Chicago: University of Chicago Press.
Kiss, Miklós, and Steven Willemsen. 2017. *Impossible Puzzle Films: A Cognitive Approach to Contemporary Complex Cinema.* Edinburgh: Edinburgh University Press.
Kovács, András Bálint. 2007. *Screening Modernism: European Art Cinema, 1950–1980.* Chicago: The University of Chicago Press.
Kövecses, Zoltán. 2000. *Metaphor and Emotion: Language, Culture, and Body in Human Feeling.* Cambridge: Cambridge University Press.
Lakoff, George. 1987. *Women, Fire and Dangerous Things: What Categories Reveal about the Mind.* Chicago: University of Chicago Press.
Lakoff, George, and Mark Johnson. 1980. *Metaphors We Live By.* Chicago: University of Chicago Press.
———. 1999. *Philosophy in the Flesh: The Embodied Mind and its Challenge to Western Thought.* New York: Basic Books.
Manovich, Lev. 2001. *The Language of New Media.* Cambridge, MA: The MIT Press.
Metz, Christian. 1985. 'Aural Objects', in Elisabeth Weis and John Belton (eds), *Film Sound: Theory and Practice.* New York: Columbia University Press, pp. 154–61.
Núñez, Rafael E., Benjamin A. Motz and Ursina Teuscher. 2006. 'Time After Time: The Psychological Reality of the Ego- and Time-Reference-Point Distinction in Metaphorical Construals of Time', *Metaphor and Symbol* 21(3): 133–46.
Núñez, Rafael E., and Eve Sweetser. 2006. 'With the Future Behind Them: Convergent Evidence from Aymara Language and Gesture in the Crosslinguistic Comparison of Spatial Construals of Time', *Cognitive Science* 30(3): 401–50.
Pearlman, Karen. 2017. 'Editing and Cognition beyond Continuity', *Projections: The Journal for Movies and Mind* 11(2): 67–86.
Tversky, Barbara. 2019. *Mind in Motion: How Action Shapes Thought.* New York: Basic Books.
Varela, Francisco J., Evan Thompson and Eleanor Rosch. 1991. *Embodied Mind: Cognitive Science and Human Experience.* Cambridge, MA: MIT Press.
Walsh, Martin. 1975. 'The Passenger: Antonioni's Narrative Design', *Jump Cut: A Review of Contemporary Media* 8: 7–10.
Zettl, Herbert. 2017. *Sight, Sound, Motion: Applied Media Aesthetics*, 8th edn. Boston, MA: Cengage Learning.

CHAPTER 8
The Most Difficult Riddle
Paradoxical Personalities in Puzzle Films

András Bálint Kovács

Introduction

In this chapter, I aim to provide support to my conjecture that the relative popularity of 'puzzle films' or 'complex' narratives produced in the past decades – films that make it difficult or impossible for the viewer to construct them as temporally linear, causally logical or spatially coherent stories – has a certain limit. This limit is related to the coherence of the protagonist's identity.

Why have puzzle films, in general, become more popular since the late 1980s than they were before? Some argue that sociocultural developments in the late twentieth century explain the increasing popularity of 'mind-blowing' Hollywood productions, focusing especially on those representing uncertain character identities (Eig 2003). Others hold that the emergence of this type of film in Hollywood is due to a change in spectatorship practice: shifting from a passive position into an active, participatory position (Elsaesser 2011; Mittell 2015). Yet others argue that the emergence of alternative storytelling experiences in video games foster young audiences' sensibilities for puzzling narration (Panek 2006). All of the above may be simultaneously true, as no single explanation is sufficient in such complex cultural matters as the popularity of works of art.

Accepting that each of these explanations has truth in them, I would like to add two ideas. The first is that cultural habituation – in other words, sustained exposure to narrative complexity of a sufficiently large audience segment – may have allowed Hollywood productions to try out narrative forms that previously seemed impossible to be brought to success. However, the limited number of such films produced during the past three decades bears witness to the limited extent of this audience segment. The second is that complicating narrative fluency (the ease of following and understanding a narrative) has a certain limit, beyond which large-scale enjoyability of this type of film dramatically decreases. I argue that this limit is related to the break of the identity of the characters and their motivations. I suggest that as long as character identity is not questioned in a narrative, space-time paradoxes in themselves do not represent too big a challenge for the majority of the general audience of puzzle narratives.

Split character identities and uncertain motivations, however, seriously risk large-scale enjoyability, as proven by the limited popularity of this type of film. This makes it a distinctive category of complex narratives that can be considered the 'most difficult' to figure out, as the anchor of the viewer's engagement – solid and identifiable character motivation – is not certain to maintain the audience's involvement. Paradoxical character identity considerably threatens wide-scale enjoyability, but it can be compensated by various techniques that still allow a certain level of popularity to be reached. When not compensated, the overwhelming majority of the viewers inescapably lose their grip on the overall coherence of the narrative.

It is to be noted that I am talking about wide-scale enjoyability here; experimental/avant-garde narratives abound in paradoxical narratives and character identities, and they have a solid but restricted audience. Neither do I claim that naturalistic understanding of character identity is always a precondition of aesthetic enjoyment. My claim is that the more identity paradox determines the narrative, the more limited the audience who can enjoy it. Identity paradox, rather than space-time paradox, limits the enjoyability of the narrative; however, it does not reduce it to zero for all audiences.

Accommodating the Prototype of the Puzzle

Puzzles are essential for all narratives, as investigation fiction's huge popularity in film and literature shows. Cinematic storytelling adds to the necessary narrative puzzles due to the fact that temporal, spatial and causal coherence cannot be unambiguously stated in a film. Whatever image sequence the spectators see in a film, the connections have to be constructed by inferential mental operations rather than simply reading and understanding common words such as 'after', 'because', 'the reason why' and 'before'. In a film, understanding these relations needs more complicated mental operations. It took some twenty years in the evolution of cinematic narrative before the techniques of seamless temporal, causal and spatial continuity crystallized – or, to put it differently, before filmmakers figured out the techniques of representing continuity that the human mind could accommodate in the easiest way. Narratives that utilize these techniques (99 per cent of fiction films, that is) are the easiest puzzles to solve, but they are puzzles, nonetheless.

The idea that narrative understanding, in general, is a problem-solving process goes back to the 1970s. David Rumelhart put forward the argument that if the protagonist of a story solves problems, understanding the protagonist's story also needs a problem-solving strategy from the reader or viewer (Rumelhart 1977). Later, he compared narrative understanding to an investigation by which the reader builds hypotheses and constantly modifies them along the way as the story develops (Rumelhart 1980). In the case of coherent narratives, we solve temporal and causal puzzles almost automatically if they satisfy some basic criteria: the story is about one or multiple characters whose actions are understandable in terms of human motivations, and they have to solve a problem in a physical world that can be imagined by the listener/reader/viewer (Yussen and Glisch 1993). These criteria rest on four basic physical axioms, which are the basis of our everyday experience:

1. Time has a direction.
2. A cause precedes its effects.
3. No object can be at more than one location at the same time.
4. Movement in space is continuous.

These criteria ensure narrative coherence, which appears in the form of causal logic, temporal order and realistic spatial relations. Actions, problem solving and motivation relate to axioms 1 and 2; the recognizable physical world relates to axioms 3 and 4. Narrative puzzles that do not respect these criteria or violate any of these axioms will be harder to solve. That is, when fluent, almost automatic narrative processing is not sufficient, slower and more conscious problem solving comes into play, and the spectator is confronted with the experience of a puzzle.

The mildest forms of narrative puzzles include crime investigation and mystery stories, which are often at the top of bestseller and blockbuster lists. Narrative art also created powerful prototypes for violations of some of the basic axioms of natural processing of events in the genres of fairy tales, science fiction and fantasy films. This is how we know for sure that puzzles resulting from a violation of physical axioms are not necessarily obstacles to aesthetic pleasure in themselves. More challenging cases are represented by 'impossible puzzle films' (Kiss and Willemsen 2017), where more than one basic axiom is violated, or the identity of the protagonist is broken. These films considerably reduce their audiences; nevertheless, many viewers do still find pleasure in watching them.

The enjoyability of easy narrative puzzles can be explained by referring to the inverted U-shaped relation between complexity and aesthetic pleasure, as defined by Berlyne (1971), predicting that a too low or a too high level of complexity or familiarity will reduce aesthetic pleasure. This means that, as a general rule, reducing ease of aesthetic processing may also increase aesthetic pleasure up to a certain point, beyond which complexity negatively correlates with aesthetic pleasure. The emergence of the relative popularity of difficult puzzles needs another explanation.

The theory of 'aesthetic fluency' (Reber, Schwarz and Winkielman 2004) may serve this purpose. This theory holds that aesthetic pleasure is contingent on ease of cognitive processing. Ease of processing has objective properties (large contrast, symmetry, clear contours, etc.) that can be demonstrated reliably in many art forms (painting, music, narrative, etc.). However, this does not mean that only the easiest forms to process are the most popular. The effects of objective properties are highly modulated by other factors, such as repeated exposure to specific forms, or expertise. One of the main factors for ease of processing is prototypicality. (A prototypical form is recognized as the model of something that we often encounter in different contexts.) Martindale (1984) also held that prototypical forms are generally preferred over new or unknown patterns. However, as Principe and Langlois (2012) proposed, the recognition of prototypicality is dependent on repeated exposure to forms based on a given prototype. Familiarity needed for aesthetic pleasure is born with habituation, which means that the attractiveness of a prototype is also highly sensitive to experience. Especially in the arts, a 'prototypical' form is subject to cultural variations. The change of cultural fashions is a clear indicator of the dependence of prototypicality on experience; the attractiveness of puzzles and the complexity of forms are no exceptions.

Here is an anecdotal example: I ask my students every year which of the two paintings of Picasso they would choose to hang in their living rooms – the one from 1896 representing his mother, a beautiful, and entirely realist painting (Museo

Picasso, Barcelona, see https://www.mutualart.com/Artwork/Tete-De-Femme/26FD28BDF6540047) or the one from 1935, his late abstract period, titled 'Head of Woman' (private collection, see: https://www.flickr.com/photos/gandalfsgallery/27485858810).

Over the years, the preference of the large majority of students, both in Europe and in California, has bent towards the 1935 'Head of Woman'. If it were only the ease of processing objective perceptual properties that determines aesthetic pleasure, then the consistent lean towards modernist forms could not be explained. Likewise, the wide popularity of impressionist art since the mid-twentieth century, compared with the general refusal and ridiculing of it in the nineteenth century, would be a mystery. If prototypicality is a factor of ease of processing, the historical habituation to new prototypes is a moderating factor. Simply put, we like what we recognize as carrying known prototypical features, but the familiarity with the features of a prototype is subject to historical and cultural habituation. It is reasonable to suppose, therefore, that the appearance of difficult or 'impossible' puzzle films in the 1990s within popular genres, after their dominance in the art-film sector in the 1960s and 1970s, is also due to a kind of cultural adaptation, within a large enough audience segment, to forms hitherto considered unacceptable due to their unfamiliarity (Klecker 2011).

It is undeniable that narratives violating the above-mentioned axioms were only sporadically present in mainstream Hollywood cinema until the end of the 1980s, but were a widespread phenomenon in European modernist art cinema (Kovács 2007). It would be hard to argue against this historical succession, but the causal explanations can be a matter of debate. It would be difficult to support with hard evidence the argument that American audiences, accustomed to the Hollywood norm, accommodated the non-classical forms of complex narratives of European art films. However, it is undeniable that with the spread of film studies education beginning in the 1970s, and the availability of these films on videotape from the late 1980s onwards, a certain audience became acquainted with a narrative prototype different from what they were used to in classical Hollywood films.

The role of prototypes in ease of processing explains how refused, 'unacceptable', 'disgusting', 'tasteless', 'immoral', 'confusing' or 'nonsensical' aesthetic forms can become acceptable or even popular over time. Some of these forms become mainstream, like impressionism or cubism, while some never make it into the mainstream but still become more acceptable, or maybe subcultural hits. Except for some blockbusters (*Inception*, 2010; *Edge of Tomorrow*, 2014), the latter can be said about most puzzle films. The question is not so much why this is so, but rather whether there is a limit to complicating a narrative to a point beyond which wide enjoyability of the film suffers and no cultural habituation is likely to occur.

Degrees of Puzzles

I propose that it is possible to categorize puzzle films into three groups according to the ease of their narrative processing. The first degree of difficulty is represented by violating physical axioms of everyday experience, keeping character motivation and identity coherent. This is the easiest puzzle to accommodate, making it the most likely to be widely enjoyed. This explains how a first-degree puzzle film such as Christopher Nolan's *Inception* (2010) can become a blockbuster. The film was an immense hit, grossing more than twice as much ($60.4m) in ticket sales in the first weekend as one of the lead actor's earlier blockbusters, the classical melodrama *Titanic* (1997) ($28m) (IMDb 2021). The film grossed more than 860 million dollars worldwide, gaining a place among the sixty highest grossing films of the 2010s.

As one critic noted, '[f]or all the talk of layers and keeping track of the movie's science, it's not a terribly complex story' (Rosenberg 2010). The reason it is not is that the protagonist's mission and internal motivations are clear from the outset and remain intact throughout the jumps from one dream layer to another, and from one storyworld to another. Even if not every viewer can follow the space-time jumps in the story, and viewers may not always know exactly when or where they are in a given scene, the narration makes sure that the local motivations and the overall reasons for the actions they see remain clear and in a causal development. The protagonist's identity is never broken and never questioned. This is the line this film does not cross, and what most likely makes it so accessible to mainstream audiences, even though no film with such a complicated narrative would ever have made it to a Hollywood studio before the 1990s. The same can be said about *Vanilla Sky* (2001), which is far less complicated than *Inception*. As confusing as the reality status of the scenes may be, the protagonist's personality and trajectory are entirely linear and coherent, and support his final decision (to live his real life).

The second degree of difficulty is represented by breaking the protagonist's identity, thereby making it difficult for the viewer to engage with the protagonist. However, films in this category still save some consistency in the characters with the help of two main compensating techniques: framing and compartmentalizing. Framing includes (a) representing the identity paradoxes as the result of mental illness (*Donnie Darko*) or different mental states (*Coherence*), and (b) using genre frameworks such as mystery (*Mulholland Drive*), horror (*Triangle*) and science fiction (*Predestination*). Compartmentalizing consists of revealing the paradox only at the closure of the narrative. Second-degree puzzle films that do cross the line of breaking the protagonist's identity pay the price of dropping popularity and become, in the best case, cult films for a restricted audience.

The third degree of difficulty includes paradoxical identities in the narrative without the above-mentioned compensatory techniques, thereby entirely losing the coherence of the main characters. Making character identity uncertain or paradoxical is one of modernist art film's main strategies. In most modernist art films, however, uncertain identities are represented in a physically coherent environment and do not violate rules of real-world physical experience. As 'puzzling' as they may seem for an audience attuned to classical narration, most modernist art films with unstable or undefined character identities have little to do with popular puzzle films (see Kiss and Willemsen 2017). Lack of character motivation (e.g. Wim Wenders' *The Goalie's Anxiety at the Penalty Kick*, 1971), lack of purposeful action (e.g. Jim Jarmusch's *Stranger than Paradise*, 1983), lack of causal connections between events (e.g. Chantal Ackerman's *Les Rendez-Vous d'Anna*, 1978), lack of realistic situation or background (e.g. Jean-Luc Godard's *Le Gai Savoir*, 1968), and the merging of dreams, fantasy and reality (e.g. Fellini's *8½*, 1962) are all narrative devices that divert the viewer's attention from problem-solving strategies rather than offering narrative puzzles to solve.

However, uncertain or paradoxical identities, together with the violation of axioms of physical experience, ignite problem-solving strategies, and only these types of modernist art films can be considered as the antecedents of contemporary third-degree puzzle films. Films written or directed by Alain Robbe-Grillet, especially *L'année Dernière a Marienbad* (1961), *L'Immortelle* (1962), *Trans-Europe Express* (1964), *L'homme Qui Ment* (1968), as well as Bergman's *Persona* (1966),

Bertolucci's *Partner* (1968) and Andrej Tarkovsky's *Zerkalo* (1974), disrupt spatial and temporal coherence through calling the coherent identity of the characters into question. Modernist art films of this type do not compensate for their representation of paradoxical character identity.

There is no mention of psychoses or any other mental state detaching the character from reality – the paradoxes appear early in the films, and there is no trace of any prototypical genre framework. Still, there is also an interpretive framework for these films, even though it is a theoretical one and available only for an initiated audience. This is the conceptual framework of the 'author film', according to which anything that happens in a narrative is the intentional creation of an author and must be interpreted as an authorial statement. The primary interpretive framework of a narrative is not real-world logic but an author's fantasy in which anything is possible. This idea originated in literature and was put into a theoretical form by Alain Robbe-Grillet (1963), which explains why most films of this type were made by Robbe-Grillet and his co-author Alain Resnais. But I would not call this another compensating technique because it does not have clear or distinct indicators recurring the same way in other art films. Inherent to the concept of authorism is uniqueness and the refusal of stereotypes, which incites authors to constantly search for hitherto unknown and original solutions. Third-degree puzzle films are often commonly classified as 'experimental films' (see Wikipedia entry for *Inland Empire*).

Framing and Compartmentalizing Paradoxical Identity

The most common procedure of framing the protagonist's incoherent behaviour is to hint at a disturbed mental state. Films with paradoxical character identity, like *Jacob's Ladder* (1990), *Donnie Darko* (2001), *Triangle* (2009), *Mulholland Drive* (2001), *Fight Club* (1999) and *Predestination* (2014), all expose the disturbed personality of their protagonists right at the outset. Donnie Darko's schizoid personality disorder is revealed very early in the film. Rita/Camilla (Laura Harring) is introduced as an amnesiac woman who does not know who she is, and the first half of *Mulholland Drive* is about the investigation of her real identity. Jess in *Triangle* appears as disturbed, which is confirmed in several dialogues. In the exposition of *Fight Club*, the protagonist explains at length his deeply depressed state of mind. In *Jacob's Ladder*, the whole narrative is about Jacob's personality disorder and his investigation of how this is related to what happened in Vietnam. At the beginning of *Predestination*, the protagonist is warned that the plastic surgery done to his burnt face might also have had mental effects, and 'psychosis' is written in his file. This type of framing provides the viewer with a feeling of reassurance that they can explain what otherwise could not be understood by means of rational problem solving. Even though paradoxical scenes cannot be rectified in the way it was done with *Inception*, the framework of the disturbed mental state allows virtually any event to be explained as a projection. By far the most frequent incoherence includes double/mirrored/split personalities and short nightmare scenes. In the mental disturbance framework, double/mirrored/split identities appear as the imagination or nightmares of the person in question.

Another basic compensation procedure is compartmentalization or temporal reduction of the paradoxical portion of the narration. As Kiss and Willemsen (2017) note, one of the main procedures used in 'impossible puzzle films' for maintaining a viewer's engagement with the narrative is simply to keep the largest part of the narrative within the classical norms – but what counts as the 'largest part'?

In *Mulholland Drive*, even if there are many mysterious scenes and characters in the film that are difficult to fit into the narrative, it is only in the final thirty minutes that the easy solution of interpreting Rita/Camilla (Laura Harring) as an amnesiac becomes untenable. From the moment when blonde Betty/Diane (Naomi Watts) unexpectedly disappears, there are no clues to help the viewer understand who is who in the story. It is only then that interpretative strategies of classical narration are no longer working; but this is only 21 per cent of the film's running time. Up to this point (79 per cent of the total running time), there is enough time to engage the spectator with the characters and the story, and generate emotional bonds with the characters, and thus to raise interest and create traditional suspense.

In *Predestination*, a similar proportion can be found. The truly confusing part starts when the 'error' warning appears on the time machine – when the identities of the two distinct main characters start to merge. This happens at around 82 per cent of the film's running time. Once the viewer understands the science fiction framework of time travel, nothing seems incomprehensible in this large portion of the film. In *Fight Club*, in the first 83 per cent of the narrative, nobody would possibly suspect that Tyler and the Narrator are the same person. *Donnie Darko* has the same structure, but in this film the confusing time loop lasts only 7 minutes out of the 127 minutes running time, so 94 per cent of the narrative, although not entirely coherent, is rather straightforward.

Limit cases are represented by *Coherence* (2013) and *Triangle* in this respect. Both films use framing as a compensation technique (science fiction, horror, mental disturbance), but the identity paradoxes are contained in a much larger portion of the narrative than in earlier examples. In *Triangle*, it is at around 50 per cent of the film's running time when Jess first confronts herself as her own enemy, which then happens twice more in the rest of the film. From this point on, it is impossible to determine if there is a 'real' and an 'imagined' Jess. In *Coherence*, four of the characters meet different versions of themselves in the street at 39 per cent of the film's running time. From this point on, the viewer has to accept that there is more than one version of each of the characters in this storyworld, and the paths of these alternative characters may even cross so that it is uncertain which character version encounters which other character version. This portion represents more than 60 per cent of the film's running time.

Both films are generally less popular and less widely known than those containing around 80 per cent of relatively coherent narration. To be sure, several reasons may be behind the restricted popularity and notoriety of these films. It may be argued, for example, that it is due to their restricted budget. However, only *Coherence* can be called a low budget film with its $50,000 production cost. *Triangle*'s budget of $12m is, in fact, higher than the median budget of Hollywood horror movies, which is about $8m (Follows 2019). Moreover, a film's budget is always proportional to the producer's expectations regarding attendance, and this expectation is highly dependent on the script. Therefore, I would argue that the relatively low budget of these films is a result of their respective scripts' structure representing their protagonists' paradoxical identities for more than 50 per cent of the running time, rather than a direct cause of their lack of popularity.

Many of these films end with one version of the split identity killing or attempting to kill the other – a plot turn that seems to be another recurring compensating technique of this type of narrative. The technique goes back as far as the 1910s, when *Der Student von Prague* (Stellan Rye, 1913) introduced the idea of killing the shadow personality. This solution reappears in a later German expressionist version (*Student von Prague*, Henrik Galeen, 1926). But even in the few exceptions where the protagonists do not kill themselves (*Jacob's Ladder* and *Donnie Darko*), they do not survive the story either. Both films are of a narrative prototype introduced into modern cinema by the short film *Occurrence at Owl Creek Bridge* (1961) by Robert Enrico, which was adapted from a short story by Ambrose Bierce of the same title (1890). The narrative idea of this prototype is to freeze a moment before death, from which an alternate universe of a possible extended lifespan is narrated, which eventually leads back to the point of departure where death happens.

These examples suggest that to reach, at least to some extent, wide-scale popularity, the disruption of character identity in puzzle films must be compensated for in one way or another. But why is the coherence of the protagonist the dividing line in the enjoyability of puzzle films?

The Primacy of Character Integrity

Even the most basic scriptwriting manuals note that characters are the key to whatever happens in the story. Syd Field, for example, cites Henry James in this regard: 'What is a character but the determination of incident? What is incident but the illustration of character?' (Field 2005). Character identity is the focal point of narrative coherence. The integrity of the characters vouches for clear motivations, motivations vouch for causal consistency of the narrative, and causal consistency is the basis of the reconstructability of temporal linearity, even when the narration is non-chronological. Probably the most important factor of narrative coherence, I propose, is the coherence of motivations behind the characters' actions, detected by what is called in psychology 'theory of mind' (ToM). Most significantly, it is through coherent character identity that viewers become engaged with a story, by way of processes like empathy, identification, mentalization, and so on. When this anchor becomes unstable, difficulties of understanding become much more disturbing than in the case of simple space–time confusion. No matter how complicated or complex a puzzle film's jumps through time and space may be, if the motivation and goal of the protagonist are consistent, the relative ease of narrative processing is ensured.

Preliminary research results (Papp-Zipernovszky, Kovács and Drótos 2019) allow for formulating a hypothesis that I call 'the primacy of character integrity' in cinematic narrative comprehension. This proposes that character consistency is a more important factor for the ease of processing in narrative films than space–time structure. Consequently, as long as the integrity of the protagonist is ensured, large-scale enjoyability can be reached by cultural habituation to different puzzle prototypes. By contrast, decreased large-scale enjoyability is caused by an increased degree of disruption of character integrity, which seems to be very resistant to being overridden by cultural habituation. This makes non-compensated types of paradoxical identity puzzle films look incoherent in the eyes of most viewers, as shown by the minimal popularity of such films. The results of this research have to be tested in further studies, which is why they are referred to here as tentative.

In the study, the cortical activations of viewers were measured by EEG while they were watching both coherent and incoherent narrative segments. Results showed that the cortical regions responsible for anticipation of action, recognition of temporal context, topographic memory, temporal coherence, episodic memory, goal attribution, and all the areas that are involved with the attribution intention to others (ToM) were significantly more active when following a film with no coherent space–time–causal structure, and when the protagonist's actions in each scene were unrelated. Areas involved with spatial attention, however, were consistently more active when watching a causally coherent narrative. The most consistent network showing relatively high activation was related to theory of mind. This result may suggest an increased workload in the areas involved with the function of understanding the actions of the character.

This hypothesis is consistent with Starbuck et al. (2000), which argues that increased cortical activations when solving problems are a sign of greater difficulty in processing. In our case, increased ToM activation can be interpreted as a sign of a greater effort in processing characters' goals and motivations, whereas lower activation (in the case of the coherent film) can be interpreted as a sign of fluent, automatic processing. This may suggest that when a viewer is confronted with a narrative representing incoherent character actions, it requires more effort to try to resolve the 'puzzle'.

Why were areas involved with spatial attention more active in the case of the coherent narrative? A possible hypothesis explaining the difference between ToM activation and spatial attention activation, in the case of the two types of narrative segments, is that a viewer's first concern is to understand the character's actions, regardless, or in spite of, incongruent spatial segments in the story. As lack of spatial contiguity is very common in cinematic narration (think of frequent jumps from one location to another), the effort goes into constructing a coherent narrative space, but only if character consistency (in terms of goals and motivations) is fluently processed. The hypothesis to be tested would be this: activation measured in areas involved with spatial orientation is systematically lower in cases when characters are inconsistent than in cases when they are not. And the reverse is assumed to be true concerning areas involved with ToM.

If tested directly, the primacy of character integrity hypothesis could explain the relatively low activity in areas involved with spatial attention and the increased relative effort in ToM in the case of incoherent narrative segments. It could also explain why time-travel, time-loop, travel-in-the-mind, travel-in-memory or -dream types of puzzles are the most common among the popular puzzle films, whereas paradoxical identity puzzles are less common and less popular. The latter need strong compensation to help to decrease processing efforts by introducing known prototypes of interpretive frameworks.

When not compensated, the ease of understanding, and thus popularity, of these films suffers. Yet, even if it is compensated, split personality puzzle films considerably reduce the possibility of viewers' engagement in following the protagonist's destiny, as the trajectory of this destiny is ambiguous. As the above examples suggest, the enjoyability, and hence the popularity, of the doppelgänger stories is proportional to the amount of time the viewer does not have to face the identity paradox that results in the loss of coherence of motivations. As we have seen, for popular film cases, this is typically around the first 80 per cent of the total running time of the film.

Uncompensated Identity Paradox

A rare example of uncompensated radical disruption of character identity by a well-known Hollywood director is represented by *Inland Empire* (Lynch, 2006). This film contains no more complicated or paradoxical twists than other popular 'impossible' puzzle films; however, a lack of the above-discussed compensating procedures remains enjoyable only for a small initiated audience.

To begin with, the frame story only starts after 8.5 minutes. Before that, we see four unrelated scenes that seem nonsensical in themselves. In the first scene, the two characters' heads are blurred, so their identities are concealed. In the second scene, a crying young woman watches a television on which there is no programme, with only occasional snippets of later scenes from this film appearing. In the third scene, we see a rather theatrical set with three rabbit-headed characters uttering nonsensical sentences. The context of a theatrical performance is also suggested by the sounds of applause and laughter from an audience. The fourth scene exposes recognizable characters once again on a luxurious set, but their dialogues are also mysterious. The rabbit-headed characters connect three of the four scenes as they appear on the television set in the second scene, and one of them enters the luxurious set at the beginning of the fourth scene. These four scenes are the introduction of the four alternate realities the main character from the frame story will pass through. Each represents different identities, which is suggested by the blurred or absurd identity concealment in two of the four scenes.

Contrary to the popular doppelgänger films, *Inland Empire* already exposes its blurred and concealed character identity in the beginning, and not as a result of a mental disturbance or generic framework, such as science fiction. The next thirty minutes offer a relatively linear and coherent narration of the frame story in which Nikki (Laura Dern), a Hollywood actress, receives an important role that could be her breakthrough. The role involves an adulterous relationship with the male lead, played by an actor called Devon (Justin Theroux), who has the reputation of being a womanizer. He is warned that, this time, he should avoid any sexually motivated approaches to Nikki because her husband is a dangerous person. Later on, threateningly, the husband also warns Devon to stay away from his wife, explaining to him that his wife is not a free agent because he does not allow her that. Nevertheless, Devon invites Nikki for dinner, and she agrees. That is when Nikki's identity starts to split, as she confuses the film's narrative with her own life. And this is where her journey starts, during which she enters into different worlds in different times and locations on different continents.

This happens at fifty-two minutes into the film, but as the first ten minutes also belongs to the portion of the narrative containing the paradoxical realities, the relatively coherent part of the film represents only 27 per cent of the total running time of the entire film. The viewer is confronted with blurred, split or parallel identities in more than 70 per cent of the narrative, with no generic stereotypes of horror, fantasy, science fiction or mystery, and with no hints of mental disturbance. This proportion of coherent and incoherent narrative parts is reversed compared to other popular puzzle films representing paradoxical identities, as illustrated in Figure 8.1.

Not only do identity paradoxes dominate the narrative, but the protagonist's motivation and goal remain blurred as well. When Nikki appears in the story, we

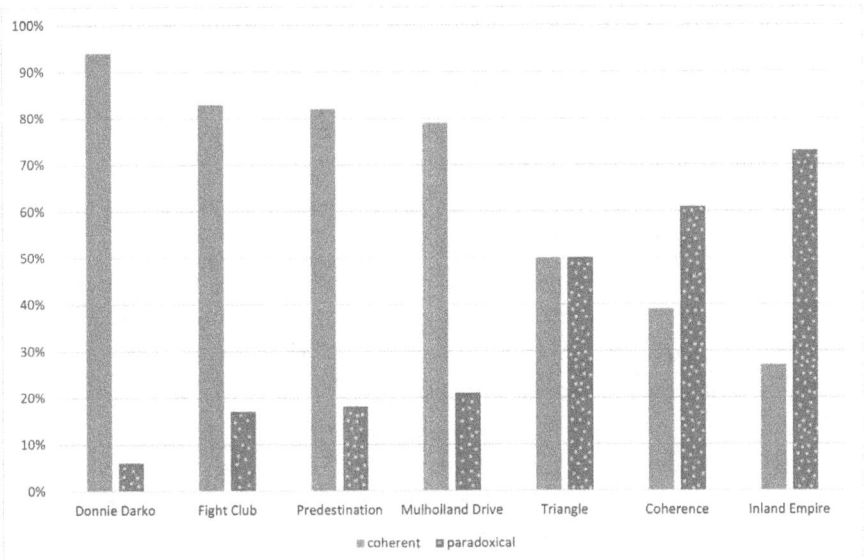

Figure 8.1. Proportion of narrative portions representing coherent vs. paradoxical identities in some 'impossible puzzle films'. © András Bálint Kovács.

learn that she is waiting for a role in a film. Very soon, she is informed that she has got the role and so rehearsals for the film begin. At this stage, we know nothing about her: her life, her marriage, her environment, or why this role is so important for her. The story seems to focus on the potentially dangerous relationship between Nikki and Devon, which could build up motivations and goals, but before it gets to that point, reality melts into the fictional world of the film to be shot and the legend about the mysterious circumstances of its making. This prevents the viewer from engaging with the protagonist, who, from this point onwards, constantly jumps from one world into another as if she has found herself in different roles with different personalities and destinies. Most of the time, she looks surprised and anxious as if lost in unknown worlds among unknown and dangerous people.

Mental travel or time travel narratives in which a protagonist passes through various incongruent and incompatible space and time fragments are not rare in popular genres, but as long as the protagonist's goal and motivation are consistent and the individual narrative fragments are coherent in themselves, these leaps of time and space do not excessively challenge the easy processing of the narrative, as proven by the frequency of this narrative type in children's tales. A quest, an investigation, a mission to accomplish, or an escape from danger are the most frequent motivations and goals of this type of adventure story. In *Inland Empire*, Nikki does not escape, nor does she have an explicit mission, a mystery to investigate, or anything to look for.

Her mental state suddenly detaches her from reality, which probably has to do with Devon's invitation to take her out for dinner. The next scene is a shooting scene of an erotic encounter between the two of them, as if it is a direct continuation of them starting a relationship. The following scene is again a shooting scene, but in this one, Nikki gets confused. In her role as Susan, frightened, she says: 'Something's happened. I think my husband knows about you. About us. He'll kill you and me. He'll...' Suddenly, she steps out of her role, looks around surprised and laughing, and says out loud: 'Damn! This sounds like the dialogue of our script!' Then we hear the voice of the director: 'Cut, cut it. What's going on?' It is clear that Nikki was talking as Nikki in the role of Susan, confused by the realization that the relationship she just accepted to initiate with Devon makes her identify with her role as Susan, who is in a similar situation in the story of the film they are shooting.

This scene is followed by a producer explaining to Devon that there is no proof that this film is cursed; Hollywood is full of stories, and they are just stories grown out from imagination that surround us every day and should not be taken as truths. This sounds like another warning to Devon to stay away from Nikki. Nonetheless, the next scene shows Nikki and Devon making love. But Nikki is entirely confused now. She talks about a memory of yesterday, of which she knows that it is tomorrow, and she tells Devon that she is Nikki, but Devon calls her Sue.

This sequence of scenes suggests that it is her adulterous sexual desire that triggers the confusion, with this feeling pushing her into different imaginary roles and situations. What her husband told Devon about Nikki's unfree status as a wife and his right to control her may provide some background for this feeling. This allows for an interpretation according to which one of the links connecting subsequent scenes in the film is the abuse of women, which is confirmed by the closure of the structure being represented by the return of the young woman we saw at the beginning crying while watching the television, who was later battered by a pimp, now reuniting with her husband and son. The young woman is associated with the prostitute in the first scene whose head was blurred (as both rooms contain some of the same furniture), and is also associated with Nikki, who appears in this room and kisses her as if liberating her, before disappearing like a ghost.

No concrete motivation or goals result from this recurring theme for Nikki. Instead of a practical motivation, a certain feeling of being threatened or endangered links the different scenes. She finds herself in situations in various roles that can be associated with this theme of abused women: as a prostitute, as a woman who takes revenge on the man who tried to rape her, and as a battered wife whose son has died. None of these realities is coherent in itself; each of them represents fragments of possible stories. Not only does Nikki not have a coherent motivation throughout these segments, but the segments have no internal narrative arcs either. This structure can only be found in films usually categorized as 'art cinema', where the mental travel type of narration does not suppose any active goal-oriented behaviour from the protagonist, and where narrative coherence is more commonly ensured by the wandering through and exploration of different mental states, memories and fantasies loosely associated through certain themes.

Conclusion

As I have tried to show, narrative puzzles complicating time and space represent no considerable obstacle for enjoyability for a statistically large audience, as evidenced by the outstanding popularity of some puzzle films. The biggest threat to large-scale acceptance by an audience is when the narrative breaks the protagonist's identity, though some compensating techniques can considerably attenuate the disturbing effects of paradoxical character identity.

I proposed that the reason for this is that the identity of the protagonist is the anchor of the viewer's engagement in the narration: as long as the coherence of character motivation and goal is assured, a lot of space–time inconsistencies can be tolerated. I also proposed that the wider popularity and, supposedly, the enjoyability of such films is contingent on the coherent portion of the narrative, which is typically around 80 per cent of the running time. For most audiences, the real difficulty in comprehension (and thus enjoyability) arises when disruption of character coherence is not compensated, either by generic prototypes or compensation techniques (such as hinting at mental disturbances) or a large amount of linear and coherent narration.

Uncompensated representations of paradoxical identities form a long tradition that goes back to early avant-garde cinema. Prototypicality is one of the main criteria of ease of aesthetic processing, and hence, the widespread enjoyability of works of art. Recognizing a prototype is subject to exposure to forms based on that prototype; therefore, cultural evolution may transform refused forms simply through habituation – making the unacceptable acceptable. However, I suggested that narrative consistency is anchored first and foremost in the coherence of character identity, goal and motivation. Unity of time and space may, in this respect, be secondary. My conjecture is, therefore, that uncompensated disruption of character identity and motivation is the strongest obstacle in this habituation process.

András Bálint Kovács is Professor at the Film Department of ELTE University, Budapest, Hungary. He teaches history of modern cinema, film analysis and psychology of film perception. He has been a visiting professor at École Normale Supérieure, Paris, Université de la Nouvelle Sorbonne, Paris, University of Stockholm and is a recurring visiting professor at U.C. San Diego. He has been an artistic and script advisor for a number of films, including films of Béla Tarr. For eight years, he has been a board member of the Hungarian Film Fund. Currently, he conducts research into the perception of shot scales and causal thinking in film viewing. His books include *Screening Modernism* (University of Chicago Press, 2008) and *The Cinema of Béla Tarr* (Columbia University Press, 2013).

References

Berlyne, Daniel E. 1971. *Aesthetics and Psychobiology*. New York: Appleton-Century-Crofts.
Eig, Jonathan. 2003. 'A Beautiful Mind(Fuck): Hollywood Structures of Identity', *Jump Cut* 46.
    Retrieved 3 October 2020 from www.ejumpcut.org/archive/jc46.2003/eig.mindfilms/index.html.
Elsaesser, Thomas. 2011. 'James Cameron's Avatar: Access for All', *New Review of Film and Television*
    Studies 9(3): 247–64.
Field, Syd. 2005. *Screenplay: The Foundation of Scriptwriting*. New York: Delta.
Follows, Stephen. 2019. 'How much does the average movie cost to make?' Retrieved 25 October
    2020 from https://stephenfollows.com/how-much-does-the-average-movie-cost-to-make/.
IMDb. 2021. *Titanic*. Retrieved 12 October 2021 from https://www.imdb.com/title/tt0120338/?ref_=
    fn_al_tt_1.

Kiss, Miklós, and Steven Willemsen. 2017. *Impossible Puzzle Films*. Edinburgh: Edinburgh University Press.
Klecker, Cornelia. 2011. 'Chronology, Causality ... Confusion: When Avant-Garde Goes Classic', *Journal of Film and Video* 63(2): 11–27. https://doi.org/10.5406/jfilmvideo.63.2.0011.
Kovács, András Bálint. 2007. *Screening Modernism*. Chicago: Chicago University Press.
Martindale, Colin. 1984. 'The Pleasures of Thought: A Theory of Cognitive Hedonics', *The Journal of Mind and Behavior* 5: 49–80.
Mittell, Jason. 2015. *Complex TV: The Poetics of Contemporary Television Storytelling*. New York: New York University Press.
Panek, Elliot. 2006. 'The Poet and the Detective: Defining the Psychological Puzzle Film', *Film Criticism* 31(1–2): 62–88.
Papp-Zipernovszky, Orsolya, András Bálint Kovács and Gergely Drótos. 2019. 'Narratív és nem narratív filmes szerkezet befogadásának összehasonlítása EEG-vel és verbális szóasszociációval', *Literatura* 45(4): 422–38.
Principe, Connor P., and Judith H. Langlois. 2012. 'Shifting the Prototype: Experience with Faces Influences Affective and Attractiveness Preferences', *Social Cognition* 30(1): 109–20.
Reber, Rolf, Norbert Schwarz and Piotr Winkielman. 2004. 'Processing Fluency and Aesthetic Pleasure: Is Beauty in the Perceiver's Processing Experience?', *Personality and Social Psychology Review* 8: 364–82.
Robbe-Grillet, Alain. 1963. *Pour un Nouveau Roman*. Paris: Éditions de Minuit.
Rosenberg, Adam. 2010. 'The Unusual Success of "Inception" as Everything a Hit Movie Isn't...Anymore', *MTV*. Retrieved 12 October 2021 from http://www.mtv.com/news/2437181/the-unusual-success-of-inception-as-everything-a-hit-movie-isnt-anymore/.
Rumelhart, David E. 1977. 'Understanding and Summarizing Brief Stories', in David LaBerge and S. Jay Samuels (eds), *Basic Processes in Reading and Comprehension*. Hillsdale, NJ: Lawrence Erlbaum Associates, pp. 265–304.
———. 1980. 'Schemata: The Building Blocks of Cognition', in R. Spiro, B. Bruce and W. Brewer (eds), *Theoretical Issues in Reading Comprehension*, Mahway: Erlbaum Associates, pp. 33–58.
Starbuck, V.N., G.G. Kay, R.C. Platenberg, C.S. Lin and B.A. Zielinski. 2000. 'Functional Magnetic Resonance Imaging Reflects Changes in Brain Functioning with Sedation'. *Human Psychopharmacology* 15: 613–18.
Yussen, Steven R., and Randall L. Glysch. 1993. 'Remembering Stories: Studies of the Limits of Narrative Coherence on Recall', in Steven R. Yussen and M. Cecil Smith (eds), *Reading Across the Life Span: Recent Research in Psychology*. New York: Springer, pp. 293–321. https://doi.org/10.1007/978-1-4612-4376-2_14.

PART III
Novel Pleasures in Contemporary Serial Television

From Complexity to Confusion

CHAPTER 9
Multiform Television

Matthew Campora

Introduction

In the early 2000s, *New Yorker* film critic David Denby wrote about a wave of films with complex narratives that hit global movie screens in the years after *Pulp Fiction* (1994). He suggested that the success of these films marked the discovery by mainstream audiences of something long known in the art cinemas of the world: *the pleasures of narrative complexity*. He further speculated that the formal play offered by films such as *Eternal Sunshine of the Spotless Mind* (2004) and *Babel* (2007) might be understood to expand the spectator's view of what art and entertainment could offer. Since then, there have been significant developments in the journey of these kinds of narratives into the mainstream – most notably, in drama series on cable, commercial and streaming television platforms. Examples range from the playful genre-blending and alternate timelines of *Community* (2009–2015) to the radical fragmentation of *Twin Peaks* Season 3 (2017).

This chapter will explore the rise of complex narrative television and take a closer look at *Mr. Robot* (2015–2019), *Maniac* (2018) and *Russian Doll* (2019–), considering these series' use of multiple ontologies to create narratives that demand more active engagement from viewers, as well as, perhaps, expanding their sense of the pleasures that television can offer. It will contextualize these series through a consideration of complex television and its relationship to the art cinema and the complex narrative films it resembles, demonstrating the ways in which cinematic conventions have been adapted to the series/serial hybrids of the HBO-TV and streaming era. The emergence of complex narrative television parallels the rise of complex narrative cinema, and can be seen as addressing audiences' growing appetite for the pleasures offered by the formal play of these more challenging forms of audiovisual storytelling.

The approach taken draws from cognitive narratology and textual analysis. It will reference the work of television scholars Jeffrey Sconce and Jason Mittell, film scholar David Bordwell, and formalist literary theorist Tzvetan Todorov. In addition, it will build on some of the categories developed in my work on narrative complexity in *Subjective Realist Cinema* (Campora 2014). The three case studies considered were selected on the basis of their use of multiple ontologies, or 'multiform narratives', and while the multiplicity of *Mr. Robot* and *Maniac* result from the combination of a standard, 'objective' (classical realist) mode of narration in tandem with 'subjective realist' levels of narration – which represent a character's imagination as if were just as real as other levels of the narrative – *Russian Doll*'s additional ontologies are 'magical realist' in origin.

Case Studies

Russian Doll is a Netflix series set in New York City and follows Nadia Volvokov (Natasha Lyonne), a computer game developer who experiences a *Groundhog Day*-like spiral of death and rebirth on the night of her 36th birthday: she repeatedly relives a 24–48-hour period, dying at the end of each iteration. Nadia spends the bulk of the series seeking to understand why she is trapped in the spiral and how she might escape it. That she is a game designer provides viewers with a clue as to how to read her experience and the kind of problem solving she must undertake in each iteration of the cycle. *Russian Doll* presents a game-like puzzle narrative for both the central character and the audience as they seek to understand the mystery of what is happening and why, which is part of its pleasure.

Maniac is also set in New York City, though in a dystopian near future. It follows Owen Milgrim (Jonah Hill) and Annie Landsberg (Emma Stone), whose stories come together in the laboratory of Neberdine Pharmaceuticals, where they are participants in a profitable but dangerous trial of experimental drugs meant to be able to cure any malady. Owen is the recently unemployed son of a wealthy industrialist who needs money in order to maintain independence from his toxic family. He also suffers from schizophrenia, which is represented via hallucinations and a recurring delusion featuring a character named Grimsson. Annie is already addicted to one of the drugs being trialled by Neberdine. Viewers learn that she has been traumatized by the death of her younger sister in a recent car accident, and the drug allows her to relive the events of the tragedy over and over again. The alternate ontologies of *Maniac* include the hallucinations and altered states of Owen and Annie, as well as the dream-like experiences that are generated when they begin the drug trial itself, which combines psychoactive chemicals with a computer-generated virtual reality to create a series of simulations that Owen and Annie must navigate and ultimately escape. Like *Russian Doll*, one of its pleasures is the ongoing challenge of assembling its multiform narrative into a coherent story.

Mr. Robot follows computer programmer and hacker Elliot Alderson (Rami Malek) over four seasons as he seeks to topple one of the world's largest financial institutions: E-Corp. In a thematic nod to David Fincher's *Fight Club* (1999), the goal of his first hack is to eradicate the consumer debt records held in E-Corp's databases. In a structural nod to *Fight Club*, each of the seasons of *Mr. Robot* features a narrative twist derived from the unreliable narration of Elliot. It is through him that viewers gain access to the diegesis via a fourth-wall-breaking direct address to a 'friend' (the viewer). The use of narration that is largely restricted to the unreliable perspective of Elliot allows for the creation of a number of subjective realist levels in the narrative that are indistinguishable from the objective level. The unmarked shifts between these levels of narration create an ontologically fragmented narrative that does not resolve until the very last moments of the series. In this way, *Mr. Robot* resembles (and regularly references) complex narrative films such as *The Sixth Sense* (1999), *Abre Los Ojos* (1997) and *Vanilla Sky* (2001). In addition, *Mr. Robot* has narrative similarities to TV series such as *The Sopranos* (1999–2007) (Elliot's relationship with his therapist plays an important role in several seasons) and *Dexter* (2006–2013) (Elliot is a cyber-vigilante acting against criminals such as child pornographers, serial philanderers and murderous corporations who have escaped the justice system).

The narratives of *Mr. Robot*, *Maniac* and *Russian Doll* feature characters who experience varying types of psychosis, and in all three, psychoactive drugs play important roles. This is not coincidental but reflects the close relationship between the style of narration they employ and the unstable and/or delusionary experience of their characters. Multiform narratives have been present since the birth of cinema, and refer to stories with parallel or alternate realities in one or more of their strands. While common in science fiction, horror and fantasy films, with examples ranging from *The Wizard of Oz* (1939) to *The Matrix* (1999), they have also been a mainstay of international art cinema where they have been used to represent the subjective perspectives of characters for nearly a century. Examples from this stream include Robert Weine's *The Cabinet of Dr. Caligari* (1919), Akira Kurosawa's *Rashomon* (1950), Ingmar Bergman's *Wild Strawberries* (1957) and Federico Fellini's *8 ½* (1962), to name but a few.

In TV series such as *Maniac* and *Mr. Robot*, multiform narratives are employed to represent the hallucinations, memories, dreams, nightmares or psychoses of their central characters. The use of the term 'multiform' to describe narratives with multiple ontologies originates with Janet H. Murray, whose *Hamlet on the Holodeck* (1997) considers the roots of multiform narrative in literature, and explores examples from cinema (Murray 1997: 30). Before looking more closely at their migration into the current long-form series of the streaming television era, it is worth considering the rise of 'complex television' more generally and the kinds of pleasure it offers its viewers, including the meta-reflexive mode of viewing that it engenders (Mittell 2015: 42).

Complex Television

When Jeffrey Sconce set out to write about the poetics of television in 2004, he felt he first had to address the concern of critics that such an exploration might not be a valid undertaking (Sconce 2004: 93). For much of its history, television was considered a purely commercial endeavour with little-to-no artistic value. Since the late 1990s, however, this view has changed, and it is now taken for granted that we are in the midst of a golden age of television (McNamara 2015: 21). What started as a handful of HBO series, such as *The Sopranos* and *Six Feet Under* (2001–2005), has become a global competition for supremacy between a group of wealthy American media/technology corporations, with many spending billions of dollars a year to create series with budgets previously unheard of for television. These series are often made by auteur-showrunners, many of whom have migrated from the cinema to the small screen for the freedoms they have been offered and the innovative potential of long-form narrative.

In his exploration of televisual aesthetics, Sconce maps the evolution of the narrative structures underpinning this new style of television. He does this, in part, by tracing Horace Newcomb's typology of four distinct formats of narrative drama that emerged over the course of television's short history: the anthology, the episodic, the serial and the cumulative. The *anthology* format emerged in the 1950s and consisted of live teleplays, with each episode featuring a distinct, self-contained story and a different troupe of actors. The age of anthology television was brief and critically acclaimed. The productions were regarded as being 'on a par with the theatrical stage', and were written by playwrights such as Rod Serling and Paddy Chayefsky (Sconce 2004: 96). Anthologies, however, quickly gave way to the *episodic* format, which offered 'the profound economic and programming advantages of a series featuring standing sets, a continuing cast, and increased durability in syndication', where the self-contained nature of series structure allows for viewers (occasional or otherwise) to experience the pleasure of narrative closure in each episode: for example, crimes are solved and criminals punished, patients' illnesses are cured, and the lonely find love (ibid.).

The next format, the *serial*, existed alongside the episodic drama series from the earliest days of television. It evolved from the serialized fiction of the nineteenth century, as well as from radio soap operas. Daytime serials such as *The Bold and the Beautiful* (1987–) and *Neighbours* (1985–2022) feature ensemble casts and offer narrative structures that are ongoing and open, with each episode containing multiple narrative strands that are interwoven and intercut. Some narrative questions may be resolved in an episode, while numerous others are left open. Prime-time serials of the 1980s, such as *Dallas*, took the formula into the evenings, and required viewers to watch regularly to stay informed of plot developments. These served as important precursors of the fourth format, the *cumulative* narrative (Sconce 2004: 96).

Cumulative narratives were featured in episodic series that also drew on serial elements, allowing 'nuances of plot and character' to accumulate over episodes or even seasons (ibid.). Series of this type existed as early as the 1970s, and include *M*A*S*H** (1972–1983) and *The Mary Tyler Moore Show* (1970–1977), among others. The cumulative narrative was developed further in the 1980s in series such as *Hill Street Blues* (1981–1987) and *St. Elsewhere* (1982–1988), and, importantly, in HBO's original series produced in the late 1990s that added new characteristics to the cumulative narrative to create HBO's own house style.

Both the prime-time serials and the HBO series that followed them are instances of what Jason Mittell refers to as 'complex narrative television', exemplified by the combination of serialized plots with regular or occasional instances of narrative closure at the episodic level (Mittell 2006: 29). The retention of episodic elements in serialized narratives enables the infrequent viewer to experience the pleasure of resolution at the episodic level while rewarding the regular viewer with longer arcs. The combination of ongoing, long-form stories with occasional closure is a key pleasure offered by complex television, with multi-season seriality allowing for character and plot development on a similar scale to that of the novel.

One of HBO's early original productions, *Six Feet Under*, offers an example of how the kind of series/serial hybridity described by Mittell works. Developed by Alan Ball, the academy-award-winning writer of *American Beauty* (1999), *Six Feet Under* comprises roughly one-hour episodes, each of which features an episodic element: a death-and-burial of the week. These self-contained mini-narratives, which resolve in each episode independently of the larger, ongoing serial stories, also have thematic links to the personal lives of the central characters of the series – the Fisher family – who run the funeral home in which the drama is set. The overarching serial elements of the family narrative, by contrast, 'stretch across many episodes, seasons, and the entirety of a series' (Newman 2006: 23). These focus on both the funeral home as a workplace, as well as the personal lives and relationships of the Fisher family. As a result of the critical success of HBO series such as *Six Feet Under*, the series/serial hybrid format had become the dominant mode of scripted dramatic television for cable networks by the early 2000s.

While series/serial hybridity is a key characteristic of these shows, many also feature other types of complexity. For instance, they might include subjective realist narration (*Six Feet Under*), unreliable narration (*Mr. Robot*), metafictional narration (*Russian Doll*) and/or expositionless dialogue (*The Wire*, 2002–2008). As a result, a range of innovative styles of television narrative have emerged that, like the cinema described by Denby, expand viewers' understanding of the possibilities and pleasures of narrative. HBO's influence has been crucial to these developments, and extends beyond their series/serial hybridity to include the use of cinematic genres, the graphic depiction of sex and violence, and the deployment of explicit language. In addition, some of their series are notable for their adaptations of the conventions of complex narrative cinema to long-form drama, all of which work to create an expanded palette of narrative pleasures for audiences.

The HBO Style

HBO's motto from 1996 to 2009, 'It's Not TV, it's HBO', gives an indication of some of the characteristics that defined its series as distinct from those of commercial, free-to-air networks. Some of these innovations developed as a result of their subscription-based freedom from the constraints faced by commercial broadcasters and non-subscription cable competitors. These benefits included the absence of advertisement interruptions, flexible running times, and higher production budgets. They were also free from Federal Communications Commission content regulations regarding 'obscene, indecent, or profane content' (FCC 2016). HBO used this freedom to develop series that were seen to be aesthetically analogous to cinema, pushing episodic drama into cinematic territory in their explicit language, sexual content and graphic violence. In doing this, HBO cultivated a brand based on stylistic traits that contrasted markedly with those of commercial television, and their series have offered an alternative to the increasingly conservative output of Hollywood's teen and global audience-oriented blockbusters and comic book films.

What emerged is an aesthetic regime that film scholar R. Colin Tate referred to as the 'HBO house style of realistic verisimilitude' (Tate 2008: 55). Many of their series are based on film genres: for instance, *The Sopranos* and *Boardwalk Empire* draw on the gangster film; *Deadwood* the western; *Rome* (2005–2007) the epic; *Sex in the City* (1998–2004) melodramas and romantic comedies; *The Wire* the social problem film; and *Game of Thrones* (2011–2019) fantasy (ibid.). Each borrows from and expands on existing generic paradigms as well as the regimes of verisimilitude that regulate them (Tait 2008: 51). What Tait sees as the transformation of genres at the hands of HBO results from the aforementioned house style of realism, in combination with the greatly expanded possibilities of characterization allowed by serialization and long-form drama. The expanded storyworlds and sophisticated characterization, combined with a more adult tone (both in terms of content and mode of address), have become standards of the form. Regarding complexity, series/serial hybridity is the first level, but crucial for this discussion is the fact that many of these early HBO series, and those that have followed, have also incorporated conventions of complex narrative cinema to create another level of complexity and, thus, another level of narrative pleasure.

The Sopranos, for instance, in episodes one and two of season five, employs an embedded, subjective realist narrative strand depicting the subconscious experience of Tony Soprano (James Gandolfini) while in a coma in an intensive care unit after being shot. Tony, in the alternate reality of his dream-like state, has taken on the identity of a character called 'Kevin Finnerty', a businessman in a foreign city who has lost his briefcase. When Tony's heart stops on the objective level of the narrative, Finnerty is invited to join 'his family' in a brightly lit house, where a woman who looks like Tony's deceased mother is seen waiting at the door. As Finnerty hesitates to enter the house (clearly a metaphor for death), the muted voice of Tony's daughter, who is at his bedside in the hospital, can be heard as if coming from the sky: 'Daddy, don't leave us'. Her voice has travelled across the ontological boundary separating the embedded, subjective level of the narrative from the objective level, momentarily dissolving it in an instance of what William Eggington refers to as 'reality bleeding', a form of ontological *metalepsis* (2001: 208).

Metalepsis is the narratological term used by Gerard Genette to describe this kind of effacement of diegetic boundaries (Genette 1980: 236), and 'reality bleeding' of this type was employed in the art cinema of the 1950s and 1960s, particularly in Bergman's *Wild Strawberries* and Fellini's *8½*, in which the central characters' nightmares, daydreams and memories are seamlessly blended with the objective level of the narration. It is not surprising, then, to find critics like William Siska (2011) who have read *The Sopranos* in terms of its relationship to art cinema.

HBO's *Six Feet Under* uses similar conventions, yet on a larger scale. In the first episode of the series, Nathaniel Fisher (Richard Jenkins), the patriarch and founder of 'Fisher & Sons' funeral home, is killed in a car accident as he drives to the airport to pick up his son Nate (Peter Krause). Throughout the five seasons of the series, however, the deceased Nathaniel regularly appears to and converses with the individuals of his family. These manifestations are treated as subjective rather than supernatural: Nathaniel is not a ghost, but his memory continues to influence the thoughts and lives of his family members. Dialogues with other deceased characters are a regular feature of the series, and contribute to what might be considered its subjective realist structure.

In addition, there are other excursions into the characters' imaginations, including an episode in which Nate, a sex addict, has a hallucinatory vision of all the children he has fathered who have been miscarried or aborted over the years. In the scene, he imagines dozens of children of various ages filling the house, and the vision ends with one of them addressing Nate: 'We have the secret to everything, but you'll never know it because you killed us'. In another sequence, from the beginning of the third season, Nate's heart stops during a surgical procedure, and spectators are shown a range of possible/alternative realities that might ensue. Spectators are not certain of the nature of these realities. Are they Nate's imagination, or alternate universes, or just a metafictional tease of the possible choices available to the writers before they settle on the one required by the linearity of the dramatic form? Whatever the case, *Six Feet Under* regularly employs a style of narration that depicts the imagination of its characters in the same way it depicts the empirical world, as well as other, more ambiguous forays that leave spectators on their own to decide how to make sense of them.

Prior to *Six Feet Under* and *The Sopranos*, there had been instances of what Kristin Thompson (2003) described as 'art television' in her analysis of Dennis Potter's BBC miniseries *The Singing Detective* (1986) and the first two seasons of David Lynch's *Twin Peaks* (1990–1991). *The Singing Detective* is a complex, multi-stranded and mixed-ontology miniseries, while *Twin Peaks* is a prime-time serial with a cumulative narrative that combines a murder mystery with serial arcs and multiple levels of narration. Thompson's 'art television' was a direct translation of David Bordwell's characterization of 'art cinema' (1979, 1985) to these series, based on their creators and modes of narration.

Mittell argues that Thompson's attempt to attribute credibility to television via an alignment with art cinema is part of a reactionary tendency of some film scholars to legitimate selected auteur-driven television series while, intentionally or not, denigrating the rest (Mittell 2015: 18). (This is perhaps a further illustration of the challenges faced by television scholars in establishing the legitimacy of television, as mentioned by Sconce.) It also illustrates how previously established art forms are used to bolster the credentials of newer forms, as initially happened with cinema's use of literary and theatrical adaptations to establish its own legitimacy. With HBO, we can see how the network used established Hollywood genres in the first instance, and art cinema conventions in the second, as a part of their strategy to build critical legitimacy for their original series. While shows like *Twin Peaks* and *The Singing Detective* marked key moments in the development of complex narrative television, the HBO series of the late 1990s and onwards continued this movement – ultimately codifying a formal and stylistic model that has been imitated in the productions of a range of networks, including subscription cable outlets such as Showtime, Starz, AMC and the USA Network, as well as Subscription Video On Demand (SVOD) providers such as Amazon, Hulu, Apple and Netflix. The combination of cumulative narratives with the conventions of complex narrative cinema has, in many of the series, yielded genuinely new narrative forms, and new kinds of narrative pleasure as a result.

Understanding Complex Narratives

To better understand these new modes of narration, their conventions, and the pleasures they offer, we can use David Bordwell's cognitive theory of film narration, which considers both the way narratives are structured and how they are perceived; as a theory, it focuses not simply on the formal and stylistic elements that make up a narrative but also on the ways in which audiences make sense of these elements. When considering complex narratives, it investigates how variations on the default mode of visual storytelling – the continuity style of classical narration – create challenges for viewer comprehension. The theory draws from cognitive psychology, which posits that spectators enter the storyworld of a film with an internalized set of expectations 'known to cognitive theorists as *schema-based knowledge*' (Bordwell 2007: 137). The spectator generates a hypothesis or multiple hypotheses based on narrative clues as well as on their knowledge of stories, which are expected to follow a predictable pattern of exposition: 'the introduction of setting and characters – explanation of a state of affairs – complicating action – ensuing events – outcome – ending' (Bordwell 1985: 35).

In regard to narrative construction, Bordwell uses the formalist distinction between 'story' (*fabula*) and 'plot' (*syuzhet*) to describe the difference between the way visual stories present material and the way this material is arranged into a narrative. A plot is the arrangement of the events in the order they are presented, which the spectator must arrange into the story: the coherent, linear arrangement of the events in a cause–effect relationship. In the ongoing process of viewing, however, the story is in a constant state of change (in the mind of the spectator) due to plot variations, and a major element of film style revolves around the structure of the plot. Visual storytellers construct their narratives with an understanding of the ways in which spectators will make meaning from the information presented. Classical narratives employ a style meant to be invisible, and are characterized by their continuity, coherence and cathartic resolution, which is an important facet of the pleasure it offers. But when the predictable patterns of classical exposition are disrupted, when the style is foregrounded, or resolution is withheld or deferred, spectators are forced into different modes of sense-making that, in turn, yield different types of pleasure.

Complex narratives can be understood in contrast to the coherence and continuity of the classical style, and are characterized by their difficulty or inscrutability. They may have temporal or spatial regimes that are fragmented, or their causality may not be clear. Characters may have traits that are contradictory or inconsistent, or there may be doppelgängers or duplicates. There may be important events or information that is missing, or resolution may be withheld, and part of the appeal they offer is their unpredictability. These forms require viewers to entertain multiple and changing hypotheses regarding the story, and offer the pleasure of putting the puzzle together once all of the pieces of the plot have been revealed.

While this may not always be possible – as in the instance of some aspects of *Twin Peaks* season three or in the kinds of impossible puzzle films considered in Kiss and Willemsen's work (2017), which offer different types of pleasure – most films and television series do offer a resolution. The television series that are the focus of the next section are no exception. *Russian Doll*, *Maniac* and *Mr. Robot* feature multiform narratives that are puzzling but not impossible, and as a result, they offer the careful and committed viewer the pleasure of arranging their multilayered plots into coherent stories (in addition to the normal rewards of the occasional resolutions at the episodic level and the in-depth character development of long-form narrative series). In these ways, they all use what Mittell refers to as an 'operational aesthetic' – a self-conscious mode of storytelling that encourages viewers to care as much about the mechanics of the narration as they do about the story itself (2015: 46).

Russian Doll

In the first episode of *Russian Doll*, viewers are introduced to the protagonist, Nadia, as she stares into a bathroom mirror on the night of her birthday. Nadia then exits the bathroom; has a conversation with her friend Maxine (Greta Lee), with whom she smokes a Ketamine-laced joint; hooks up with literature professor Mike Kershaw (Jeremy Bobb); goes for a walk to search for her lost cat; and then is struck by a taxicab and killed. She immediately wakes up back in the bathroom, staring into the mirror, where the episode began, but with complete recollection of what has just transpired. Confused, Nadia begins the cycle over again, dying again, then again, and again – over twenty times across the first season's eight episodes.

While there is significant repetition, each iteration represents a different ontology with different features. For instance, each time Nadia exits the bathroom, there are fewer guests at the party. This creates a distinct sense that her world is shrinking and that she has a finite number of lives in which to solve the puzzle. Nadia's experience of the spiral is reminiscent of *Groundhog Day*'s Phil Connors (Bill Murray). Like Phil, she remembers each iteration, allowing her to learn from them, and the episodic aspect of the series is built around this growth of knowledge resembling that of video gameplay. In addition, the repetition of the temporal spiral forces Nadia to respond to the punishment-by-death aspect of the plot by seeking to 'master the rules of the game' (Buckland 2014: 1988). While the narrative logic is similar to that of a video game, the process she undertakes to master the rules is also similar to the cognitive challenge the viewer is experiencing, which, in turn, is similar to one described by Tzvetan Todorov in his work on *uncanny* and *marvellous* narratives (1973: 41).

Todorov posits that when a reader/viewer is confronted with a seemingly supernatural event in an otherwise naturalistic narrative, they experience a hesitation – a cognitive pause during which they must decide how to make sense of the event. Is the event actually supernatural? Or is there a naturalistic explanation? Depending on how these matters are resolved – whether by the text itself (if it provides an explanation) or by a decision of the reader (where left ambiguous) – a generic determination can be made (Todorov 1973: 25). If the events are supernatural and occur in an otherwise realist narrative – as in films like *Being John Malkovich* (Jonze, 1999) – we might say it is 'magic realist' (Todorov's 'fantastic') (ibid.: 32). If the events prove to be naturalistic, the genre may be determined on the basis of the kind of explanation offered; if it is scientific (or even quasi-scientific), as in *Solaris* (Tarkovsky, 1972), wherein the doppelgängers are explained as manifestations made possible by space travel to the planet Solaris, it is science fiction ('marvellous') (ibid.: 41). If the events are imaginary, whether the result of hallucination, dreams, drugs or psychosis – as in *Mulholland Drive* (Lynch, 2001) – it is 'subjective realist' ('uncanny') (ibid.).

Russian Doll situates its central character within a mystery, and Nadia's response follows a similar process to the one described by Todorov, with her hesitation transposed to the viewer – who is initiated into the puzzle aspect of its complex narrative along with her – and a focus on the mechanics of the narration itself. Initially, Nadia suspects the events must have a rational explanation. She considers that she may be hallucinating as a result of the drugs she has taken or possibly be having a psychotic episode. After investigating these possibilities, however, she rules out the uncanny and considers supernatural (fantastic) explanations: first, that Maxine's apartment, located in a former Yeshiva school, might be haunted. After eliminating this as a possibility, however, Nadia meets Alan (Charlie Barnett), who is trapped in his own death spiral. As the two of them work together to solve the mystery, they eventually come to understand that, much like one of the video games that Nadia has designed (and Alan has played), there is a 'glitch' in the code of their narratives. To repair the glitch, they conclude that they must return to the night of their respective deaths and try to save each other. What they discover in the final iterations of their respective loops, however, is that each has gone back to a different reality than the other, and that they must save a version of the other who has no memory of previous iterations. This narrative twist results from a subversion of the typical 'foldback' structure of a video game, where the plot *folds back* to a single ontology: *Russian Doll* folds back to dual ontologies, where the characters are once again strangers to one another (Buckland 2014: 189).

The conclusion of *Russian Doll* thus provides a range of pleasures. Nadia and Alan's developing romance, their progressive elimination of possibilities, and their work towards resolving the season's primary enigma offer the viewer a great deal of satisfaction. Yet, several questions are still left unanswered: will the two universes merge back together? Are all the other possible universes, in which Nadia and Alan have died, actual existing universes or merely figments of Nadia's imagination (and thus, subjective/uncanny)? Thus, while viewers may have experienced a satisfying resolution in terms of the diegesis, they are also left with open questions. In this way, *Russian Doll* offers the pleasure of resolution typical of the classical style (and episodic drama series) while also offering a degree of openness and ambiguity more common to seriality and narrative complexity. Further, it creates what Mittell refers to as an operational reflexivity – a mode of viewing that offers pleasures beyond the simple focus on 'diegetic action' to a greater awareness of the storytelling mechanics themselves (Mittell 2015: 47).

Maniac

In contrast to *Russian Doll*, Netflix's *Maniac* is a limited miniseries and concludes with a high degree of resolution. It features a multiform structure resulting from a standard level of narration combined with a series of embedded narratives.

The embedded levels are generated by the dream-like experiences of the characters while under the influence of the drugs they take in some clinical trials. These experiences are influenced by the simulations of an artificially intelligent supercomputer, GRTA – named after and voiced by Greta Mantleray (Sally Field), the pop-psychologist mother of one of the researchers. Although the GRTA was originally programmed to assist the researchers in their attempts to resolve their subjects' trauma, 'she' has become depressed after the death of one of the study's head researchers. As a result of her grief, GRTA tries to trap the test subjects in the simulation to save them from future pain. Spectators learn that this would result in the subject becoming permanently comatose in the real world, euphemistically referred to by the Neberdine staff as a 'McMurphy'. There are three pills taken by the subjects in the trial, and the dream-like states of consciousness induced by the pills are guided by the GRTA. Owen and Annie's experiences under the influence of the second and third pills are shared as the result of a hardware malfunction in which the circuits connecting them to the computer are fused together. These experiences are intercut with the diegetic level of the story to create a complex, multilayered and multi-ontological plot, and part of the pleasure of watching *Maniac* is, once again, the meta-reflexive mode of viewing that it requires: in this instance, the attempt to understand how the multiple layers relate to one another.

According to Genette, all fictional narratives have at least two levels: an *extradiegetic* and an *intradiegetic* (1980: 162). The extradiegetic is the level at which the narration happens, which in visual storytelling is the level of the camera-narrator. The intradiegetic (or simply 'diegetic') is the primary level of the story being told – where the action takes place – which, in *Maniac*, is a dystopian New York City of the near future. Additional, *metadiegetic* levels exist when embedded narratives occur within the diegetic world – as with *Maniac*'s mini-narratives that result from the psychoactive drugs in tandem with the computer simulations. These experiences represent metadiegetic levels and take the form of episodic narratives set in what might be described as short genre films, in which Owen and Annie play central roles.

The first of the embedded narratives is a kind of heist film in which Annie appears as a nurse called Lin, who, with the help of her husband Bruce (Owen), must kidnap a rare ring-tailed lemur from a furrier who has stolen it from her. The initial appearance of their doppelgängers is confusing for the viewer, as their appearance, names and demeanour have all been transformed within the metadiegetic narrative. The second takes the form of a period mystery in which they feature as Ollie and Arlie – a pair of con artists who attend a seance at the mansion of a wealthy antiquities collector to steal the lost chapter of Cervantes' *Don Quixote*, which is rumoured to have the power to allow its reader to remain in their fantasy world forever (much as GRTA seeks to do with the subjects of the trial itself). Here, the plots and themes of the metadiegetic narratives begin overlapping with events on the diegetic level, and it is also here that Annie begins a kind of metaleptic toggling between different instances of the embedded narratives. Her boundary crossing is enabled by her growing awareness that she is in a simulation, which also yields an increasing sense of agency. This is paralleled by the viewer's growing awareness of the rules that govern the narration and its uncanny nature. In this way, there is a similarity to *Russian Doll*, as both transpose the characters' experiences to the viewer through a kind of epistemic doubling.

The multiple metadiegetic layers and the metaleptic boundary crossings create a roller coaster ride of a narrative. In Todorovian terms, the naturalizing of the uncanny events via Owen's schizophrenia and drugs on the one hand, and the computer simulations on the other, offer both subjective realist and science-fiction-based explanations (uncanny and marvellous) of the questions raised by the hallucinations, doppelgängers and magical events. *Maniac*, like *Russian Doll*, weaves together its multiple ontologies into a complex but ultimately comprehensible story, offering its viewers the pleasures of a complex puzzle that concludes with a high degree of resolution and catharsis. In addition to the appeal of traditional narrative, it also adds the operational aesthetic in which the awareness and challenges of its complex plot structure also offer the viewer pleasure (Mittell 2015: 43).

Mr. Robot

Mr. Robot, like *Maniac*, features multiple subjective metadiegetic levels. These are generated via the unreliable narration of its central character, Elliot, who is the focalizer of much of the narrative, and the series begins with Elliot directly addressing the audience: 'Hello, friend'. This breaking of the fourth wall is naturalized through the later revelation of Elliot's mental illness – the audience is simply one of his imaginary friends, and their close alignment with his perspective allows for a number of the narrative twists that occur across the series. These twists offer shock and surprise for viewers, functioning as instances of what might be described as 'narrative special effects' (Mittell 2015: 43). For instance, near the end of the first season, it is revealed that the mysterious Mr. Robot (Christian Slater), who resembles Elliot's deceased father, is not actually a separate being, but that Elliot has dissociative personality disorder and that he and Mr. Robot are one and the same person – or rather, they share the same body. This revelation resembles the twist in *Fight Club* when it is revealed that Tyler Durden (Brad Pitt) is actually Jack's (Edward Norton) alter ego.

In the next season, another twist takes place when it is revealed that much of the action (at least the action that centres on Elliot) has actually taken place inside the prison where he is incarcerated. This fact has been concealed from the audience through the (unreliable) visual representation of his experience, which is achieved through a form of subjective narration that visually depicts the delusions Elliot experiences rather than a typical objective depiction of the world as it would be if he were not delusional, much like in *A Beautiful Mind* (Howard, 2001). In the fourth and final season, Elliot has interactions with another alter ego, his eight-year-old self, who helps him to uncover the repressed childhood trauma revealed to be the source of his fragmented psyche, as well as the antisocial aspects of his activism. And finally, *Mr. Robot* ends with the revelation that the narrator himself, whom viewers have come to know as 'Elliot Alderson', is not actually Elliot, but yet another of his alter egos – referred to as 'The Mastermind' – who was, in fact, responsible for the hack of E-Corp and many other major events of the four seasons, including the destruction of the mysterious machine built under the nuclear power plant where Elliot's father worked.

These progressive revelations culminate in the real Elliot Alderson reawakening in its closing scene. The twists are designed as narrative special effects to shock and amaze viewers, who have been primed to watch the series in a meta-reflexive mode, attuned to the complex structures at play. Of course, it is not until the final episode of *Mr. Robot* that the full scope of its unreliable narration is revealed, and that the numerous layers that have made up its multiform narrative become evident to the viewers – viewers who are finally in a position to make determinations regarding its uncanny narrative and fragmented ontology, and thus, to assemble all the events of the plot into one story.

In contrast to the continuity and coherence of the classical style of narration, which generally offers viewers a reliable, objective diegesis, *Mr. Robot* is thus characterized by its unreliability and fragmented diegesis. While shifts between ontological levels are normal in classical narratives with multiple levels, they are marked for the sake of coherence. For instance, a transition from a dream to a waking state (or vice-versa) would usually include a point when the transition is indicated; at the end of some shocking event in a dream, the dreamer awakens, and audiences are reoriented in the diegesis.

Classical narration features a range of markers to signal dreams or other ontologies, including soft-focus photography, canted camera angles, distorted decor, slow-motion cinematography and slurred sound, among others (Bordwell 2006: 15). These kinds of markers are used to keep different levels of narration clearly demarcated. Ontological fragmentation results when shifts between ontologies are not marked, as in *Mr Robot*, which often leaves viewers without essential information regarding the ontological status of the world depicted.

The subjective realist representation of Elliot's experience is the mechanism through which *Mr. Robot* surprises its viewers, season after season. Its systematic subversion of the conventions of realist narration can be seen as part of a new phase in the evolution of narrative complexity to which each of these series belongs. Like *Russian Doll* and *Maniac*, *Mr. Robot* offers the pleasure of complex puzzle solving. Its multiple, subjective, metadiegetic layers evoke operational reflexivity on the part of the viewer, whose cognitive experience is of a constantly changing set of narrative hypotheses as a result.

Conclusion

Russian Doll, *Maniac* and *Mr. Robot* are exemplars of new modes of televisual narration. At the episodic level, each offers occasional resolution and season-long narrative arcs that occasionally resolve while also leaving open questions for the subsequent seasons to address. They conclude with (mostly) definitive and cathartic endings, offering both the expected pleasures of the series/serial hybrid, as well as those offered by the operational aesthetic in which there is pleasure in the spectacular moments of the narrative and focus on the complex mechanics of the plot itself (Mittell 2015: 42). As such, these series resemble the kinds of complex narrative films discussed by David Denby at the beginning of this chapter, and can be seen to offer their viewers an expanded set of narrative pleasures.

In *Subjective Realist Cinema*, I argued that the style of narrative complexity developed in the independent cinema since the 1990s offers audiences an exciting alternative to the big-budget spectacle of the Hollywood blockbuster in a kind of 'low-budget cinema of attraction' (Campora 2017: 54). Using techniques developed in what Tom Gunning refers to as the 'avant-garde trajectory of the cinema of attractions' (1990: 61), complex films such as *Memento* and *Eternal Sunshine of the Spotless Mind* subvert audience expectations with shocking narrative twists and/or the complex construction of time and space. These films, and others like them, have roots that can be traced back through the experimental and art cinema of the postwar era to the formalist silent cinema and ultimately back to the trick films of Georges Méliès. The exhibitionistic techniques they employ add shock and surprise as additional pleasures to those already inherent in narrative.

The complex narrative drama series under consideration in this chapter can be seen to expand this tradition of cinematic storytelling to the creation of new televisual modes. *Russian Doll*, *Maniac* and *Mr. Robot* all use complex, long-form narratives to create novel and, at times, shocking experiences for their viewers. Each features the kind of series/serial hybridity described by Mittell, and is part of the multiform narrative tradition that, itself, extends back through the art cinema of the 1950s and further back to the German expressionism of the 1920s. In combining conventions common to complex narrative cinema with long-form narrative, they represent the synthesizing of a range of different styles and modes of film and television narratives into a form of complex and often puzzling television series that offer viewers similar kinds of narrative pleasure to those known by readers of modernist and postmodernist literature, as well as denizens of the art house cinemas of the world, for well over a century.

Matthew Campora is the Head of Screen Studies at the Australian Film Television and Radio School in Sydney, and the author of *Subjective Realist Cinema: From Expressionism to Inception* (Berghahn Books, 2014).

References

Bordwell, David. 1979. 'The Art Cinema as a Mode of Film Practice'. *Film Criticism* (Fall): 56–64.
———. 1985. *Narration in the Fiction Film*. Madison: University of Wisconsin Press.
———. 2006. *The Way Hollywood Tells It*. Berkeley: University of California Press.

———. 2007. *The Poetics of Cinema*. Oxford: Taylor & Francis.
Buckland, Warren. 2014. '*Source Code*'s Video Game Logic', in Warren Buckland (ed.), *Hollywood Puzzle Films*. New York: Routledge, pp. 185–97.
Campora, Matthew. 2014. *Subjective Realist Cinema: From Expressionism to Inception*. New York: Berghahn Books.
Denby, David. 2007. 'The New Disorder: Adventures in Film Narrative,' *New Yorker*, 5 March. Retrieved 24 September 2020 from http://www.newyorker.com/arts/critics/atlarge/2007/03/05/070305crat_atlarge_denby.
Eggington, William. 2001. 'Reality Is Bleeding', *Configurations* 9: 207–29.
Federal Communications Commission (FCC). 2016. Retrieved 1 October 2016 from https://www.fcc.gov/media/television/television.
Genette, Gerard. 1980. *Narrative Discourse Revisited*. Trans. Jane Lewin. Ithaca, NY: Cornell University Press.
Gunning, Tom. 1990. 'The Cinema of Attractions: Early Film, Its Spectator, and the Avant Garde', in Thomas Elsaesser (ed.), *Early Cinema: Space, Frame, Narrative*. London: British Film Institute, pp. 56–62.
Kiss, Miklós, and Steven Willemsen. 2017. *Impossible Puzzle Films: A Cognitive Approach to Contemporary Complex Cinema*. Edinburgh: Edinburgh University Press.
McNamara, James. 2015. 'The Golden Age of Television?' *Australian Book Review* (April): 21–31.
Mittell, Jason. 2006. 'Narrative Complexity in Contemporary American Television', *Velvet Light Trap* (58) (Fall): 29–40.
———. 2015. *Complex TV: The Poetics of Contemporary Television Storytelling*. New York: NYU Press.
Murray, Janet. 1997. *Hamlet on the Holodeck: The Future of Narrative in Cyberspace*. New York: The Free Press.
Newman, Michael Z. 2006. 'From Beats to Arcs: Towards a Poetics of Narrative Television', *Velvet Light Trap* (58) (Fall): 16–28.
Sconce, Jeffrey. 2004. 'What If? Charting Television's New Textual Boundaries', in Lynn Spigel and Jan Olsson (eds), *Television after TV: Essays on a Medium in Transition*. Durham, NC: Duke University Press, pp. 93–112.
Siska, William. 2011. '"If All This is for Nothing": *The Sopranos* as Art Cinema', in David Lavery, Douglas L. Howard and Paul Levinson (eds), *The Essential Sopranos Reader*. Louisville: The University of Kentucky Press. Retrieved 16 September 2019 from https://www.yumpu.com/en/document/read/12353281/sopranos-david-lavery.
Tait, R. Colin. 2008. 'The HBO-ification of Genre', *Cinefile* 4(1): 50–57.
Thompson, Kristin. 2003. *Storytelling in Film and Television*. Cambridge, MA: Harvard University Press.
Todorov, Tzvetan. 1973. *The Fantastic: A Structural Approach to a Literary Genre*. Trans. Richard Howard. Cleveland, OH: Case Western Reserve University.

CHAPTER 10
'I Can't Keep Track of Any of It Anymore'
Cognitive Challenge and Other Aesthetic Appeals in *Community*

Jason Gendler

Introduction

This chapter will discuss an episode of the television series *Community*, inquiring into how it creates aesthetic appeal by playing with notions of narrative complexity and cognitive challenge. *Community* is a comedy about a diverse group of students at a community college, but the series often devotes entire episodes to hilarious, reflexive parody and pastiche of other television shows, films, or even entire genres, such as *Law and Order*, *My Dinner with Andre* (1981), spaghetti westerns, zombie films, stop-motion animated Christmas specials, and clip shows, among many other subjects. This chapter will focus on the ninth episode of season two, 'Conspiracy Theories and Interior Design', which hilariously parodies the conspiracy theory genre, paying particular attention to the climax, which features a dizzying series of plot twists, reversals and double-crosses that offer viewers the cognitive challenge of recasting each character's motivations and behaviour with each new revelation. Accordingly, the scene would seem to be characterized by what Jason Mittell (2015: 43–44) calls a 'narrative special effect', or a particularly heightened moment of 'operational aesthetics' – a feature of complex television where the reflexive foregrounding of the narration's self-consciousness invites viewers to marvel at how the story is told rather than being fully immersed in the narrative diegesis.

However, while this climax certainly invites viewers to marvel at the storytelling, I will argue that the episode's parody of the conspiracy theory genre and the genre's accordant narrative complexity actually alters the scene's aesthetic appeal. While there may be some pleasure to derive from the cognitively challenging activities Mittell describes as central to appreciating narrative special effects or operational aesthetics (such as performing formal analysis or 'forensic' work regarding the narration's manipulation of information), operating alongside and, in this case, likely superseding these potential pleasures (both in the climax and in the episode more broadly) are a different set of aesthetic appeals. These appeals include recognizing how the episode cleverly parodies conspiracy theory genre tropes, how the episode's conspiracies deftly incorporate *Community*'s serial qualities, like ongoing relationships and well-established character traits, and the humour that results from absurd contrasts in general. Ultimately, I will show that narratively complex television comedy can create different kinds of aesthetic appeal aside from (or in addition to) the cognitive challenge of appreciating operational aesthetics or engaging in forensic fandom. In turn, I will be speaking more broadly to the general appeal of *Community* and its tendency towards reflexive parody, as well as the kinds of pleasure generated from parodying very difficult cognitive challenges.

The Pleasures and Limitations of the 'Operational Aesthetic' in the Climax

In 'Conspiracy Theories and Interior Design', one of the main characters, Jeff – a fairly selfish disbarred lawyer who has tried to coast through life by relying on his charm and sharp rhetorical skills – has created and enrolled in a fake course, 'Conspiracy Theories in US History', in order to get a free credit. When the dean of the college catches him, Jeff is surprised to discover a stranger claiming to be the course's instructor, Professor Professorson, vouching for both Jeff and the course. Jeff spends much of the episode reluctantly trying to get to the bottom of this conspiracy: who Professorson really is, and why he helped prevent Jeff from getting caught in his lie. He is prodded into this investigation by his study group partner Annie, a highly strung, earnest overachiever. Eventually, they discover that the dean had conspired with Professorson (who is really a drama professor named Garrity) to concoct a fake conspiracy about the college's night school being riddled with fake courses, all in an effort to manipulate Jeff into actually learning something about conspiracies. Irritated by the dean's attempt to manipulate him, Jeff then asks Garrity if the theatre department has any prop guns, initiating a conspiracy with Annie and Garrity to make the dean regret his conspiring against Jeff.

In the dizzying climax that follows, Annie, Jeff and Garrity meet with the dean to 'expose' the fake night school conspiracy. The dean feigns mild surprise over the news, but when he is on the cusp of forgiving Garrity, Annie pulls out a gun and shoots Garrity. The dean appears to be genuinely shocked and dismayed by this turn of events, and as Annie begins justifying murder as a punishment befitting Garrity's crime, the dean pulls out his own gun and shoots Annie. Jeff reacts to Annie's murder with what seems to be genuine surprise and anger, and reveals what viewers have likely surmised: Annie's gun was a fake, and they had staged Garrity's murder to punish the dean for being deceitful. When the dean levels the same accusation against Jeff, Jeff brandishes his own gun and shoots the dean. Now it is Annie's turn to appear genuinely shocked and dismayed, rising from her apparent murder to frantically explain to Jeff that she had helped the dean devise the original conspiracy (fake night school classes) and that her staged murder was the final step in teaching Jeff a lesson about academic integrity. Jeff momentarily appears to be horrified over having needlessly shot the dean, until he walks over to the dean and helps him up from the ground, revealing to Annie that the dean's murder was really a part of yet another conspiracy – Jeff and the dean's – to teach Annie a lesson about not conspiring behind the backs of your friends. Annie appears to be genuinely hurt by the revelation, protesting that she only conspired with the dean because she loves Jeff, and then brandishes yet another gun and trains it on Jeff. The dean is taken aback by Annie's vengefulness as she explains how hurt she was by Jeff ignoring her all summer after they had kissed at the end of the previous school year. Jeff appears to react with a mixture of regret and fear, especially after Annie reassures him that her gun is real, and reminds him of her history of mental instability. When she finally shoots Jeff, the dean screams in horror over what he thinks is a real murder, and when he bemoans Annie's actions, she confronts him over why he conspired against both her *and* Jeff, at which point the dean snaps, screaming, 'I don't know! I can't keep track of any of it anymore! I just keep teaming up with whoever suggests it!' Upon the dean's admission, Jeff rises from the ground (soliciting more shocked screams from the dean), and together with Annie, the two chastise the dean for his willingness to conspire with anyone who approached him. At this point, Garrity collects all of the prop guns, only for a policeman to barge into the room and shoot Garrity, horrifying the other three. However, after the policeman chastises them for their cavalier use of prop guns, Garrity surprises the other three again when he arises from the ground to declare the 'scene' over – and the series of twists with it.

This climax offers viewers a lot to unpack. Certainly, it can be described partly by Mittell's operational aesthetic. I agree with Mittell (2015: 47) that some of its pleasures 'are embedded in a level of awareness that transcends the traditional focus on diegetic action typical of most mainstream popular narratives'. However, because this episode is a parody, this transcendence differs from what Mittell suggests in his description of the activities solicited by operational aesthetics. Mittell consistently equates appreciation of operational aesthetics with viewers behaving like formal analysts: figuring out how the narration 'guides, manipulates, deceives, and misdirects viewers', and 'dissecting the techniques used to convey spectacular displays of storytelling craft' (ibid.: 43, 47). Later, he describes operational aesthetics as encouraging 'the conscious accumulation, analysis, and hypothesizing of information concerning how the story is told' (ibid.: 169–70). In this example from *Community*, consciously analysing how the story is told could conceivably include appreciating how the scene executes its parody of conspiracy theory genre conventions. After all, understanding a parody as such requires viewers to be familiar with the style or conventions of the original work or genre to which the parody refers, and to recognize how the parody applies those same conventions to inappropriate subject matter (Genette 1997; Chatman 2001: 36). In other words, parody involves drawing attention to artifice, to a work's formal features.

However, recognizing how a work is in dialogue with others – or, more basically, simply noticing form – seems to be a different mode of viewer engagement than the much more deliberate probing or analytical efforts that Mittell describes through operational aesthetics. Engaging with genre parody rewards intertextual or generic knowledgeability more than pouring over the narration to gain insight into how it 'guides, manipulates, deceives, and misdirects viewers'. In 'Conspiracy Theories and Interior Design', the latter might involve unpacking each of the climax's new revelations in terms of how they accord with the characters' previous behaviour (particularly the discrepancies between their perceived and actual ranges of knowledge), determining precisely when each of the characters hatched their conspiracies and began lying to each other, and, in turn, reconstructing the narrative in light of the many elided scenes of conspiring revealed by the characters during the climax. While these kinds of effortful or challenging cognitive tasks are certainly available to viewers in this example from *Community*, we can more fully account for why the scene is enjoyable by also considering the pleasure derived from genre parody.

First, though, let us approach this climax from the perspective of operational aesthetics to assess precisely what sorts of aesthetic pleasures can be derived from analysing how the narration manipulates viewers, using Annie as an example. Annie's behaviour corresponds with her range of knowledge and ultimate motivation throughout the scene, and it is possible to make plausible moment-by-moment inferences about her mental state as she plays out the string of the many overlapping conspiracies in which she is involved. She shoots Garrity as a part of the conspiracy that Jeff concocted in the scene preceding the climax, which was meant to teach the dean not to manipulate Jeff. She then plays along with getting shot by the dean because she is enacting the conclusion of the initial conspiracy she had hatched with the dean to teach Jeff a lesson about academic fraud, and she wants to trick the dean into thinking that she is unaware that he has been conspiring with Jeff behind her back. Then, when Jeff shoots the dean, she feigns surprise and dismay to convince the dean that his conspiracy with Jeff (to teach Annie a lesson about being a good friend) is successful. However, her reaction here is actually a part of the scene's *fourth* conspiracy: Jeff and Annie teaching the dean a lesson about conspiring with whoever approaches him. Her feigned pain over being the subject of their conspiracy against her, when combined with the serial information she raises, motivates her shooting of Jeff and draws out the dean's confession that he became too confused to follow all of the conspiracies he was involved in. Annie (along with Jeff and the dean) is unaware of the fifth and final conspiracy between Garrity and the police (meant to teach the others that prop guns should be treated more seriously), hence her genuine surprise and horror over Garrity being shot a second time.

Her ultimate goal is to chastise the dean for conspiring with anyone who approached him, and it dictates her behaviour throughout the scene. However, discerning how her range of knowledge and motivation corresponds both with what she knows and what she wants others to *think* she knows – especially in light of all of the elided scenes revealed by the characters – yields only minimal aesthetic dividends. Once one has full command of all of the conspiracies and each character's involvement, it becomes clear that Annie and Jeff are faking all of their reactions to each surprise (except the final one). They know about the other conspiracies and are just playing along, and the entire scene becomes somewhat of a rote exercise in how the conspiracies are affecting the dean, as he is the only character in the dark. More importantly, knowing that Annie and Jeff are faking their surprise does not add any nuance or complexity to their behaviour, or any anticipatory pleasure for viewers, both because they play nearly all of it straight and because there is not enough time for the characters to exhibit much behaviour that takes on retrospective significance. The closest the scene comes to providing retrospective significance or added nuance is when Jeff glances twice at the dean to scan his reaction after Annie brandishes the fourth prop gun, and when Annie motivates her shooting of Jeff with an inflated account of their romantic liaisons. However, the former is a brief performative note, and the latter is made pleasurable not because it provides retrospective hints that Annie and Jeff are manipulating the dean into believing their conspiracy, but because it calls on serial knowledge – a point discussed in greater detail below.

More significantly, whatever aesthetic pleasures are derived from appreciating the operational aesthetics of this scene might be cancelled out by the difficulty of arriving at them. Reasoning out Annie's range of knowledge and motivations is a moderately difficult cognitive activity to engage in even retrospectively, let alone when watching the scene for the first time. Indeed, it is likely to be nearly impossible to do so upon a first viewing, simply because viewers are not given enough time to sift through the complex layers of mental attribution arising from each twist before the scene quickly barrels past it to get to the next twist, which recasts her behaviour yet again. Instead, we must take Annie's explanations at their word, shunting off to the side the cognitive challenge of aligning her previous behaviour and range of knowledge with each twist.

This difficulty is compounded further when considering that one can perform a similar task for the scene's other characters (it is especially challenging for the dean because his involvement in the conflicting, independent conspiracies with both Annie and Jeff makes some of his behaviour contradictory). Indeed, squaring each character's deceptive behaviour with their true knowledge and intentions might actually be counterproductive to enjoying the scene, decreasing its pleasure for some viewers. While the characters do explain themselves after each twist, the effort of reconstructing the characters' hierarchy of knowledge might be so overwhelmingly challenging that, for some viewers, it could stray from pleasurable into unpleasant aesthetic territory. The complexity might increase past a 'maximal level', as Todd Berliner (2017: 26) theorizes of an artwork's potential for positive hedonic value, 'at which point subjects start to become overwhelmed, and their pleasure diminishes and eventually turns to displeasure'.[1] Depending on viewers' expertise, appreciating the complexity of the scene's most prominent operational aesthetics (i.e. mapping a hierarchy of knowledge) seems just as likely to drain the scene of some of its pleasure as it is to (minimally) enhance it. However, the scene avoids such potential displeasure because it does not insist on viewers appreciating its operational aesthetics in order to enjoy it, and because it offers pleasures aside from mastering its cognitive challenges.

The principal appeals of the climax, and more broadly the entire episode, rest not in dissecting how the narration is built to deceive viewers or how each character's behaviour corresponds to their role in the multiple, overlapping conspiracies, but in recognizing how the episode reflexively pushes genre tropes to ludicrous extremes, incorporates serial knowledge, and creates hilariously absurd contrasts. While these pleasures certainly transcend a focus on following the story and are clearly a part of appreciating the narration's 'baroque' formal qualities, because the episode is a parody, much of its pleasure actually relies on other forms of engagement aside from the effortful or analytical cognitive activities that Mittell emphasizes in his discussion of operational aesthetics. In the case of the climax, these pleasures include the surprising speed and number of the twists, the large disparity between the stakes of the conspiracies and their outcomes ('murdered' characters), that the characters are all involved in multiple overlapping conspiracies against each other, and that the conspiracies are all in an effort to teach the other participants relatively banal life lessons, among other qualities.

Appeals Derived from Parodying Plot Twists

Conventionally, regardless of genre, plot twists are often given room to breathe: the narration lingers on the revelation of the twist, at the very least allowing viewers some time to process the implications of the new information, and sometimes even walking viewers through how previous parts of the plot can be recast in light of the twist, either via dialogue or, more recently, brief flashbacks. Examples abound: *Stage Fright* (1950), *The Blue Gardenia* (1953), *Psycho* (1960), *The Conversation* (1974), *The Sixth Sense* (1999), *The Prestige* (2006) and even the conspiracy film *The Manchurian Candidate* (1962). However, 'Conspiracy Theories and Interior Design' parodies this convention by giving most of the plot twists no such breathing room. The first three practically trip over one another, all taking place within twenty-three seconds, allowing viewers scant time to recast the characters' previous behaviour in light of the new information. Indeed, after Annie shoots Garrity, the dean shoots her before she even finishes her sentence explaining her actions, and just as the dean seems like he is about to chastise Jeff for his academic fraud, Jeff suddenly shoots the dean.

The speed of these twists is not only surprising but potentially confusing. Sometimes, conspiracy narratives make the shape of the conspiracy difficult to grasp by obfuscating its scale, goals and players. John Caughie, in describing the narration of the BBC conspiracy miniseries *Edge of Darkness* (1985), states: 'The narrative itself conspires to heighten our bafflement, our sense of things out of control leaving deductive reasoning with no purchase' (2007: 88). Part of *Community*'s parody, then, is that this potential bafflement does not result from the complexity of the conspiracies but from the speed with which the twists are revealed, as well as their overlapping nature. In the DVD commentary track, Dan Harmon – *Community*'s showrunner and the unofficial co-writer of 'Conspiracy Theories and Interior Design' – states that the speed of the twists was meant to be deliberately hard to follow: '[T]he distance between finding out you don't know what's going on keeps decreasing until everything just sort of falls apart'.

Another related aspect of the parody in this scene is the number of twists themselves. Conventionally, plot twists do not come in bunches. A narrative might feature one or two shocking revelations or reversals in knowledge, but the more twists there are, the more the convention draws attention to itself, potentially reducing the narration's capacity for surprise. In other words, too many twists can be counterproductive, at least for narratives that want viewers to actually be surprised by plot twists: the more twists there are, the less surprising each one becomes. Thus, by featuring five plot twists, the climax of this episode of *Community* parodies conventional plot twists, not only by exaggerating them into a running gag but also by diminishing the potential surprise of some of the twists, particularly the last two, as there is a minute-and-a-half gap between the third and fourth twists that allows viewers more time to anticipate that the scene will feature more surprises (although the fourth plot twist mitigates this effect somewhat by incorporating serial knowledge).

The speed and the large number of plot twists in this climax certainly *gesture* towards the kinds of cognitive activities encouraged by complex television's 'baroque variations on themes and norms', as Mittell puts it, which in the case of plot twists means reconsidering 'all that we have viewed before in the episode' (Mittell 2015: 45). However, in this case, *Community* makes fun of precisely this cognitive activity by including too many twists that are too closely packed together, in turn actively discouraging us from reconsidering previous narrative information and instead encouraging us just to laugh at the ludicrously Byzantine nature of the twists. In other words, some of the pleasure of the scene is derived precisely from forgoing trying to make sense of it. The notion is akin to Steven Willemsen and Miklós Kiss's comments on complex film narratives, where they argue that, in some cases, 'formal play' rather than narrative sense-making is 'the "point" of their concept' (Willemsen and Kiss 2017: 2), or where they suggest that 'cognitive overload' can create deliberately puzzling viewing experiences (Kiss and Willemsen 2017: 46–48). Rather than deriving much of its pleasure from the kind of analytical or forensic work that Mittell argues is central to the operational aesthetic, the absurd difficulty of this scene's cognitive challenges instead encourages viewers to throw their hands up and simply go with the flow, parodying not just conspiracy theory narratives but also the analytical activity to which complex television lends itself.

Appeals Derived from Genre Parody

By mocking the cognitive activities involved in appreciating the operational aesthetics of plot twists, this scene also parodies the conspiracy theory genre itself, because conspiracy theory narratives tend to foster viewing behaviour very much akin to appreciating operational aesthetics. As Stephanie Kelly-Romano (2008: 113) writes of the conspiracy theory genre, '[s]easoned conspiracy viewers are taught to dismiss nothing and to scan the visual scene for clues and cues to solve the mystery ... Because of basic visual clues, fans learn to look closely at texts. On one level then, these references condition viewers to process information differently'. While Kelly-Romano is referring to diegetic mysteries, the same could be said of a work's formal qualities: we might hold the narration in suspicion, looking for places where information seems to have been elided, or for misleading stylistic manipulation (camera angles that conceal important actions, scenes that begin or end abruptly, and so on). In short, conspiracy theory narratives cast doubt on the narrative and the narration. Everything can be suspicious in these narratives; thus, viewers are encouraged to approach the genre with their eyes open to its machinations (or operational aesthetics).[2]

Yet, *Community* parodies these operational aesthetic-like activities by making such scanning for clues irrelevant: the episode does not provide enough of them to allow viewers to come even close to anticipating how most of the climax's surprises will unfold. At most, viewers might anticipate the first time Garrity is shot, because it is the plot 'twist' that relies the most on information provided by previous scenes; but overall, the episode has elided too many other scenes for viewers to be able to anticipate most of the climax's surprise conspiracies. This difficulty of anticipating the surprises of the climax is made clearer by summarizing what likely transpired in all of the elided scenes that the characters allude to when they explain their conspiracies (a task that falls squarely within appreciating operational aesthetics, but that seems largely subordinate to the many other pleasures this scene offers).

After the dean discovers Jeff's fake class, he approaches Annie to conspire with her to teach Jeff a lesson. Then, when Jeff realizes he is being manipulated by Annie, he goes to the dean to conspire with him to teach *Annie* a lesson. However, Jeff then realizes that the dean was working *with* Annie all along, and so he goes to Annie to conspire with her to teach the *dean* a lesson. Garrity, tired of being a pawn in all of their conspiracies, then conspires with the police to teach everyone a lesson about not treating prop guns like toys. There is simply too much withheld information here – and too few hints provided about it – for viewers to figure out the conspiracies ahead of time, or even to find much behaviour that retroactivity points to there being multiple conspiracies, as conventional conspiracy narratives would have it.[3] Thus, the episode further parodies the conspiracy theory genre by providing so few clues about the true nature of the conspiracies, creating aesthetic appeal (rather than frustrating viewers) in the process. It is as if the episode were chiding viewers for any analytical energy they might expend trying to anticipate who is involved in the conspiracy that Jeff and Annie set out to investigate by actively stymieing viewing behaviours encouraged by operational aesthetics, essentially extending the episode's parody to the analytical activities fostered by complex television.

The climax also parodies conspiracy theory genre tropes by having all of the characters involved in multiple, overlapping conspiracies against each other. Similar to how the climax parodies plot twists by including so many of them, one aspect of the parody here simply involves the number of conspiracies. Conventionally, conspiracy theory narratives involve a single conspiracy; it can be far ranging and involve hundreds of conspirators, but it stands alone. In *JFK* (1991), for instance, Jim Garrison does not suddenly switch from investigating the Kennedy assassination to UFOs landing in Roswell.[4] Yet the climax of 'Conspiracy

Theories and Interior Design' reveals five independent and overlapping conspiracies: independent in that each has different goals, and overlapping in that they are causally related and play out simultaneously.

Their unfolding simultaneously is particularly important for how the episode parodies conventions regarding the complexity of conspiracies. Unlike the genre's conventional conspiracies, each conspiracy here is relatively straightforward, but they appear to be more complex because they overlap one another, obfuscating what is real and what is part of another layer of conspiracy (and whether the characters' actions match their range of knowledge and motivation, as described previously). In other words, the conspiracies appear complex because they seem to possess a recursive structure, like Russian nesting dolls, with each layer of conspiracy nestled inside another. However, the conspiracies are really hatched sequentially, with each caused by the one preceding it, and with the penultimate conspiracy superseding and invalidating all the others (Jeff and Annie merely go through the motions of the others to manipulate the dean).[5] Adding to the complexity is that, when taken together, the overlapping conspiracies fold in on themselves, as the scene is (nearly) bookended by Annie and Jeff trying to teach the dean *two* lessons (do not manipulate Jeff, and do not become mired in too many conspiracies), the absurdity of which can be appreciated even without familiarity with the conspiracy theory genre.

While the individual conspiracies themselves are relatively straightforward, the complexity resulting from their overlapping is also potentially confusing, and *Community* hilariously parodies possible viewer confusion by having some of the characters echo it. Typically, even if viewers are confused about some aspect of the conspiracies, the characters are not. Here, though, the dean collapses and bemoans that he cannot keep track of the conspiracies after Annie confronts him over why he double-crossed her to conspire with Jeff. His confusion is reiterated when Garrity is shot a second time and the dean responds apoplectically, screaming, 'You've got to be kidding me!' As Dan Harmon (*Community* 2011) notes, 'the Dean becomes us [the viewers]'. The characters' overlap-derived confusion is further parodied in the epilogue when Jeff wonders if they have actually learned anything. Conventionally, the outcomes of conspiracies are clear: either they are foiled, as in *The Manchurian Candidate*, or their goals are achieved, as in *Arlington Road* (1999). Here, however, the conspirators wonder whether or not they have achieved anything because their goals have been diluted by such circuitous conspiring.

The genre parody is extended further by having the roles of the participants shift, depending on the conspiracy. In discussing intelligence agency conspiracy films, Barna William Donovan (2011: 18) writes that double-crosses are common: 'In these stories, secret agents' worst enemies can – and often do – turn out to be the very people they are working for'. Likewise, John Caughie (2007: 83–84) writes that one of the characteristics of conspiracy theory narratives is that protagonists have difficulty identifying friends and enemies (especially friends). In conspiracy thrillers, everyone's roles tend to be cast into doubt; characters that seem like the protagonist's allies might end up being antagonists, and vice versa. However, the main protagonists themselves are usually unassailable, and our range of knowledge rarely waivers from theirs. *Community* parodies conventional double-crosses and betrayals by having characters who function as protagonists in one conspiracy serve as antagonists in others, and by having all of the heroes turn out to be conspirators themselves. For instance, Jeff is the protagonist in his efforts to uncover the dean and Annie's conspiracy but is then a conspiratorial antagonist in his and the dean's conspiracy against Annie, and viewers are unaware of it until he reveals that he conspired with the dean behind Annie's back.

The episode also parodies conventional double-crosses via the dean, whose involvement in the conspiracies against Jeff and Annie is contradictory: his professional goal (guard the college's academic integrity) conflicts with his personal goal (feel included and spend time with Jeff); thus, he becomes a willing participant in two conspiracies that mutually undermine each other. Here, the parody resides in the absurdity of the dean's participation in both conspiracies and is motivated by his being kind of dumb, which both Annie and Jeff point out in explaining their conspiracies (hilariously, the dean even agrees with them).

The dean's commitment to two oppositional conspiracies also parodies the supposed complexity of plot twists by showing how such twists can be pretty straightforward if they need not actually add up to anything. It is a relatively simple matter to surprise viewers with a plot twist if the twist does not make sense in the context of previous narrative information.[6] Such plot twists might give the appearance of spectacular complexity but are actually just the product of poor execution, and *Community* pokes fun at shoddy twists via the dean, who lacks a master plan for committing to so many conspiracies and does not seem to care (or understand) that the conspiracies are at cross purposes. While his conflicting motivations are ultimately coherent (both are consistent with his character traits), his inability to fully realize the implications of his actions parodies narratives where twists are surprising largely because they do not actually make sense. As Annie tells the dean in her criticism of his haphazard machinations, 'if you conspire with every person that approaches you, you're not even really conspiring with anyone; you're just doing random crap'.

Another related aspect of the parody here concerns the types of role each character plays. Donovan (2011: 15) describes some of the conventional protagonist types in conspiracy theory films, including the idealist outsider or naive rookie whose eyes become open to a system's corruption, the grizzled veteran or cynical burnout who rediscovers their ideals, and the protagonist's 'world-weary superiors who might warn the heroes about rocking the boat upon discovery of the conspiracy' and who are often revealed as traitors. Annie, Jeff and the dean each seem to correspond to these character types of the idealistic rookie, the grizzled veteran and the world-weary superior, respectively, except that the episode parodies these archetypes through the characters' persistent traits and through revealing all of them to be conspirators.

Annie runs closest to the conventional character type; her idealism is motivated by her type-A personality, and she initially conspires with the dean because she is miffed that Jeff's fake class devalues all of her real ones. However, Jeff contrasts with the grizzled veteran type. Yes, Jeff is a cynical character, but he is bemused by Professorson's first appearance rather than resigned or cynical about it, and, initially, he refuses to investigate the conspiracy not because he is burned out or because his idealism has been shattered by the college course system's corruption, but because he is apathetic and wants to benefit from the conspiracy's protection of his lie. If a stranger appears out of thin air to corroborate his fake class, he would prefer not to ask questions about it. Indeed, his dumbfounded glee over Professorson's initial appearance is a particularly hilarious moment of the parody as it so strongly contrasts with the concern or suspicion a typical conspiracy theory protagonist would show in this situation. Likewise, while the dean fulfils the role of traitorous superior, he is not world-weary but dumb and needy, and he only embarks on his initial conspiracy with Annie once he discovers that Jeff is cheating the system, rather than in an attempt to prevent Jeff from 'rocking the boat'.

The parodying of generic character types speaks to one of *Community*'s frequent tactics for creating humour in general: commenting on genre conventions by filtering them through its characters' dispositions. In parodying other genres from week to week, the series never loses sight of its characters, who sometimes fit oddly into the parodied genre's conventional character types. The friction created between the show's characters and archetypical genre roles often creates room for humour, both by parodying the genre and by reflexively commenting on characters' roles within *Community* itself. (This reflexivity is often aided by many characters' self-awareness and media literacy, particularly Abed, another member of Jeff and Annie's study group who sometimes seems to know that he is in a television show.)[7]

This aspect of *Community*'s humour – using its characters to comment on genre conventions – is also made clear through the large disparity between the low stakes of the conspiracies (fake course credits) and their outcomes (supposedly murdered characters), as well as each conspiracy's goals: teaching other characters relatively banal life lessons. Conventionally, the actual conspiracies in conspiracy theory narratives are vast, and their stakes high. Donovan describes them as involving

> *the abuse of power, the hidden manipulation of the political, economic or legal systems, the manipulation of the entire country and culture, in effect. These films are about the unseen operations of the powerful few and the effect they have on the lives of the powerless masses. Conspiracy films deal with the use of power to subvert rules, laws for personal gain and the illegal amassing of wealth, [and tap into fears about] being manipulated by unseen cabals of amoral, even murderous, power brokers. (Donovan 2011: 13)*

Likewise, Stephanie Kelly-Romano (2008: 105) describes the conspiracies in these stories as concerning sinister forces working against good people, while Gordon Arnold (2008: 4) describes them as being about a small group of believers with little power fighting against 'enormous external forces'. Jovan Byford (2011: 77) offers further narrowing criteria, asserting that conspiracy theories are not about individuals but larger, carefully worked-out plans that persist no matter who is in charge, and that those plans usually involve 'the creation of a "New World Order"'. More significantly, Byford (ibid.: 21) also argues that the label 'conspiracy theory' is rarely used to describe events consisting of 'a petty and obvious plot, or one with straightforward or benevolent objectives'. Instead, conspiracy theories 'allege the existence of a plot with nefarious and threatening aims'.

In nearly every respect, all of the actual conspiracies in 'Conspiracy Theories and Interior Design' correspond with – but are the exact opposite of – the conventions these scholars describe.[8] The conspiracies are not large scale but small scale, orchestrated not by unseen cabals but by only a handful of conspirators. Their plots are petty and, in places, obvious or sloppy (like when Jeff discovers Professorson's real identity when he passes a poster for Garrity's college production of *Hamlet* in the hallway, allowing him to easily dismantle the fake conspiracy about the night school).[9] Likewise, the objectives of these conspiracies are ultimately benevolent, if sometimes misguided: teaching characters moral lessons about academic integrity, friendship, committing to too many conspiracies, and the seriousness of prop guns. Indeed, the dean and Annie's creation of a fake conspiracy for Jeff to investigate is itself quasi-altruistic, in that it is an attempt to make Jeff actually learn about conspiracies (or, as Jeff puts it, they are making him do real work for his fake class).

The parody of the actual conspiracies is furthered by having the characters attempt to trick each other into thinking that their conspiracies have resulted in murder. Murder is a convention of conspiracy theory narratives, often initiating the conspiracy's investigation or serving as a step in the conspiracy's plan or even its ultimate goal. However, in this case, turning towards convention furthers the parody because murder is incommensurate with the conspiracies' low stakes. This is an aspect of the humour that can be appreciated even by viewers unfamiliar with conspiracy theory genre conventions: imparting a lesson about friendship, for instance, does not usually entail pretending to be shot dead. Thus, the humour rests in the absurd contrast between the conspiracies' low stakes intentions and high stakes outcomes. This humour is further bolstered – or, more appropriately, enabled – by our knowledge that the characters are using prop guns, and that no one is actually killed. As Dirk Eitzen (1999: 268) writes of Gregory Bateson's concept of a play frame, '[h]umor requires that we suppose no genuine harm is intended by behaviours or situations [that] might otherwise appear harmful or challenging'. Much like how *Community* creates humour by imbuing generic character archetypes with its characters' ill-fitting specificities and self-awareness, the episode also creates humour by merging generic plot conventions (like murder) with the incongruous settings and circumstances of the series (a community college).

All of the ways in which this climax (and the episode more generally) parodies the conspiracy theory genre – the overlapping conspiracies, the shifting roles of the participants, the incongruity between the *Community*'s characters and generic archetypes, and the size, scope and goals of the conspiracies – correspond to Mittell's conception of operational aesthetics in the broadest sense: they transcend narrative immersion by drawing attention to the narration. But they do so less by making viewers wonder how the show pulled off its 'narrative pyrotechnics' and more by humorously commenting on conventions themselves through various means, like the creation of self-evident running gags, absurd contrasts and incongruity, and exaggeration or contradiction of genre conventions. While the climax certainly relies on viewers having familiarity with conspiracy narratives in order to fully appreciate many aspects of its humour, this sort of genre literacy is distinctly different from what Mittell characterizes as the effortful pleasures of operational aesthetics, and from the kinds of cognitive challenge typically associated with narrative complexity in general.

Appeals Derived from Serial Knowledge

Aside from genre parody, another part of the pleasure of 'Conspiracy Theories and Interior Design' rests in how it weaves in serial knowledge, using it to both motivate some of the characters' behaviour and play with viewers' expectations. Generally, having a scene call on serial knowledge is pleasurable because it rewards long-time viewers' intimacy with the characters, enriching the inferences they might make about characters' behaviour (Blanchet and Bruun Vaage 2012; Gendler 2016). Such pleasures characterize the episode's climax, however, just as with the pleasure created by the scene's genre parody, they do not derive from the cognitively challenging activities involved in appreciating operational aesthetics but instead derive from the pleasures offered by serialized storytelling in general. For instance, the dean's eagerness to betray Annie and conspire with Jeff is motivated by the dean's oft-suggested infatuation with Jeff. Thus, when Jeff explains to Annie that he was able to deduce her involvement in the dean's original conspiracy because the dean is 'too stupid to orchestrate anything' on his own, our serial knowledge of the dean's infatuation enriches the humour of the dean happily agreeing with this insulting description, which he is perfectly willing to do if it means he can enjoy becoming Jeff's close confidant in some capacity.

A more complicated example involves Annie and Jeff's attempt to convince the dean that Annie really murders Jeff, which references small serial details like Annie's history of nervous breakdowns, and her living in a bad neighbourhood (thus explaining why she has a 'real' gun), as well as more prominent plot arcs like her and Jeff's hesitant attraction. Their hesitancy is a product of their dispositions: Annie is young and inexperienced, and Jeff is callous and self-conscious about their age difference (she is nineteen, he is in his late thirties). These dispositions, in turn, lend plausibility to the story that Jeff really did blow her off over the summer after their kiss at the end of the previous school year and that this really did hurt Annie. Thus, their ability to trick the dean into believing Annie could actually murder Jeff calls on and rewards viewers' (and presumably the dean's) knowledge of what has transpired in previous episodes. More importantly, this incorporation of serial knowledge also contributes to the surprise that Jeff and Annie have staged their romantic conflict as part of yet another conspiracy. By the point when Annie shoots Jeff, viewers have had time to recognize the running gag of escalating plot twists and are primed to anticipate that yet another twist will follow from Annie training a prop gun on Jeff (despite Jeff's explicit suggestion that the gun is real). However, even if viewers are sceptical that Annie will actually murder Jeff (both are regular characters, after all), incorporating the characters' romantic serial history makes their conflict seem more plausible, not just for the dean but for viewers too. Thus, yet another pleasurable (and reflexive) surprise here – aside from Annie and Jeff conspiring against the dean – stems from Annie and Jeff seeming to advance their serial romantic arc, only to reveal that this development was merely a part of their ruse.

Of course, this very analysis of how this scene incorporates serial knowledge would seem to support Mittell's point that complex television is at its best when it adds 'the operational possibilities of formal engagement' to the other general pleasures of serialized television, as doing so enriches the experience of the scene. However, just as with the pleasure derived from appreciating the genre parody, the pleasure of performing this analysis (or reading it) seems to be of a different order from the aesthetic pleasure of engaging with the scene sans analysis. Calling upon serial knowledge to enrich a scene is an aspect of complex television that is pleasurable, even if viewers do not stop to think about *why* it is pleasurable. Rather than being derived from operational aesthetics, the pleasure of calling on serial knowledge is simply one of the core features of serialized television, and of narrative complexity in particular (as Mittell and others have persuasively argued), because it can yield not only surprises or a deeper understanding of character psychology (as in this exchange between Jeff and Annie) but also other possible effects, like increased suspense or a sense of how characters have changed, among other possibilities.

Appeals in Non-climax Scenes

Other scenes aside from the climax also demonstrate how the episode's appeal resides more in genre parody, serial knowledge and absurd contrasts than it does in the appeal of the potential cognitive challenges it raises. For instance, in a scene midway through the episode, Jeff receives a voice-altered phone call threat that leads him to tackle Annie to 'save' her from a 'car bomb', which is really just a firecracker hidden in a toy car on Annie's school project diorama. This scene raises questions about who planted the firecracker and who called Jeff to warn him about it (retrospectively, Annie herself seems a likely candidate for the former, and Garrity for the latter), and just as Mittell claims of operational aesthetics, this scene offers other prominent pleasures aside from answering these questions. Yet the primary pleasures it offers reside less in analysing or marvelling at the narration and more in appreciating the parody of genre conventions like car bombs, threatening phone calls, and a last-minute tackle to save someone, as well as our serial knowledge of Jeff and Annie's hesitant attraction, emphasized here in their breathless sexual tension as Jeff lies on top of Annie after tackling her. Likewise, we can also derive pleasure from the absurd contrast between Jeff's reaction to the phone call and the thoroughly underwhelming 'explosion' of the toy car. Both of these are emphasized via slow motion, and the latter is emphasized again through the editing, which repeats the car's explosion three times from different camera angles (the last of which is presented in step-frame slow motion) as if the firecracker's shower of sparks were a special effect in which viewers would want to luxuriate. Indeed, the stylistic treatment of the explosion itself parodies how moments of high spectacle are often stylized in big-budget action films. All of these pleasures are central to the scene's humour, and are exemplary of the show's narrative complexity; however, because they derive from the scene's genre parody, they are distinctly different from those that describe other cases of cognitively challenging operational aesthetics in complex television.

Appeals Derived from Homage

The stylization of the explosion raises yet one more important aspect of the aesthetic appeal of this episode's parody, namely its homage. Thus far, I have equated parody with ridicule or mockery, but for audiences to understand how a parody ridicules an original work or genre, a parody also often entails paying homage to the original's stylization or conventions in some capacity. As Linda Hutcheon (1985: 78) puts it, the parody 'authorizes' the original. Mittell (2004: 160) has commented on this aspect of parody as well: 'While the host genre is usually mocked within parodies it can still provide more conventional associations and pleasures'. For instance, stylistic homage is plentiful throughout 'Conspiracy Theories and Interior Design', particularly in the music, which is often indistinguishable from the kind of dramatic, suspenseful music one might find in a mystery thriller.[10] For example, the scene where the dean initially accuses Jeff of making up his conspiracy class features musical accompaniment suggesting something sinister is afoot, while a later chase sequence is accompanied by stabbing, fast-paced strings and percussive stingers. This musical homage is prevalent throughout, and is yet another reason why the episode's parody generates humour so effectively: the music lends intrigue and dramatic weight to the mystery of the conspiracies but is incongruous with their low stakes and the characters' ridiculous behaviour.

The pleasure of the episode's homage also extends to its mysteries, which are occasionally genuinely compelling, soliciting curiosity over their details and, more importantly, suspense over their resolutions. However, much like with the music, this intrigue also feeds into the parody's ridicule: the intrigue is undermined by the episode's alternating between its A and B plots. The A plot (or the plot with the most time devoted to it) consists of the conspiracy story described thus far (Newman 2006: 18). In the B plot, two other members of Jeff and Annie's study group, Troy and Abed, build a large-scale blanket fort that eventually encompasses a significant part of the college campus. This B plot is largely independent of the A plot, and its independence furthers the humour of the parody: every few minutes, the episode takes a break from the conspiracy plot to check in on a silly B plot, effectively undercutting whatever suspense the A plot generates by momentarily shifting focus away from the mounting tension.

Later, the A and B plots briefly intertwine once Annie and Jeff track down Garrity and chase him through the blanket fort. Here, the B plot contributes to the parody more directly through setting details. Rather than a high-octane chase through city streets, ala *The French Connection* (1971) (which Harmon's DVD commentary claims this scene is supposed to resemble), the characters crawl through blanket- and pillow-lined tunnels full of pyjama-clad students eating snacks and playing board games. Much like the low stakes of the conspiracies or the banality of their aims, funnelling the A plot's chase through the B plot's setting furthers the parody by scaling down the scope of genre conventions (like suspenseful chase sequences) to make them fit within the series' wackadoo community college setting.[11]

This fluid interplay of homage and ridicule does not present the same kind of cognitive challenge for viewers as the plot twists of the episode's climax. If anything, successfully manoeuvring between homage and ridicule is a challenge for *Community*'s producers rather than its viewers, as it is the writers and other creative personnel who must attempt to strike a proportional balance between genuinely compelling intrigue and humour (for viewers, the shift from homage to ridicule might actually be a relief from the more cognitively challenging aspects of the conspiracies). However, homage and ridicule also represent the principal pleasures offered by the climax, which are based less on the effortful analytical activities of appreciating its operational aesthetics and more on generic knowledgeability and the easily accessible pleasures generated by absurd contrasts.

Conclusion

Of course, the cognitive activities that Mittell emphasizes in his description of operational aesthetics certainly still apply to *Community* in a macro sense, where there is pleasure in seeing what shape a given episode's parody might take. Likewise, once the shape of the parody is clear, there is also pleasure in discovering how the creators will execute it, which is akin to Mittell's description of the operational aesthetic on comedies like *Seinfeld*, *Arrested Development* and *Curb Your Enthusiasm* (Mittell 2015: 42–43, 199). However, this episode of *Community*, and the climax in particular, offers a different calibre of experience from the specific cognitive challenges that comprise the operational aesthetics usually associated with plot twists (or 'narrative special effects'), and which are characteristic of puzzling stories.

As this chapter has argued, 'Conspiracy Theories and Interior Design' gestures towards the cognitive challenge that such stories offer, but actually accepting that challenge is beside the point because *Community* is parodying the kinds of cognitive activities that conspiracy theory narratives – and plot twists in particular – usually foster. To put it another way, *Community* is such an intelligent and self-aware comedy that it is reflexive even about its own use of parody, suggesting that viewers turn away from the challenges offered by complex television, betting instead on their deriving pleasure from exaggerations in both the conventions of the conspiracy theory genre and trends in narrative complexity. Ultimately, the effortful analytical activities that are central to operational aesthetics, while certainly illuminating and often pleasurable, are not always central to all iterations of complex television. The pleasures offered by complex television are more robust and, as I hope I have shown, can rely on other forms of viewer engagement, such as appreciating genre parody, serial information and absurd contrasts.

Jason Gendler holds a PhD in Film and Television, and, as an Adjunct Professor, he has taught at various Southern California institutions, including UCLA, Chapman University, and CSU Long Beach. He has published in *Projections*, the AFI reader *Color and the Moving Image* and *Nebula*. He is currently revising various articles and manuscripts for publication. His interests include narration in film and television, style and aesthetics, cognitive psychology, media history and popular film and television criticism. He also semi-regularly writes popular film and television criticism for various publications, which are collected at jasongendler.com.

Notes

1. Of course, aesthetic experiences need not be pleasing in order to have value. Some genres, like horror, derive aesthetic value partly from arousing unpleasant emotions. Moreover, aside from hedonic value, or how pleasing a work is, another component to aesthetic pleasure that Berliner discusses is epistemic value, or how *interesting* a work is: how it arouses '"knowledge emotions" ... associated with thinking and comprehending', challenging our ability to master the work's aesthetic properties (like reasoning out complex character motivations and behaviour, as in this example from *Community*) (Berliner 2017: 27–28). Unlike with hedonic value, epistemic value increases linearly with complexity. That is, interest in a work continually increases along with the work's complexity, even if it becomes so complex that it becomes less pleasing or even unpleasant. However, the climax of 'Conspiracy Theories and Interior Design' avoids such potential displeasure by actively discouraging viewers from attempting to derive epistemic value from it, as this chapter will subsequently argue.
2. Perhaps not incidentally, holding anything and everything in suspicion is an attitude that many conspiracy theorists take towards evidence when crafting their theories (Pipes 1997; Kelly-Romano 2008: 105–21; Byford 2011).

3. The closest the episode gets to providing hints is when the dean nods along vigorously to Annie's objections over Jeff's fake class when he first confronts Jeff about it, Annie's rehearsed-sounding 'whoa!' when Jeff reveals Garrity's real identity, and the long look Jeff gives Annie shortly thereafter, which perhaps indicates the moment when he realizes that Annie is conspiring with the dean. However, these moments still provide scant clues for anticipating the many twists of the climax.
4. While solitary conspiracies are a convention of the conspiracy theory genre, cordoning off one conspiracy from another is not typical of actual conspiracy theories or theorists, who are often eager to fold incongruous facts into ever-wider networks of conspiracies (Pipes 1997; Byford 2011).
5. My thanks to David Bordwell for drawing my attention to the conspiracies' seemingly recursive structure.
6. My thanks to Robert Blanchet for suggesting this aspect of the parody to me.
7. To take just one other example from another episode, season two's 'Epidemiology' clearly features characters reflexively pushing against genre conventions. The episode parodies zombie films: an infectious disease breaks out at the campus's Halloween party, and many of the characters' persistent traits end up parodying zombie or horror film archetypes. Jeff becomes an image-conscious hipster zombie, for instance, while Britta, a virtue-signalling poser largely unaware of her own privilege, endangers the others after becoming infected because of her delusional hope that she might be 'special' and able to resist the disease. Likewise, Troy becomes the last remaining uninfected protagonist, which could be homage to *Night of the Living Dead* (1968), but which also seems like a parody of horror films' tendency to kill off African-American and other characters of colour first, as well as the 'final girl' slasher film convention, where the last remaining protagonist is a woman.
8. While Jeff's initial attempt to create a fake class for a free credit could be described as the subversion of an institution's rules for personal gain, his ploy is merely a lie rather than a conspiracy.
9. Another part of the episode's parody of actual conspiracy theories includes the list of obviously fake night school courses that Annie discovers during their investigation, which feature hilarious titles like 'History of Something', 'Principles of Intermediate', and 'Learning!' This list parodies conspiracy theories by making fun of the belief that secret documents reveal parts of conspiratorial plans (Byford 2011: 78).
10. In the DVD commentary, the episode's writer, Chris McKenna, notes that the music 'really made the episode', and Harmon agrees, stating of *Community* in general that 'there's no other comedy to which sound is so important' (*Community* 2011).
11. This chase scene also furthers the parody by adding a splash of reflexivity that subtly incorporates serial knowledge. Upon entering the blanket fort, Annie tries to solicit Troy and Abed's help, announcing to them, 'We're in a chase!' By stating it this way, she is framing her and Jeff's actions in generic terms: they are not 'chasing someone' but *in* a chase, as though their actions are a component of an ongoing story (which they are, from our perspective). This is a reflexive joke that also slyly calls on serial knowledge. Abed thinks of his life in terms of his being a character in a film/television narrative; thus, Annie's phrasing is a way of putting her and Jeff's actions in terms that Abed will immediately react to with a genre-appropriate level of gravitas. It works too: Abed and Troy spring into action to help them.

References

Arnold, Gordon B. 2008. *Conspiracy Theory in Film, Television, and Politics*. Westport, CT: Praeger.
Berliner, Todd. 2017. *Hollywood Aesthetic: Pleasure in American Cinema*. New York: Oxford University Press.
Blanchet, Robert, and Margrethe Bruun Vaage. 2012. 'Don, Peggy, and other Fictional Friends? Engaging with Characters in Television Series', *Projections* 6(2): 18–41.
Byford, Jovan. 2011. *Conspiracy Theories: A Critical Introduction*. London: Palgrave Macmillan.
Caughie, John. 2007. *Edge of Darkness*. London: British Film Institute.
Chatman, Seymour. 2001. 'Parody and Style', *Poetics Today* 22(1): 25–39.
Community Season 2 DVD. 2011. Los Angeles: Sony Pictures.
Donovan, Barna William. 2011. *Conspiracy Films: A Tour of Dark Places in the American Conscious*. Jefferson, NC: MacFarland & Company.
Eitzen, Dirk. 1999. 'The Emotional Basis of Film Comedy', in Carl Plantinga and Greg M. Smith (eds), *Passionate Views: Film, Cognition, and Emotion*. Baltimore, MD: The Johns Hopkins University Press, pp. 84–99.
Gendler, Jason. 2016. 'The Rich Inferential World of *Mad Men*: Serialized Television and Character Interiority', *Projections* 10(1): 39–62.
Genette, Gérard. 1997 *Palimpsests: Literature in the Second Degree*. Lincoln: University of Nebraska Press.
Hutcheon, Linda. 1985. *A Theory of Parody: The Teachings of Twentieth-Century Art Forms*. New York: Methune.
Kelly-Romano, Stephanie. 2008. 'Trust No One: The Conspiracy Genre on American Television', *Southern Communication Journal* 73(2): 105–21.
Kiss, Miklós, and Steven Willemsen. 2017. *Impossible Puzzle Films: A Cognitive Approach to Contemporary Complex Cinema*. Edinburgh: Edinburgh University Press.
Mittell, Jason. 2004. *Genre and Television: From Cop Shows to Cartoons in American Culture*. New York: Routledge.
———. 2015. *Complex TV: The Poetics of Contemporary Television Narratives*. New York: New York University Press.
Newman, Michael Z. 2006. 'From Beats to Arcs: Toward a Poetics of Television Narrative', *The Velvet Light Trap* 58: 16–28.
Pipes, Daniel. 1997. *Conspiracy: How the Paranoid Style Flourishes and Where It Comes From*. New York: The Free Press.
Willemsen, Steven, and Miklós Kiss. 2017. 'Resistance to Narrative in Narrative Film: Excessive Complexity in Quentin Dupieux's *Réalité* (2014)', *Global Media Journal - Australian Edition* 11(1): 25–39.

CHAPTER 11
How Not to Comprehend Television
Notes on Complexity and Confusion

Jason Mittell

Fargo's second season opens with a spectacularly incomprehensible five minutes of television. Originally airing in 2015, this season of the anthologized miniseries offers no essential continuities from the first season; thus, a viewer knowing nothing about *Fargo*'s previous incarnations (as either television series or feature film) is poised to make just about as much sense of this opening as anyone else might. The episode begins with a black-and-white version of the iconic MGM lion roaring before fading up on a pan across an old-time battlefield littered with corpses, arrows, wagons and a Gatling gun – all signalling a late nineteenth-century setting. Soon, a graphics overlay displays a title '*Massacre at Sioux Falls*' followed by credits: 'starring Ronald Reagan and Betty LaPlage'. With the tinny musical score, black-and-white imagery, and rounded corners of the image, we are presumably meant to think that this is the opening to a 1940s-era film – although the 16:9 aspect ratio situates it in twenty-first-century television more than the era's typical Academy ratio.

The image pans to a solitary American Indian dressed in a stereotypical headdress standing silently, surveying the field of arrow-ridden white soldiers, and we linger on him for an uncomfortably long fifteen seconds as the theme music ends. The image wobbles as if a projected film is glitching, and he finally speaks to someone off-screen: 'Am I, uh... what are we waiting for?' After some off-screen noise, a man enters dressed in a hat, tie and sweater that clearly do not belong in this scene, explaining that they are waiting for wardrobe to secure the arrows on Reagan. As the conversation continues, it becomes clear that this footage is from the film shoot itself, as the actor playing Running Dog converses with the film's assistant director Syd Schwartz about this delay in shooting.[1] They speak awkwardly for two minutes, with Schwartz referring to the site as the 'real location' for the Massacre at Sioux Falls (a fictional battle), the actor mentioning that he is from

New Jersey, and Schwartz suggesting that Reagan (a.k.a. Dutch) is 'a prince, a real class act'. They both smoke cigarettes.

The scene runs for more than three minutes in a single unbroken take, presenting no meaningful narrative information or character introductions, until it cuts abruptly to President Jimmy Carter addressing the nation on television from the White House, giving his renowned 1979 'crisis of confidence' speech in full colour. The next minute intercuts Carter's speech with other archival footage from the late seventies era, and introductory shots of fictional characters who will be featured throughout the season, presented in dynamic split screen and fast editing (all in 4:3 aspect ratio) over the rollicking 1969 Fleetwood Mac song 'Oh Well'. During this montage, the episode presents the most consistent feature of the various film and television iterations of *Fargo*: a sequence of captions reading: 'This is a true story. The events depicted took place in Minnesota in 1979. At the request of the survivors, the names have been changed. Out of respect for the dead, the rest has been told exactly as it occurred'. After this sequence, the ratio expands back to the contemporary television standard of 16:9, and the season's narrative commences with a dialogue scene between Dodd, Rye and Hanzee, all members of the Gerhardt crime family who will be central to the season's story; neither Running Dog, Schwartz, nor the *Massacre at Sioux Falls* film will ever appear or be referenced again on *Fargo*.

At the scenic level, this sequence is resolutely incoherent: the opening credits and score suggest a finished feature film, only to seamlessly shift to what appears to be unedited production footage that would never have been released or probably even shot. The first three minutes of the season presents an incomprehensible sequence intermixing a real actor (Reagan) with a fictional one (LaPlage) on the set of a non-existent film based on an allegedly true story that never happened. The shift to 1979 is entirely unmotivated, with only a tenuous link between the credit of Ronald Reagan and the real image of President Jimmy Carter, who would face each other in the 1980 election. Reagan does appear in a later episode, in a fictionalized campaign stop in Minnesota, but there are no further narrative connections to these opening moments. In the context of the rest of the season, this fake film in the opening will never be addressed or referenced, but instead, another massacre at Sioux Falls will take place in 1979: a shootout at a motel involving competing mobsters, police and an inexplicable UFO.

Certainly, we can see some thematic resonances for the season's tale: the episode's title 'Waiting for Dutch' refers both to this moment for Running Dog and

Schwartz and to the 1979 era when Reagan was on the cusp of being elected and transforming American politics. The titular allusion to *Waiting for Godot* undercuts Reagan's predicted efficacy, and presages some of *Fargo*'s absurdist tendencies. Additionally, the battle's aftermath connects to the post-Vietnam experiences of many of the season's characters, and the troubling treatment of American Indians becomes central to Hanzee's narrative arc. The presence of fictional history being presented as truth is an overarching motif of *Fargo*, as all of its incarnations are misleadingly framed as true crime. But television storytelling does not typically present an extended incomprehensible scene solely to create thematic foreshadowing or echoes of motifs, suggesting something new is in play. The opening sequence is a total narrative anomaly, inexplicable in terms of diegetic storytelling and only vaguely evocative in terms of tone, theme and setting, but more disruptive and confounding than enlightening.[2] In short, this opening sequence seems designed to provoke the very reaction that I had upon my first viewing: 'What the fuck did I just watch?'

This is not how fictional television is supposed to tell stories. I would argue that, at its core, narrative television must strive first and foremost to be comprehensible. In fact, I have argued just that in my book *Complex TV*. I begin the chapter on narrative comprehension with this claim:

> *At the most basic level, nearly all viewing starts with the core act of comprehension, making sense of what is happening within an episode. This might seem obvious, and certainly much of television storytelling aims to make comprehension easy, invisible, and automatic. However, complex television has increased the medium's tolerance for viewers to be confused, encouraging them to pay attention and put the pieces together themselves to comprehend the narrative. While television rarely features an avant-garde level of abstraction or ambiguity, contemporary programming has embraced a degree of planned confusion. (Mittell 2015: 164)*

This was true when I first wrote it in 2012, and even when it was published in spring 2015 there were few exceptions to this claim. Still today, as I write in 2021, most complex television series prioritize comprehension, even if deferred, as found with prominent recent examples across a range of genres, from *This Is Us* to *The Good Place* to *Westworld*. In most such programmes, moments of confusion are tied to carefully planned narrative enigmas designed to be resolved later in the series, prompting viewers to respond to cognitive challenges through close attention and forensic fandom.

But over the last few years, a number of series have downplayed comprehension while ratcheting up confusion. Certainly, the standard-bearer here is the 2017 return of *Twin Peaks*, which shattered numerous norms of television storytelling by featuring the very 'avant-garde level of abstraction and ambiguity' I had previously doubted. A David Lynch series should never be held up as representative of broader trends, as his core work is always enigmatically unique, but just as the original 1990s *Twin Peaks* presaged much of complex TV that emerged a decade later, we can look at *Twin Peaks: The Return* as an extreme version of a larger phenomenon where confusion has shifted from being a temporary condition to be tolerated, to becoming an outright aesthetic goal. A number of recent so-called 'prestige television' series present a lack of narrative comprehension as a feature, not a bug – programmes that encourage us to forgo comprehension, inviting us to experience storytelling amidst confusion. Often, these are temporary forays into perplexing ambiguity within an otherwise coherent narrative, as in *Hannibal, Fargo, Atlanta* and *Transparent*. A few series build narrative ambiguity into their core storytelling engines, with uncertainty as to what is happening and how it coheres, as with *Twin Peaks: The Return, The Leftovers, Russian Doll, American Gods, Mr. Robot* and *Legion*. I believe that together they add up to something new happening in the realm of commercial television storytelling, and this chapter aims to make sense of the particular brands of nonsense they are serving up.

The dominant affective response that pervades this mode of television is bewilderment, as I felt at the start of *Fargo*'s second season. I considered a number of different names for this narrative mode, but keep coming back to the term that best captures this reaction: batshit TV. I use the term 'batshit' to evoke the combination of excessive unpredictability and the absence of rationality. I first assumed that the word was shorthand for 'batshit crazy', but in the interesting etymology of 'batshit', it appears that it was used as a lone term before it was attached to 'crazy' (Elliott 2016). As such, my use of 'batshit' does not strive to evoke mental illness or so-called madness, but rather a state untethered from norms of causality, coherence and reality, with a radical sense of unbounded possibility – all of which capture the televisual pleasures of this emerging mode of storytelling.

The most relevant scholarly precedent for batshit TV is the concept of 'unnatural narrative', an umbrella term used to study storytelling that violates the conventions of the real world in either depiction or narration by rejecting the underlying mimetic assumption of most narratological theory (see Alber et al. 2010; Alber, Nielsen and Richardson 2013). While this scholarly subfield is insightful in its depth of consideration of a broad array of narrative properties, it is somewhat limited for understanding this mode of television storytelling. First off, it is highly grounded in the written word – where prominent techniques (such as first-person narration) offer little explanatory power for television storytelling – and cannot account for the entire mimetic basis of performed, time-based media like film and television, where the real world in front of the camera nearly always exerts its presence in the final edit.[3] Additionally, unnatural narratives encompass a far wider range of possible examples than batshit TV, as entire television genres (like science fiction and fantasy) might be considered unnatural due to their overtly unreal storyworlds; thus, series with highly straightforward mimetic narrative strategies (like *Star Trek* and *Game of Thrones*) might create 'unnatural' worlds, but they have little in common with the batshit storytelling of the mostly realist worlds of *Fargo* or *Hannibal*. Most importantly, unnatural narratives do not describe what they are but more what they are not. The usefulness of a term like batshit TV is that it evokes the defining attribute of the category: the off-kilter experience of watching such programmes.

I do believe that unnatural narratology might be useful to explain the extreme nether regions of batshit TV, where comprehension and mimesis are completely jettisoned for an embrace of disorienting affect. I would point to the legendary episode 8 of *Twin Peaks: The Return* as the most unnatural television I know of – an hour within a serialized story that strives to create an affective response with no pretences to narrative continuity or comprehension. As critic Matt Zoller Seitz writes, the episode 'owes as much to expressionistic and surreal painting, musical performance, and installation art as it does to narrative and experimental cinema', and as such might be productively analysed using the tools of unnatural narratology (Seitz 2017). But as a whole, that episode is an exception in an already exceptional series, as even the most batshit moments of other television programmes seem too connected to a core of narrative mimesis, continuity and comprehension as to be best understood through the lens of the unnatural.

Batshit TV's lack of comprehension differs from the planned confusion found in complex TV. As I wrote concerning the latter, complex TV programmes 'invite temporary disorientation and confusion, allowing viewers to build up their comprehension skills through long-term viewing and active engagement'

(Mittell 2015: 51). In batshit TV, there is an additional level of confusion, where viewers are often unsure to what degree such disorientation is temporary before being resolved via serialized comprehension; for instance, I watched the second season of *Fargo* wondering whether the *Massacre at Sioux Falls* film sequence would ever become diegetically relevant or just remain a perplexing thematic overture for the season. Indeed, rather than 'confusion' being a defining feature of batshit TV viewing, the term 'perplexion' seems more apt, in part because the word itself sounds a little bit batshit. Such moments are perplexing in lacking clear causality and rationality within the storyworld, as well as embracing operational ambiguity in terms of how we are supposed to make sense of them within the larger serialized whole.

Other narrative traditions certainly operate in similar registers of batshittery, notably experimental literature, absurdist drama and art cinema – as *Hannibal* showrunner Bryan Fuller proudly touted, he informed every new director who worked on the series, 'We are not making television. We are making a pretentious art film from the 80s' (Thurm 2015). The influence of David Lynch on batshit TV reinforces these continuities, and perhaps raises the question of whether there is anything new here, or if we would be better off labelling these programmes 'experimental TV', 'absurdist TV' or even 'art TV'. For me, the key distinction is the melding of batshit TV's emphasis on experiencing perplexion alongside comprehension within the structure of serial television, where story development and resolution typically forge the primary narrative drive, rather than a full-on dive into an anti-mimetic, unnatural or experimental ethos. In *Fargo*, the opening minutes give way to a much more grounded and coherent narrative experience to keep us coming back each week – such moments of incoherence function more as a colourful garnish than as the main course. It is hard to imagine *Fargo* working as a series where every few minutes we are given a different narrative moment that lacks a direct connection to the next, in the way that the transition between the fake 1940s film gives way to the real 1970s news footage. Even *Twin Peaks: The Return* – the most extensively incoherent example of batshit TV – still clings to moments of causality, suspense, curiosity, character development and narrative resolution (aside from the truly incomprehensible episode 8), providing a skeletal framework of comprehension to frame its moments of deep perplexion, utter bewilderment and excessive sensory experience.

This is not to say that batshit TV is just complex TV with some extra weird stuff sprinkled on top. I have found my own experiences of watching batshit programmes to be distinctly different from how I watch complex TV. Viewing complex TV allows for, or even requires, great attention to detail, as we try to make sense of both gaps in narrative information and the operational norms of storytelling at work – we pay close attention, lean forward, and try to rise to the cognitive challenge (Mittell 2015). Batshit TV invites a different mode of viewing where we give up on trying to make rational sense of the story and allow ourselves to go on an experiential journey – we lean back and go for an unpredictable ride. Such an approach to narrative consumption echoes Elizabeth Alsop's excellent discussion of how excessive duration in *Twin Peaks: The Return* simultaneously alienates viewers from the narrative while deepening their emotional investment in it. Although Alsop does not use the term 'batshit TV', she does characterize these programmes by 'their resistance to narrative condensation: the fact that they function as texts to be *experienced* and *appreciated* … rather than recapped' (Alsop 2018, emphasis in original; see also Alsop 2020). Trying to reduce a batshit series like *Twin Peaks* or *The Leftovers* to a plot summary elides the very thing that makes these series worth watching: the transcendent, indescribable experience of watching them.

Such recap-resistance also presents a challenge for critical analysis; describing the programmes does not do justice to the experience of viewing them. These facets make such series appropriate subjects for videographic criticism (such as Alsop 2020), as a written-only analysis cannot fully capture the affective pleasures of a series like *Legion*, which is arguably the most experimental, incomprehensible, excessive and outright batshit series not produced by David Lynch. Loosely based on a Marvel superhero connected to *The X-Men*, the series follows the story of David Haller, who has been institutionalized for severe mental illness but slowly realizes that he actually has mutant telepathic powers and is possessed by a psychic parasite named The Shadow King, who incarnates in his mind in the form of a drug addict friend named Lenny (played by Audrey Plaza). In the episode 'Chapter 6', David and his fellow mutant friends Syd and Ptonomy have been captured in the astral plane, where The Shadow King is holding them hostage in a psychic projection of the mental institution where David had previously lived. (As noted, batshit TV is resistant to recapping!) As they sit at the cafeteria table, Syd eats a piece of cherry pie (a potential *Twin Peaks* allusion), only to discover it is crawling with beetles. The camera tracks along the pie remnants thrown across the floor as the image dissolves to Lenny staring into the camera with the music of Nina Simone's 'Feeling Good' rising on the soundtrack. She flips her head back and begins to strut towards the camera as the music's beat kicks in and the background lighting becomes bright red. The next ninety seconds features a non-narrative dance number, with exaggerated graphic effects juxtaposing Lenny dancing over clips of previous moments between David and Lenny, and scenes of Lenny rhythmically destroying David's apartment and a laboratory. As the music fades, Lenny tamps down her destructive exuberance, puts on glasses, and returns to her incognito role as a doctor in the illusory institution where she has captured David and his friends.

Even if you understand what is happening in the narrative at this point in *Legion*'s run, this sequence still resists comprehension. The diegetic realities in the scene straddle various layers of fantasy and hallucination, and the presentational style pivots into an experiential realm that transcends sense. I would contend that such moments of batshit TV defy interpretation for deeper meanings of theme or symbolism. Instead, we watch scenes like this to be perplexed, to be impressed by the ambition and risk-taking, to wallow in the chaos and stylistic excess, and to ask, 'What the fuck did I just watch?' We are still having a narrative experience, as we care about the characters and want to see how they might move forward from their current predicaments, and the unreal tone does reinforce numerous themes and character traits. But ultimately, we are here for the affective ride, willing to wade into the realm of batshit and forsake the comforts of narrative complexity and comprehension.

It is telling that this sequence is set in a mental institution (albeit one that Lenny recreates in the astral plane), as much of batshit TV emerges in moments highlighting mental illness and instability. Characters in *Legion*, *Hannibal*, *Mr. Robot*, and *Russian Doll* are explicitly diagnosed as psychologically troubled, and many of the most batshit moments emerge in the uncertain boundary between subjective and objective narration from the perspective of unreliable characters. It is easy to dismiss such moments as fantasies or 'unreal' (although within the context of a fictional television series, all moments are unreal at their core), but we experience them as an audience and must grapple with how to process them nonetheless. As Fuller notes in discussing *Hannibal*, the camera frequently drifts into subjective experiences without clear demarcation from objective reality, providing 'a veil of surreality through which we see the show', and where murderous acts are highly aestheticized and experienced via the off-kilter subjectivity of both killers and victims (Thurm 2015).

Moments of unnatural narrative – including unreliable narration and counterfictionality – abound throughout complex television, pushing the medium's storytelling boundaries towards the realm of batshit, typically by foregrounding subjective presentation (see Butter 2017). A good point of comparison is with *The Sopranos*, where Tony's psychotherapy anchored the show with dream sequences to provide frequent glimpses into characters' subconscious lives. Such dreams feature numerous unrealistic and confounding moments; yet, I would not label them as batshit due to their narrative function and explicit framing as dreams: they are designed to be interpreted to uncover character motivations, beliefs and, in one notable instance, plot revelations, when Tony realizes that Pussy has become a snitch in a dream. Such dream sequences in *The Sopranos* are more in keeping with the surrealist tradition, in which fantastic imagery and nonsensical events reveal deep unconscious meanings in keeping with psychoanalytic theory. Batshit TV fantasy sequences are more like Dadaism than surrealism, rejecting both surface rationality and subtextual psychological interpretation. Even on *Hannibal*, with narratively central therapeutic relationships and prevalent subconscious subtexts, the unnatural imagery is far less bounded by overt dream sequences; instead, they seep into waking moments, presented as unsettling experiences to be immersed in, rather than an externalization of interior meanings to be decoded and analysed.

The experience of watching batshit TV often evokes an irrational state of mind in viewers, diving into a subjective experience of perplexion and disorientation. While those mental states may connect with on-screen dreams, fantasies or delusions, they are also akin to the altered state of being intoxicated – a mode of spectatorship explored by Caetlin Benson-Allott (2021). Many of the experiences evoked by watching batshit TV – perplexion, bewilderment, amusement at unlikely moments, and immersion into a world of awe-inspiring transcendent nonsense – mirror being stoned, as the experience can be a real trip. Personally, I have often watched *Hannibal*, *Mr. Robot*, *Legion* and *Twin Peaks* late at night, when I will often enter a trance-like (but sober) state between awake and asleep as I let the images wash over me without trying to follow precisely what is going on. These are still narrative experiences, and sometimes I will replay such moments in daylight in order to make a little more sense of what I have seen; but I do not regard such trance-like viewing as an aberrant or subpar viewing mode. Instead, it functions as an approach to experiencing something new and unexpected without my ingrained habits of narrative comprehension and cognitive decoding – akin to the 'Zen way of reading' that Kiss and Willemsen discuss as how viewers might forgo comprehension for embracing poetic disorientation (2017: 117–18).

We can see the parallels between stoned viewing and batshit TV storytelling in *Atlanta*, a comedy that embraces Afrosurrealism as an aesthetic (see Francis 2013). *Atlanta*'s storyworld is seemingly realistic, lacking the supernatural elements that pervade many batshit series, but the mundanity of realism is tinged by two distorting factors: the frequent weed-smoking of most of the characters and the omnipresent irrationality of living in a racist, anti-Black society. Per Benson-Allott, moments of Afrosurrealism, like when a character drives off in an invisible car, create 'a structure of paranoia wherein the spectator must keep questioning the show's reality and their own', grounded in a racial critique of an irrational world (Benson-Allott 2021: 208). In *Atlanta*, batshit elements are not simply absurdist nonsense devoid of meaning but are carefully constructed absurdism designed both to further a social critique and to evoke affective disorientation in response to the irrationality of living under white supremacy (see also Bruce 2021).

Atlanta's distinctive approach to Afrosurrealist storytelling peaks in its lauded episode 'Teddy Perkins', where stoner Darius wanders into the mansion of the reclusive title character, who has a frozen white mask for a face, feeds him an ostrich egg and shares tales of childhood abuse while plotting to murder his bandaged, silent brother trapped in a wheelchair. This harrowing batshit affective experience resembles a bad drug trip, but the illicit substance is laced with racial trauma; the episode's meaning is less about imposing a rational explanation for what is happening in the narrative, but more the experiential dimension of living through Darius's witness to this unnatural world forged by an abusive parent and a white supremacist society. 'Teddy Perkins' points towards one crucial aspect of batshit TV: how we respond to perplexion is cued by the characters within the narrative itself. As Darius realizes the uncanny situation he finds himself in, his approach is less to try to figure out or resolve what exactly is going on, but more to observe and experience the strangeness. He is not a puzzle-solving hero trying to take control but a passive spectator, who eventually witnesses the brothers' climactic murder-suicide and walks away from the batshit experience to never directly refer to it again. Yet we, the audience, are changed from the disorienting experience, and are left to ponder Teddy's identity and the social impacts of racial trauma and parental abuse.

Such an observational mode runs in direct contrast to complex series in which decoding the confusing moments is part of both the characters' diegetic behaviour and the viewing experience. Take *WandaVision* – the high-profile 2021 Marvel television series that bewilderingly casts titular heroes Wanda and Vision in a succession of slightly uncanny classic sitcom homages. While the first few episodes offer few explanatory contexts or answers, by the fourth episode the entire series has been reframed as a simulation being constructed by Wanda, with a number of secondary characters employing overt forensic fandom techniques in watching her diegetic sitcom broadcasts to figure out what is actually happening. However, the series' final two episodes go to great lengths to explain every possible ambiguity and close down any pleasures of perplexion. One could imagine the series being played more as a batshit version following the hypothetical logic of Marvel's comic series *What If?* – 'What if Wanda Maximoff and Vision starred in a classic sitcom?' – and jettisoning the 'real world' frame of characters trying to solve the puzzle. As I have previously discussed, many transmedia extensions of a serialized narrative can posit a 'What If?' approach, mimicking the playful logic common to fan productions, and many such extensions can certainly embrace a batshit rejection of continuity, causality and comprehension (Mittell 2015: 315–18; see also Sconce 2004). Yet *WandaVision* pivots towards a more typical mode of puzzle solving via layered clues, overt explanation, and clear viewer identification with the characters hoping to restore realism to the perplexing narrative scenario.

Another useful concept for making sense of batshit TV is authorship, or more specifically, the *inferred author function*. As I explored in *Complex TV*, 'the inferred author function is a viewer's production of authorial agency responsible for a text's storytelling, drawing on textual cues and contextual discourses' (Mittell 2015: 107). In other words, as we watch a programme, we construct a figure to attribute intentionality to, which becomes vital for guiding our comprehension towards rational decoding, or perhaps for accepting perplexing batshit as inscrutable. This concept is similar to Jan Alber's concept of 'hypothetical intentionalism' as we watch a film; but, for serialized television, the role of paratextual contexts becomes more central due to the extended duration of a series and the gaps between episodes, which invite the construct of authorial intentionality to help viewers make sense of the narrative (Alber 2010). Alber notes that hypothetical intentionalism is particularly useful for understanding experimental narrative films that he frames as 'unnatural narration', using the example of David Lynch's *Lost Highway*; certainly, knowledge of Lynch's career and oeuvre as part of his inferred author function helps us to make sense of Lynch's batshit TV work on *Twin Peaks* and the more-obscure *On the Air*, as well as his unique television-to-film masterpiece *Mulholland Drive* (see Mittell 2013). In watching a Lynch-made text, we not only accept perplexion but come prepared to both expect and enjoy it.

Likewise, dedicated fans who embraced *Fargo*'s playful garnishing of batshit were likely primed for a more overwhelming dose of perplexion in Noah Hawley's follow-up series *Legion*, a pattern repeated in Bryan Fuller's dual series *Hannibal* and *American Gods*.

Few television creators have had such a prominent but fraught authorial career as Damon Lindelof, showrunner of *Lost*, *The Leftovers* and *Watchmen*, whose work has straddled the complex and batshit modes. If reduced to a plot summary, all three of these series would likely read as equally incomprehensible and perplexing; however, the different ways that each constructs its complex storytelling suggests different relationships to the batshit mode. *Lost* is one of the most important exemplars of complex television, whose narrative innovations I have written about at length (Mittell 2009, 2012, 2015). The series features many moments of unnatural narration, where dead characters manifest on the tropical island, a monster made of black smoke threatens the protagonists, and the final season features a parallel dimension whose reality status is never fully clarified. Despite such inscrutable moments, *Lost* never embraces the batshit aesthetic, but attempts to explicate the inexplicable, as all of the island's oddities are framed as mysteries to be solved. These moments fuel forensic fandom and drive the narrative to answer every posed question, rather than letting the ambiguities linger at the heart of the series.

A good example is the second season's episode 'Dave', which focuses on Hurley's vision of an old friend appearing on the island. Via narrative flashbacks, we see that Dave was a negative influence on Hurley during his time in a psychiatric institution, who encouraged him to boycott his medication and escape. Eventually, however, Dave is revealed to be a psychological construct that Hurley uses to process his guilt, rather than an actual person. In the narrative present, Dave tries to convince Hurley that the island itself is a delusion and that he is still a patient at the hospital, imagining his life while in a coma; but Hurley eventually rejects Dave and embraces the reality of the island. Such ambiguous reality status of a character is a trope seen in many batshit series, including *Legion*, *Hannibal*, *Mr. Robot* and *Russian Doll*, but *Lost* does not allow the ambiguity to linger beyond this single episode. Dave's illusionary presence is a device used for him to process his anxiety about growing closer to Libby, and she helps him to process his feelings and discard the delusion. Notably, Dave never appears or is even mentioned again in the series, making it a clear example of a question that is quickly resolved and moved past. While many of *Lost*'s questions linger across seasons, this example typifies the overall approach to answering questions, as modelled by character motivations, actions and psychology.

Lindelof's next series swings towards the opposite approach to answering questions: the theme song for the second season of *The Leftovers* is Iris DeMent's 'Let the Mystery Be', which explicitly articulates the programme's choice not to answer the major questions it raises. The series begins with the greatest mystery that remains unanswered throughout three seasons: why did a seemingly random 2 per cent of the world's population spontaneously disappear at a single moment, known as the 'Sudden Departure'? The programme's entire dramatic momentum focuses on the aftermath of this traumatic event once it becomes clear that no conclusive answers will be offered by science or religion, reframing the action by asking how people might cope with such uncertainty. But this is far from the only inexplicable event in the series, as the post-departure storyworld is full of unexplained phenomena – dogs going feral, a deer rampaging inside a character's house, a faith healer able to absorb people's pain with a hug, and a mysterious character who credibly claims to be God, among many others. But unlike *Lost*, the narrative is not structured around the discovery of answers to any of these questions; most *Leftovers* characters do not try to solve these mysteries but rather try to process them and learn to live within the enigmatic situations that have been forced upon them.

A good example is the enigma at the heart of one of the main characters, Kevin Garvey, who inexplicably seems unable to die. In the second season, Kevin seems to die by poisoning, but then spends an episode in a strange version of the afterlife: a hotel where he is tasked with being an international assassin who must kill a presidential nominee embodied by Patti Levin, a character who died in the first season but has haunted Kevin throughout the second season. 'International Assassin' is the most fully batshit episode of the series – until, that is, Kevin returns to this undead realm in the third season's 'The Most Powerful Man in the World (and His Identical Twin Brother)'. In the *New York Times*, critic Jen Chaney calls 'International Assassin' 'a brain-shredding masterpiece', 'a fantastic work of "what-the-hell?" TV' and 'a slice of brazenly surreal storytelling that dazzles, confuses, [and] amuses', effectively writing around the term 'batshit' that probably violates the *Times*'s content standards (Chaney 2015). Kevin inexplicably returns to life at the end of the episode – having been buried for eight hours – only to be killed two episodes later when his neighbour John Murphy shoots him, sending Kevin back to his purgatorial afterlife. Kevin returns to life again, and John finds him covered in blood. Shocked, John says, 'I killed you', to which Kevin replies, 'Nope'. After seeing the severity of Kevin's gunshot wound, John tries to treat it but breaks down in tears and says haltingly, 'I don't understand what's happening'. Kevin's response is 'Me neither', as they both laugh through tears at the absurdity of their situation, and Kevin reassures him, 'It's okay' as the musical score rises with a solo piano version of The Pixies' iconic song 'Where Is My Mind?'

In this scene, John's emotionally wrought perplexion over why Kevin did not die mirrors our own, as we have witnessed Kevin being killed twice by this point, with no explanations for his apparent immortality. Kevin's response that ends the scene provides the clearest explanation we will get: 'Fuck it'. This scene demonstrates – both through character reactions and the evocative musical cue of 'Where Is My Mind?', which references the canonical batshit film *Fight Club* – that our ideal response to such narrative uncertainties is not to ask 'why did that happen?', but rather 'how should I feel about that happening?' Shifting our attention to affective experience rather than narrative comprehension helps to explain the appeal of batshit TV, as it invites us to engage in an ongoing story where emotional response and subverting expectations are privileged over narrative coherence and causality. Once a strict adherence to comprehension and coherence is let go, batshit TV can explore situations that provoke a wider range of affective responses than are seen in typical narratives found on television.

The Leftovers concludes with a striking return to the core enigma inciting the narrative: what happened to the 2 per cent of the world's population who disappeared during the Sudden Departure? The series finale jumps forward around ten years from the core narrative timeline to find main characters Kevin and Nora reuniting after a long separation. After an awkward reunion (where Kevin inexplicably feigns never knowing Nora, despite their multi-year romantic relationship), Nora invites him to her home, makes some tea, and tells him the story of what happened to her during the temporal gap. She describes how she used a form of experimental technology to send her to the place where the departed had gone so that she could find her children. Nora discovered a parallel world where 98 per cent of the population had disappeared to leave only the 'departed' of her own world; she eventually realized that her children did not need her, and so she returned to her original world. We experience this explanation via an emotionally powerful ten-minute monologue that ends with her fear that Kevin would not believe her; he tearfully responds, 'I believe you', and they clasp hands across the table as the series ends.

This finale, which I would rank high atop any list of great television endings, delivers the emotional pay-offs that we want from serialized drama, providing character closure with tears and embraces. Additionally, it suggests the resolution of a core narrative enigma, but in a style that is true to the programme's batshit sensibility: we have no way of knowing whether Nora's story actually happened to her or if it is an imagined tale she tells herself to provide post-traumatic comfort and closure. Unlike in *Lost*'s 'Dave', where ambiguity is quickly resolved for narrative momentum and comprehensibility, *The Leftovers* leans into the enigma to leave us emotionally satisfied but eternally perplexed as to what exactly happened. This neat trick is accomplished through a well-established method of creating ambiguity: the first-person narration of a story that may or may not have happened, rendered as a monologue rather than subjective flashback or dramatization. While far less batshit than an immortal character visiting an afterlife hotel as an assassin, the affective impact is similar in forcing us to reject coherence and clarity, and to let the mystery be. The episode's description on the HBO website summarizes its inherent poetic incoherence: 'Nothing is answered. Everything is answered. And then it ends'.

Lindelof's next series falls between his previous two offerings on the spectrum of complex versus batshit TV: *Watchmen* offers fewer anomalies and inexplicable mysteries than *The Leftovers* but still revels in ongoing perplexion, and it defies straightforward comprehension more than *Lost*. Part of its approach stems from its status as an extension to the narrative world of the original *Watchmen* comic series from the 1980s – as it appeared three decades after the comic, the HBO series needed to be both accessible to viewers who had never read the original, and compelling to diehard fans of the cult classic comic. Lindelof makes this dichotomy explicit in an interview:

> *I want two people watching the pilot, one of whom knows* Watchmen *chapter and verse, the other knows nothing about it. At the end of the pilot, the one who knows nothing about it turns to the one who knows everything about it and says, 'What the fuck just happened?' And the one who knows everything about it says, 'I do not know'. We're all in it together moving forward. (Quoted in Bernardin 2019)*

Thus, when faced with the obstacle of viewers having widely different intertextual frames of reference to make sense of the new series, Lindelof chose to make confusion the universally shared reaction. Rather than pitch the series primarily to *Watchmen* fans or newbies, he united all viewers under the banner of batshit.

Watchmen's storytelling scope is much wider ranging than most limited-run series, jumping across a full century, venturing into outer space, and regularly leaving viewers disoriented concerning continuity in setting, character and events. Its format as a nine-episode miniseries enables a different relationship to seriality and comprehension from Lindelof's previous ongoing series, as the finite storytelling canvas allows perplexing moments and uncertainties to linger across episodes while giving viewers a bounded scope to suggest that things will coalesce and make sense by the finale. *Watchmen*'s use of atemporality and multiple narrative perspectives pushes beyond earlier precedents set by *Lost*, offering a moment-by-moment viewing experience that is among the more disorienting examples of television storytelling, even as many of its incongruities and ambiguities are eventually resolved and clarified by the finale more than in *The Leftovers*. Lindelof explicitly notes that the writers were inspired by *Legion*, *Mr. Robot* and *Atlanta* to push the boundaries of 'absurdity' and 'narrative bravado' beyond what is typically possible within television norms, situating *Watchmen* as clearly part of the broader trend of batshit TV (Hill 2019). As with other such series, many of these moments of absurdity are simply accepted by characters as part of their world rather than framed as mysteries to be solved, as with the regular outbursts of squid raining from the skies, or the presence of masked avengers fighting alongside (also masked) police. Watching the first few episodes is a disorienting excursion into an alternative universe for which the 1980s comic is an insufficient travel guide, confounding the expectations of hardcore fans. While most of the underlying confusions and absurdities in *Watchmen*'s main Tulsa-based storyline are eventually contextualized or explained as part of its unique storyworld, the affective response of perplexion remains central.

The series embraces the batshit aesthetic most overtly in the Adrian Veidt storyline, which runs as a separate narrative detached from the main story for most of the series – whereas the central story focusing on police, white supremacy and family history takes place in Tulsa, six of the seven first episodes pivot to a segment chronicling Veidt's life in a stately country manor (devoid of temporal or spatial contextualization), dealing with his servants, putting on plays, and feuding with a local game warden. Nearly every other detail of these sequences reads as truly batshit when either recapped or viewed: Veidt's servants are all identical clones of one woman and one man, revealed to be grown from foetuses that Veidt fishes out of a local lake. Veidt writes a play about Dr Manhattan (referencing their shared past in the comics), culminating in burning one of his servants alive as part of their performance staged only for him. The servants repeatedly and inexplicably give Veidt a secret horseshoe, which eventually comes in handy for him to dig his way out of prison in episode eight. Veidt accumulates dozens of dead bodies of his cloned servants and catapults them into the sky, where they disappear – and we eventually see him use the bodies to spell out words on the surface of Europa, moon of Jupiter. By the end of the series, all of this makes 'sense', at least in terms of providing narrative causality and explanation, but still remains mostly inexplicable, retaining its underlying absurdity and enigmatic quality. This batshit perplexion outlasts our narrative comprehension, making *Watchmen* function simultaneously as a well-constructed complex narrative that comes together in the end with precision and unity, and a batshit experience with a level of absurdity that underscores the thematic focus on racial trauma – as with *Atlanta*'s Afrosurrealism, perplexion is used to convey the affective disorientation that is a by-product of living under white supremacy.

So what are we to ultimately make of batshit TV? As an experience, it should remain inexplicable, designed to provoke intense emotional reactions that defy analysis or taxonomic classification. As a trend, there is a bit more to be said. Clearly, the narrative innovations of complex TV that have expanded globally in the twenty-first century are still dominant and widespread, with new possibilities and iterations certainly yet to come. But just as such innovations were fostered by the shifts in industrial norms, technological interfaces and viewer engagements that I detailed in *Complex TV*, these ongoing transformations have allowed for this new iteration of groundbreaking television storytelling. I doubt that batshit TV will become as pervasive as narrative complexity has been, as it is a considerably more acquired taste that tends to alienate more viewers than it appeals to – most of the programmes mentioned here are niche successes at best, garnering a cult following and critical accolades rather than the strong ratings of complex hits like *Lost*, *24* and *This Is Us* – but these innovations will certainly continue to open up new possibilities for narrative experimentation. As Lindelof characterized in his reaction to watching *Legion* and *Atlanta*, it is comparable to The Beatles and The Beach Boys listening to each other's work in the mid-1960s and thinking, 'you can do that?' (Hill 2019). Thus, even though I refuse to try to understand batshit TV as a viewer, I still believe that we can learn a lot about what the medium has to offer by embracing and analysing this experience of not comprehending television.

Jason Mittell is Professor of Film & Media Culture and American Studies at Middlebury College in Vermont, USA. His books include *Television and American Culture* (Oxford University Press, 2009), *Complex Television: The Poetics of Contemporary Television Storytelling* (New York University Press, 2015), *Narrative Theory and* Adaptation. (Bloomsbury, 2017) and *How to Watch Television* (co-edited with Ethan Thompson; New York University Press, 2020). He has created a number of video essays about film and television, and is the project manager for *[in]Transition*.

Notes

1. These character names are never mentioned in the series, but have been taken from the episode script found online, retrieved 15 October 2021 from http://mzp-tv.co.uk/tv_scripts/Fargo/Fargo_2x01_-_Waiting_for_Dutch.pdf.
2. For more on narrative anomalies, see Iampolski 1998.
3. For instance, very few of the references to films in *Poetics of Unnatural Narrative* (Alber, Nielsen and Richardson 2013) account for cinematic form, treating them more as medium-less narratives without significant differences from literary norms. A more effective application of unnatural narratology to moving images is by Kiss and Willemsen (2017), who consider its usefulness for understanding 'impossible puzzle films'.

References

Alber, Jan. 2010. 'Hypothetical Intentionalism: Cinematic Narration Reconsidered', in Jan Alber and Monika Fludernik (eds), *Postclassical Narratology: Approaches and Analyses*. Columbus: The Ohio State University Press, pp. 163–85.
Alber, Jan, Stefan Iversen, Henrik Skov Nielsen and Brian Richardson. 2010. 'Unnatural Narratives, Unnatural Narratology: Beyond Mimetic Models', *Narrative* 18(2): 113–36.
Alber, Jan, Henrik Skov Nielsen and Brian Richardson. 2013. *A Poetics of Unnatural Narrative*. Columbus: The Ohio State University Press.
Alsop, Elizabeth. 2018. '"Dead Time": Cinematic Temporalities in *Twin Peaks: The Return*'. Society for Cinema and Media Studies, Toronto.
———. 2020. 'The Television Will Not Be Summarized', *[in]Transition* 7(3). Retrieved 15 October 2021 from http://mediacommons.org/intransition/television-will-not-be-summarized.
Benson-Allott, Caetlin. 2021. *The Stuff of Spectatorship: Material Cultures of Film and Television*. Oakland: University of California Press.
Bernardin, Marc. 2019. 'Blackman Special: Damon Lindelof on *Watchmen*'. Retrieved 15 October 2021 from https://youtu.be/lmCo8TGaMFI?t=1702.
Bruce, La Marr Jurelle. 2021. *How to Go Mad without Losing Your Mind: Madness and Black Radical Creativity*. Durham, NC: Duke University Press.

Butter, Michael. 2017. 'Think Thrice, It's Alright: *Mad Men's* "The Wheel" and the Future Study of Television Narratives', *Narrative* 25(3): 374–89.

Chaney, Jen. 2015. '"*The Leftovers*" Season 2, Episode 8: Stop Thinking in Straight Lines', *The New York Times*, 23 November. Retrieved 15 October 2021 from https://www.nytimes.com/2015/11/22/arts/television/the-leftovers-season-2-episode-8-review-assassin.html.

Elliott, Chris. 2016. 'The Etymology of "Batshit Crazy"', *The Grammar Dance* (blog). Retrieved 15 October 2021 from https://thegrammardance.blogspot.com/2016/02/the-etymology-of-batshit-crazy.html.

Francis, Terri. 2013. 'Introduction: The No-Theory Chant of Afrosurrealism', *Black Camera* 5(1): 95–111. Retrieved 15 October 2021 from https://doi.org/10.2979/blackcamera.5.1.95.

Hill, Libby. 2019. 'Damon Lindelof and the Extra-Textual Brilliance of *Watchmen*', *IndieWire Millions of Screens*. Retrieved 15 October 2021 from https://www.indiewire.com/2019/12/damon-lindelof-watchmen-millions-of-screens-episode-10-1202198191/.

Iampolski, Mikhail. 1998. *The Memory of Tiresias*. Berkeley: University of California Press.

Kiss, Miklós, and Steven Willemsen. 2017. *Impossible Puzzle Films: A Cognitive Approach to Contemporary Complex Cinema*. Edinburgh: Edinburgh University Press.

Mittell, Jason. 2009. '*Lost* in a Great Story: Evaluation in Narrative Television (and Television Studies)', in Roberta Pearson (ed.), *Reading LOST: Perspectives on a Hit Television Show*. London: IB Tauris, pp. 119–38.

———. 2012. 'Playing for Plot in the *Lost* and *Portal* Franchises', *Eludamos: Journal for Computer Game Culture* 6(1): 5–13.

———. 2013. 'Haunted by Seriality: The Formal Uncanny of *Mulholland Drive*', *Cinephile* 9(1): 27–32.

———. 2015. *Complex TV: The Poetics of Contemporary Television Storytelling*. New York: New York University Press.

Sconce, Jeffrey. 2004. 'What If? Charting Television's New Textual Boundaries', in Lynn Spigel and Jan Olsson (eds), *Television After TV: Essays on a Medium in Transition*. Durham, NC: Duke University Press, pp. 93–112.

Seitz, Matt Zoller. 2017. 'The Eighth Episode of *Twin Peaks: The Return* Is Horrifyingly Beautiful', *Vulture*. Retrieved 15 October 2021 from https://www.vulture.com/2017/06/twin-peaks-the-return-part-8-atom-bomb-flashback.html.

Thurm, Eric. 2015. '*Hannibal* Showrunner: "We Are Not Making Television. We Are Making a Pretentious Art Film from the 80s"', *The Guardian*. Retrieved 15 October 2021 from http://www.theguardian.com/tv-and-radio/2015/jun/03/hannibal-tv-showrunner-bryan-fuller.

PART IV
Reading, Viewing, Engaging

Conceptualizing the Pleasures of Being Challenged

CHAPTER 12
Challenges of Enjoying Morally Ambiguous Character Drama
The *Dexter* Case

Ed S. Tan, Monique Timmers, Claire M. Segijn, Suzanna J. Opree and Guus Bartholomé

Introduction

Since its rise in the 1950s, television drama has been considered more an entertainment commodity than an art form with its own intricacies. Yet television scholars such as Schlütz (2016), Mittell (2006, 2015) and Dunleavy (2017) have signalled the increasing complexity of serial television drama over the years, especially since the emergence of multiplatform broadcasting and the related practice of VOD binge-watching.

According to Mittell, American dramas – from popular series such as *Seinfeld, Lost, The West Wing* and *The X-files* to HBO successes like *The Sopranos, Six Feet Under, Curb Your Enthusiasm* and *The Wire* – are characterized by demanding narrative forms. How can such complex drama be enjoyed? Mittell (2006) argued that viewers build up decoding competence in the use of the 'local' conventions of a series over time. The viewer's pleasure is felt through competent decoding in answer to narrative and stylistic challenges. Thus, the joys of complex television drama include aesthetic appreciation. Another complexity of recent television drama has also been noted: especially the quality series feature of morally ambiguous primary characters' (Schluetz 2016: 113). It may lend moral and psychological complexity to them and introduce moral considerations in viewers' understanding and possibly enjoyment of such series.

The present chapter deals primarily with the complex experience of ambiguous morality – a challenge to viewers that is more affective than cognitive. It aims to substantiate the engaging potential of this affective moral challenge. In this way, we hope to add to the chapters of this volume that address complexity as formal-structural experimentation, setting a cognitive-aesthetic challenge to viewers of film and television. The analytic focus is on a recent subgenre of complex serial television drama, namely Morally Ambiguous Character or 'MAC' drama. Traditional television crime drama has predominantly featured straight detectives dealing with mean crooks. Audiences enjoyed these simple narratives mainly because they witnessed a sympathetic protagonist succeeding in giving immoral characters what they deserved. By contrast, MAC drama storylines revolve around ambiguous protagonists who commit immoral acts, thus making it unclear whether they deserve our sympathy. This is mainly because the story raises uncertainty about how bad the protagonist really is. In spite of its complexity, however, the genre is firmly established as a form of entertainment, as illustrated by the success of series such as *Breaking Bad*, *The Wire*, *House of Cards* and *Dexter*.

The question, then, is how television dramas featuring protagonists who display questionable moral intent and actions can be enjoyed or appreciated as entertainment. In this chapter, we investigate, from a psychological point of view, what challenges are posed by MAC drama. We will use an already classic example of MAC drama, *Dexter*, for analysis. We propose an explanation of enjoyment of such series despite, or perhaps due to, moral discomfort. More specifically, our explanation is based on elaborate emotion regulation strategies resulting in an appreciation of the moral dilemmas posed by the MACs and their actions.

Fiction as a Game of Make-Believe: Challenge and Reward

Our account of enjoyment of morally ambiguous character drama is based on the notion that watching a television drama is equivalent to participating in a game of fiction. We follow philosopher Kendall Walton's (1990) conception of fiction as a game of make-believe (or pretence) in which recipients are invited to engage in a make-believe world with make-believe events and characters. Playful imagination of fictional worlds is led by 'props' or cues presented in a narrative or drama. Cues are immediate representations, more or less similar to objects or events in the real world. The typical example in make-believe games is that a banana can be used suggestively as a revolver. Walton proposes that, in a fictional story, every object or event is taken as a cue to imagine it as being real for the moment. For example, in *Casablanca*, the event of Humphrey Bogart looking at a group of figurants singing the Marseillaise cues viewers to imagine Rick Blain approvingly watching the French colony demonstrating their patriotic pride, momentarily taking it all as real.

Participation in fiction as a game of make-believe is appreciated as much for the activity as it is for the generated fictional world itself (see Tan and Visch 2018). Absorption in the generation and active participation in a game is rewarding because it satisfies basic psychological needs, according to Przybylski, Rigby and Ryan (2010). These researchers have argued that pleasant absorption in gaming activity is not due to any external incentive for the activity; instead, players of games experience pleasant absorption associated with the satisfaction of basic human needs. These are competence, autonomy and relatedness. When players sense the satisfaction of these needs, they experience intrinsic reward in the activity, are more deeply absorbed in it, and want to pursue it, enjoy it and feel happier. Game activity satisfies certain needs: for competence, when players feel their activity is effective; for autonomy, when players feel their activity is deliberate and under their personal volition; and for relatedness, when players sense belongingness to a game's player community or partners.[1]

Sherry (2004) likewise proposed that absorption in the activity of a game is due to experiencing it as intrinsically rewarding. He refers to absorption as 'flow', a concept he borrowed from Csikszentmihalyi (1997). The notion of balancing challenge and reward in games of fictional make-believe is the basis for our analysis of MAC drama as a playful exercise. It is diagrammed in Figure 12.1.

The game of fiction in drama sets challenges to recipients that are different from those in video gaming. In video games, recipients need to accomplish aims in the make-believe world as make-believe protagonists. In drama, protagonists meet challenges posed by the storyworld; recipients identifying with them have to follow the protagonist's acts and deal with their own emotions due to these and their outcomes.

The precise nature of the challenge depends on the genre. For example, in an adventure drama, recipients must empathize and side with the protagonist, following them through the obstacles (e.g. Zillmann 2000). In watching horror movies, viewers need to master their fear. In meeting the challenge set by a fictional game of make-believe – be it a video game or a drama – the recipient incurs 'costs', by which we mean generally unpleasant efforts and, especially, unpleasant affect. Efforts and costs are the exercise side of the coin of meeting the challenge. The flipside is the experience of the activity as a playful activity that is

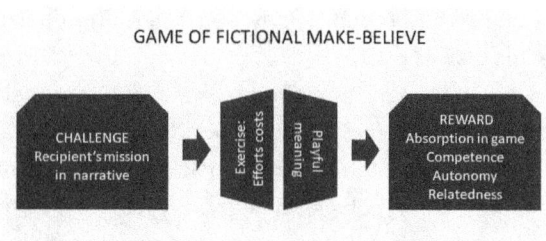

Figure 12.1. Playful exercise in games of fictional make-believe. Diagram by the authors.

in itself rewarding because of its meaning: meeting a game's challenge. In an absorbing experience, enjoyment of the game comes from dealing with the challenge. In the next sections, we introduce the challenge of MAC drama, discuss efforts and costs spent on meeting it, and then consider its rewards.

The Game of MAC Drama and Its Moral Challenge

MAC drama is a rather recent genre that is too complex to be categorized as just crime drama. The most complete analysis of the genre has been achieved by Margrethe Bruun Vaage (2015). Vaage uses the term 'antihero drama' rather than MAC drama. Anti-heroes are main characters who commit crimes as serious as murders. The protagonist's moral flaws are profound as well as persistent: the protagonist is 'no saint – he truly is immoral, in the sense that he is continually violating moral principles' (ibid.: xi).

American anti-hero television narratives may be quite demanding because of intricate narrative structures and self-conscious style. However, the profound challenge they confront the viewer with, is the need to deal with anti-heroes' moral transgressions. These would never be approved of if they were encountered in real life, and real-life perpetrators are downright disliked, to say the least. A classic example of MAC drama is *Dexter* (creator: Manos; directors: Rosenberg and Lieberman, 2006). It is a prototypical MAC drama because its moral complexity seems an attractive feature of the show. The show's protagonist, Dexter Morgan (Michael C. Hall), is a forensics analyst who leads a double life as a serial killer. He is a respectable member of a vice squad serving the cause of finding murderers; yet, at the same time, he is also a seriously disturbed vigilante individual hunting after criminals who have escaped justice. He kills them mercilessly, in cold blood and with technical finesse.

Like ourselves, Vaage considers MAC dramas – such as *Dexter* – as fictional games of make-believe. Our analysis of the challenge posed by the genre and its effects on aesthetic experience draws on her book *The Antihero in American Television*. However, we will conceive of the game of make-believe implied in Vaage's analysis somewhat more explicitly than she does, seeing it as a test of the viewer's moral stamina. This conceptualization is reminiscent of rather rare proposals of researchers in television fiction and fictional video games. For example, Hill (1997) mentions boundary testing as a gratification of watching violent films; Zillmann and Gibson (1996) point to the opportunity that horror films offer to some male viewers to prove their masculinity; and Jansz (2005) points to the use of violent video games for experiencing socially controversial emotions.

We propose, specifically, that the game of MAC drama poses the following challenge to the viewers: testing one's capacity to not only watch horrific events that are outcomes of immoral acts but also to enjoy the show. This is the challenge that makes efforts and costs meaningful to the individual viewer. Rewards are that 'winners' prove to themselves that they can stand watching the horror and even like the drama. For example, viewers of *Dexter* have to witness and endure – in lengthy and gruesome detail – how the protagonist murders his victims, and like it. 'Losers' receive the penalty of proving themselves unable to endure the horrors and immorality. They may quit the game altogether – that is, stop viewing the current episode and dislike it to the point that they will not want to watch any episode ever again.

In our conception, viewers accept the challenge and the efforts and costs involved in meeting it. To the degree that they do, they will be absorbed in the activity of meeting the challenge. The cornerstone in Vaage's explanation of why anti-hero drama is enjoyable is what she calls 'fictional relief'. It refers to a temporary suspension of 'fully considering the moral and political consequences of one's engagement with fiction, from considering whatever relevance the fiction film may have for the real world, and from whatever realistic basis the narrative has' (Vaage 2015: 235).

Fictional relief is associated with attention to and transportation into the fictional world, and low-cognitive-effort affective responding. In fictional relief, the evaluation of characters tends towards fully intuitive judgement, doing away with any elaborate moral reasoning. Moral evaluations that would hold in the real world are suspended. According to Vaage, viewers may be cognizant throughout the show that the MAC is acting immorally, but fictional relief keeps the thought dormant. *Reality check moments* involve a sudden confrontation of the self with real threats to one's moral integrity; views of a gruesome killing, and the anti-hero enjoying it, act as wake-up calls to consider the immorality of the acts presented, and recall the consequences that their siding with immoral characters would have if they were individuals acting in the real world. Scrutinous deliberate moral reflection ensues.

We would emphasize the positive role of deliberate reflection somewhat more than Vaage does, and the efforts it takes in the experience of the drama as a whole. In our view, absorption is the major pleasurable state in the game of fiction (see Kuijpers et al. 2014; Kuiken and Douglas 2017; Kuijpers and Hakemulder 2017). Absorption is the experience of progress in meeting a game's challenge. Seemingly automated imaginations of witnessing events in a fictional world are part of absorption. This is because, in absorption, the recipient's attention is drawn away from the constructive efforts involved in make-believe (see, e.g., Busselle and Bilandzic 2009). But deliberate reflection can also add to absorption instead of interrupting it. The most intensely emoting moments may be accompanied by reflection but, all the while, the game's challenge – testing one's capacity to stand such horrible scenes – is felt the strongest, and absorption in the game is maximal.

The rewards offered to the viewer of MAC drama, as we understand from Vaage (2015), are the following. Fictional relief as an escape from the moral conventions and other constraints of real life enables rewarding engagements with MACs. Among these are the pleasures of partiality or siding with the MAC, suspense based on empathy, interest in or fascination for the MAC, and aesthetic appreciation. Her analyses of anti-heroes convincingly suggest that fictional relief is key to the engagement with characters such as Dexter, Hannibal, Tony Soprano and others. Finally, there is a role for expertise in the rewards offered by anti-hero drama: Vaage (2015), like Mittell (2006), argues that competence in decoding anti-hero series increases familiarity, partiality, empathy and generally fictional relief, including moral forgiveness and aesthetic appreciation.

Before we are ready to discuss the challenges posed by MAC drama following Vaage's analysis, we first need to settle on the use of related terms. Conceiving drama as a game, we will reserve the word 'challenge' for the mission assigned to the viewer as a player of the game of fiction. We are interested in evaluating the demands posed to viewers of MAC drama – instead of speaking of 'challenges', here we will stick to 'efforts and costs': (cognitive) efforts, in the next sections, are demanding cognitive processes such as taxing executive operations, problem solving and deliberate reasoning; (affective) costs are unpleasant affective experiences unwanted in (hedonic) principle, such as disgust and fear.

In Vaage's 2015 analysis, costs and efforts spent engaging with MAC drama seem rather low throughout, except for moments of reality checks. Moral scrutiny here presents substantial cognitive efforts and affective costs. We explicitly propose that the demands posed by such moments represent the norm, especially for affective costs of MAC drama as a genre. Taking Vaage's analysis as our starting point, we consider and deliberate the viewer's reflection on moral evaluation of the acts, the protagonist and the self when watching these as a means to an end – the end being the regulation of unpleasant emotions. Downregulating these unpleasant emotions is necessary for watching and enjoying the immoral ordeal we have been made to believe – the challenge one is meeting. So conceived, the challenges set by anti-heroes and anti-hero drama are met by efforts spent and affective costs incurred in emotion regulation.

There is some literature on the role of negative emotions in the arts. For example, Oatley and Johnson-Laird (2008) conclude that music, literature and film induce emotions in an aesthetic context and thus help us to understand our emotions. Oliver (e.g. Oliver and Hartmann, 2010) proposes distinguishing enjoyment of cultural artefacts from appreciation. The latter response requires an appraisal of poignance and meaning in possibly intense negative emotions. Menninghaus et al. (2017) proposed an encompassing distancing-embracing model of negative emotions in the reception of art. It is postulated that unpleasant emotions such as sadness, disgust and fear are pervasive and intensely felt, but are counterbalanced by positive emotions, including enjoyment deriving from the compositional interplay of emotions and aesthetic merits of the work of art's presentation of negative emotion elicitors. Menninghaus et al. address the regulation of negative emotion regulation through aesthetic distancing. Their solution to the issue of the enjoyability of art-produced negative emotions is a major inspiration for our proposal; however, to our knowledge, no attempts have so far been made to address the role of emotion regulation in the reception of fiction or drama in ways informed by recent research in emotion regulation. We intend to make up for this lacuna by introducing the major emotion regulation strategies investigated in the research, and by evaluating their appropriateness, costs and benefits for the MAC drama viewer.

Emotion Regulation in Watching *Dexter*: Strategies, Efforts, Costs and Benefits

Following Gross, who founded the research area in emotion regulation in the 1990s (Gross 1998), people are not subjugated by their emotions but can regulate them. Negative emotions such as sadness, anger and fear can be downregulated, and positive ones like happiness, amusement and mirth can be enhanced. To this end, people use strategies of regulation either unconsciously or in acts of explicit self-regulation. Such strategies aim to control or alter the default response to an emoting situation. For example, the default emotional response to someone insulting you may be embodied and displayed aggression, and an experienced intent to attack. However, situational (e.g. when the insulter is an important customer) and personal features (when you are a particularly prudent person) do moderate default responses. All emotion regulation can take substantial executive resources, and when sustained, it can result in cognitive depletion (Wheeler, Briñol and Hermann 2007).

We discuss the possible use, costs and benefits of the major strategies of emotion regulation used by viewers of *Dexter* watching, as an example, episode 5 of season 1, 'Love American Style' (producers: Goldwyn, Colleton and Phillips; creator: J. Manos; writer: M. Rosenberg; director R. Lieberman; first aired 29 October 2006). The episode can be summarized as follows: an illegal immigrant from Cuba has been missing for days. Dexter finds a police list of possible suspects of murder in a comparable case, and follows Jorge Castillo, the owner of a salvage yard. He finds out that Castillo smuggles Cuban immigrants into Florida and kills those who cannot pay their fees. Dexter awaits him after Castillo visits a container where he keeps his victims imprisoned, and leads him to a trailer at his salvage yard. As Dexter prepares to kill him, Castillo's wife Valerie arrives at the scene, and Dexter decides to kill them both as they confess to cooperating in the murders. (This summary has been adapted from Author unknown, no date).

Emotion Regulation Strategies

The two most studied emotion regulation strategies since Gross (1998) are suppression and reappraisal.

Expressive suppression of immediate negative affect targets the emotional response. It consists of preventing one's bodily reactions from being displayed to others by inhibitive efforts. The climax scenes of the episode show Dexter about to kill, and then kill, a victim. Graphic portrayals of preparations are shown: the Castillos tied to beds and gagged, terrified, awaiting what looks like their execution. Dexter questions them and speaks an indictment, making incisions with a scalpel and producing and manipulating surgical instruments. The torture is followed by the execution. We see the knife being raised above the head, and a downward stabbing movement is suggested. These moments are likely to induce automated expression of gut feelings such as tension, fear and disgust. These expressions cause kinaesthetic sensations that, in turn, intensify the unwanted feeling. An immediate and virtually automated regulation answer to these emotions can be suppression of the expression.

Reappraisal of morally offensive acts targets the mental representation of the emoting situation. The person assumes a distanced cognitive set (as in most of Gross's studies) or reinterprets the emoting situation (e.g. Ochsner and Gross 2005), and the altered perception or understanding can then modify the emotional response (e.g. Gross and Thompson 2006). The immoral acts of torturing and killing the Castillo victims at the episode's climax presumably activate morally inspired negative emotions such as fear, disgust and revulsion. By 'morally inspired', we mean that fear, disgust and revulsion are not just gut reactions to violent imagery but are based on appraisals of the violation of moral principles: for example, the revulsion one feels when witnessing the fearful looks of the Castillos when they are tied up, and watching Dexter prepare his instruments for the killing. It is based on the realization that one's moral convictions are at stake: no one should be tortured or killed like that. Reappraising – that is, changing the meaning of the acts – is a strategy that fits a critical purpose. In order to enjoy the drama as entertainment, viewers need to overcome negative moral emotions connected to Dexter and his acts, and maintain sympathy for him.

Moral disengagement is the perfect form that reappraisal can take when immoral acts threaten sympathy and enjoyment in MAC drama. The concept was first launched by Bandura (1999). He referred to it as a set of manoeuvres that people use when they perceive themselves agentive of morally reprehensible or inhumane conduct. These manoeuvres evade moral self-sanctions. They include moral justification, sanitizing language, advantageous comparison, downplaying personal agency by diffusion or displacement of responsibility, minimizing harm done by one's actions, and blaming or dehumanizing victims. Moral disengagement applies to the perceived agency of the self but can also be applied in the control of moral responses to others' conduct. Raney (2004) was the first to propose that viewers of MAC drama employ moral disengagement as a strategy for maintaining sympathy for a MAC in order to enjoy the drama (see also Raney 2005, 2011; Shafer and Raney 2012; Janicke and Raney 2015: 201). The moral judgement of a MAC is adapted to the sympathetic disposition.

Bartholomé and Segijn (2011) interviewed viewers of the example episode of *Dexter* and identified uses of moral disengagement by their test viewers. For example, viewers can find the Castillos guilty of the assault of innocent people and serial killing for money. They can then blame the victims in order to morally justify the acts. Alternatively, they can downplay Dexter's personal agency due to his split personality: a dark side balanced by a humane spirit. Thus, moral disengagement reappraises the acts and downregulates morally inspired fear, disgust and related antipathy for Dexter. Effects of moral disengagement on sympathy for MACs, and/or enjoyment of MAC drama have been documented by empirical researchers such as Raney 2004, 2011; Eden, Grizzard and Lewis 2011; Tsay and Krakowiak 2011; Krakowiak and Oliver 2012; Krakowiak and Tsay-Vogel 2013; Hartmann 2013; and Janicke and Raney 2018.

Vaage (2015) argues that the climax moments, such as the killing of the Castillos, are reality check moments in that viewers become aware that they are watching acts that violate their moral principles. Sensing the guiltiness of their pleasure potentially gives rise to moral embarrassment and shame. A more drastic reappraisal than moral disengagement is then called for – namely, fictionalizing the witnessed acts. Fictionalizing is the moral disengagement manoeuvre exclusive to the domain of fiction; it is not among the well-known manoeuvres proposed by Bandura (1999). Watching the torture and killing of the Castillos, viewers of *Dexter* can fall back on the meta-fictional realization that there is no harm in witnessing such torture and killing as fictional constructions.

We propose that cognitive reappraisal is the dominant strategy in the regulation of negative emotions induced by MAC drama. It is dominant because the ambiguity of the protagonist and his predicament invite apologetic accounts of immoral acts, and moral disengagement in particular. Moreover, as we will see in the next section, reappraisal has a more favourable cost-benefit ratio than other strategies.

Acceptance of immoral acts and negative affect, as an alternative regulation strategy, has received much less attention than suppression and reappraisal. This strategy bets on an optimal experience of the emotion, even if it is a negative one. Acceptance is a mindful way of dealing with negative emotions that, according to Troy et al. (2018: 74), allows 'individuals to nonjudgmentally engage with the full range of human experiences and promote increased self-awareness, self-compassion, and behavioral flexibility'. The instruction given to participants in the experiment of Troy et al. (2015) illustrates this mindset: 'Please watch the following film clip carefully. ... [A]s you watch, try to experience [your] feelings fully and do not try to control or change them in any way' (ibid.).

It should be noted that acceptance is, somewhat paradoxically, a strategy that excludes any of the other emotion regulation strategies. We can surmise that the ideal accepting viewers of *Dexter* would experience fear and disgust to the full in the face of the torture and killing. They would not resist their expressions or empathy with the terrified Castillos. Ideal acceptance would exclude limitations to the imagination and impact of these scenes by reappraisal strategies such as moral disengagement and fictionalizing strategies. To make the argument consistent, we consider that ideally mindful accepting viewers could also accept the fact that their moral convictions are violated by Dexter's torture and killing. They would even allow the insight that their voluntary watching of the terrible acts is morally dubious. Hence, they would also experience unpleasant self-aware emotions, such as shame and guilt, more intensely than non-accepting viewers.

Costs and Benefits Associated with Emotion Regulation Strategies

Costs and benefits of suppression and reappraisal are known from several empirical studies in emotion regulation. Suppression has been shown to result in depletion: experimental studies have shown that induced attempts to avoid showing emotional reactions in response to fear, sadness, or disgust-inducing films lead to impaired memory performance, fatigue and decreased tolerance of pain (see, e.g., Muraven, Tice and Baumeister 1998; Richards and Gross 2002; Ochsner and Gross 2005; Troy et al. 2018). As important for a cost-benefit assessment, it is apparent from these studies that expressive suppression is generally not very effective.

We can be more specific on the costs and efforts of moral disengagement as a form of cognitive reappraisal. Moral disengagement is, in our view, not a matter of simply switching off an appraisal of immorality; we argue that cognitive efforts involved in this may, in cases, be so considerable as to rival the complexity of moral scrutiny, as referred to by Vaage (2015) in her characterization of the reflective processing of reality-check moments. Furthermore, we argue that moral disengagement comes with unpleasant self-related emotions, such as shame and guilt, that can count as affective costs.

The cognitive efforts of moral disengagement seem negligible at first sight. Raney (2004) was the first to suggest that the strategy is facilitated by MAC story schemas. Their effectiveness has been demonstrated by Krakowiak and Tsay-Vogel (2013) and Grizzard et al. (2018). From their studies, it would seem that retrieval and handling of such schemas is easy because of their familiarity. However, Eden, Daalmans and Johnson (2017) concluded from their own and previous empirical studies that MACs are not based on familiar clear-cut hero vs. villain schemas. We would therefore more specifically argue that the defining characteristic of MACs is ambiguity of characterization; a variety of schemas are applicable in understanding their moral intent.

The moral ambiguity of *Dexter* has been qualitatively analysed by Vaage (2015).[2] Moral disengagement is supported by a compound schema, the vigilante-psychopath 'Dark Passenger'. In this schema, the vigilante is the bright heroic side of the MAC, and the psychopath the evil side – the latter with childhood trauma as a foundation. A variety of component schemas, like the competent judge or the psychiatric patient, have each been shown to support moral evaluations of *Dexter* (van Ommen et al. 2017). In morally disengaging from torture and killings, we would argue that viewers of *Dexter* need to consider the available options. Mentally performing 'seeing *Dexter* as' simulations, they can decide which schema is the best for disengaging from a particular immoral or revulsive act. The exercise of 'seeing as' is then complicated by conflicting cues from Dexter's thoughts presented to viewers through voice-overs. Metonymic and metaphorical inferences must often bridge the gap between immediately perceived actions and one of the other schemas. The outcome may not be that the winning schema takes all, but rather some weighed combination of schemas that allows for the moral disengagement best fitting a particular moment. The operations involved require more or less elaborate reasoning. Moral disengagement comes with considerable affective costs. Affective challenges, we propose, are associated with moral objections to moral disengagement.

Moral disengagement piggybacks on profound empathizing. Watching Dexter, viewers take his immoral perspective and are thus led to morally disengage from his heinous acts, just as he does himself. Empathizing with an immoral protagonist often entails a violation of the viewer's own moral convictions. Fictionalizing, in our view, also requires cognitive efforts. It may take some effort to grasp the constructions that conjure up the storyworld in which one is absorbed, and in the end, there may be viewers for whom schema-based disengagement and fictionalizing do not suffice to deal with the sense of guilty pleasure. They may keep a nagging awareness of engaging with an immoral persona, even if only in the imagination. All they can do is accept their feelings of shame and guilt.

Chambers, Gullone and Allen (2009) reviewed research into efforts and costs of mindful acceptance of unpleasant emotions. Acceptance takes conscious effort because engagement with negative emotions and applying downregulation to these is, as the authors say, an ontogenetically and phylogenetically long-term habit. Overcoming downregulation in mindful acceptance takes a great deal of attentional resources. The authors, for an illustration, point at the known effort that it takes to achieve mindfulness. It can require thousands of hours of meditation training before the right attentional processes in acceptance can become automated. Troy et al. (2018) compared acceptance with reappraisal strategies induced in viewers of a sad film. The reappraisal instruction invited participants to see sad events in a positive light and find positive lessons within them. Acceptance effectively upregulated negative emotions – especially sadness – while psychophysiological manifestations diminished, which points to a decoupling of embodied response from feeling responses. Reappraisal downregulated felt sadness and associated psychophysiological responses. Acceptance proved to be the far more cognitively taxing strategy.

The effects of acceptance as an emotion regulation strategy have received less attention from researchers than those of suppression and reappraisal. Moreover, it may be too challenging a strategy to be applied in watching MAC drama. For these reasons, we must be careful in considering acceptance as a serious candidate for the default downregulation of unpleasant emotions triggered by revulsive scenes in MAC drama. However, it can also be argued that its successful application helps to reap to the full the emotional rewards that MAC drama has to offer. This will be considered in the next section.

Playful Reward in MAC Drama

We have proposed that meeting the challenge posed by watching an MAC drama can be identified with an exercise in regulating unpleasant, morally inspired emotions. Now that we have evaluated the efforts and costs invested by viewers in the exercise, we turn to its reward side (see Figure 12.1). Emotion regulation in MAC drama is not just a demanding exercise but also a meaningful one; it has meaning as a challenge of one's spectator stamina, rendering efforts and costs meaningful to the viewers' self. We propose that the primary rewards associated with MAC drama as a game of fiction are, first, absorption in emotion and emotion regulation, and second, the satisfaction of the basic needs of competence, autonomy and relatedness. The balancing of challenge and rewards required for absorption is realized by the MAC drama's narrative and style. On the one hand, they invite viewers to downregulate morally inspired negative emotions, increasing the likelihood of successful regulation. On the other hand, narrative and stylistic devices bring rewards within reach: notably, pleasant absorption and satisfaction of competence, autonomy and relatedness needs.

We elaborate in more detail on how the various strategies of regulation by the viewer are supported by narrative and style in *Dexter*. In the examples, the viewer's regulation is demonstrated by the protagonist or argued by the narrator. First, suppression of expression is displayed by Dexter in his act of torture and killing for the viewer to mirror: an efficient operation by a composed professional sustaining a perfect poker face and addressing his victims in a distant way. The empathetic viewer is invited to follow the behavioural example. Second, the manoeuvres of moral disengagement are demonstrated to the viewer. The efficient surgery depiction of the killing is equivalent to the use of sanitizing language, first of all blaming the victim – Dexter's indictment is confirmed by the Castillos, rendering them guilty victims.

An important stylistic device helps the viewer to understand the argument for moral justification: throughout the episode, Dexter observes the evil intent and practices of the Castillos, and makes these explicit in voice-over comments. Throughout the episode, too, his voice-over comments point at the inability of the justice system to deal with serial killing perpetrators. Thus, viewers are prepared to consider the vigilante killings as necessary and to use the responsibility displacement manoeuvre as Dexter does. Subjective flashback sequences lend viewers access to Dexter's past that provides excuses for his immoral conduct (the origin of his emotional handicap is a childhood trauma). In-depth access to Dexter's motivation throughout the episode provides ground for downplaying his agency in torture and killing.

We can be brief about the third emotion regulation strategy – acceptance. We surmise that *Dexter* as a drama exhibits a multitude of cues indicating to viewers that they are engaging in a game of fiction. Stylistic excess, such as the blood motif and wry humour, have been observed by Vaage (2015) in her analyses. The effect of an awareness of fictionality is a readiness to let go of critical disbelief. We argue that the downregulations of fear and moral disgust are thus modelled to the viewer: virtually all they have to do is follow the demonstrations and subscribe to the arguments provided by the narrator.

After discussing the support for emotion regulation strategies in the drama, we come to the viewer rewards associated with successful use of the strategies. Two rewards are associated with the outcome of all strategies, namely, pride – the self-aware sense of competent gameplay – and the pleasure of being absorbed in Dexter's world.

Successful moral disengagement comes with the reward of felt competence. As argued above, moral disengagement from the acts of MACs takes efforts of disambiguation. In resolving the moral ambiguity of *Dexter*, viewers need to construct motivations that underly Dexter's seemingly immoral actions. Viewers may, in particular, enjoy their success in finding the appropriate schemas for a persona that cannot help but commit the killings, especially in view of the inconsistency among schemas. Executioner vs serial killer, and psychopath vs traumatized child, are examples. Viewers can not only enjoy their resolution of ambiguities but can also appreciate the character's ambiguity as a playful challenge. Furthermore, by putting their moral convictions on hold, viewers may experience a rewarding sense of freedom for their imagination – a sense of autonomy. They can be aware that they have the option to go along in immoral reasoning and illicit imaginations. Being given the option to consume forbidden fruits can be experienced as an enjoyable teasing game. Actual consumption of these is also enjoyed: imaginatively standing in the shoes of the protagonist, viewers may empathetically enjoy the killing as a victory of justice. We propose that it is this empathic act that makes for the core rewarding experience. It meets the challenge of enjoying the immoral act, a need for competence is satisfied, and viewers experience pride. The achieved empathic understanding of Dexter's actions and their appraisal as morally right allow for sympathy to grow. Growing sympathy for Dexter, in turn, satisfies a basic relatedness need, heightening enjoyment of the show.

We should hasten to add to our proposal on the pleasures of competent moral disengagement that there is a downside to the success. As said, we propose that the costs of moral disengagement are not fully balanced by rewarding fun in games. Reality-check moments owe their label to the viewers considering the reality of violating their own moral convictions. Successful moral disengagement may incite pride while also remaining a cause for embarrassment and guilt. In sum, sympathizing with a morally ambiguous character and going along with their immoral acts may be an ambiguous pleasure.

We propose that the third emotion regulation strategy – acceptance – is, in principle, the most rewarding one, even if it is also the most demanding. Mindfully watching, imagining and letting go of any coping efforts, viewers can be fully absorbed in the drama and the game of make-believe. Even more importantly, to have mindfully watched and listened to horrible events, and gone through all the morally inspired emotions they provoke, is the most uncompromised evidence of one's capacity to stand witnessing the horrific acts being committed by Dexter. Thus, the reward is a maximal sense of competence in playing the game. A mindful, open attitude is also rewarded by the most intense absorption in the storyworld and the widest range of emotions. Positive emotions, such as sympathy and positive empathic emotions, co-occur with negative ones like disgust and moral revulsion. Acceptance allows for the full experience of competing appraisals and emotions resulting from Dexter's moral ambiguity.

Accepting the full range of positive and negative emotions would have paradoxical implications for self-aware emotions. One can feel satisfaction in standing the test of watching gruesome immoral acts and, at the same time, experience guilt and shame about the pleasure. In our example, the aesthetics of *Dexter* may, on the one hand, scaffold acceptance and, on the other, provide rewards for successful acceptance. Mindful watching allows the viewer to appreciate the aesthetic qualities of MAC drama described by Vaage (2015: 2–47). An example of such aesthetic qualities is splendid views, such as the path pegged out in the nightly dark by dozens of burning wax candles that lead Castillo to the place where Dexter is to kill him. Open-minded observation may also leave room for contemplation on the connotations beyond the portrayed action. For example, Dexter's wry humour and the producer's black comedic intentions can be appreciated.

Whether or not acceptance leads to imagining the horrific torturing and killing scenes as real presents an interesting question. On the one hand, an open attitude and attentive watching may enhance awareness of fictional constructions, which would undermine the perception of reality in these scenes. Especially in Menninghaus et al.'s (2017) model of emotion regulation referred to earlier, fictionalizing is the major distancing factor in aesthetic appreciation. However, acceptance, as the term implies, involves abstinence from any emotion downregulation. This means that fictionalizing, as a negative emotion downregulation strategy, is precluded by acceptance. We propose that a way out of this issue is to surmise that acceptance involves an awareness of fictionality but that this awareness is not used to reappraise negatively emoting events. Instead, signs of fictionality are taken for what they are: cues that invite, license and scaffold a full imagination of the presented events as real.

We can conclude that, while acceptance is very hard to accomplish, it makes for the most intense and variegated experience of emotions, both positive and negative. Yet, one may wonder whether the mélange, including extreme valence opposites, can truly be enjoyed. Following Oliver and Hartmann (2010), we propose that it can be appreciated rather than enjoyed, because it is meaningful rather than hedonically gratifying.

Skilled Playful Exercise in MAC Drama: Viewer Expertise

The balancing of challenge and reward in a game depends on the player's (or, in this case, the viewer's) expertise. Complex television, according to Mittell (2006), has its aficionados who can meet challenges thanks to mastery and skills developed in repeated dedicated viewing. MAC drama conceived of as a game of fiction is a case in point.

The effects of repeated viewing on fictional relief have been established in media-psychological empirical research (Eden, Grizzard and Lewis 2011; Shafer and Raney 2012). In her analyses, Vaage (2015) has pointed to the role of connoisseurship, specifically in the enjoyment of MAC drama, that enables the viewer to find rewarding experiences in the drama that go far beyond the pleasure of fictional relief. In line with her reasoning, we consider that, whereas first-time viewers may be overwhelmed by the story of heinous acts, regular viewers have recognized the drama as a playful test of coping ability and have developed skills that lighten efforts and reduce the costs of suppression and reappraisal. Repeated and dedicated viewing may transform suppression and cognitive reappraisal from downregulation strategies into playful explorative efforts.

We consider that aficionados are good at mentally performing 'seeing Dexter as' exercises, trying out which schema is the best for disengaging from a particular immoral or revulsive act, as well as dealing with conflicting cues in Dexter's actions. The seeing-as exploration, as we noted, involves recognizing metonymic and metaphorical allusions in the characterization of Dexter. Expertise due to viewing experience may, perhaps most importantly, consist of a readiness to involve the self in the simulation. We propose that aficionados who are already trained to stand in the shoes of Dexter may also more easily wonder and imagine what they themselves would do in the situation, and deliberate on what that would mean to their moral self. If there is truth in this conjecture, the MAC drama functions as what Hakemulder (2000) called a moral laboratory.

We propose specifically that aficionados of MAC dramas, more than naive viewers, can use acceptance as their strategic answer to the challenge of regulating negative emotions. An open-minded attitude allows for curiously exploring the moral ambiguity of the character, and freely imagining what it is like to stand in the MAC's shoes. Unhindered by a need to sympathize with him or suppress unpleasant feelings, one can also consider his darkest sides; when the immorality of his acts is accepted, there is space left for the aesthetic qualities of the drama to be appreciated. Here, reality-checking may be traded for aesthetic attention to, and the savouring of, narrative qualities, *mise en scène* and visual motifs.

Perhaps, accepting the pleasure of watching immoral acts as a guilty one, and even experiencing unpleasant self-aware emotions, may add to the feeling of competence. In addition to competence, autonomy and relatedness, too, may be rewarded more than for incidental, inexperienced viewers. The self's open and playful attitude towards moral deviance may be appreciated as freedom from conventions. Moreover, the experienced viewer may realize they are in the virtual company of other 'experts', and derive from it a fan's satisfaction of basic relatedness needs.[3] Paradoxically, the expert's guilt and shame can be a ground for pride at being one of the few who can appreciate both the pleasure and its guiltiness.

Conclusion: Challenge and Reward Balance in the Aesthetic Experience of MAC Drama

What have we learnt about the role of challenge in the aesthetic experience of morally ambiguous character drama? The genre is associated with the popular aesthetic experience of entertainment, but it goes beyond the challenges offered by the fictional game of traditional crime drama. There, viewers are required to side with morally straight detectives, to guess 'who done it', and endure the adversities detectives meet with in restoring justice (Cooke 2006). Self-involvement can be rather low. By contrast, MAC drama fits into a trend of growing complexity in television drama signalled by Mittell (2015). Select, competent audiences seek challenging and thought-provoking complex serial forms, the complexity of which would border on that of art film cinema narration (Bordwell 1985).

Siding with the detective in MAC drama requires some understanding of the ambiguity of the character. The added cognitive effort can be sufficient to result in deep reading of the character's mind – deeper than, for instance, the 'mind reading' afforded by watching real people in documentaries. Black and Barnes (2015) found that watching complex television can contribute to better performance on Theory of Mind tasks, such as the 'Reading the Mind in the Eyes' test. In line with Mittell's reasoning, we would position the demandingness of complex serials such as MAC drama somewhere between traditional popular television drama and the most complex current streaming platform drama titles, such as *Dark*, *Westworld* and *Twelve Monkeys*.

The most typical challenge posed by MAC drama is more affective than cognitive. It aims at the viewer's self and their core values. Standing the test of watching and enjoying gruesome immoral acts is a moral-emotional challenge. We have proposed that meeting it requires the regulation of negative morally inspired emotions. The downregulation of these emotions brings along considerable cognitive effort, and affective costs are even higher. Viewers taking up the challenge to the full put their own moral values at stake, possibly self-mockingly exposing to conflicting morals, as Vaage (2015: 46, 51) puts it. As in all good games, the high stakes and corresponding efforts and costs are balanced by rewards that go beyond the nice mood ensuing from a satisfactory story-outcome. It is the self that is rewarded. Feelings of competence follow on from passing the test, and having explored controversial moral stances adds to a sense of autonomy of mind. A basic need for relatedness has been satisfied by identification with an extraordinary human, and possibly also by an awareness of being part of a competent entertainment elite that seeks and finds appreciation in exploring the moral limits of oneself and others.

Discussion and Outlook

Our account of enjoyment of MAC drama as a fictional game is not meant to predict responses by the audience of the genre or even of *Dexter* in actual viewing. It is a typology of different ways that viewers can deal with the challenge posed by the genre. We have proposed that an ideally accepting viewer can have the pleasure of maximal competence in enjoying terrible events.

But such ideal viewers do not exist (except in theory) as the endpoint of a continuum that ranges from a total refusal to imagine morally deviant acts (see Black et al. 2019) to complete acceptance. Empirical research can identify viewers who fit the theoretically ideal ways of meeting the challenge and enjoying the genre. For example, in survey research, aficionados of a MAC series can be identified as a select category of viewers to be compared with non-aficionado viewers. It can be tested whether aficionados appreciate the drama more, have more intense and varied emotions, and do better than non-aficionados in recognizing and accepting the challenge of enjoying immoral acts. In addition, it can be tested whether their appreciation of the drama is more strongly related to acceptance regulation than with moral disengagement, and whether feelings of guilt and shame contribute to their appreciation. Controlled observation studies of high- vs low-aficionado groups may highlight differential emotion profiles in the actual viewing of an entire episode.

More specifically, continuous empirical measurement could establish how morally inspired emotions develop within and across episodes. We envision that regulation is not limited to the highlight moments when a MAC is shown to commit repulsive acts, such as killings, but may also be functional in dealing with less morally offensive plans, intentions, thoughts and feelings. For example, in between the acts of killing, Dexter is shown feigning ignorance, scheming and burgling. These acts may be only interesting to morally disengaging viewers but amusing to the more accepting viewers. Empirical measurements using surveys could help to assess whether viewers may continue, in between episodes, to reappraise immoral acts and their own watching and enjoyment of these. Perhaps aficionado viewers use the interval to forgive Dexter and, as a consequence, like him even better and excuse themselves, while non-aficionados' moral upset just habituates.

Ed S. Tan is Professor of Film, Media and Communication at the University of Copenhagen and an emeritus professor of the Amsterdam School of Communication Research. Trained as a research psychologist, he taught and conducted research at arts, media and communication departments in the Netherlands, especially on emotion, film and media. He was among the founders of the Society for the Cognitive Study of the Moving Image. His current research interests include the social dimension to cognition and experience of film and narratives, and the design of playful experiences for training participation and self-reliance.

Monique Timmers holds a PhD in Psychology (University of Amsterdam) and is currently at the Department of Communication Science at the University of Amsterdam. Her research focuses on emotions and media, and she is published in top-ranked journals, such as *Cognition and Emotion* and the *Personality and Social Psychology Bulletin*.

Claire M. Segijn (PhD, University of Amsterdam) is an associate professor at the Hubbard School of Journalism and Mass Communication, University of Minnesota. Her research focuses on attention and how the use of multiple media simultaneously affect information processing and advertising effectiveness. Her work has been published in top-tier journals in the field of communication and advertising (e.g. *Communication Research, Human Communication Research, Journal of Advertising, International Journal of Advertising*), and she has been honoured with awards from the International Communication Association and the American Academy of Advertising. She makes use of different methods of research, such as experiment, media diaries, content analysis and eye-tracking.

Suzanna J. Opree (PhD, University of Amsterdam) is an Associate Professor in Quantitative Methods in Media and Communication at the Department of Media and Communication, at the Erasmus School of History, Culture and Communication of Erasmus University Rotterdam, the Netherlands. Her main research line, 'The good(s) life', focuses on the effect of advertising and commercial media on materialism and well-being in youths. Suzanna's work has been published in top journals in the fields of communication, marketing and (developmental) psychology, and has been recognized with several awards. In 2017, she received the Research Prize of the Erasmus University Rotterdam, which honours the university's most promising postdoctoral researcher.

Guus Bartholomé (PhD, University of Amsterdam) is, at present, a researcher at the Dutch Broadcasting Agency (NPO), specializing in online data collection and analysis. His research has predominantly been focused on the roles of framing of conflict and viewpoint in political news.

Notes

1. Przbylski et al. present an account of motivation in video-gaming; however, it is sufficiently general as to apply to fictional games of make-believe as well. The basic needs that feature are rooted in Deci and Ryan's (2000) self-determination theory.
2. Ch. 1 41/67, ch. 1 59/67. Reference to page numbers follows the in-chapter page numbering of the e-book edition.
3. Evidence has been found that suggests that video game aficionados find satisfaction in basic relatedness needs. Expert gamers seem to feel more connected with the gamer community than gamers who are less skilled and enthusiastic (Neys, Jansz and Tan 2014).

References

Author unknown. n.d. 'Love American Style (Dexter)'. In *Wikipedia*. Retrieved 2 July 2020 from http://en.wikipedia.org/wiki/Love_ American_Style_(Dexter).

Bandura, Albert. 1999. 'Moral Disengagement in the Perpetration of Inhumanities', *Personality and Social Psychology Review* 3(3): 193–209. doi:10.1207/s15327957pspr0303_3.

Bartholomé, August J., and Claire M. Segijn. 2011. 'Verslag Pretest Moral Disengagement' [Report of moral disengagement pretest]. Unpublished research report, University of Amsterdam.

Black, Jessica E., and Jennifer L. Barnes. 2015. 'Fiction and Social Cognition: The Effect of Viewing Award-Winning Television Dramas on Theory of Mind', *Psychology of Aesthetics, Creativity, and the Arts* 9(4): 423–29.

Black, Jessica E., Yomna Helmy, Olivia Robson and Jennifer L. Barnes. 2019. 'Who Can Resist a Villain? Morality, Machiavellianism, Imaginative Resistance and Liking for Dark Fictional Characters', *Poetics* 74: 1–13.

Bordwell, David 1985. *Narration in the Fiction Film*. Madison: University of Wisconsin Press.

Busselle, Rick, and Helena Bilandzic. 2009. 'Measuring Narrative Engagement', *Media Psychology* 12(4): 321–47.

Chambers, Richard, Eleonora Gullone and Nicholas B. Allen. 2009. 'Mindful Emotion Regulation: An Integrative Review', *Clinical Psychology Review* 29(6): 560–72.

Cooke, Lez. 2006. 'The Crime Series', in Glen Creeber (ed.), *The Television Genre Book*, 2nd edn. London: BFI, pp. 29–34.

Csikszentmihalyi, Mihaly. 1997. *Finding Flow: The Psychology of Engagement with Everyday Life*. New York: Basic Books.

Deci, Edward L., and Richard M. Ryan. 2000. 'The 'What' and 'Why' of Goal Pursuits: Human Needs and the Self-determination of Behavior', *Psychological Inquiry* 11(4): 227–68.

Dunleavy, Trisha. 2017. *Complex Serial Drama and Multiplatform Television*. London: Routledge.

Eden, Allison, Serena Daalmans and Benjamin K. Johnson. 2017. 'Morality Predicts Enjoyment But Not Appreciation of Morally Ambiguous Characters'. *Media Psychology* 20(3): 349–73. doi:10.1080/15213269.2016.1182030.

Eden, Allison, Mathew Grizzard and Robert J. Lewis. 2011. 'Disposition Development in Drama: The Role of Moral, Immoral and Ambiguously Moral Characters', *International Journal of Arts and Technology* 4(1): 33–47. doi:10.1504/IJART.2011.037768.

Grizzard, Matthew, Jialing Huang, Kaitlin Fitzgerald, Changhyun Ahn and Haoran Chu. 2018. 'Sensing Heroes and Villains: Character-schema and the Disposition Formation Process', *Communication Research* 45(4): 479–501.

Gross, James J. 1998. 'The Emerging Field of Emotion Regulation: An Integrative Review', *Review of General Psychology* 2(3): 271–99.

Gross, James J., and Ross A. Thompson. 2006. 'Emotion Regulation: Conceptual Foundations', in James J. Gross (ed.), *Handbook of Emotion Regulation*. New York: Guilford, pp. 3–24.

Hakemulder, Jameljan. 2000. *The Moral Laboratory: Experiments Examining the Effects of Reading Literature on Social Perception and Moral Self-Concept*. Amsterdam: Benjamins.

Hartmann, Tilo. 2013. 'Moral Disengagement during Exposure to Media Violence', in Ron Tamborini (ed.), *Media and the Moral Mind*. London: Routledge, pp. 109–31.

Hill, Annette. 1997. *Shocking Entertainment*. Luton: University of Luton Press.

Janicke, Sophie H., and Arthur A. Raney. 2015. 'Exploring the Role of Identification and Moral Disengagement in the Enjoyment of an Antihero Television Series', *Communications* 40(4): 485–95.

———. 2018. 'Modeling the Antihero Narrative Enjoyment Process', *Psychology of Popular Media Culture* 7(4): 533–46.

Jansz, Jeroen. 2005. 'The Emotional Appeal of Violent Video Games for Adolescent Males', *Communication Theory* 15(3): 219–41. https://doi.org/10.1111/j.1468-2885.2005.tb00334.x.

Krakowiak, K. Maja, and Mary B. Oliver. 2012. 'When Good Characters Do Bad Things: Examining the Effect of Moral Ambiguity on Enjoyment', *Journal of Communication* 62(1): 117–35. https://doi.org/10.1111/j.1460-2466.2011.01618.x.

Krakowiak, K. Maja, and Mina Tsay-Vogel. 2013. 'What Makes Characters' Bad Behaviors Acceptable? The Effects of Character Motivation and Outcome on Perceptions, Character Liking, and Moral

Disengagement', *Mass Communication and Society* 16(2): 179–99. doi:10.1080/15205436.2012. 690926.

Kuijpers, Monique M., Frank Hakemulder, Ed S. Tan and Miruna Doicaru. 2014. 'Exploring Absorbing Reading Experiences: Developing and Validating a Self-report Scale to Measure Story World Absorption', *Scientific Study of Literature* 4(1): 89–122.

Kuijpers, Moniek M., and Frank Hakemulder. 2017. 'Narrative Absorption: Introduction and Overview', in Moniek M. Kuijpers, Ed S. Tan, Katalin Bálint and Miruna M. Doicaru (eds), *Narrative Absorption*. Amsterdam: John Benjamins, pp. 1–7.

Kuiken, Don, and Shawn Douglas. 2017. 'Forms of Absorption that Facilitate the Aesthetic and Explanatory Effects of Literary Reading', in Moniek M. Kuijpers, Ed S. Tan, Katalin Bálint and Miruna M. Doicaru (eds), *Narrative Absorption*. Amsterdam: John Benjamins, pp. 217–49.

Menninghaus, Winfried, Valentin Wagner, Julian Hanich, Eugen Wassiliwizky, Thomas Jacobsen and Stephan Koelsch. 2017. 'The Distancing-Embracing Model of the Enjoyment of Negative Emotions in Art Reception', *Behavioral and Brain Sciences* 40: 1–63.

Mittell, Jason. 2006. 'Narrative Complexity in Contemporary American Television', *The Velvet Light Trap* 58(1): 29–40.

———. 2015. *Complex TV: The Poetics of Contemporary Television Storytelling*. New York: New York University Press.

Muraven, Mark, Dianne M. Tice and Roy F. Baumeister. 1998. 'Self-control as a Limited Resource: Regulatory Depletion Patterns', *Journal of Personality and Social Psychology* 74(3): 774–89.

Neys, Joyce L., Jeroen Jansz and Ed S. Tan. 2014. 'Exploring Persistence in Gaming: The Role of Self-determination and Social Identity', *Computers in Human Behavior* 37 (August): 196–209.

Oatley, Keith, and Philip Johnson-Laird. 2008. 'Emotions, Music and Literature', in Michael Lewis, Jeannette M. Haviland-Jones and Lisa Feldman Barrett (eds), *Handbook of Emotions*, 3rd edition. New York: Guilford Press, pp. 102–18.

Ochsner, Kevin N., and James J. Gross. 2005. 'The Cognitive Control of Emotion', *Trends in Cognitive Sciences* 9(5): 242–49.

Oliver, Mary Beth, and Tilo Hartmann. 2010. 'Exploring the Role of Meaningful Experiences in Users' Appreciation of "Good Movies"'. *Projections* 4(2): 128–50.

Przybylski, Andrew K., C. Scott Rigby and Richard M. Ryan. 2010. 'A Motivational Model of Video Game Engagement', *Review of General Psychology* 14(2): 154–66.

Raney, Arthur A. 2004. 'Expanding Disposition Theory: Reconsidering Character Liking, Moral Evaluations, and Enjoyment', *Communication Theory* 14(4): 348–69. doi:10.1111/j.1468- 2885.2004.tb00319.x.

———. 2005. 'Punishing Media Criminals and Moral Judgment: The Impact on Enjoyment', *Media Psychology* 7(2): 145–63. doi:10.1207/S1532785XMEP0702_2.

———. 2011. 'The Role of Morality in Emotional Reactions to and Enjoyment of Media Entertainment', *Journal of Media Psychology* 23(1): 60–63.

Richards, Jane M., and James J. Gross. 2002. 'Emotion Regulation and Memory: The Cognitive Costs of Keeping One's Cool', *Journal of Personality and Social Psychology* 79(3): 410–24.

Schlütz, Daniele M. 2016. 'Contemporary Quality TV: The Entertainment Experience of Complex Serial Narratives', *Annals of the International Communication Association* 40(1): 95–124, doi: 10.1080/23808985.2015.11735257.

Shafer, Daniel M., and Arthur A. Raney. 2012. 'Exploring How We Enjoy Antihero Narratives', *Journal of Communication* 62(6): 1028–46. doi:10.1111/j.1460-2466.2012.01682.

Sherry, John L. 2004. 'Flow and Media Enjoyment', *Communication Theory* 14(4): 328–47.
Tan, Ed S., and Valentijn T. Visch. 2018. 'Co-imagination of Fictional Worlds in Film Viewing', *Review of General Psychology* 22(2): 230–44.
Troy, Allison S., Amanda J. Shallcross, Anna Brunner, Rachel Friedman and Markera C. Jones. 2018. 'Cognitive Reappraisal and Acceptance: Effects on Emotion, Physiology, and Perceived Cognitive Costs', *Emotion* 18(1): 58–74.
Tsay, Mina, and K. Maja Krakowiak. 2011. 'The Impact of Perceived Character Similarity and Identification on Moral Disengagement', *International Journal of Arts and Technology* 4(1): 102–10. doi: 10.1504/ijart.2011.037773.
Vaage, Margrethe B. 2015. *The Antihero in American Television*. New York: Routledge.
van Ommen, Merel, Serena Daalmans, Addy Weijers, Allison Eden, Rebecca N.H. de Leeuw and Moniek Buijzen. 2017. 'A Vigilante Serial Killer as Ethics Educator? An Exploration of Dexter as a Tool for Moral Education in the Professional Domain', *Journal of Moral Education* 46(4): 378–95.
Walton, Kendall. 1990. *Mimesis as Make-believe: On the Foundations of the Representational Arts*. Cambridge, MA: Harvard University Press.
Wheeler, S. Christian, Pablo Briñol and Anthony D. Hermann. 2007. 'Resistance to Persuasion as Self-regulation: Ego-depletion and its Effects on Attitude Change Processes', *Journal of Experimental Social Psychology* 43(1): 150–56.
Zillmann, Dolf. 2000. 'Basal Morality in Drama Appreciation', in Ib Bjondeberg (ed.), *Moving Images, Culture, and the Mind*. Luton: University of Luton Press, pp. 53–63.
Zillmann, Dolf, and Rhonda Gibson. 1996. 'Evolution of the Horror Genre', in James B. Weaver and Ron Tamborini (eds), *Horror Films*. Mahwah, NJ: Erlbaum, pp. 15–32.

CHAPTER 13

The Fascination of Failure
On Predictability, Unpredictability and Postdictability in Art

Marina Grishakova

The Predictive Processing Framework and the Experience of Art

The predictive processing framework (Hohwy 2013; Clark 2016b) seeks to bridge the Cartesian gap by integrating internal and external resources of cognition into an overarching predictive-corrective loop. Arguably, the brain is prediction-hungry, and 'naturally intelligent systems' do not passively wait for stimuli but are 'trying to predict the streams of sensory stimulation before they arrive'; rather than triggering a response, a sensory signal is 'just providing a corrective feedback on the emerging top-down predictions' (Clark 2016a: 264). The proactive predictive dynamics, as Clark contends, also extend to social and cultural processes (ibid.: 301–2).

However, concerns have been raised about the capacity of the predictive processing framework to adequately account for higher cognitive processes, such as reasoning and deliberating, decoupled from immediate sensory flow (Williams 2018). Likewise, the predictive processing theory seems to encounter difficulties in explaining the work of imagination, unconstrained by immediate sensory inputs (Jones and Wilkinson 2020). The deliberate act of imagination detached from sensory flow remains tolerant to prediction errors, ambivalence, indeterminacy (the tolerance that John Keats called 'the negative capability'), keeping on hold and exploring improbable hypotheses: 'It corresponds to perceptual decoupling from the world; it allows your brain to hold on to hypotheses that do not adequately predict the world' (ibid.: 97). Jones and Wilkinson suggest that, in the absence of immediate perceptual constraints and in 'linguistically saturated environments' (106), language and narrative mould the scope of the imagination. They also contend that the role of language in shaping human cognition is still to be fully understood.

Similarly, Newsome (2013) and Kesner (2014) refer to the constitutive role of culture-related skills and knowledge – the 'cultural hyperpriors' – in higher cognition. In these ways, it has been argued that multidisciplinary methodologies, rather than the predictive processing framework alone, are required to approach complex processes of imagination and higher cognition. However, the humanities have already accumulated considerable knowledge on the constraints that language and other symbolic systems (such as expressive systems of verbal and non-verbal arts) put on the work of imagination. The human capacity to imagine and manipulate phenomena beyond immediate reach, to refer to absent or even non-existent entities (a 'semiotic' capacity in Piaget) was triggered and enhanced by the development of language and other symbolic systems. A work of art is separated from its environment and made 'special' through the mediating acts of human symbolic imagination that manifest in such ways as the projections of colour on a canvas surface, linear and non-linear perspective, the rules of composition, or narrative conventions of beginnings and endings. Ellen Dissanayake refers to the sustained and protected *salience* of certain objects (artefacts) and their function of capturing and holding attention as essential factors in the evolution of art (Dissanayake 1992).

Further integration of research in psychology, philosophy and art studies may yield more adequate results in explaining the role of predictability and unpredictability in the engagement with art. As Kesner observes, such integration would allow us to revisit 'some long-standing questions in image studies, the psychology of art and art history' (2014: 2). This chapter explores some hypotheses and approaches to predictability and unpredictability in experimental aesthetics and cognitive humanities, as well as the challenges that a work of art – dissociated from the sphere of mundane applied practices, and unconstrained by any immediate sensory input – may offer to the predictive processing framework. Various stratification models suggest that the perception and comprehension of complex semiotic texts are modulated by formal patterns and layers of meaning. Complex stratified processes invest in *postdiction* rather than *prediction*. The postdictive 'backward reference' (see Lampert 1995) re-enters and integrates what seem to be prediction errors but are, in fact, variations of the available cultural templates in a new artistic form, which, in turn, modify and extend our repertoire of perceptual-cognitive habits.

Prediction Failure and Surprise Evoke Pleasure

Art's tendency to amplify (rather than minimize) prediction errors and enhance surprise challenges the predictive processing theory. Creative works engage humans' ability to tolerate ambiguity and sustain interest in exploring alternate or controversial meanings (see, e.g., Empson 1947; Steiner 1978). Research in experimental aesthetics reveals the relevance of perceptual challenges to the appreciation of a work of art, particularly when combined with contrasting visual determinacy (Muth, Raab and Carbon 2016). A work of art defies predictability and resists the explaining away of surprise. This effect has been identified as 'defamiliarization' or 'making strange' in Russian Formalist and other modernist theories of art.

Experimental research shows that art's unpredictability and uncertainty evoke pleasure (Van de Cruys and Wagemans 2011) and call for the work of interpretation while opening up ever-new spaces of possibility, propelling new hypotheses and involving its audience in the dynamics of expectation and surprise. In Kesner's view, 'the basic tenet of the Bayesian framework that the brain minimizes unpredictability is at odds with the ontological nature of works of art' (2014: 4).

It has been proposed that 'prediction errors or delayed prediction confirmation can be an important tool for artists to amplify the subsequent positive affect of prediction confirmation, in a sort of contrast effect' (Van de Cruys and Wagemans 2011: 1041). In this way, the viewers' ability to tolerate an extent of uncertainty or ambiguity may be rewarded by the postponed gratification, as they undergo a reduction of surprise (similar to the cathartic release of a challenging, difficult experience) and its transformation into a positive affect. However, empirical evidence also shows that the perceptual and cognitive challenge may be enjoyable and valuable per se. By opening up multiple layers of meaning, and fostering ever-new interpretation cycles without a clear resolution or closure, complex artistic forms challenge our ideas of how the world works, rather than allowing ease of processing or precise prediction.

In their book on 'impossible puzzle films', Miklós Kiss and Steven Willemsen list the following factors that make controversial, cognitively dissonant experiences of art appealing: a fascination with both infinity (e.g. evoked by multiplication and reversibility of interpretive frames and the lack of closure) and existential anxiety (caused by a collapse of fiction/non-fiction boundaries or metaleptic transgressions across narrative levels), effort justification, fascination with failure, and *eudaimonic* motivations – such as the pursuit of meaning, truth or self-development – see Oliver and Raney 2011 (Kiss and Willemsen 2017: 185–208).

Complex experimental forms of art often cultivate and amplify uncertainty and unpredictability to the extreme. A paradox, aporia or riddle inherent in such works may not yield a coherent explanation; it retains the recipient in a state of unknowability and puzzlement that may, nonetheless, be pleasurable. In (post) modern experimental art, 'an overload of prediction errors …, despite our best efforts, cannot be reduced to a more predictable, sparser explanation' (Van de Cruys and Wagemans 2011: 1052). Works of modernist writers, such as Samuel Beckett and Gertrude Stein, include 'impossible sentences', conjure 'impossible worlds' and abound in 'egregious gaps', pushing our understanding to the limits (Abbott 2013: 82). The failure to grasp the elusive, unspeakable or meaningless lies at the very heart of Beckett's creative method: '[T]o be an artist is to fail as no other dare fail' (*Proust and Three Dialogues with Georges Duthuit*, cited in Koczy 2018: 54).

The difficult, experimental poetics that challenge cognitive uptake pave the way to innovation and change in established practices. On the contrary, the processes that reduce prediction errors could not drive innovation in these practices (Menary 2016). I shall argue that innovation, nevertheless, operates through the knowledge and memory of convention, and may, ultimately, result in the modification or extension of the repertoire of conventions.

The Role of the Predictable: A Stereotype or a Learned Pattern?

The role of the predictable and schematic in works of art should not be underestimated. Classical aesthetics prioritizes imitation of models over originality, as do canonical genres (such as Menippean satire, medieval fairy tales, Romantic and Gothic fiction, eighteenth-century philosophical tales and novels, canonical genres in music and lyric poetry, and many others). Obviously, the 'familiar' is defined differently in each case – as formal (rhetorical, poetic, narrative) conventions; aesthetic, philosophical or religious frameworks; and analogies, schemas or stereotypes.

The 'schema' or 'frame' may refer to any kind of habitual patterns that are based on repeated experiences, such as generic and cultural conventions, habits or stereotypes. For Bartlett, 'schema' is 'an active organization of past reactions, or of past experiences, which must always be supposed to be operating in any well-adapted organic response' (1995: 201). In my 2009 paper, I used the broad meaning of 'schema' – as a social or cultural template, rather than as a mental representation pulled out on demand – to show that certain types of experimental (complex, 'difficult') fiction interestingly combine controversial tracks of schema-consistent and schema-inconsistent reading, or even paradoxically sustain a more trivial predictable reading (i.e. 'primary processing' that may suppress prediction errors and inconsistencies) and foreground stereotypical information in order to alleviate the cognitive load that schema-inconsistent or counter-stereotypical information presents the reader. The naturalizing immediate uptake, which seems more secure and easy than processing the ambivalent or difficult data, may be provocatively supported by the narrative itself (see below on the 'naturalizing' reading, reducing or obliterating of cognitive dissonance that such narratives afford).

Both in real life and art, intuitively grasped interpretive schemas or scenarios are used to come to terms with new situations. Commonly, schema- or stereotype-consistent knowledge facilitates seamless and quick rule-based behaviour in familiar contexts, but its role may be misleading in unfamiliar contexts and new situations. As social psychologists Daniel Katz and Kenneth Braly observe in their pioneering work on racial stereotypes, 'a stereotype is a fixed impression, which conforms very little to the fact that it pretends to represent, and results from our defining first and observing second' (Katz and Braly 1935: 181). In other words, it is a result of hasty conceptualization. Events are experienced as self-evidently valid on the basis of a stereotypical 'low-level gut feeling', despite countering cognitions (Burton et al. 2007). The experiential system is spontaneous, intuitive and has the appeal of immediacy. By contrast, rationality is mediated, effortful and lags behind.

It often proves difficult to distinguish between the different meanings of 'schemata'. This concept has been understood, first, as referring to cognitive biases; second, as 'folk wisdom', 'culture in mind' (Hinton 2017) or 'tacit knowledge' (Polanyi 1966) – that is, relatively stable cultural associations, beliefs and dispositions that are taken for granted, thereby serving as an intuitive basis for everyday judgement and behaviour; and third, as a stock of learned conventions – that is to say, part of expert knowledge. The question of where the line should be drawn between 'nature' and 'nurture' – with inborn dispositions (schemas) as part of the human cognitive equipment or schemas as learned conventions – remains debated. Nevertheless, one could try to define the functions of those schemas predictably found in art.

In the perception of art, the strategy of ignoring prediction errors, contradictions and discrepancies for the sake of familiar schemas is not unlike the robust 'fast and frugal' heuristics used in real-life situations. Both are motivated by the necessity of quick rough estimate, and justified in the long run by avoiding the risks of 'overfitting' (that is to say, non-transferable adaptation to local conditions) and simply learning from any kind of discrepancy or error (Kaaronen 2018: 11; see also Todd and Gigerenzer 2012). Based on Festinger's theory of cognitive dissonance, Kaaronen lists the following strategies for reducing cognitive dissonance and suppressing prediction errors: first, focusing on supportive beliefs and reducing the importance of conflicting beliefs; second, adding cognitive elements or hypotheses that may reconcile dissonant cognitive elements, and, finally, an arbitrary change in beliefs and attitudes (Kaaronen 2018: 5). For example, a reader of Kafka's *Metamorphosis* may reduce the cognitive dissonance by focusing on Gregor Samsa's human features, ignoring his insect features and looking for 'natural' explanations of his condition (such as illness, hallucination or dream), or, on the contrary, by ignoring the human underpinnings of the story and reading it as fantasy fiction. In this way, readers focus on the factors supporting a reductive interpretation and ignore the conflicting information. These strategies have been exploited in various adaptations of Kafka's story to different media (cf. McEwan's ingenious 2019 version of *Metamorphosis* in which the bug Jim Sams transforms into a human, a UK prime minister). Similarly, a reader reading 'for the plot' may downplay complex allusions and metaphors or multiple controversial layers of meaning in the works of Vladimir Nabokov, Umberto Eco, Kazuo Ishiguro, Don DeLillo, Margaret Atwood and other complex novels – instead, reading them as detective, family or romance fictions (an option suggested or anticipated by authors themselves).

An alternative strategy for reducing cognitive dissonance, which requires changing beliefs and attitudes, may involve the audience taking inconsistencies and contradictions in their stride, trivializing and accepting them as regular features of certain types of worlds. For instance, a reader could perceive Boris Vian's worlds – which occasionally include inanimate objects coming to life and animals speaking – as realistic, including any deviating details that do not change these worlds substantially.[1]

On the other hand, expert knowledge includes *learning* predictable patterns: a repertoire of generic, stylistic, compositional conventions or schemata that can be modified in artistic practices. Studies of stylistic expectations for higher levels of musical structure, using the probe-tone method (Krumhansl and Shepard 1979; Schmuckler 1989), suggest that

> *melodic expectations of non-experts typically rely on salient surface features, such as pauses, register changes, and frequency of occurrence in the local probe-tone context, whereas those of enculturated experts are more dependent on abstract schemas relating to tonal hierarchies and global transitional probabilities within a given style of music; [thereby,] expert listeners incorporate schema-driven, top-down processing to a greater extent than non-experts.* (Hansen, Vuust and Pearce 2016: 2)

David Huron distinguishes four types of surprise in music, in accordance with four types of expectation and the degree of their predictability: schematic (learned, associated with stylistic conventions), veridical (based on familiar works or patterns), dynamic (evoked in the course of listening to a specific work), and conscious (based on explicit conjectures) (Huron 2006: 237–40).

In the predictive processing framework, low-level (neurobiological) predictions do not reach consciousness – only prediction errors do. Conversely, cultural 'priors' and skills are learned and used intentionally; even if understood as experiential 'tacit knowledge' or habitual 'fast thinking', they are easily retrieved and tend to retain their semi-active status as the background from which artistic unpredictability, surprise, and breaking of conventions develop and operate. Prediction errors do not discard the role of conventions or templates in art.

Surprise Triggers Sense-Making

Recent psychological research shows that problem-solving situations that decrease information-processing capacity through high cognitive load (e.g. difficulty of the task, multiple task demands or emotional excitement) may increase the stereotypicality of the perceiver's judgement. By contrast, the conceptual fluency of stereotypical or familiar information allows for allocating attention to and processing informationally more valuable *schema-inconsistent* data by freeing up additional cognitive resources (Bessenoff et al. 1998). From the perspective of the distribution of attentional-cognitive resources, the function of a schema is twofold: it may confirm expectations, but it also channels attention to the missing parts of schematic patterns or the information that contradicts expectations (Graesser 1981: 34, 69). Interpretive dynamics combine familiar (habitual) smoothly processed predictive-interpretive patterns, as well as counter-intuitive assumptions or images with high effort- and attention-demanding potential (Boyer 1994). The effect of surprise is precisely due to the stereotypical expectations that provide the effortless processing of information, whereas critical attitude and rationality lag behind. The deviation from a predictable pattern makes the recipients revise their tacit assumptions. This type of attention distribution and corrective reading has been referred to more recently by Anthony J. Sanford and Catherine Emmott (2012) as *secondary processing* or a *double take* and by Kahneman (2011) as *fast* and *slow* thinking.[2] Fast thinking is effortless, whereas slow thinking is effortful, and allows the mistakes of fast thinking to be corrected.

Sanford and Emmott's (2012) experimental research on narrative is based on the conception of scenario-mapping: arguably, texts allow the readers to fill out textual gaps by making inferences from real-world situations or scenarios evoked by the text. The reader's brain activity was measured by Sanford and Emmott using EEG and fMRI methods. The measurements revealed that rapid 'primary processing' predominantly utilized situation-specific world knowledge. The scenario-mapping theory has been combined with the rhetorical processing framework and rhetorical focusing principle, the latter being 'a psychological version of the humanities ideas of foregrounding and defamiliarization, in which unusual stylistic items are forefronted in attention, and receive a different, more thorough than usual, analysis by readers' (ibid.: 7). The experiments revealed that whenever mapping the real-world situational knowledge onto the text (a predictive hypothesis) fails, the 'secondary processing', which is more time- and cognitive resource-consuming, is triggered.

In this way, the secondary processing recruits internal (in-text) resources, rather than real-life knowledge, to come to grips with a surprise. From an epistemic perspective, any narrative closure is provisional: the dynamics of comprehension is guided by epistemic drive – that is, the time-bound attending to and elimination of possibilities, and the negotiation of what counts as relevant knowledge. We are led to surprise by what we have known or expected – in other words, a piece of tacit knowledge, the relevance of which has thus far not been obvious. In natural narratives, the 'story-takers' or recipients often readily take the stance of positive ignorance, owing to a lack of knowledge about the narrated events. The readers or listeners of fictional stories take this stance voluntarily, knowing that available interpretive schemata often prove to be inadequate or irrelevant in fiction.

Fictional narratives introduce hypothetical connections between events, and open up further negotiations for meaning by throwing in and elaborating on incremental detail, displaying ever-new perspectives and introducing fuzzy causality,[3] all while the relevance status of narrated events remains suspended due to their framing as incomplete and only suggestive of the future. In this way, fictional narratives work as attunement tools, factoring in multiple processing and increases in complexity: whenever the first take does not result in a satisfactory interpretive hypothesis, the repeated parsing reveals previously unattended details, and stitches them into ever-new patterns. Fictional narratives enhance the reader or listener's attunement to increasing cognitive load (Grishakova 2019).

This process may be described as a trade-off between goal-directed thought and mind-wandering, an alternation between exploitative and exploratory modes of thought – previously considered as polar opposites, but which have recently been reconceived as a continuum in psychological literature (e.g. Sripada 2018). In contrast with its previous bad reputation as a distraction and an obstacle to achieving a goal or performing a task, mind-wandering has been related to creativity and pattern recognition as a mode of thought that enhances tolerance to variability and change in the visual field (van Leeuwen and Smit 2012; Sripada 2018). The function of mind-wandering is exploratory: by attending to the environments in a more random or dispersed way than the goal-targeted thought, it allows the viewer to detect and capture ever-new details and shades of meaning, from which new patterns and structures of meaning arise (van Leeuwen and Smit 2012: 123).

Postdiction and the Backward Reference

Ultimately, primary processing based on real-world expectations is of limited applicability in the experience of the works of art, which engages but also challenges recipients' perceptual and cognitive habits, and thrives on novelty. The dynamics of 'secondary processing' builds on *postdiction* resulting from retaining and keeping multiple predictive hypotheses on hold.

While conducting experiments exemplifying the predictive-corrective dynamics of discourse, Emmot and Sanford have been working with sentences or short segments of text. As they note, various attention-grabbing 'pre-announcement devices' (i.e. italics or emphases that mark shifts in meaning) act as precision improvement tools:

> *On the argument that change detection reflects the precision of semantic representation, sentential processing load thus reduces precision, while focus and emphasis effects improve precision. In this way, change detection appears to be a suitable tool for investigating the effects of devices that might be expected to modulate the precision of semantic representations, including a wide range of literary devices.* (Sanford and Emmot 2012: 125)[4]

However, while it may be relatively easy to pinpoint shifts in meaning at the level of sentences or paragraphs, a work of art involves a more complex orchestration across a hierarchy of layers and patterns of meaning: it engages the recipient via long-distance and inter-textual links on various levels, considerably delayed or ambiguous references (e.g. the reference of pronouns in fiction: see Gibbons and Macrae 2018) and information gaps. Discourse psychology considers text-stratification levels to be congruent to the levels of a reader's comprehension (see, e.g., Kintsch 1980). A number of models (structural-semiotic, hermeneutic, discourse-psychological and others) describe text stratification, starting from micro-level formal and stylistic entities to intermediate-level syntactic narrative structures, to macro-level thematic and semantic units, with the formal micro-units blending into patterns and constraining macro-level units. In a work of art, the natural regularities we are accustomed to seeing – such as natural combinations of colour, gestures or sounds of speech (as compared with painted combinations, dance or poetry) – are disrupted and reconfigured by the use of metaleptic transgressions, and blends of distinct levels, conjuring entirely new types of meaning. The resulting semantization or thematization of formal features that are not meaningful in the natural language, but become meaningful in art, evokes an instant increase in semantic richness through the activation of inner expressive resources. For instance, graphic and syntactic tools such as italics, emphases and clefting, considered by Sanford and Emmott solely as attention-grabbing and focusing devices, could be ascribed a semantic or thematic value in poetry and fiction. Similarly, a graphic-compositional organization in painting, or sound polyphony in poetry, produces semantic effects. Consider the contrast in Gerard Manley Hopkins' poem between the heaviness of tide and lightness of a skylark, which encrypts a complex Welsh medieval poetic sound patterning (Cynghanedd) in 'natural' sounds imitating a tide's noise and a skylark's song:

> On ear and ear two noises too old to end
> Trench – right, the tide that ramps against the shore;
> With a flood or a fall, low lull-off or all roar,
> Frequenting there while moon shall wear and wend.
> Left hand, off land, I hear the lark ascend,
> His rash-fresh re-winded new-skeinèd score
> In crisps of curl off wild winch whirl, and pour
> And pelt music, till none's to spill nor spend. (Hopkins 1970: 68, orig. 1877)

Being contingent on their function in the overall artistic design, and captured in hindsight, the meaning of the semanticized formal elements is manifested by the whole patterning of stratified relations and spreads across various layers of meaning, rather than by the direct referential interpretation of each element or application of real-life scenarios. In Hopkins' poem, urban civilization ('shallow and frail town') appears paradoxically insignificant when juxtaposed to the unique blend of nature and poetry.

The 'postdictive' scanning may reveal a significance of recurrent patterns of light and dark in painting (for instance, in Caravaggio's paintings, figures and objects with scrupulously rendered realistic detail, rising out of the contrasting background darkness as if levered forward, symbolizing divine humility that reveals itself in mundane, humble circumstances), recurrent patterns of cinematographic editing and camerawork in film (for example, aggressive, fast editing used to render violence or addiction), or recurrent sound patterns with occasional (poetic) synonyms and antonyms as constituents of verse semantics. In this way, postdiction introduces a retroactive, hermeneutic causality to aesthetic works: the elements perceived as surprising and unpredictable in the forward perspective may appear as motivated parts of an overall design in hindsight, while, nevertheless, evoking 'intellectual' surprise and wonder as the pieces of the puzzle suddenly come together to reveal an image.

Hindsight hermeneutics capitalizes on the dynamics of retention and protention, that is the dynamics of the retained past and anticipated future in the mobile horizon of the present, and on the phenomenon of 're-entry', that is reinsertion of memories in the current perceptions, as Bergson (1999) puts it, and ongoing revision of memories through the new perceptions.[5] The process entails a reconfiguration and reintegration of all constituents of stratified levels into aesthetic patterns. Garcia Landa (2019) points out the pervasive role of what he calls '"retroprospective structures in cognition", including a kind of paradoxical bootstrapping closely related to the fallacies and paradoxes studied in narrative theory – whereby emergent meanings present themselves as already being awaited by the past' (432).

In his book on simultaneity and delay, Jay Lampert discusses Benjamin Libet's experimental data on the 'backward referral of subjective time perception' (Lampert 2012: 112). Libet's experiments revealed a delay between the brain activity necessary for a physical act and the test subject's awareness of and reporting on having carried out this physical act. The implications of Libet's experiments have been discussed and contested, and are, of course, open to further debate. Lampert offers an epistemological explanation, leaving aside the conditions of the test itself. Lampert argues that this kind of 'fraudulent backward reference' is necessary to synchronize the awareness of certain events with the occurrence of these events: 'Whenever the consciousness is present, it takes itself to have been present earlier' (ibid.: 117).

It is easy to see the analogy between Libet's interpretation of 'backward referral' and the discussion on narrative explanation in the philosophy of history, particularly Arthur Danto's (1985) celebrated work on narrative sentences, and his example: 'The Thirty Years' War began in 1618'. The meaning of the sentence is only available in hindsight: when the Thirty Years' War began, nobody knew it was the Thirty Years' War. However, once the event is defined and embraced as the Thirty Years' War, it is also redefined as an antecedent of subsequent events – a narrative sequence defined in terms of the Thirty Years' War. The backward reference restructures the past as if it were intended towards the future and, in turn, reworks the future as a fulfilment of premises and possibilities that germinated in the past.

In neuroscience, postdiction has been studied as a mechanism of perception and integration of information after the event – a kind of a reverse-causality or an 'authentic (objective) illusion' of forward-causality. Psychologist Shinsuke Shimojo

(2014) pointed out that postdictive effects are observed in the study of perceptual phenomena (when a stimulus presented later seems to causally affect the percept of the stimulus presented earlier), but also in higher-level cognition and memory, particularly in the 'memory revision' or its alignment to various new contexts.

The retrospective restructuring of the past as predictive of the future is known as 'hindsight bias'. The hindsight bias accounts for the suppression of cognitive dissonance, reorganization of the memory for consistency, information compression and the ease of retrieval: for example, in retelling or interpreting complex stories (see the examples of discarding a cognitive dissonance above). In Bartlett's study of remembering and repeated reproduction (retelling), a North American folk tale, 'The War of the Ghosts', served as experimental material. In the course of reproduction, the subjects of the study rationalized the story, replaced less-familiar terms with more modern and conventional ones, imposed coherence, and omitted elements that seemed to be inconsistent or supernatural details (Bartlett 1995: 64–82). The output was a considerably simplified and 'flattened' story. However, as I suggest below, if the hindsight is understood in epistemic terms – as an extended hermeneutic awareness or insight – postdiction may defy the hindsight bias. In a work of art – due to its stratification, interaction and transgressions between various layers – postdiction may introduce an increase in complexity and a concurrent modification of schematic expectations.

Perspectives on Postdiction in Complex Narratives

In his article 'Learning from Text, Levels of Comprehension, or: Why Anyone Would Read a Story Anyway', Walter Kintsch (1980) argues that 'postdictability' defines the place (function, motivation, importance or cognitive interest) of every textual constituent and, in hindsight, serves the explanation of how 'it all fits together'. However, for Kintsch, the interest is determined by a knowledge structure (cognitive schemata and frames) that, in turn, defines textual coherence for the reader. This knowledge structure may change and be replaced by a new one in the process of reading; interesting texts modify readers' expectations. Kintsch's perspective has a strong computational-cognitive bent, and it hypostatizes the integration, coherence and functionality of constituents in both literary and non-literary texts. However, Kintsch's two levels of text comprehension – stylistic and narrative – may be divergent or conflicting, as, for example, in the case of parodic or weakly narrative texts with stylistic 'overkill'. Similarly, symbolic, philosophical, rhetorical or affective motivations contributing to the hypothetical aesthetic whole may clash, and work against coherence and closure.

Many complex first-person narratives, or narratives exploiting cited monologue (such as stream-of-consciousness novels), start and end *in medias res*, as consciousness has neither a beginning nor an end. They may include multiple 'fake' beginnings and endings (the 'ragged edge' of beginnings that stretches beyond endings in Woolf, as Melba Cuddy-Kean puts it), with the fictional world extending beyond the storyworld, or playing off the metaphor of the real world as the 'otherworld' of the storyworld: 'Not everyone who lives is alive; nor is death a portal that only opens in one direction' (from Hjalmar Bergman's *Memoirs of a Dead Man*, 2007: 342).

Another means for challenging and undermining 'backward' predictability is a surprising ending that ascribes new functions to narrative sequence, reconfiguring previous events and changing their meaning: such as the endings in Patrick McGrath's *Trauma* (2007) or Margaret Atwood's *The Blind Assassin* (2000). In the latter, the last sections of the framing (embedding) narration disclose the narrator, Iris, to be the embedded novel's author (rather than her sister Laura, as the readers tend to presume) and the lover of the young leftist Alex Thomas. Within this new configuration, the roles of Iris and Laura appear interchangeable. The multiple encodings or framings appear similarly detrimental for a hindsight bias, as they provide an opportunity to read and interpret the narrative in different ways, and present a discrepancy between the frames of reference that prompts the reader to loop back in search of further clues.

Opportunities for alternative (but neither contradictory nor mutually exclusive) interpretations are also offered by the fusion of the mundane with the mysterious, fantastic or magic, or the flickering and fibrillation of the mysterious at the margins of realistic worlds: think of the 'leakage' of realistic ontologies in Ambrose Bierce's stories, and intrusions of the supernatural in the novels of Mikhail Bulgakov, Boris Vian and García Márquez, as well as alternate versions of realistic worlds in John Fowles or Ruth Ozeki, which are so distant and dissimilar as to appear less real or fantastic. Ambrose Bierce's 'The Mockingbird' may be read both as a mystery story of a double (with a long list of predecessors from Stevenson to Oscar Wilde) or as a realistic Civil War story about twin brothers who happen to be fighting on opposite sides on the front line, with one brother accidentally killing the other. In these ways, complex narratives accustom the reader to coordinating several cognitive processes, monitoring several tracks of meaning, and suspending a prediction rather than proceeding to its immediate acceptance or rejection.

In his article on cognition in the non-indicative contexts (with multiple choices), Christopher Mole highlights the function of voluntary attention in non-indicative contexts that the principle of prediction error minimization cannot explain (Mole 2011; Ransom et al. 2017). Indeed, a work of art is itself such a context in which surprise and deviation from the predictable do not nullify the role of conventions. As Kiss and Willemsen justly note (2017: 185), readers and viewers of complex narratives enjoy interpretive multiplicity – the hermeneutic play and complexity. These are also, as I have sought to show, reasons why art and literature are 'necessary, and not just nice' (Gerrig 2012). By defying hindsight bias and the habit of retrospective streamlining, the transformative experience of prediction error enhances reading or seeing skills, sensitivity to future 'failures', and openness to a multiplicity of interpretations – the episodic memory of failure being re-entered and re-instantiated as part of long-term memory and cultural knowledge.

Conclusions

Art engages the human ability to tolerate ambiguity and uncertainty and to sustain interest in exploring alternate meanings and scenarios. The reception of a work of art borders on the real-life experiences of the uncertain, ambivalent, challenging, extreme, sublime or repulsive, but, ultimately – owing to the artfully deferring, impeding and 'defamiliarizing' nature of these effects, as described by Shklovsky – such experiences also invite reflection on the ways they appear and are brought to our awareness through the delayed recognition of aesthetic experience.

The observations disseminated in Shklovsky's works reveal various ways in which the experience of a literary work is made 'strange' and difficult: from the unusual use of language (e.g. erotic language in non-erotic contexts, or vice versa), uncanny perspective or prominent detail, to intricate forms of composition and plot construction. Robust real-life heuristics often downplay prediction errors, cognitive dissonance and surprise, but enable quick decisions and sustain 'ecological rationality' (Todd and Gigerenzer 2012). Conversely, art slows down perceptions through 'secondary processing', amplifies prediction errors and enhances cognitive dissonance in order to activate and intensify semiotic and artistic resources, exploiting them as vehicles of aesthetic effect. This 'secondary processing' invests in *postdiction* (rather than *prediction*) and introduces a retroactive causality in aesthetic works: the elements perceived as surprising and unpredictable in the forward perspective may appear as motivated parts of an overall design in hindsight. The *backward reference* 're-inserts' and integrates what seem to be prediction errors but are, in fact, variations of the available cultural templates and conventions in a new artistic form, which, in turn, realigns and enhances the reader's or viewer's repertoire of cognitive habits, and makes them more sensitive to the transformative effects of failure.

Evidence from experimental science indicates that experiments allow estimation and stimulation of interfering factors and errors for the sake of robustness: 'an excellent way of learning from error is to deliberately magnify it ... By magnifying distortions, mere whispers can be made to speak volumes' (Mayo 2014: 68). Any experiment involves a deliberate manipulation, transformation or distortion of certain features or properties of a research object, with the purpose of better understanding its standard behaviour or structure. Amplifying error or 'distortion' is also characteristic of ethical experiments or imaginary scenarios that include the deception and deliberate misleading of its participants in order to study their reactions and explore the impact of the experimental conditions on the participants' behaviour (see Grishakova, Gramigna and Sorokin 2019) – experiments that, as a variety of playful fictional modelling, are akin to experimentation in art.

Marina Grishakova is Chair Professor of Literary Theory and Intermedial Studies at the Institute of Cultural Research, University of Tartu. Her scholarly interests include intermedial and interart studies, narratology, cognitive humanities, and the semiotics of culture. Among her recent publications are *Intermediality and Storytelling* (De Gruyter, 2010), *Theoretical Schools and Circles in the Twentieth-Century Humanities: Literary Theory, History, Philosophy* (Routledge, 2015), *Narrative Complexity: Cognition, Embodiment, Evolution* (University of Nebraska Press, 2019) and *The Gesamtkunstwerk as a Synergy of the Arts* (Peter Lang, 2020).

Notes

Research for this chapter was supported by the Estonian Research Council (Grant 1481, 'The Role of Imaginary Narrative Scenarios in Cultural Dynamics') and the European Regional Development Fund (Center of Excellence in Estonian Studies).

1. Obviously, there is a difference in degree between what Jan Alber refers to as 'recuperation of inexplicable elements' or 'making impossible scenarios readable' (Alber 2009: 81) and my typology of reduction of cognitive dissonance based on Kaaronen 2018. The latter amounts to the overt reduction of the plurality of meanings and investment in quick estimate.
2. Clark suggests a possible revision of Kahneman's model by accepting the fast, habitual, automatic response (Kahneman's 'fast thinking') as the default mode, 'within which a large variety of possible strategies may be available' (Clark 2016a: 276). In Clark 2016b, he reproduces, almost verbatim, Kahneman's distinction between 'fast, cheap modes of response' and 'more costly, effortful strategies' (244). Indeed, Kahneman also acknowledges a variety of strategies of dealing with cognitive biases. Nevertheless, 'fastness' and 'slowness' remain important empirical criteria of processing 'easy' and 'difficult' information (for instance, the sentences or text fragments including gaps and ellipses, figurative language, counterfactuals, etc. in Sanford and Emmott 2012). From this perspective, 'fast thinking' refers to the default mode of response and 'slow' to the *effortful interpretation*, rather than to the actual speed of reading.
3. See, e.g., Lemon (1995) on narrative causality as non-deterministic, and Grishakova 2011 on non-implicative types of causality.
4. In the introductory sections, I have argued – citing recent philosophical polemics – that a specific form and medium make a work of art distinct and relatively independent from the immediate sensory environment, thereby changing conditions of its perception: the literary text is not identical to the 'designed sensory flow' (Kukkonen 2020: 7ff). In spite of such occasional straightforward definitions, Karin Kukkonen's *Probability Designs* offers a valuable analysis of in-textual and inter-textual 'precision expectations', guiding a reader's attention through the development of the plot.
5. Bergson suggests that, by summoning recollections and reinserting them in perception, the act of heightened attention intensifies memories and, concurrently, extends and enriches the experience of perception (Bergson 1999: 110). Drawing on the work of the mathematician Spenser-Brown, Kauffman and Varela (1980) consider re-entry as a self-reference or recursion: a (biological or social) form operates on itself by way of re-entry and therefore retains continuity despite being affected by the contingencies of the environment. In terms of the broadly understood information theory, I would define 're-entry' as a process of *auto-communication* that ensures both the organism's autonomy and its openness as regards the environment.

References

Abbott, H. Porter. 2013. *Real Mysteries: Narrative and the Unknowable*. Columbus: Ohio State University Press.

Alber, Jan. 2009. 'Impossible Storyworlds and What To Do with Them', *Storyworlds* 1: 79–96.

Bartlett, Frederic C. (1932) 1995. *Remembering: A Study in Experimental and Social Psychology*. Cambridge: Cambridge University Press.
Bergman, Hjalmar. 2007. *Memoirs of a Dead Man*. Trans. Neil Smith. University of East Anglia, Norwich: Norvik Press.
Bergson, Henry. 1999. *Matter and Memory*. New York: Zone Books.
Bessenoff, Gayle R., Leigh A. Frost, Angela Y. Lee and Jeffrey W. Sherman. 1998. 'Stereotype Efficiency Reconsidered: Encoding Flexibility Under Cognitive Load', *Journal of Personality and Social Psychology* 75: 589–606.
Boyer, Pascal. 1994. *The Naturalness of Religious Ideas: A Cognitive Theory of Religion*. Berkeley: University of California Press.
Burton, Chad M., Stephen M. Drigotas, Joshua A. Hicks and Laura A. King. 2007. 'Ghosts, UFOs, and Magic: Positive Affect and the Experiential System', *Journal of Personality and Social Psychology* 92: 905–19.
Clark, Andy. 2016a. 'Embodied Prediction', in Thomas Metzinger and Jennifer M. Windt (eds), *Open Mind: Philosophy and the Mind Sciences in the 21st Century*, Vol. I. Cambridge, MA: MIT Press, pp. 263–84.
———. 2016b. *Surfing Uncertainty: Prediction, Action, and the Embodied Mind*. Oxford: Oxford University Press.
Danto, Arthur C. 1985. *Narration and Knowledge*. New York: Columbia University Press.
Dissanayake, Ellen. 1992. *Homo Aestheticus: Where Art Came From and Why*. New York: Free Press.
Empson, William. 1947. *Seven Types of Ambiguity*. New York: New Directions.
Garcia Landa, Jose Angel. 2019. 'In Hindsight: Complexity, Contingency, and Narrative Mapping', in Marina Grishakova and Maria Poulaki (eds), *Narrative Complexity: Cognition, Embodiment, Evolution*. Lincoln: Nebraska University Press, pp. 414–36.
Gerrig, Richard. 2012. 'Why Literature Is Necessary, and Not Just Nice', in Isabel Jaén and Julien Jacques Simon (eds), *Cognitive Literary Studies: Current Themes and New Directions*. Austin: University of Texas, pp. 35–52.
Gibbons, Alice, and Andrea Macrae (eds). 2018. *Pronouns in Literature: Positions and Perspectives in Language*. Basingstoke: Palgrave Macmillan.
Graesser, Arthur C. 1981. *Prose Comprehension Beyond the Word*. New York: Springer-Verlag.
Grishakova, Marina. 2009. 'Beyond the Frame: Cognitive Science, Common Sense, and Fiction', *Narrative* 17(2): 188–99.
———. 2011. 'Narrative Causality Denaturalized', in Jan Alber and Rüdiger Heinze (eds), *Unnatural Narratives – Unnatural Narratology*. New York: De Gruyter, pp. 127–44.
———. 2019. 'Predictive Mind, Attention, and Cultural Evolution', in Marina Grishakova and Maria Poulaki (eds), *Narrative Complexity: Cognition, Embodiment, Evolution*. Lincoln: Nebraska University Press, pp. 367–90.
Grishakova, Marina, Remo Gramigna and Siim Sorokin. 2019. 'Imaginary Scenarios: On the Use and Misuse of Fiction', *Frontiers of Narrative Studies* 5(1): 112–29. https://doi.org/10.1515/fns-2019-0008.
Hansen, Niels Chr., Peter Vuust and Marcus Pearce. 2016. '"If You Have to Ask, You'll Never Know": Effects of Specialized Stylistic Expertise on Predictive Processing of Music', *PLoS ONE* 11(10): e0163584. doi:10.1371/journal.pone.0163584.
Hinton, Perry. 2017. 'Implicit Stereotypes and Predictive Brain: Cognition and Culture in "Biased" Person Perception', *Palgrave Communications* 3: 17086. https://www.nature.com/articles/palcomms201786.

Hohwy, J. 2013. *The Predictive Mind*. Oxford: Oxford University Press.
Hopkins, Gerald Manley. 1970. *The Poems*. Oxford: Oxford University Press.
Huron, David. 2006. *Sweet Anticipation: Music and the Psychology of Expectation*. Cambridge, MA: MIT Press.
Jones, Max, and Sam Wilkinson. 2020. 'From Prediction to Imagination', in Anna Abraham (ed.), *The Cambridge Handbook of the Imagination*. Cambridge: Cambridge University Press, pp. 94–110.
Kaaronen, Roope Oskari. 2018. 'A Theory of Predictive Dissonance: Predictive Processing Presents a New Take on Cognitive Dissonance', *Frontiers in Psychology* 9: 2218. doi: 10.3389/fpsyg.2018.02218
Kahneman, Daniel. 2011. *Thinking, Fast and Slow*. New York: Farrar, Straus & Giroux.
Katz, Daniel, and Kenneth W. Braly. 1935. 'Racial Prejudice and Racial Stereotypes', *Journal of Abnormal Social Psychology* 30: 175–93.
Kauffman, Louis H., and Francisco J. Varela. 1980. 'Form Dynamics', *Journal of Biological and Social Structures* 3: 171–206.
Kesner, Ladislav. 2014. 'The Predictive Mind and the Experience of Visual Art Work', *Frontiers in Psychology* 5(1417). https://doi.org/10.3389/fpsyg.2014.01417.
Kintsch, Walter. 1980. 'Learning from Text, Levels of Comprehension, or: Why Anyone Would Read a Story Anyway', *Poetics* 9: 87–98.
Kiss, Miklós, and Steven Willemsen. 2017. *Impossible Puzzle Films: A Cognitive Approach to Contemporary Complex Cinema*. Edinburgh: Edinburgh University Press.
Koczy, Daniel. 2018. *Beckett, Deleuze and Performance: A Thousand Failures and Thousand Inventions*. Newcastle upon Tyne: Palgrave Macmillan.
Krumhansl, C.L., and R.N. Shepard. 1979. 'Quantification of the Hierarchy of Tonal Functions within a Diatonic Context', *J Exp Psychol Hum Percept Perform* 5(4): 579–94. doi: 10.1037/0096-1523.5.4.579 PMID: 528960.
Kukkonen, Karin. 2020. *Probability Designs: Literature and Predictive Processing*. Oxford: Oxford University Press.
Lampert, Jay. 1995. *Synthesis and Backward Reference in Husserl's Logical Investigations*. Dordrecht: Springer.
———. 2012. *Simultaneity and Delay*. London: Bloomsbury.
Leeuwen, Cees van, and Dirk J.A. Smit. 2012. 'Restless Minds, Wandering Brains', in Shimon Edelman, Tomer Fekete and Neta Zach (eds), *Being in Time: Dynamical Models of Phenomenal Experience*. Amsterdam: John Benjamins, pp. 121–48.
Lemon, Michael C. 1995. *The Discipline of History and the History of Thought*. London: Routledge.
Mayo, Deborah G. 2014. 'Learning from Error: How Experiment Gets a Life (of Its Own)', in Marcel Boumans, Giora Hon and Arthur C. Petersen (eds), *Error and Uncertainty in Scientific Practice*. London: Pickering & Chatto, pp. 57–79.
McEwan, Ian. 2019. *The Cockroach*. London: Jonathan Cape.
Menary, Richard. 2016. 'What? Now. Predictive Coding and Enculturation. A Reply to Regina E. Fabry', in Thomas Metzinger and Jennifer M. Windt (eds), *Open Mind: Philosophy and the Mind Sciences in the 21st Century*, Vol. 1. Cambridge, MA: The MIT Press, pp. 1041–48.
Mole, Christopher. 2011. *Attention is Cognitive Unison*. New York: Oxford University Press.
Muth, Claudia, Marius H. Raab and Claus-Christian Carbon. 2016. 'Semantic Stability Is More Pleasurable in Unstable Semantic Contexts: On the Relevance of Perceptual Challenge in Art Appreciation', *Frontiers in Human Neuroscience*, Vol. 10, article 43. doi: 10.3389/fnhum.2016.00043.

Newsome, Will. 2013. 'Complementing Predictive Coding'. *Frontiers in Psychology* 3: 554. doi: 10.3389/fpsyg.2012.00554.

Oliver, Mary Beth, and Arthur A. Raney. 2011. 'Entertainment as Pleasurable and Meaningful: Identifying Hedonic and Eudaimonic Motivations for Entertainment Consumption', *Journal of Communication* 61(5): 984–1004.

Polanyi, Michael. 1966. *The Tacit Dimension*. London: Routledge & Kegan Paul.

Ransom, Madeleine, Sina Fazelpour, and Christopher Mole. 2017. 'Attention in the Predictive Mind.' *Consciousness and Cognition* 47: 99–112. http://dx.doi.org/10.1016/j.concog.2016.06.011.

Sanford, Anthony J., and Catherine Emmott. 2012. *Mind, Brain and Narrative*. Cambridge: Cambridge University Press.

Schmuckler, M.A. 1989. 'Expectation in Music: Investigation of Melodic and Harmonic Processes', *Music Percept* 7(2): 109–149.

Shimojo, S. 2014. 'Postdiction: Its Implications on Visual Awareness, Hindsight, and Sense of Agency', *Frontiers in Psychology* 5(196). https://doi.org/10.3389/fpsyg.2014.00196.

Sripada, Chandra S. 2018. 'An Exploration/Exploitation Trade-off between Mind-Wandering and Goal-Directed Thinking', in Kieran C.R. Fox and Kalina Christoff (eds), *Oxford Handbook of Spontaneous Thought*. Oxford: Oxford University Press, pp. 23–34.

Steiner, George. 1978. *On Difficulty and Other Essays*. Oxford: Oxford University Press.

Todd, Peter M., and Gerd Gigerenzer. 2012. *Ecological Rationality: Intelligence in the World*. New York: Oxford University Press.

Van de Cruys, Sander, and Johan Wagemans. 2011. 'Putting Reward in Art: A Tentative Prediction Error Account of Visual Art', *I-perception* 2: 1035–62.

Williams, Daniel. 2018. 'Predictive Coding and Thought', *Synthese* 197: 1749–75. https://doi.org/10.1007/s11229-018-1768-x.

CHAPTER 14
Expressive Challenge and the Metaphoricity of Literary Reading

Don Kuiken

Introduction

Cognitive challenge is a multidimensional construct, as is the aesthetic experience that it potentially facilitates or obstructs. One conception of the challenge inherent in literary reading identifies formal deviations from routine language use that create uncertainty, retard reading, and evoke an appreciation of *how* textual content is presented. An alternative framework emphasizes two forms of challenging deviation: the first involves cross-domain resemblances that are generated by extended metaphoric and quasi-metaphoric structures; the second involves explanatory relations between temporal intervals and the viewpoints that frame them.

Both forms of deviation are evident in a poem entitled, 'The Conversation of Prayer', by Dylan Thomas (1996). The poem contrasts a man's prayer 'as he climbs the stairs to the room of his dying love' with a child's bedside prayer 'for safe sleep'. The poem's primary metaphor accentuates the 'sameness' of their prayers:

> *The sound about to be said in the two prayers*
> *For the sleep in a safe land and the love who dies*
> *Will be the same grief flying ...*

Despite such metaphoric sameness, the man in the 'fire of his care ...'

> *... shall find no dying but alive and warm ...*
> *... his love in the high room*

while the child 'not caring to whom he climbs his prayer ...'

> *Shall drown in a grief as deep as his made grave,*
> *And mark the dark-eyed wave, through the eyes of sleep*

While the poem's primary metaphor marks the sameness of the man's and the boy's prayer, the poem also portrays contrasting plot-like progressions from these moments of prayer: the man 'shall' find life and warmth in the 'high room', and the boy 'shall' drown in the dreamy grief that drags him 'up the stairs'. The metaphoric structure invites a form of reflective engagement that 'finds' how praying and grief are 'the same'. The plot-like progressions invite a form of reflective engagement that 'explains' what follows these moments of prayer.

This chapter examines these two contrasting forms of reflective engagement: (a) *expressive explication* of the recurrent cross-domain resemblances generated by metaphoric (and quasi-metaphoric) structures and (b) *interpretive explanation* of separate temporal intervals, and the viewpoints that frame them. This analysis leads to the identification of two modes of deeply absorbed reading engagement: *expressive enactment* and *integrative comprehension* (Kuiken and Douglas 2017, 2018). Related research indicates that expressive enactment, but not integrative comprehension, is associated with response to the type of reading challenge that derives from metaphoricity, including movement towards a mode of aesthetic response involving sublime feeling. Conversely, integrative comprehension, but not expressive enactment, is associated with plot assembly, including movement towards a mode of aesthetic response that depends upon heightened curiosity. Mounting evidence of discriminant validity substantiates the distinctiveness of expressive enactment and integrative comprehension as sources of aesthetic response to the challenges of literary reading.

Expressive Challenge and the Metaphoricity of Literary Reading

Frameworks for understanding the relations between cognitive challenge and aesthetic experience regularly address four aspects of readers' encounters with narrative texts: difficult linguistic structures, modes of attention to those structures, modes of reflection on their meaning, and forms of aesthetic response. *Difficult linguistic structures* can range from non-standard orthography and phonological anomalies to poetic metaphor and impossible narratives. Difficult linguistic structures can elicit *modes of attention* that range from surprise to fascination. Forms of attention can trigger *modes of reflective engagement* that range from explication and elucidation to inference and explanation, and reflective engagement can precipitate *forms of aesthetic response* that range from pleasure and disgust to being moved and experiencing a feeling of the sublime. Without conceptual and empirical precision at all four levels of analysis, nuances within the interplay between cognitive challenge and aesthetic experience may be obscured. Contemporary models of narrative reading have identified two primary paths through this multileveled terrain.

Traditional Dualities Revisited

Epistemic and Aesthetic Functions

The nearly unavoidable – but usually qualified – separation between form and content continues to influence empirical studies of literature. Because of its influence, the form/content duality remains a useful point of departure for discussion of difficult textual structures. Although no longer suggesting that stylistic variations merely adorn invariant (untransformed) content (Leech and Short 2007: 11–16), attempts to separate the functions of form and content continue to influence models of literary reading. One influential account (Hakemulder and Van Peer 2016) emphasizes stylistic deviations from routine language use. These stylistic deviations ('foregrounding') purportedly (a) evoke uncertainty ('defamiliarization'), (b) retard reading, and (c) prompt 'appreciation' of the style in which textual content is presented. The transition from uncertainty to appreciation marks movement from the fragile epistemic import of the text's referential claims (i.e. uncertainty) to aesthetic valuation of its stylistic linguistic structures (i.e. appreciation).

This fundamentally formalist heuristic framework persists even though, during literary reading, (a) linguistic structures construed as stylistic (e.g. a poetic metaphor) and (b) linguistic structures construed as content (e.g. an underlying *fabula*) jointly contribute to a (Fregean) 'sense' of the imagined world that is perhaps even more fine-grained than the text's referential intensions (i.e. conceptual meanings). This global sense of the imagined world is the nexus within which both stylistic linguistic structures and those that represent untransformed narrative content establish their conceptual (epistemic) import. Although the former structures are often opaque (e.g. Stein's *A Carafe, that is a Blind Glass*) and the latter are often transparent (e.g. Hemingway's *The Old Man and the Sea*), readers are regularly challenged both by the difficult stylistic structures (e.g. the opening 'musings' of Joyce's *Portrait of the Artist as a Young Man*) and the difficult narrative developments (e.g. the 'story' lurking in Robbe-Grillet's *Le Voyeur*) that shape the world of the text.

Dual Epistemic Functions

The traditional duality (see Jakobson 1960) between form (with its poetic function) and content (with its referential function) should be reconfigured as a duality involving (a) textual structures that motivate (without determining) readers' categorial explicative efforts and (b) textual structures that motivate (without determining) readers' narrative explanatory efforts. There is a fundamental contrast between the epistemic import of *explication-centred* response to stylistic linguistic structures and the epistemic import of *explanation-centred* response to narrative development. For example, there is a fundamental contrast between reflective explication of what is 'the same' about prayer and 'grief flying', and reflective elaboration of what 'shall' occur after the boy's and the man's moments of prayer.

Epistemic affirmations are traditionally grounded in deduction (deriving an inference from established premises), induction (reaching a generalized conclusion from a sample of instances), and sometimes abduction (reasoning that generates plausible hypotheses). Abduction is especially relevant when portrayed – as in Peirce's original sense – as reasoning that facilitates the discovery of causal hypotheses (Schurz 2008). Such 'abduction to best explanation' anticipates and advances the epistemic import of deduction. Eco (1983), for example, described this kind of abduction as supporting discovery of the deductive inferences that guide resolution of the enigmas in Doyle's Sherlock Holmes stories and Voltaire's philosophical novel *Zadig ou la Destinée*. In the Dylan Thomas poem, this form of abduction may also guide articulation of the inferences that explain the relief that follows the man's prayers and the grief that follows the boy's prayers.

Another kind of abduction supports the epistemic import of induction.[1] Abduction, in this form, anticipates and advances the explication of categorial constructs, including the explication of 'equivalences', such as those provided by the metaphoricity of lyric poetry (Jakobson 1960). This kind of abduction warrants comparison with Husserl's (1989) seminal discussion of categorial intuition – a process by which the essential attributes of sensuously present instances of a category are disclosed and elucidated.[2] Following this lead, Chernavin and Yampolskaya (2019) propose that something like the 'phenomenological reduction' contributes to the sensuous – and yet categorial – explication that shapes literary reading (see also Natanson 1998). Expressive explication begins when abstractly conceived categorial instances are apprehended as if they were not familiar – as though freshly seen or, better, freshly sensed (Berlina 2017). In the Dylan Thomas poem, this form of abduction may involve explication of how the man's and the boy's prayers are 'the same'.

Differential Openings for Creative Response

The epistemic duality that frames the challenges of literary reading (i.e. explication-centred vs explanation-centred response to literary texts) is given impetus by research concerning attention and creativity. Reference to this research is justified to the extent that literary reading is an opportunity to creatively engage a sensuous-affective imaginal artefact by drawing on distinctive attentional resources. Conceptions of attention were crucial within the ill-fated discussions of 'the aesthetic attitude' during the last century (Dickie 1964; Stolnitz 1978); now, as noted by Mullennix (2019), a somewhat similar distinction between automatic and controlled attentional processes is central in dual-processing approaches to aesthetic experience. For example, controlled attentional processes hypothetically guide response to novel (rather than prototypic) stimuli (Hekkert, Snelders and van Wieringen 2003), or to early, automatic and intuitive impressions of aesthetic stimuli (Graf and Landwehr 2015).

However, a quite different attentional duality contributes to explication-centred and explanation-centred reading. Specifically, during literary reading, creative response to difficult linguistic structures depends, in part, upon two attentional dispositions, each involving a subtly different process. Also, each of these attentional dispositions supports the individual differences in cognitive flexibility that are characteristic of the global personality trait called 'openness to experience'. One involves an aspect of this global trait called 'openness', which enables cognitive flexibility in sensuous-affective domains (e.g. the function of 'openness' in the arts); the other involves an aspect of this global trait called 'intellect', which enables cognitive flexibility in abstract conceptual domains (e.g. the function of 'openness' in the sciences; (DeYoung, Quilty and Peterson 2007; DeYoung 2015; Kaufman et al. 2016)).

The importance of these contrasting attentional dispositions may be made clearer with an example that involves an especially ambiguous linguistic anomaly. The Dylan Thomas poem includes linguistic structures that quite unambiguously invite either explication-centred or explanation-centred reflection. That is, the primary metaphor invites explication of the 'sameness' of the man's and the boy's prayers; the plot-like progressions invite explanatory inferences about what causes the man to find relief and the boy to find grief. In contrast, the following example does not obviously invite either explication-centred or explanation-centred reflection; rather, whether the reader engages in one or the other depends upon individual differences in openness to experience (openness, intellect). The general principle is that examining the *interaction* between textual structures and individual differences is necessary to predict either of these forms of reading engagement.

A short story by Sean O'Faolain entitled *The Trout* begins with the following anomalous locution: 'One of the first places Julia always ran to when they arrived in G— was The Dark Walk'. If the criterion for foregrounding is detection of deviant linguistic structures (Hakemulder 2020), noticing 'G—' almost certainly qualifies. But how does this deviation function? On the one hand, its detection may invite the cognitive flexibility that supports *explanatory interpretation* of the narrative events that have caused Julia to give this location an anonymizing identity; on the other hand, its detection may invite the cognitive flexibility that supports the *expressive explication* of what Julia's anonymizing impertinence 'is like' (perhaps in contrast to the veneration suggested by the adjacent capitalization of 'The Dark Walk'). Each of these alternatives depends upon detection of the deviant linguistic structure, but the issue is more basic: what kind of attentional disposition is activated by detection of such a linguistic structure? Is it the openness to experience ('openness') that supports cognitive flexibility in sensuous-affective domains? Or, is it the openness to experience ('intellect') that supports cognitive flexibility in abstract conceptual domains?

Response to these questions requires consideration of aspects of attention that exceed sustained selective attention (Sanford and Emmott 2012: Chapter 4). Instead, it may require consideration of evidence that, during creative task engagement, attention depends upon the co-activation of subsystems that support both sustained attention and flexible attention (Zabelina 2018). Recent evidence indicates that – among individuals whose openness to experience supports creative response to constrained abstract problems (e.g. multiple uses tasks, interpreting analogies) – sustained selective attention is complemented by an executive function ('updating' working memory) that facilitates access to 'different problem solutions' (Zabelina, Friedman and Andrews-Hanna 2019). On the other hand, among individuals whose openness to experience supports a creative response to extended imaginative problems (e.g. remote associates tasks, metaphor interpretation), sustained selective attention is complemented by an executive function ('shifting' between mental sets) that facilitates perspective changes to 'different dimensions' (Zabelina, Friedman and Andrews-Hanna 2019) and 'levels of analysis' (Zabelina, Saporta and Beeman 2016).

The contrast between (a) attentional openness to alternative solutions for abstract conceptual problems and (b) attentional openness to different levels or dimensions of sensuous-affective categories is congruent with a distinction between *instrumental* and *experiential* sets (Tellegen 1981). While a creative instrumental set may allow flexible reconsideration of alternative solutions to a constrained abstract problem, a creative experiential set allows attention to shift across different levels and dimensions of a categorial image or percept in an extended sensuous-affective problem. This duality suggests that, for some individuals, linguistic structures that capture attention precipitate an instrumental set in which attention is oriented towards different problem solutions (e.g. determining *how it came about* that Julia's destination was called 'G—'). For other individuals, the same linguistic structures may precipitate an experiential set in which attention is oriented towards different dimensions or levels of sensuous-affective categorial constructs (e.g. contrastively determining *what kind of place* was venerably named The Dark Walk).

Difficulties That Motivate Resemblance-Seeking

To clarify the creative path that moves towards experiential reading, close examination of a few exemplary experimental studies of foregrounding is useful. In one attempt to compare the effects of foregrounded and background textual structures, Hakemulder (2004) replaced deviant (foregrounded) linguistic structures in Nabokov's poem *The Old Bridge* with semantically similar but mundane (background) linguistic structures. Among the numerous foregrounding features that were replaced, words with double meanings were replaced by less ambiguous ones (e.g. 'bird' replaced 'swift'). Comparison of the effects of these two versions indicated greater appreciation of the original (foregrounded) version during a second reading. In this study, words with double meanings – or metaphoric semantic structures – were among numerous manipulated linguistic devices.

In a similar effort, Bohrn et al. (2012) also compared the effects of foregrounded and background linguistic structures. They modified a proverb that is sufficiently familiar to constitute background (e.g. 'knowledge is power' – *Wissen ist Macht*) to create two altered versions: one in which the substituting word produced a proverb that was roughly (and literally) synonymous with the original (e.g. 'information is power' – *Kenntnis ist Macht*), and another in which the substituting word twisted the original meaning (e.g. 'conscience is power' – *Gewissen ist Macht*). Comparison of these versions on fMRI indices indicated that response to the meaning-twisting substitution induced activation of cortical areas associated with affective evaluation (e.g. dmPFC) as well as with information integration (e.g. left IFG). On the other hand, response to the roughly synonymous version activated cortical areas associated with cognitive evaluation and error detection (e.g. the dorsal ACC and right dlPFC [BA 10]).

These two studies stand out not only as experimental exemplars but also because the results of both suggest that the 'deviations' (Hakemulder) and 'twists' (Bohrn et al.) that comprise foregrounding initiate the exploration, and perhaps explication, of 'hidden similarities' (Jacobs 2016: 160) – for example, the metaphoric 'equivalence' of the quickness of swifts and fleeting affections (Hakemulder 2004) or of guidance by a moral conscience and by factual knowledge (Bohrn et al. 2012). That is, the attentional set elicited by the deviant/twisted linguistic structure invited openness to subsequent articulation of the different levels and dimensions of metaphoric categories (Glucksberg 2008).

Recent accounts of literary reading begin to circumscribe the linguistic structures that initiate sustained and yet flexible attentiveness to levels and dimensions of metaphorically generated categories. The simplest forms of these structures are noun–noun compounds (e.g. a grief prayer) and nominal metaphors (e.g. praying is grieving). Jacobs and Willems (2018) focus on an array of figurative forms (e.g. metaphors, similes, irony), presenting affectively bivalent compounds (e.g. erotic-angel, rather than leper-misery) as the prototype (Forgács et al. 2012;

Kuhlmann et al. 2016). The authors emphasize a resemblance-seeking process that integrates incongruous affective words into a single 'meaning gestalt' (Jacobs and Willems 2018: 152).

Similarly, Kuiken and Douglas (2018) refer to textual structures that support reflection on recurrent cross-domain resemblances ('equivalences'; Jakobson 1960). These include explicit metaphoric structures (Goatly 2011: 215): 'the eye was a raindrop' (copula), 'the raindrop of an eye' (genitive), 'the raindrop eye' (noun premodifier), 'the eye-raindrop' (compound), 'the eye, a raindrop' (apposition) and 'the reyendrop' (blend). In addition to these direct resemblance-seeking structures, there are some indirect (quasi-metaphoric) structures that depend upon readers' construal to exert their metaphoric effect (Goatly 2011: chapters 6–8), such as 'the eye, as though a raindrop'. These quasi-metaphoric markers include structures that are often independently considered stylistic devices, including the recurrent intonation patterns (Lea et al. 2008), enjambments (van 't Jagt et al. 2014), and functional shifts (Keidel et al. 2013) that juxtapose potentially metaphoric topics and vehicles. Collectively, this family of metaphoric and quasi-metaphoric structures contributes to extended metaphors, often involving discontinuous text passages (see Kuiken and Douglas 2018: Study 1).

The process by which a metaphoric vehicle and topic generate a 'meaning gestalt' (Jacobs and Willems 2018) suggests a conception of metaphoric meaning that is not reducible to the salient attributes of the metaphoric vehicle or topic considered separately. Rather than a unidirectional 'mapping' of vehicle onto topic (which selectively retains salient attributes of the vehicle), interaction between the vehicle and topic may generate novel meanings that emerge in the same manner that configural properties of a percept emerge from – and yet exceed – the sum of its component parts (Wagemans et al. 2012). The interactive process that generates emergent meanings may involve the bidirectional categorial interplay through which the vehicle and topic are fused to create a non-additive blend. Such bidirectional integration may occur especially when (a) the metaphoric vehicle and topic come from distant conceptual domains (e.g. presidents and scorpions, rather than presidents and lieutenants), and (b) the vehicle and topic concepts are semantically dense (e.g. prayers and grief, rather than sanctuaries and museums; Katz and Al-Azary 2017). As with poetic metaphor more generally (Goodblatt and Glicksohn 2017), openly creative readers plausibly 'find' integrated categorial meanings that are coherently dependent upon both the vehicle and the topic, but not previously salient in either. To do so requires a reader to engage in an experiential mode of open and focused reflection that enables explication of levels and dimensions of an emergent categorial meaning.

Difficulties That Motivate Explanation-Seeking

As just argued, some 'deviations' precipitate an *experiential* attentional set that, in general, is attuned to textual metaphoricity. Within such an experiential set, the levels and dimensions that delimit metaphoric categorial constructs are potentially blended and integrated to generate emergent meaning. In contrast, another array of 'deviations' precipitate an *instrumental* set that is attuned to textual indicators of coordinated temporal intervals and character/narrator viewpoints. Going beyond the contrasts between *fabula* and *suzjet* (Toolan 2001), first- and third-person narration (Kaufman and Libby 2012), and inclusion or exclusion of characters' thoughts and feelings (van Krieken, Hoeken and Sanders 2017), recent studies have examined these markers of coordinated temporal intervals and viewpoints, including shifts in verb tense (Sanders 2010), demonstrative deictics (Dancygier 2019), and free indirect discourse (Nikiforidou 2012).

As Sanders and van Krieken (2019: 284) argue, these linguistic markers shape three basic structures. In one, several temporal intervals are embedded recursively within a single viewpoint. Zunshine demonstrates this structure by paraphrasing embedded viewpoints within Virginia Woolf's *Mrs Dalloway*: 'Woolf *intends us to recognize* ... that Richard *is aware* that Hugh *wants* Lady Bruton and Richard to *think* that because the makers of the pen *believe* that it will never wear out, the editor of the *Times* will *respect* and publish the ideas recorded by this pen' (Zunshine 2006: 33, italics in original). Van Duijn and Verhagen (2019) complicate this portrayal of embedded viewpoints by emphasizing the narrator's overall perspective on characters' viewpoints, but the vertical embedding principle is primary.

In a second basic structure, successive temporal intervals correspond one-to-one with episodic viewpoints (van Krieken, Sanders and Hoeken 2016). Each episodic viewpoint entails coherent time, space, and character relations, and temporal movement from one episodic viewpoint to another constitutes a storyline. Van Krieken et al. identify prototypic instances of this structure in news stories, such as the following excerpt from *The Washington Post* coverage of a killing spree on the Virginia Tech campus in 2007:

[Viewpoint 1] The first attack came in Room 206, advanced hydrology taught by Loganathan. There were 13 graduate students in the class, all from the civil engineering department. There was no warning, no foreboding sounds down the hallway ... [Viewpoint 2] In Jamie Bishop's German class, they could hear the popping sounds. What was that? Some kind of joke? Construction noises? More pops ... [Viewpoint 3] Trey Perkins knocked over a couple of desks and tried to take cover. [Viewpoint 4] No way I can survive this, he thought.

The authors complicate this portrayal of successive viewpoints by emphasizing the narrator's construction of a 'virtual observer', but the horizontal temporal principle is primary.

In a third basic structure, several viewpoints are blended into a single temporal interval that is marked by parallel, superimposed viewpoints. Fletcher and Monterosso (2016) experimentally examined this structure by modifying passages from Jane Austen's *Emma*. A comparison of their control and experimental (free indirect discourse) texts helps to clarify this structure. A section of their control text read: 'Amerigo Bonasera remembered the judge's pledges, his vows, and all his great promises that he would be just. And Amerigo felt betrayed.' The experimental version read: 'Amerigo Bonasera remembered the judge's pledges, his vows, and all his great promises. Just. He called himself just. And Amerigo felt betrayed.' While the control text was entirely third-person, the experimental text began in third-person ('Amerigo Bonasera remembered ...') and pivoted into the first ('Just ...') before pivoting back into the third ('And Amerigo felt betrayed'). Additional nuances of such blended viewpoints have been studied empirically (see Sopčák, Kuiken and Miall 2020).

Little is known about the distribution of, or variations in, these three basic structures across genres (e.g. narrative fiction vs lyric poetry vs news stories). However, in general, readers assemble an 'actual' timeline (i.e. a plot) by considering the temporal intervals – and the viewpoints that frame them – across an entire narrative. As part of plot assembly, coordinating an array of temporalizing frames poses complex explanatory questions. Beyond the narrated events through which narrative personae overcome obstacles or deficiencies (external causes), the coordination of temporalizing frames entails exploration of their motives or intentions (internal causes; Zwaan and Rapp 2006). To portray a temporal frame from a narrator's or character's viewpoint is to present events as momentarily perceived, interpreted and evaluated by that character.

The quest for explanations (external causes and internal intentions) during plot assembly resembles the interplay between prospection, retrospection and recognition that Sternberg (1990, 1992, 2006) attributes to narrative comprehension. However, the difficulties faced during plot assembly (e.g. while reading Nabokov's *Pale Fire*) evoke a more nuanced response than is captured by the emotions that Sternberg attributes to prospection (suspense), retrospection (curiosity) and recognition (surprise). Similarly, the challenging complexities of temporal intervals and character/narrator viewpoints, as summarized above, are often incompatible with the effortless attention, affective empathy and immersive emotions that Jacobs (2016) describes as background to foregrounded linguistic structures in his model of literary reading (Jacobs and Lüdtke 2017).

Functionally Coordinated Linguistic Structures

Some studies of response to difficult linguistic structures involve the manipulation of individual (usually local) deviant features (Emmott, Sanford and Dawydiak 2007; Bohrn et al. 2012). However, the array of deviant structures is extraordinarily diverse, ranging from alliteration (Lea et al. 2008) to supra-natural narrative events (Hsu, Conrad and Jacobs 2014). Other studies of response to difficult linguistic structures attempt simultaneous alteration of numerous linguistic structures across phonetic, syntactic and semantic levels of analysis (e.g. Hakemulder 2004; Kuijpers and Hakemulder 2018). The guiding assumption is that these difficulties function as an aggregate array of deviant linguistic structures.[3] However, in general – as Sanford and Emmott (2012) argue – it remains very difficult to identify the 'cohesive chains' of language structures that integrate 'referential choice' (e.g. noun terms, anaphoric terms) with 'stylistically marked' forms of reference (e.g. metaphoric predication, syntactic repetition). Such chained structures are the coherent but, nonetheless, 'rule breaking' categories (ibid.: 102) for which computer algorithms are not available.

In this light, it may be more useful to empirically determine whether there are *theory-guided* and *functionally coordinated* subsets of difficult linguistic structures. The present version of the traditional dual-process model identifies two such subsets. The first is composed of metaphoric structures and quasi-metaphoric structures, including the phonological and syntactic variations that facilitate the juxtaposition of potentially metaphoric topics and vehicles (Kuiken and Douglas 2018). The second subset is composed of linguistic markers of temporal intervals and character/narrator viewpoint, including shifts in verb tense and temporal adjectives, demonstrative deictics and free indirect discourse (Sanders and van Krieken 2019).[4]

If the specification of nominal metaphoric structures is already daunting, detecting cohesive chains of metaphoric structures (e.g. extended metaphors) is even more so. Nonetheless, Steen et al. (2010) have tried to address that task systematically, using Metaphor Identification Procedures (VU; see also Steen 2016). Similarly, although challenging, systematic specification of the subset of structures that identify temporal intervals and character/narrator viewpoint has begun. Eekhof, van Krieken and Sanders (2020) offer the ViewPoint Identification Procedure (VPIP) as a systematic method for identifying perceptual, cognitive and emotional viewpoint markers in narrative discourse. There is reason to be optimistic that a combination of computational procedures and expert judgement will enhance these efforts (Herrmann 2017).

Other Sources of Difficulty

Several sources of difficulty are not directly addressed within the traditional duality, perhaps especially in the form that duality has been revisited here. First, the difficulties that motivate resemblance-seeking are responses to linguistic structures that focus specifically on metaphoricity. However, that restriction is tempered by the inclusion of quasi-metaphoric structures that depend upon readers' construal to exert their metaphoric effect (including the recurrent intonation patterns, enjambments and functional shifts that juxtapose potentially metaphoric topics and vehicles). Second, the difficulties that motivate explanation-seeking are responses to deviations in linguistic structures that focus specifically on markers of temporal intervals and character/narrator viewpoint (including shifts in verb tense, demonstrative deictics and free indirect discourse). However, that restriction is tempered by the fact that these applications of the conceptual blending model (e.g. Fauconnier and Turner 2002) address structures that span the entire narrative.

On the other hand, several sources of difficulty are not addressed by the preceding dualistic model. Castiglione (2019) has reviewed discussions of the difficulty of literary reading, beginning with landmark essays by Shklovsky (Berlina 2017), Empson (1930), Steiner (1978) and Diepeveen (2013). Crucial to his discussion – and model – is the distinction between textual structures that foster difficulty (at the discourse level) and obscurity (at the thematic level). Castiglione's model warrants close comparison with the kinds of difficulty addressed in the dualistic model reviewed here, but that task is beyond the scope of this chapter.

Also, the duality as offered here does not address what may be called the difficulties of intertextual interpretation. One form of intertextual interpretation involves detection within a target text of imitative structures (e.g. quotation, allusion, parody). A second involves detection of similarities between the genres, themes or style of the target text and other texts. The difficulties posed by both of these forms of intertextual interpretation will be less of a liability for literary experts than for novice literary readers. As important as those sources of difficulty may be (see Goldman, McCarthy and Burkett 2015), they are not addressed here.

Immediate Attentional Responses to Difficult Textual Structures

These functionally coordinated subsets of linguistic structures are expected to have quite different effects on attention, especially on the co-activation of subsystems supporting sustained and flexible attention (see Zabelina 2018). Direct assessment of such attentional patterns may only be possible in research paradigms that involve the manipulation of very brief text segments (e.g. Bohrn et al. 2012; Forgács et al. 2012). Research in this domain has relied instead on readers' self-reported attentional response to aggregates of linguistic structures within longer texts. In foregrounding research, it has seemed necessary to rely on self-reported 'defamiliarization' (e.g. surprise, strikingness) or on ratings that are plausibly correlated with defamiliarization (e.g. discussion value).

However, there have been almost no systematic psychometric studies of self-report measures of defamiliarization (e.g. content validation, confirmatory factor analyses, convergent and discriminant validation). Also, rather than focusing on defamiliarization and its derivatives, it may be useful to examine the contrasting effects of the subsets of linguistic structures articulated here. They may elicit quite different modes of self-reported attention.

Inexpressible Realizations

The immediate attentional response to metaphoric and quasi-metaphoric structures (e.g. extended metaphor) may resemble what Shklovsky called *ostranenie* (usually translated as 'defamiliarization'). He compared *ostranenie* to an encounter with an intentional object as though it is 'seen for the first time' (Berlina 2017: 81), rather than as abstractly conceived (77), routinely named (81), or merely recognized (88). Chernavin and Yampolskaya (2019) compare this encounter with the 'attentional doubling' that derives from a similar gap between abstract understanding and sensuous intuition within the phenomenological *epoché*.

A cognitive psychological version of this account posits differentiation between abstract (amodal, symbolic) representational systems and grounded (enactive, embodied, embedded and extended) representational systems (Ward, Silverman and Villalobos 2017). Grounded representational systems have their origin in comprehension of the enactive, embodied, embedded and extended 'here-and-now' of directly lived situations. During literary reading, these same representational systems are reactivated during comprehension of the grounded 'here-and-now' of imaginally lived situations.

Mahon and Caramazza (2008; see also Lambon Ralph et al. 2017) describe how the activation of abstract representations potentially flows, over time, *towards* activation of grounded representations. For example, reading the word 'flying' initially activates an abstract representation (e.g. an abstract conception of 'transportation') that, in turn, flows towards activation of various enactive, embodied, embedded and extended representations (e.g. a kinaesthetic sense of 'bodily ascent', a visual sense of a 'receding horizon', an auditory sense of 'wind in my ears'). This transition involves movement *from* the ability to say only what is abstractly named, conceived and recognized, *towards* the ability to say something 'more' that is captured by grounded representations. Such 'expressive' possibilities constitute *reanimating explication* of what a selected categorial object 'is like' – how it has appeared and how it might appear again.

Consistent with this proposal, self-reported strikingness is the most consistently replicated response to stylistically deviant passages (Hunt and Vipond 1985; van Peer 1986; Miall and Kuiken 1994; Sopčák 2007; Kuiken and Douglas 2018). Strikingness ratings suggest that a more fully reanimated conception of what 'this is like' will derive from subsequent explication.[5] One measure of such intimations is a brief self-report scale for *inexpressible realizations* (Kuiken, Campbell and Sopčák 2012: 270). Items include, 'I began to understand something that could not be put into words', and 'I sensed something that I could not find a way to express'. Such intimations may occur specifically in response to difficult metaphoric or quasi-metaphoric linguistic structures.

Persistent Curiosity

The immediate attentional response to markers of temporal intervals and character or narrator viewpoint is perhaps *persistent curiosity* – that is, the interactive combination of retrospective curiosity (e.g. 'I wonder how this [moment] came about'), concurrent curiosity (e.g. 'I wonder what is happening here') and prospective curiosity (e.g. 'I wonder what will happen next'). Cognitive coordination between these temporal frames and viewpoints can occur in a variety of ways: they may contrast with one another, reinforce one another, be causally linked, or become mixed (van Duijn and Verhagen 2019). Thus, the immediate (and generic) effect of detected markers of temporal intervals and character or narrator viewpoint may be the *interactive* (not additive) combination of retrospective, concurrent and prospective curiosity.[6]

Modes of Reflective Engagement with Difficult Linguistic Structures

Open Reflection

Although the aspect of openness to experience that is suited to constrained abstract problems (intellect) can be distinguished from the aspect of openness to experience that is suited to extended imaginative problems (openness), both involve co-activation of sustained and flexible attentional subsystems (see above). However, whether a reading moment supports the instrumental orientation (intellect) or the experiential orientation (openness) may depend upon an *interaction* between each of these traits and the presence of a situated commitment to 'dwelling silently' in the world of the text.[7] Following Ihde's (2007) phenomenological account, it may be appropriate to compare such 'dwelling' with silently listening for the farthest sound; the more closely one listens in silence, the more readily *unanticipated* sounds show themselves. An analogous form of 'dwelling silently' characterizes reflective openness to an unanticipated 'something more' or 'something else' within an imaginally present text world.[8]

    The situated commitment to 'dwelling silently' is especially pertinent when considering the family of contemporary constructs that describe absorption in the narrative world (e.g. flow, transportation, engagement, immersion; see Hakemulder et al. 2017). However, rather than assuming that each of these constructs imperfectly reflects the same underlying process (see Walter et al. 2020), Kuiken and Douglas (2017, 2018) have examined the contrast between two kinds of narrative absorption – each rooted in one of the two paths through reading difficulty articulated here (see above). The first, called expressive enactment, becomes concretely evident during inexpressible realizations – that is, during immediate response to resonances between metaphoric or quasi-metaphoric categorial objects. The second, called integrative comprehension, becomes concretely evident during peak moments within persistent curiosity – that is, during immediate response to successive, contrasting, or overlapping temporal intervals and viewpoints. However, each describes a continuing mode of reflective engagement that follows the immediate attentional response to difficult textual structures.

Integrative Comprehension

Integrative comprehension is a form of absorbed reflective engagement that supports an instrumental orientation and is explanation-centred. This orientation accentuates the distal senses (seeing, hearing) and provides an impression that the text world is 'beyond reach' (but navigable); objects, locations and people seem positioned relative to each other and 'over there' (*extra-personal space*). It also involves the activation of memory categories that concern what is familiar to people in general ('world knowledge') and that facilitate allocentric (object-to-object) coordination of the perspectives of text personae (*cognitive perspective-taking*). Finally, this form of reflection supports an inference-driven impression that fictional events are portrayed as they might 'actually' occur (*generalizing realism*).

Expressive Enactment

In contrast, expressive enactment is a form of reflective engagement that accentuates the proximal senses (reaching, touching, holding) and provides an impression that the text world is 'close'; objects, locations and people seem almost palpably 'within reach' (*peri-personal space*). This form of reflection activates memory categories centred on what is familiar to oneself and to identifiably intimate others ('personal knowledge'), and that facilitate egocentric (self to other) coordination of these perspectives with the perspectives of imaginal text personae; the reader covertly and metaphorically anticipates the implications of saying (with a narrator) 'I am in the world of the text' or (with a character) 'I am in the world of this character' (*pre-enactive empathy*). This form of reflection supports active explication of 'what it is like' to participate in a blend of experiences that is simultaneously self-implicating and relevant for intimately known others, and yet grounded in imaginal text personae (*self-implicating givenness*).

Expressive Enactment and Contrasts with Integrative Comprehension

This final section will concentrate on expressive enactment, which has become focal within a research programme that began with studies of foregrounding and defamiliarization (Miall and Kuiken 1994) but expanded to include phenomenological studies of the fundamental features of expressive enactment (Kuiken, Miall and Sikora 2004; Sikora, Kuiken and Miall 2011) and, more recently, psychometric and structural equation models (Kuiken, Campbell and Sopčák 2012; Kuiken and Douglas 2017, 2018) of expressive enactment. Closely related concepts have also been examined among readers who have experienced loss or trauma (Sikora, Kuiken and Miall 2010; Kuiken and Sharma 2013).

Rather than reviewing that research programme, it may be more useful to articulate the characteristics and effects of expressive enactment, especially as suggested by the preceding discussion of immediate and extended response to metaphoric and quasi-metaphoric structures. Although more has been accomplished in studies of expressive enactment than in studies of integrative comprehension, some pivotal contrasts with integrative comprehension will be mentioned where appropriate.

Expressive Enactment and Inexpressible Realizations

According to the structural equation model developed by Kuiken and Douglas (2017, 2018), (a) open reflection initiates both expressive enactment and integrative comprehension, and (b) expressive enactment mediates the relationship between open reflection and inexpressible realizations (i.e. a felt sense that a reanimated conception of what 'this is like' will derive from subsequent explication). That pattern has been consistently observed (Kuiken and Douglas 2017, 2018), suggesting that an inexpressible realization is the first moment in more extended explication-centred reflection. Notably, integrative comprehension does not predict inexpressible realizations.

Expressive Enactment and Metaphor Comprehension

The framework provided here begins to identify how readers reflect on the sensed but initially inexpressible complexity of metaphoric and quasi-metaphoric textual structures. A strikingly inexpressible realization initiates *reflective* consideration of the *pre-reflective* understanding that accompanies presentation of metaphoric or quasi-metaphoric textual structures. This transition from pre-reflective to reflective consideration of such structures is neither reducible to explicit recognition of a specific syntactic type (e.g. a 'metaphoric expression'; Gibbs 1990) nor to explicit recognition that such a linguistic structure is 'deliberate' (Steen 2015). Rather, an inexpressible realization becomes evident to the reader as a reflectively accessible 'unity of presence' (simultaneous 'retention' of two or more grounded intentional objects) that is 'the foundation for … relations of likeness and similarity' (Husserl 1973: 183). During subsequent reflection, progressive explication of likeness and similarity depends upon indexical forms of reference to such an unnamed 'unity of presence' (e.g. 'this', 'that', 'here', 'now').

The implicit question – answers to which are constrained by the sensed substrate referred to by these indexical terms – is: what are the attributes by which a pre-reflective 'this' and a pre-reflective 'that' are 'the same'? For example, a pre-reflective 'this' could be a felt sense of what prayer is like, a pre-reflective 'that' could be a felt sense of what grief is like, and their 'sameness' could be how, metaphorically, prayer 'is' grief flying. Kuiken and Douglas (2017) refer to this form of exploratory questioning of initially inexpressible realizations as *expression-centred explication*.

In tests of the Kuiken and Douglas (2017, 2018) structural equation model, expressive enactment mediated the relationship between open reflection and comprehension of *unconventional literary* metaphors (e.g. 'death is a fat fly'), whereas integrative comprehension mediated the relationship between open reflection and the comprehension of *conventional nonliterary* metaphors (e.g. 'genes are blueprints'; Douglas 2019; Kuiken and Douglas 2018). More specifically, in response to normed categories of nominal metaphors (Katz et al. 1988), expressive enactment predicted readers' readiness to include an unconventional literary vehicle (e.g. 'fat fly') and topic (e.g. 'death') in the same ad hoc category (i.e. as metaphorically 'the same'). Integrative comprehension, in contrast, predicted readers' readiness to include a conventional non-literary vehicle (e.g. 'blueprints') and topic (e.g. 'genes') in the same category. This pattern underscores an asymmetry between poetic and mundane metaphors; rather than metaphoric linguistic structures in general, expressive enactment specifically predicted comprehension of metaphors with the potential to disclose emergent meanings.

Expressive Enactment and Sublime Disquietude

The specific aesthetic outcomes that emerge through expressive enactment require careful consideration. Aesthetic response traditionally involves epistemic (appetitive) *interest*, which can be distinguished from satiating (consummatory) pleasure (Silvia 2010; Panksepp and Biven 2012) and perhaps also non-satiating (anticipatory) pleasure (Koelsch et al. 2015). Perhaps epistemic interest is indeed an emotion (or feeling); if so, it must be differentiated not only from anticipatory pleasure (e.g. joy) but also from appreciation of stylistic structures that are somehow 'on top' of content (Menninghaus et al. 2019: 177) or that serve a poetic function independently of a referential function (Hakemulder and van Peer 2016).

In contrast, explication-centred reflection reanimates epistemic interest by interweaving grounded representations of emotion, feeling and mood with representations of external events and a situated self (e.g. a felt sense 'for me' of an external event). Sometimes these grounded representations involve short-term relations with specific intentional objects (e.g. momentary fear of this coyote in my backyard); at other times, they involve a relatively long-term relation with a global situation (e.g. estrangement from everyone around me; Ratcliffe 2005). Kuiken, Campbell and Sopčák (2012) laid out empirical criteria for sublime disquietude that represent a poignant epistemic blend of (a) 'unpleasure' in the 'inexpressibility' of a long-term concern and (b) the 'pleasure' of a felt shift towards a relatively complete understanding of such a long-term concern.[9]

As expected (Kuiken and Douglas 2017, 2018), expressive enactment mediated the relationship between open reflection and sublime disquietude. Moreover, as indicated in both studies, expressive enactment mediated the relationship between open reflection and being moved (Menninghaus et al. 2019). In contrast, integrative comprehension mediated the relationship between open reflection and narrative comprehension (narrator intelligibility, causal explanation and explanatory cohesion). The explanation-centred effects mediated by integrative comprehension lack the epistemic poignancy of sublime disquietude.

Conclusion

Among the questions that arise from the research on absorption-like states is whether the effects attributed to either expressive enactment or integrative comprehension generalize to other absorption-like states, such as the immersion that derives from a reader's reactive participation in narrative construction (Ryan 2001; Nilsson, Nordahl and Serafin 2016) or the side-participation derived from interactions with text personae (e.g. the narrator, story characters; Gerrig and Jacovina 2009; Bezdek, Foy and Gerrig 2013). The Kuiken and Douglas (2017) instrument assesses such reactive engagement, potentially facilitating comparison of that mode of reflective engagement with the two modes that have been considered here.

Although integrative comprehension is facilitated by the same open reflection that facilitates expressive enactment, the explanatory outcomes of integrative comprehension plausibly involve a mentalizing attribution of causes (e.g. external influences, internal intentions), rather than the explication of what it is like to be narrative personae (whether the narrator or a character). Evidence that integrative comprehension precipitates explanatory outcomes may have implications for recent studies of the effects of literary reading on social cognition. That literary reading facilitates 'simulation' of the 'thinking styles' of narrative personae suggests that empathy is an outcome of the 'mentalizing' that occurs during the explanation-centred 'construction' of situation models (Djikic and Oatley 2014). However, studies of how literary reading enhances social cognition have given insufficient attention to how some literary narratives – perhaps especially tragic narratives (Nussbaum 2001) – foster the poignant bivalence of sublime disquietude. These narratives present challenging questions about what constitutes human virtue within the context of subtle ambivalence and seemingly unavoidable conflicts (Oliver and Woolley 2011).

Ongoing research (Sopčák, Kuiken and Douglas, in preparation) suggests that a *global* moral outcome (called non-utilitarian respect) emerges from within the same nexus of processes through which expressive enactment leads to sublime disquietude. In contrast, a *specific* moral outcome (e.g. changes in attitude towards indigenous minorities) emerges from within the nexus of explanatory processes through which integrative comprehension leads to plot coherence and narrator intelligibility. Perhaps this is the difference between having a change of heart and changing one's mind.

Don Kuiken is Professor Emeritus in the Department of Psychology, University of Alberta, Canada. His continuing research addresses impactful dreams, the effects of literary reading and empirical phenomenological methods. He is past president of the International Society for the Empirical Study of Literature, and former editor of the journal *Dreaming*.

Notes

1. Schurz (2008: 219ff.) describes this stance as 'common cause induction', tracing it to the kind of reasoning that supports multivariate (factor analytic) studies of dispositional constructs. However, Borsboom et al. (2016) have reframed this family of multivariate procedures as supporting the exploration of categorial constructs. That step helps to differentiate abduction in the service of explanatory deduction from abduction in the service of categorial (ontological) induction.
2. In his discussion of the essences of material categories, Husserl (1973) allowed for inexact (morphological) essences – that is, delineation of more or less characteristic attributes or features (as in biological species). This too infrequently noted aspect of his framework complicates critiques of phenomenological 'essentialism', but it also complicates attempts to 'naturalize' phenomenology.
3. The fragility of that assumption is indicated by evidence of only modest agreement between expert judges on the levels of foregrounding in short story passages (e.g. Miall and Kuiken 1994: 396) and by failures to replicate the results of otherwise promising research paradigms (e.g. Kuijpers and Hakemulder 2018).
4. Whether the specific linguistic structures within these functionally coordinated subsets function as linear or interactive aggregates is crucial. Some of the relevant linguistic structures are expected to work interactively. Examples include (a) functional shifts and the evocation of polysemous or metaphoric meanings (Keidel et al. 2013), and (b) incongruity between the text-wide choice of verb tense (e.g. past tense) and the local choice of a proximal deictic (temporal, locative or demonstrative) in free indirect discourse (Dancygier 2019).
5. Miall and Kuiken (1994) reported that rated strikingness in response to foregrounding co-occurred with a self-reported 'feeling'. It has been tempting to describe that result as though foregrounding triggers 'powerful emotions' (Hakemulder and van Peer 2016: 194) that influence subsequent coping, empathy and identification. A viable alternative is that the 'feelings' reported in response to foregrounding involved much subtler 'feelings of knowing'.

6. Fayn et al. (2019) used an analogous but simpler index, i.e. the correlation between simple curiosity and confusion ratings. Perhaps it is noteworthy that their index of curious confusion was unrelated to openness/intellect in their study of response to a difficult poem.
7. Koopman and Hakemulder (2015) similarly suggest that the 'slowing down of readers' perceptions of the fictional world' creates moments of 'stillness'. However, their unidimensional conception of stillness differs from the integrated function of sustained attention and attentional flexibility.
8. In the Kuiken and Douglas (2017) Absorption-Like States Questionnaire, Open Reflection is composed of item parcels that separately reflect sustained attention (Resisting Personal Distraction, Resisting Task-Related Distraction) and readiness for attentional reorienting (Shift to Narrative Time, Altered Sense of Time).
9. Deligiorgi (2014) lays out a Kantian account of this sublimely poignant antinomy.

References

Berlina, Alexandra (ed.). 2017. *Viktor Shklovsky: A Reader*. New York: Bloomsbury Academic, an imprint of Bloomsbury Publishing Inc.

Bezdek, Matthew A., Jeffrey E. Foy and Richard J. Gerrig. 2013. '"Run for it!": Viewers' Participatory Responses to Film Narratives', *Psychology of Aesthetics, Creativity, and the Arts* 7(4): 409–16. doi: 10.1037/a0034083.

Bohrn, Isabel C., et al. 2012. 'Old Proverbs in New Skins: An fMRI Study on Defamiliarization', *Frontiers in Psychology* 3. doi: 10.3389/fpsyg.2012.00204.

Borsboom, Denny, et al. 2016. 'Kinds versus Continua: A Review of Psychometric Approaches to Uncover the Structure of Psychiatric Constructs', *Psychological Medicine* 46(8): 1567–79. doi: 10.1017/S0033291715001944.

Castiglione, Davide. 2019. *Difficulty in Poetry: A Stylistic Model*. Cham, Switzerland: Palgrave Macmillan.

Chernavin, Georgy, and Anna Yampolskaya. 2019. '"Estrangement" in Aesthetics and Beyond: Russian Formalism and Phenomenological Method', *Continental Philosophy Review* 52(1): 91–113. doi: 10.1007/s11007-018-9454-8.

Dancygier, Barbara. 2019. 'Proximal and Distal Deictics and the Construal of Narrative Time', *Cognitive Linguistics* 30(2): 399–415. doi: 10.1515/cog-2018-0044.

Deligiorgi, Katerina. 2014. 'The Pleasures of Contra-Purposiveness: Kant, the Sublime, and Being Human', *Journal of Aesthetics and Art Criticism* 72(1): 25–35. doi: https://doi.org/10.1111/jaac.12060.

DeYoung, Colin G. 2015. 'Openness/Intellect: A Dimension of Personality Reflecting Cognitive Exploration', in Mario Mikulincer and Philip R. Shaver (eds), *APA Handbook of Personality and Social Psychology: Personality Processes and Individual Differences*. Washington, DC: American Psychological Association, pp. 369–99.

DeYoung, Colin G., Lena C. Quilty and Jordan B. Peterson. 2007. 'Between Facets and Domains: 10 Aspects of the Big Five', *Journal of Personality and Social Psychology* 93(5): 880–96. doi: 10.1037/0022-3514.93.5.880.

Dickie, George. 1964. 'The Myth of the Aesthetic Attitude', *American Philosophical Quarterly* 1(1): 56–65.

Diepeveen, Leona. 2013. *Difficulties of Modernism*. New York: Routledge.
Djikic, Maja, and Keith Oatley. 2014. 'The Art in Fiction: From Indirect Communication to Changes of the Self', *Psychology of Aesthetics, Creativity, and the Arts* 8(4): 498–505. doi: 10.1037/a0037999.
Douglas, Shawn T. 2019. 'Narrating Identity: The Impact of Literary Reading on Storied Autobiographical Memory Development'. PhD dissertation, University of Alberta, Edmonton, Canada.
Eco, Umberto. 1983. 'Horns, Hooves, Insteps: Some Hypotheses on Three Types of Abduction', in Umberto Eco and Thomas A. Sebeok (eds), *The Sign of Three*. Bloomington: Indiana University Press, pp. 198–220.
Eekhof, Lynn S., Kobie van Krieken and José Sanders. 2020. 'VPIP: A Lexical Identification Procedure for Perceptual, Cognitive, and Emotional Viewpoint in Narrative Discourse', *Open Library of Humanities* 6(1): 18. doi: 10.16995/olh.483.
Emmott, Catherine, Anthony J. Sanford and Eugene J. Dawydiak. 2007. 'Stylistics Meets Cognitive Science: Studying Style in Fiction and Readers' Attention from an Inter-Disciplinary Perspective', *Style* 41(2): 204–25.
Empson, William. 1930. *Seven Types of Ambiguity*. London: Chatto & Windus.
Fauconnier, Gilles, and Mark Turner. 2002. *The Way We Think: Conceptual Blending and the Mind's Hidden Complexities*. New York: Basic Books.
Fayn, Kirill, et al. 2019. 'Confused or Curious? Openness/Intellect Predicts More Positive Iinterest-Confusion Relations', *Journal of Personality and Social Psychology* 117(5): 1016–33. doi: 10.1037/pspp0000257.
Fletcher, Angus, and John Monterosso. 2016. 'The Science of Free-Indirect Discourse: An Alternate Cognitive Effect', *Narrative* 24(1): 82–103. doi: 10.1353/nar.2016.0004.
Forgács, Bálint, et al. 2012. 'Neural Correlates of Combinatorial Semantic Processing of Literal and Figurative Noun Noun Compound Words', *NeuroImage* 63(3): 1432–42. doi: 10.1016/j.neuroimage.2012.07.029.
Gerrig, Richard J., and Matthew E. Jacovina. 2009. 'Chapter 7 Reader Participation in the Experience of Narrative', in *Psychology of Learning and Motivation* 51, Academic Press, an imprint of Elsevier, pp. 223–54. doi: 10.1016/S0079-7421(09)51007-9.
Gibbs, Raymond W. 1990. 'The Process of Understanding Literary Metaphor', *Journal of Literary Semantics* 19(2). doi: 10.1515/jlse.1990.19.2.65
Glucksberg, Sam. 2008. 'How Metaphors Create Categories – Quickly', in Raymond W. Gibbs (ed.), *The Cambridge Handbook of Metaphor and Thought*. New York: Cambridge University Press, pp. 67–83.
Goatly, Andrew. 2011. *The Language of Metaphors*. 2nd edn. New York: Routledge.
Goldman, Susan R., Kathryn S. McCarthy and Candice Burkett. 2015. 'Interpretive Inferences in Literature', in Edward O'Brien, Anne E. Cook and Robert F. Lorch (eds), *Inferences during Reading*. New York: Cambridge University Press, pp. 386–415. doi: 10.1017/CBO9781107279186.018.
Goodblatt, Chanita, and Joseph Glicksohn. 2017. 'Bidirectionality and Metaphor: An Introduction', *Poetics Today* 38(1): 1–14. doi: 10.1215/03335372-3716189.
Graf, Laura K.M., and Jan R. Landwehr. 2015. 'A Dual-Process Perspective on Fluency-Based Aesthetics: The Pleasure-Interest Model of Aesthetic Liking', *Personality and Social Psychology Review* 19(4): 395–410. https://doi.org/10.1177/1088868315574978.
Hakemulder, Frank. 2004. 'Foregrounding and its Effect on Readers' Perception', *Discourse Processes* 38(2): 193–218. doi: 10.1207/s15326950dp3802_3.

———. 2020. 'Finding Meaning through Literature', *Anglistik* 31(1): 91–110. doi: 10.33675/ANGL/2020/1/8.

Hakemulder, Frank, and Willie van Peer. 2016. 'Empirical Stylistics (Chapter 12)', in Violeta Sotirova (ed.), *The Bloomsbury Companion to Stylistics*. London: Bloomsbury Academic (Bloomsbury Companions), pp. 189–207.

Hakemulder, Frank, et al. (eds). 2017. *Narrative Absorption*. Philadelphia, PA: John Benjamins (Linguistic Approaches to Literature, Volume 27).

Hekkert, Paul, Dirk Snelders and Piet C.W. van Wieringen. 2003. '"Most Advanced, Yet Acceptable": Typicality and Novelty as Joint Predictors of Aesthetic Preference in Industrial Design', *British Journal of Psychology* 94(1): 111–24. doi: 10.1348/000712603762842147.

Herrmann, Berenike J. 2017. 'In a Test Bed with Kafka: Introducing a Mixed-Method Approach to Digital Stylistics', in Sally Chambers, Catherine Jones, Mike Kestemont, Marijn Koolen and Joris van Zundert (eds), *Special Issue: Digital Humanities Quarterly* 11(4). http://www.digitalhumanities.org/dhq/vol/11/4/000341/000341.html.

Hsu, Chun-Ting, Markus Conrad and Arthur M. Jacobs. 2014. 'Fiction Feelings in Harry Potter: Haemodynamic Response in the Mid-Cingulate Cortex Correlates with Immersive Reading Experience', *NeuroReport* 25(17): 1356–61. doi: 10.1097/WNR.0000000000000272.

Hunt, Russell A., and Douglas Vipond. 1985. 'Crash-Testing a Transactional Model of Literary Reading', *Reader: Essays in Reader-Oriented Theory, Criticism, and Pedagogy* 14: 23–39.

Husserl, Edmund. 1989. *Ideas Pertaining to a Pure Phenomenology and to a Phenomenological Philosophy (Second Book)*. Trans. R. Rojcewicz and A. Schuwer. Dordrecht: Kluwer Academic Publishers.

———. 1973. *Experience and Judgment: Investigations in a Genealogy of Logic*. Trans. L. Landgrebe. Evanston, IL: Northwestern University Press.

Ihde, Don. 2007. *Listening and Voice: Phenomenologies of Sound*. 2nd edn. Albany: State University of New York Press.

Jacobs, Arthur M. 2016. 'The Scientific Study of Literary Experience: Sampling the State of the Art', *Scientific Study of Literature* 5(2): 139–70. doi: 10.1075/ssol.5.2.01jac.

Jacobs, Arthur M., and Jana Lüdtke. 2017. 'Immersion into Narrative and Poetic Worlds (Chapter 4)', in Frank Hakemulder et al. (eds), *Narrative Absorption*. Amsterdam: John Benjamins, pp. 69–96.

Jacobs, Arthur M., and Roel M. Willems. 2018. 'The Fictive Brain: Neurocognitive Correlates of Engagement in Literature', *Review of General Psychology* 22(2): 147–60. doi: 10.1037/gpr0000106.

Jakobson, Roman. 1960. 'Linguistics and Poetics', in Thomas A. Sebeok (ed.), *Style in Language*. Cambridge, MA: MIT Press, pp. 350–77.

Katz, Albert N., and Hamad Al-Azary. 2017. 'Principles that Promote Bidirectionality in Verbal Metaphor', *Poetics Today* 38(1): 35–59. doi: 10.1215/03335372-3716215.

Katz, Albert N., et al. 1988. 'Norms for 204 Literary and 260 Nonliterary Metaphors on 10 Psychological Dimensions', *Metaphor and Symbolic Activity* 3(4): 191–214. doi: 10.1207/s15327868ms0304_1.

Kaufman, Geoff F., and Lisa K. Libby. 2012. 'Changing Beliefs and Behavior through Experience-Taking', *Journal of Personality and Social Psychology* 103(1): 1–19. doi: 10.1037/a0027525.

Kaufman, Scott Barry, et al. 2016. 'Openness to Experience and Intellect Differentially Predict Creative Achievement in the Arts and Sciences: Openness, Intellect, and Creativity', *Journal of Personality* 84(2): 248–58. doi: 10.1111/jopy.12156.

Keidel, James L., et al. 2013. 'How Shakespeare Tempests the Brain: Neuroimaging Insights', *Cortex* 49(4): 913–19. doi: 10.1016/j.cortex.2012.03.011.

Koelsch, Stefan, et al. 2015. 'The Quartet Theory of Human Emotions: An Integrative and Neurofunctional Model', *Physics of Life Reviews* 13: 1–27. doi: 10.1016/j.plrev.2015.03.001.

Koopman, Eva Maria, and Frank Hakemulder. 2015. 'Effects of Literature on Empathy and Self-Reflection: A Theoretical-Empirical Framework', *Journal of Literary Theory* 9(1): 79–111. doi: 10.1515/jlt-2015-0005.

Kuhlmann, Michael, et al. 2016. 'Mixing Positive and Negative Valence: Affective-Semantic Integration of Bivalent Words', *Scientific Reports* 6(1): 30718. doi: 10.1038/srep30718.

Kuijpers, Moniek M., and Frank Hakemulder. 2018. 'Understanding and Appreciating Literary Texts through Rereading', *Discourse Processes* 55(7): 619–41. doi: 10.1080/0163853X.2017.1390352.

Kuiken, Don, Paul Campbell and Paul Sopčák. 2012. 'The Experiencing Questionnaire: Locating Exceptional Reading Moments', *Scientific Study of Literature* 2(2): 243–72. doi: 10.1075/ssol.2.2.04kui.

Kuiken, Don, and Shawn Douglas. 2017. 'Forms of Absorption that Facilitate the Aesthetic and Explanatory Effects of Literary Reading (Chapter 11)', in Frank Hakemulder et al. (eds), *Narrative Absorption*. Amsterdam: John Benjamins, pp. 217–49.

———. 2018. 'Living Metaphor as the Site of Bidirectional Literary Engagement', *Scientific Study of Literature* 8(1): 47–76. doi: 10.1075/ssol.18004.kui.

Kuiken, Don, David S. Miall and Shelley Sikora. 2004. 'Forms of Self-Implication in Literary Reading', *Poetics Today* 25(2): 171–203. doi: 10.1215/03335372-25-2-171.

Kuiken, Don, and Ruby Sharma. 2013. 'Effects of Loss and Trauma on Sublime Disquietude during Literary Reading', *Scientific Study of Literature* 3(2): 240–65. doi: 10.1075/ssol.3.2.05kui.

Lambon Ralph, Matthew A., et al. 2017. 'The Neural and Computational Bases of Semantic Cognition', *Nature Reviews Neuroscience* 18(1): 42–55. doi: 10.1038/nrn.2016.150.

Lea, R. Brooke, et al. 2008. 'Sweet Silent Thought: Alliteration and Resonance in Poetry Comprehension', *Psychological Science* 19(7): 709–16. doi: 10.1111/j.1467-9280.2008.02146.x.

Leech, Geoffrey N., and Mick Short. 2007. *Style in Fiction: A Linguistic Introduction to English Fictional Prose*. 2nd edn. Harlow, England: Pearson Longman (English language series).

Mahon, Bradford Z., and Alfonso Caramazza. 2008. 'A Critical Look at the Embodied Cognition Hypothesis and a New Proposal for Grounding Conceptual Content', *Journal of Physiology-Paris* 102(1–3): 59–70. doi: 10.1016/j.jphysparis.2008.03.004.

Menninghaus, Winfried, et al. 2019. 'What Are Aesthetic Emotions?', *Psychological Review* 126(2): 171–95. doi: 10.1037/rev0000135.

Miall, David S., and Don Kuiken. 1994. 'Foregrounding, Defamiliarization, and Affect: Response to Literary Stories', *Poetics* 22(5): 389–407. doi: 10.1016/0304-422X(94)00011-5.

Mullennix, John W. 2019. 'The Role of Attention, Executive Processes, and Memory in Aesthetic Experience', in Marcos Nadal and Oshin Vartanian (eds), *The Oxford Handbook of Empirical Aesthetics*. Oxford: Oxford University Press. doi: 10.1093/oxfordhb/9780198824350.013.35.

Natanson, Maurice A. 1998. *The Erotic Bird: Phenomenology in Literature*. Princeton, NJ: Princeton University Press.

Nikiforidou, Kiki. 2012. 'The Constructional Underpinnings of Viewpoint Blends', in Barbara Dancygier and Eve Sweetser (eds), *Viewpoint in Language*. Cambridge: Cambridge University Press, pp. 177–97. doi: 10.1017/CBO9781139084727.014.

Nilsson, Niels Christian, Rolf Nordahl and Stefania Serafin. 2016. 'Immersion Revisited: A Review of Existing Definitions of Immersion and their Relation to Different Theories of Presence', *Human Technology* 12(2): 108–34. doi: 10.17011/ht/urn.201611174652.

Nussbaum, Martha C. 2001. *Upheavals of Thought: The Intelligence of Emotions*. Cambridge: Cambridge University Press.

Oliver, Mary Beth, and Julia K. Woolley. 2011. 'Tragic and Poignant Entertainment', in Katrin Döveling, Christian von Scheve and Elly A. Konijn (eds), *The Routledge Handbook of Emotions and Mass Media*. New York: Routledge, pp. 134–57.

Panksepp, Jaak, and Lucy Biven. 2012. *The Archaeology of Mind: Neuroevolutionary Origins of Human Emotions*. New York: Norton (A Norton professional book).

Ratcliffe, Matthew. 2005. 'The Feeling of Being', *Journal of Consciousness Studies* 12(8–10): 43–60.

Ryan, Marie-Laure. 2001. *Narrative as Virtual Reality: Immersion and Interactivity in Literature and Electonic Media*. Baltimore, MD: Johns Hopkins University Press.

Sanders, José. 2010. 'Intertwined Voices: Journalists' Modes of Representing Source Information in Journalistic Subgenres', *English Text Construction* 3(2): 226–49. doi: 10.1075/etc.3.2.06san.

Sanders, José, and Kobie van Krieken. 2019. 'Traveling through Narrative Time: How Tense and Temporal Deixis Guide the Representation of Time and Viewpoint in News Narratives', *Cognitive Linguistics* 30(2): 281–304. doi: 10.1515/cog-2018-0041.

Sanford, Anthony J., and Catherine Emmott. 2012. *Mind, Brain and Narrative*. Cambridge: Cambridge University Press.

Schurz, Gerhard. 2008. 'Patterns of Abduction', *Synthese* 164(2): 201–34. doi: 10.1007/s11229-007-9223-4.

Sikora, Shelley, Don Kuiken and David S. Miall. 2010. 'An Uncommon Resonance: The Influence of Loss on Expressive Reading', *Empirical Studies of the Arts* 28(2): 135–53. doi: 10.2190/EM.28.2.b.

———. 2011. 'Expressive Reading: A Phenomenological Study of Readers' Experience of Coleridge's "The Rime of the Ancient Mariner"', *Psychology of Aesthetics, Creativity, and the Arts* 5(3): 258–68. doi: 10.1037/a0021999.

Silvia, Paul J. 2010. 'Confusion and Interest: The Role of Knowledge Emotions in Aesthetic Experience', *Psychology of Aesthetics, Creativity, and the Arts* 4(2): 75–80. doi: 10.1037/a0017081.

Sopčák, Paul. 2007. 'Creation from Nothing': A Foregrounding Study of James Joyce's Drafts for 'Ulysses'', *Language and Literature*, 16(2): 183–196. doi: 10.1177/0963947007075984.

Sopčák, Paul, Don Kuiken and David S. Miall. 2020. 'The Effects of Free Indirect Style in George Eliot's Middlemarch: A Reader Response Study', *Anglistik: International Journal of English Studies* 31(1): 15–29.

Steen, Gerard. 2015. 'Developing, Testing and Interpreting Deliberate Metaphor Theory', *Journal of Pragmatics* 90: 67–72. doi: 10.1016/j.pragma.2015.03.013.

———. 2016. 'Identifying Metaphors in Language', in Elena Semino and Zsófia Demjén (eds), *The Routledge Handbook of Metaphor and Language*. London: Routledge (Routledge Handbooks in Linguistics), pp. 73–87.

Steen, Gerard, et al. 2010. *A Method for Linguistic Metaphor Identification: From MIP to MIPVU*. Amsterdam: John Benjamins (Converging Evidence in Language and Communication Research). doi: 10.1075/celcr.14.

Steiner, George. 1978. 'On Difficulty', in George Steiner (ed.), *On Difficulty and Other Essays*. New York: Oxford University Press, pp. 18–47.

Sternberg, Meir. 1990. 'Telling in Time (I): Chronology and Narrative Theory', *Poetics Today* 11(4): 901–48. doi: 10.2307/1773082.
——. 1992. 'Telling in Time (II): Chronology, Teleology, Narrativity', *Poetics Today* 13(3): 463–541. doi: 10.2307/1772872.
——. 2006. 'Telling in Time (III): Chronology, Estrangement, and Stories of Literary history', *Poetics Today* 27(1): 125–235. doi: 10.1215/03335372-27-1-125.
Stolnitz, Jerome. 1978. '"The Aesthetic Attitude" in the Rise of Modern Aesthetics', *The Journal of Aesthetics and Art Criticism* 36(4): 409. doi: 10.2307/430481.
Tellegen, Auke. 1981. 'Practicing the Two Disciplines for Relaxation and Enlightenment: Comment on "Role of the Feedback Signal in Electromyograph Biofeedback: The Relevance of Attention" by Qualls and Sheehan', *Journal of Experimental Psychology: General* 110(2): 217–26. doi: 10.1037/0096-3445.110.2.217.
Thomas, Dylan. 1996. *Collected Poems 1934–1953*. Edited by Walford Davies and Ralph Maud. London: J.M. Dent.
Toolan, Michael J. 2001. *Narrative: A Critical Linguistic Introduction*, 2nd edn. London: Routledge.
van Duijn, Max, and Arie Verhagen. 2019. 'Recursive Embedding of Viewpoints, Irregularity, and the Role for a Flexible Framework', *Pragmatics* 29(2): 198–225. doi: 10.1075/prag.18049.van.
van Krieken, Kobie, Hans Hoeken and José Sanders. 2017. 'Evoking and Measuring Identification with Narrative Characters: A Linguistic Cues Framework', *Frontiers in Psychology* 8: 1190. doi: 10.3389/fpsyg.2017.01190.
van Krieken, Kobie, José Sanders and Hans Hoeken. 2016. 'Blended Viewpoints, Mediated Witnesses: A Cognitive Linguistic Approach to News Narratives', in Barbara Dancygier, Wei-lun Lu and Arie Verhagen (eds), *Viewpoint and the Fabric of Meaning: Form and Use of Viewpoint Tools across Languages and Modalities*. Berlin: Mouton de Gruyter, pp. 145–68.
van Peer, Willie. 1986. *Stylistics and Psychology: Investigations of Foregrounding*. London: Croom Helm (Croom Helm linguistics series).
van 't Jagt, Ruth Koops, et al. 2014. 'Look Before You Leap: How Enjambment Affects the Processing of Poetry', *Scientific Study of Literature* 4(1): 3–24. doi: 10.1075/ssol.4.1.01jag.
Wagemans, Johan, et al. 2012. 'A Century of Gestalt Psychology in Visual Perception II: Conceptual and Theoretical Foundations', *Psychological Bulletin* 138(6): 1218–52. doi: 10.1037/a0029334.
Walter, Nathan, et al. 2020. 'Metacognitive Approach to Narrative Persuasion: The Desirable and Undesirable Consequences of Narrative Disfluency', *Media Psychology* 24(5): 1–27. doi: 10.1080/15213269.2020.1789477.
Ward, Dave, David Silverman and Mario Villalobos. 2017. 'Introduction: The Varieties of Enactivism', *Topoi* 36(3): 365–75. doi: 10.1007/s11245-017-9484-6.
Zabelina, Darya L. 2018. 'Attention and Creativity', in Rex E. Jung and Oshin Vartanian (eds), *The Cambridge Handbook of the Neuroscience of Creativity*. Cambridge: Cambridge University Press, pp. 161–79. doi: 10.1017/9781316556238.010.
Zabelina, Darya L., Naomi P. Friedman and Jessica Andrews-Hanna. 2019. 'Unity and Diversity of Executive Functions in Creativity', *Consciousness and Cognition* 68: 47–56. doi: 10.1016/j.concog.2018.12.005.
Zabelina, Darya, Arielle Saporta and Mark Beeman. 2016. 'Flexible or Leaky Attention in Creative People? Distinct Patterns of Attention for Different Types of Creative Thinking', *Memory and Cognition* 44(3): 488–98. doi: 10.3758/s13421-015-0569-4.

Zunshine, Lisa. 2006. *Why We Read Fiction: Theory of Mind and the Novel*. Columbus: Ohio State University Press.

Zwaan, Rolf A., and David N. Rapp. 2006. 'Discourse Comprehension', in Matthew J. Traxler and Morton Ann Gernsbacher (eds), *Handbook of Psycholinguistics*. 2nd edn. Boston, MA: Elsevier, pp. 725–64.

CHAPTER 15
Who Likes Complex Films?
Personality and Preferences for Narrative Complexity

Steven Willemsen, Katalin Bálint, Frank Hakemulder, Miklós Kiss, Elly Konijn and Kirill Fayn

Introduction

A remarkable context of the present book is the 'mainstreamization' of challenging narratives. Over the past decades, we have seen surprisingly large audiences flock to the cinemas for, and to be deeply engaged with, highly complex, confusing or ambiguous movies – qualities that were previously more common in art house films aimed at a more select audience. This makes one wonder who the people are whose particular preferences trigger unforeseen box office hits and high viewer ratings, and who contribute to a flourishing 'forensic fandom' around such productions (Mittell 2015).

The aim of this chapter is to explore whether people's preference for or dislike of complex stories is associated with their personality traits. Just like the age-old assumption that one's bookcase (e.g. Schutte and Malouff 2004) or, more recently, one's music playlist (Rochow 2010) is a reliable indication of who that person is, could the same hold for the preference for (or dislike of) complexity in stories?

The storytelling found in contemporary complex film, television and literature produces a particular kind of narrative experience – one characterized by high rates of uncertainty, ambiguity or incongruity. In everyday life, people are known to vary in their willingness and ability to cope with such uncertain or ambiguous epistemic states. Could the same personality factors influence the enjoyment of complexity in fiction? And if so, which personality traits are the most influential? Charting the relationships between preference for various forms of narrative and personality traits will allow us to speculate about the underlying mechanisms of narrative complexity and their impact on viewers. Moreover, it paves the way for future work investigating whether engagement with complexity in fiction can have carry-over effects to complexity in everyday life (e.g. boosting one's tolerance for ambiguity).

To answer these questions, we first need to find a reliable measure of this preference (currently not available), provide a clear conceptualization of the distinct experience that complex stories evoke, and formulate informed guesses as to what personality traits might be relevant. To this end, we developed the new Preference for Narrative Complexity (PNC) scale, tailored to film viewing experiences. This scale was tested in an online experiment with 101 participants, during which participants also completed several personality tests. These included the 'Big Five' of personality (Openness to Experience, Conscientiousness, Extraversion, Agreeableness and Neuroticism – Soto and John 2017), Need for Cognition (Lins de Holanda Coelho, Hanel and Wolf 2018) and Tolerance for Ambiguity (McLain 2009). Factor analyses were used to test and determine the structure of the new PNC scale, while regression analyses detected any connections between participants' personality traits and their preference for complex storytelling. The findings provide support for our hypotheses – namely, that people who are more tolerant of ambiguity in real life, or who tend to seek out more cognitively effortful activities and sensory and abstract information, also show a preference for forms of storytelling that stimulate these traits.

What Makes a Complex Narrative Experience?

Does personality influence one's preference or dislike for complexity in stories? To answer this question, we first need an understanding of what aspects can be considered to be distinctive and formative to 'complex narrative' experiences. The present study focuses on the medium of fiction film, as this is not only where narrative complexity arguably reached its widest audience but it is also been the field where the most academic literature on the phenomenon has been available (e.g. Panek 2006; Cameron 2008; Buckland 2009, 2014; Elsaesser 2009, 2018; Poulaki 2011, 2014; Klecker 2011, 2013; Kiss 2012, 2013; Campora 2014; Hven 2017; Willemsen and Kiss 2017, 2020).

In film and literary studies, some consensus has emerged that the experience of narrative complexity can be seen as the outcome of a mode of cognitive challenge: a text or film's strategic obstruction or intensification of the process of narrative comprehension (Kiss and Willemsen 2017; Grishakova and Poulaki 2019;

Magliano, Higgs and Clinton 2019). Narrative complexity, in this view, 'does not only lie in intricate narrative structures themselves, but should also be analyzed as cognitive effects and experiences that such formal disruptions bring about in viewers' (Kiss and Willemsen 2017: 5). Based on this experiential definition, no strict set of formal criteria can define what constitutes a 'complex narrative'. Stories can use a variety of formal-structural strategies to achieve complexifying effects, the experiential effect of which may also differ between viewers. For the present study, we therefore sought to identify the modes of cognitive challenge most commonly employed in contemporary cinema, as these can be seen as the main determinants of complexity as a narrative experience.

Factors of Narrative Complexity

From the available typologies and taxonomies, we identified six factors of complexification that we expect to cover the most relevant strategies for evoking complex narrative experiences in contemporary film. The factors should be seen as a set of overlapping features typical of contemporary complex films, but none of which is, by itself, necessary or common to all cases.

1. *Puzzles and Puzzling.* Complex contemporary film narratives have been described as 'puzzles' (Panek 2006; Buckland 2014) or as 'playing games' with the spectator (Elsaesser 2009): their storytelling challenges viewers to actively fit pieces of information together or invites them to engage in the formation of alternative interpretive hypotheses and extensive inferencing to make sense of the story events.
2. *Complexity and High Information Load.* Many stories also complexify the viewing experience by providing 'overstimulating' amounts of information (Kiss and Willemsen 2017: 46). This may include the presentation of a multiplicity of different plotlines, events, characters, or other narrative elements. Keeping track of the narrative events or information streams thus demands heightened attention, working memory, and/or interpretation.
3. *Alternative Temporalities.* A recurring trait of many complex narratives lies in their 'modular' (Cameron 2008) treatment of narrative time. Complex stories may demand heightened cognitive effort by presenting events out of causal or chronological order, featuring multiple timelines, or by introducing 'non-linear

storyworlds' (Willemsen and Kiss 2020) in which non-chronological temporalities are somehow the diegetic state of affairs – for example, through the existence of time-travel or multiple parallel worlds.

4. *Narrative Nonclosure*. Unlike most canonical or 'classical' narratives, complex narratives frequently withhold closure at the end of a story experience in favour of endings that retain a strong ambiguity or that leave significant gaps or indeterminacies to be filled in, thus leaving viewers with the task of prolonged and active sense-making (Bálint et al. 2016).

5. *Twists*. A significant amount of the literature has focused on so-called 'twist' or 'mind-trick narratives' (Klecker 2013). Such narratives present a restricted part of their storyworld reality, and do this in a way that encourages viewers to make misguided inferences or draw erroneous conclusions. The recognition of this misguidance – the 'twist' – typically comes later, paired with surprise and a retroactive re-evaluation of the earlier information. Some authors, it must be noted, have argued that twists are not a complexifying narrative device per se. According to this view, twists rather form a subcategory of narrative surprise, because they set out to 'mislead' rather than confuse their viewers, and thus cause no disturbance to the 'online' process of narrative comprehension, but only retrospectively and for a very short moment of revelation (Kiss and Willemsen 2017: 50). For this reason, we include this factor tentatively in the present study.

6. *Incongruities*. Lastly, many complex narratives challenge viewers by presenting salient schema-disrupting moments of incongruity or impossibility (Kiss and Willemsen 2017) – for instance, in the form of a cause-and-effect paradox, unexpected character duplication, or other inexplicable events. Such events leave it unclear how elements of the story relate to each other, and tend to evoke a sense of mystery or impossibility, introducing a clear cognitive disequilibrium into the process of narrative comprehension.

We propose that the above aspects collectively cover most of the major forms of cognitive challenge employed in contemporary complex audiovisual narratives. They, therefore, formed the basis for our Preference for Narrative Complexity scale. Popular complex fiction films can then be further subdivided into various types that employ these factors to different degrees or in different modes: for example, *puzzle films* (Buckland 2014), which introduce significant cognitive challenges but ultimately resolve these dissonances through new narrative information; *impossible puzzle films* (Kiss and Willemsen 2017), which present strong incongruities and impossibilities but do so without providing explicit resolutions or explanations for them; and *art cinema* (Bordwell 1985; Kovács 2007), which defines itself more explicitly against the classical mode of narration and its story-driven genres, and frequently uses complexifying narrative techniques as one way of doing so.

Complexity and Personality

In what ways could we expect a preference for these forms of narrative to be related to personality? As noted, complex stories typically challenge viewers through puzzles, ambiguities or incongruities in the process of narrative comprehension. Outside of narrative complexity, personality psychologists have developed several constructs that measure and describe individual differences in people's abilities and tendencies in coping with ambiguity and complexity in their lives. Can these constructs also be transposed to complex narrative enjoyment? We will argue that four central factors could be expected to moderate attitudes to narrative complexity.

The Big Five: Openness to Experience

Within the 'Big Five' (Openness to Experience; Conscientiousness; Extraversion; Agreeableness; and Neuroticism), which is the dominant model of personality, Openness to Experience describes individual differences in seeking and appreciating sensory and abstract information (DeYoung 2014). Openness is a broad construct, covering aspects of one's imagination, aesthetic responsiveness, attentiveness to feelings, preferences for variety and novelty, and intellectual curiosity (Costa and McCrae 1992). Openness has been shown to be a strong predictor of sensitivity to aesthetic stimuli in general (Silvia et al. 2015), and highly open people often display a preference and appreciation for novelty and complexity in their aesthetic and epistemic experiences (Fayn, MacCann, Tiliopoulos and Silvia 2015a; Fayn, Tiliopoulos and MacCann 2015b; Silvia, Henson and Templin 2009). Furthermore, they are less negatively affected by confusion or a lack of understanding in response to aesthetic and epistemic situations (Fayn et al. 2017, 2019), tend to enjoy puzzle-solving activities more (Rocklin 1994), and show a stronger tendency towards discovery-oriented cognitive styles and positive motivation for the resolution of uncertainty (Hodson and Sorrentino 1999).

In the context of film and media preferences, Openness is the best personality predictor of cerebral, aesthetic and alternative media preferences (Xu and Peterson 2017) and the liking of surrealist film clips (Swami et al. 2010) as well as independent and foreign films (Rentfrow, Goldberg and Zilca 2011). While relations between personality and the category of complex narrative film have not previously been researched, the indications above suggest that Openness to Experience can be expected to be central to preferences for narrative complexity in general.

Need for Cognition

The broad construct of Openness to Experience can be divided into two related yet distinct aspects: Openness and Intellect. Openness is thought to reflect engagement with sensory and aesthetic information, while Intellect reflects engagement with abstract and epistemic stimuli (DeYoung 2014; Fayn et al. 2017). The construct of Need for Cognition most closely resembles the Intellect aspect of Openness/Intellect. Originally defined as 'a need to understand and make reasonable the experiential world' (Cohen, Stotland and Wolfe 1955: 291), modern conceptualizations view the Need for Cognition less as a 'need' for conceptual order and more as an individual's 'tendency to engage into effortful cognitive endeavours' (Cacioppo et al. 1996: 197; Cacioppo and Petty 1982). People who score highly on Need for Cognition tend to derive more enjoyment from effortful cognitive tasks and engage in more thoughtful activity overall, including meta-cognitive reflections on their own thinking (Petty et al. 2009). They are also more likely to engage in activities to gather additional external information (Verplanken, Hazenberg and Palenéwen 1992). For these reasons, we expect Need for Cognition to relate positively to a preference for narrative complexity, particularly for factors such as Puzzling, Complexity or Temporality, as people with a high Need for Cognition are more likely to experience such heightened cognitive efforts as rewarding and stimulating rather than cumbersome or frustrating.

Tolerance for Ambiguity

Another construct that is empirically tied to Openness to Experience is Tolerance for Ambiguity (Jach and Smillie 2019). Tolerance for Ambiguity can be defined as one's range of typical reactions – from rejection to attraction – to 'stimuli perceived as unfamiliar, complex, dynamically uncertain, or subject to multiple conflicting interpretations' (McLain 1993: 184). The concept is closely related to neighbouring (or opposite) constructs, such as Intolerance of Uncertainty (Buhr and Dugas 2002; Carleton, Norton and Asmundson 2007), with previous research showing the measures to demonstrate 'close empirical and conceptual overlap' (Jach and Smillie 2019: 69).

People with a high Tolerance of Ambiguity demonstrate more willingness and enjoyment in engaging with uncertain and ambiguous stimuli or events. This has been found to influence many aspects of everyday life (Furnham and Marks 2013), including aesthetic preferences. For instance, Swami et al. (2010) found a link between people's Openness and Ambiguity Tolerance and their liking of short surrealist film clips. Conversely, Wiersema, Schalk and van Kleef (2012) found that people who showed more desire for a predictable and organized world gave lower liking scores for a play that featured an open ending. As complex film narratives frequently present salient ambiguities, or leave more uncertainty about key narrative events for prolonged periods, we expect that a high Tolerance for Ambiguity will have a positive effect on Preference for Narrative Complexity in general, and the factor of Nonclosure in particular.

Behavioural and Emotional Engagement with Complex Films

We propose that viewers' preference for complex films will determine the extent to which they seek exposure to complex cinema; some viewers actively seek exposure to complex narratives, while others are less attracted to this type of cinema. This engagement, therefore, results in how knowledgeable a viewer will be about complex film titles (behavioural engagement) as well as how much they enjoy the experience (emotional engagement). The question is, can personality traits alone predict behavioural and emotional engagement with complex cinema, or is the preference for complex cinema a necessary mediator? In other words, can it be that a viewer reports a high level of Need for Cognition, Tolerance for Ambiguity, and Openness but still dislikes complex narratives? We expect the new PNC scale to predict this further variation.

Aims of This Study

To test the above expectations, we formulated a six-step plan of research questions. The first two research questions address the development and validation of the PNC scale, while the other four examine its relations to personality, demographic variables and behavioural and emotional engagement with complex films.

1. Does the PNC scale factor structure fit the factors based on the theory? (i.e. do the results consistently support the six different factors we hypothesized or is another factor structure implied by the data?)
2. Is the PNC scale reliable? (i.e. are people's responses to the measures of different aspects of narrative complexity consistent?)
3. Does PNC vary as a function of personality traits?
4. Does behavioural and emotional engagement with complex films vary as a function of personality traits?
5. Is the PNC scale valid for predicting behavioural and emotional engagement with (different types of) complex narrative films beyond the influence of personality constructs?
6. Does PNC relate significantly to demographic control variables (age, gender, educational level, etc.)?

Hypotheses

To examine our main research questions, we specified our predictions as follows:

1. Openness to Experience relates positively to Preference for Narrative Complexity (PNC).
2. Need for Cognition (NFC) relates positively to PNC, particularly those factors that promote active cognitive engagement (i.e. Puzzling, Complexity and Temporality).
3. Tolerance of Ambiguity (ToA) relates positively to PNC, particularly those factors that include a confrontation with ambiguities (Nonclosure, Incongruities).
4. Openness, NFC and ToA positively predict behavioural and emotional engagement with complex films.

5. Behavioural and emotional engagement with complex narrative film is associated with higher PNC.
6. The PNC scale is a stronger predictor of behavioural and emotional engagement with complex films compared to the more general personality constructs.

Methods: Participants and Procedure

Participants were recruited via Prolific with a set age range (22–60 years old), fluent English ability and set geographical area (North America and Western Europe). These criteria were chosen to target an audience that is most likely to have social, cultural and economic access to complex audiovisual narratives, as well as the film examples included in the items list. To maximize the validity of responses, participants had to pass three attention checks and an answer consistency check (not more than one strongly inconsistent answer) with a minimum duration for completion of the survey of six minutes. Participants were compensated at a rate of 7.52£ per hour.

A total of 114 participants started the survey, but one person did not finish it and a further 12 people failed more than one attention check. Thus, the final sample had 101 participants (mean age in years = 32.84, SD = 9.15, range 25 to 60), of which 62.4 per cent were female and the rest were male (none of the participants reported 'other' for gender). The majority of the sample had completed a level of college, with 3 per cent of the sample having a doctorate, 14.9 per cent a master's, 42.6 per cent a bachelor's, and 4 per cent associate degrees. A further 21.8 per cent of participants had completed a portion of college, 12.9 per cent had completed high school, and 1 per cent reported having less than a high school degree. The majority of the participants reported their nationality as UK (67.3 per cent) and USA (19.8 per cent), with two participants each from Belgium, the Netherlands and Finland, and one each from Estonia, France, Germany, Norway, Russia, Sweden and Switzerland.

After reading an information statement and signing the consent form, participants completed some demographic questions (age, gender, level of education, nationality), followed by the questionnaires in random order. Within each questionnaire, items were also presented in a random order.

Measures

Preference for Narrative Complexity Scale

To be able to assess people's preference or dislike for various aspects of narrative complexity and empirically verify the theorized factors, we created the Preference for Narrative Complexity (PNC) scale. Starting from the six factors of complexity outlined above (Puzzling, Complexity, Temporality, Nonclosure, Twists, Incongruities), we formulated four items to assess each factor. The four items were created to reflect the subjective states we expected to be most relevant in preferences or dislikes of complexity: *interest* and *enjoyment* versus *annoyance* and *frustration*. This resulted in a total set of twenty-four items, which were balanced to represent an equal number of items expressing complexity preference and dislike (e.g. 'Open endings in films spark my interest' versus 'I am annoyed by endings of films that leave a lot of gaps to fill in'), to which participants reported their degree of agreement. Participants were asked to rate all items on a 6-point scale, from *strongly disagree* to *strongly agree*.

Behavioural and Emotional Engagement with Complex Film

As an additional measure of engagement, we added a complex film recognition set. This consisted of eighteen film items (international title, year, and the film's poster image) representing various types of complex cinema (puzzle films, impossible puzzle films, and complex art films). For each item, participants were asked whether they had seen the film and, if so, how much they had enjoyed it on a 5-point scale: did not enjoy it at all; enjoyed it a little; enjoyed it a moderate amount; enjoyed it a lot; enjoyed it a great deal.

The films were selected from three categories of complex film: Puzzle Films – *Memento* (2000), *Shutter Island* (2010), *Inception* (2010), *Looper* (2012), *Edge of Tomorrow* (2014), *Arrival* (2016); Impossible Puzzle Films – *Mulholland Drive* (2001), *Donnie Darko* (2001), *Primer* (2004), *Triangle* (2009), *Enemy* (2013), *The Shining* (1980); and Complex Art Cinema – *Persona* (1966), *2001: A Space Odyssey* (1968), *Inland Empire* (2006), *Uncle Boonmee Who Can Recall His Past Lives* (2010), *The Tree of Life* (2011), *Mother!* (2017). Two variables were calculated based on this scale. First, we calculated the total number of films seen by each participant as an indicator of behavioural engagement with complex films, overall and by category;

second, we calculated the average level of enjoyment that people reported by averaging the enjoyment ratings of participants who had seen at least two of the films.

Personality Features

Personality was assessed via the BFI-2-XS scale (Soto and John 2017) that assesses the Big Five dimensions of personality through fifteen items (three per dimension) on a Likert scale from *strongly agree* to *strongly disagree*. The internal consistency of the scales in the current samples were acceptable for Extraversion ($\omega = .79$), Conscientiousness ($\omega = .69$) and Neuroticism ($\omega = .81$), but somewhat low for Agreeableness ($\omega = .59$) and Openness ($\omega = .62$).

Tolerance for Ambiguity

Tolerance of ambiguity was assessed via the MSTAT-II scale (McLain 2009) through thirteen items on a Likert scale from *strongly agree* to *strongly disagree*. The internal consistency of the scale was excellent ($\omega = .90$).

Need for Cognition

Need for cognition was assessed via the NFC-6 scale (Lins de Holanda Coelho, Hanel and Wolf 2018) through six items on a Likert scale from *strongly agree* to *strongly disagree*. The internal consistency of the scale was good ($\omega = .87$).

The PNC Scale: Item Selection, Dimension Reduction and Psychometric Properties

For initial item selection purposes, we investigated each PNC item for its relation to all other items (item-rest correlations) as an indicator of whether some items clearly do not fit with the rest. To determine the number of dimensions that best represent the data from the PNC scale, we used principal components parallel analysis. Then, we estimated principal axis factoring with oblique oblimin rotations exploratory factor analyses, following the procedure set out by Lim and Jahng (2019), thus considering the number of factors suggested by the parallel analysis ±1 factor and considering each solution for interpretability. Following the decision on the final factor structure, we fitted a confirmatory factor analysis to test how well the data fitted the proposed model. Based on the comparative fit index (CFI) and Tucker-Lewis index (TLI), fit was evaluated at around 0.95, the root mean square error of approximation (RMSEA) close to 0.6, and the standardized root mean square residual (SRMR) at around 0.08, following the recommendations of Hu and Bentler (1999). Finally, we used McDonald's Omega (ω) as an estimate of the reliability of the scales (McNeish 2018).

Bivariate and Multivariate Tests of Relationships between Study Variables

To evaluate the relationships between age, preferences for complexity, pleasure and personality, we used Pearson's product-moment correlations and multiple regression analysis. The measures for movies seen are count variables and therefore differ in how they are distributed. Such variables are usually modelled using Poisson or negative binomial regression analyses, depending on the nature of the distributions (Gardner, Mulvey and Shaw 1995). The distribution of the total number of movies seen was best described by a negative binomial distribution, while a Poisson distribution better described the distributions of the specific categories of movies. To evaluate differences in preferences for narrative complexity between gender and education level, we used ANOVAs.

Results

The PNC Scale: Structure, Psychometric Properties and Validity

While six distinct dimensions (factors) of preference for narrative complexity were predicted, a single higher-order 'overall' preference for narrative complexity was assumed. Thus, we expected that all items would have high associations with the total scale. This was confirmed for all but one item ('films with a straightforward story disinterest me'), which had a low correlation (0.27) with the rest of the scale, and was thus removed from the analysis. A parallel analysis was conducted on the rest of the twenty-three items, which suggested two factors. Following the procedure set out by Lim and Jahng (2019), we considered one-, two- and three-factor solutions.

The single-factor solution had significant loadings of all items onto a single factor (underlining that 'overall' preference for narrative complexity is one construct). However, this solution lacks the nuance of being able to evaluate different aspects of this preference. The two-factor solution separated the Nonclosure and Twist factors, with the rest of the items having weaker loadings on these two dimensions, with substantial cross-loadings. The three-factor solution also had clear Nonclosure and Twist factors, but it also grouped the Puzzle, Complexity and Alternative Temporalities factors into one. The Incongruities items had loadings on multiple factors and failed to load on a single factor in any of the solutions. Therefore, we removed the Incongruities items and went with a three-factor solution, given its greater interpretability and compliance with the six theoretically predicted categories of narrative complexity.

Given that the analysis did not differentiate between the Puzzle, Complexity, and Alternative Temporalities items, these were grouped as one factor. This factor was labelled 'Cognitive Challenge' (as all these factors pertained to aspects causing cognitively challenging experiences during narrative engagement). To reduce the number of items within this subscale, we based decisions on (a) keeping two items from each of the three factors, (b) keeping an equal number of items that were positively and negatively worded, (c) retaining items that represented the different experiential dimensions of preference (enjoyment, interest, annoyance, frustration), and (d) keeping the highest-loading items that complied with the previous two criteria. This led to the removal of five items, leaving a total of fourteen items for the whole scale.

Next, we fitted a confirmatory factor analysis model on the remaining fourteen items. The fit of the CFA model was acceptable (χ^2 = 99.13; df = 74; p = .02; RMSEA = 0.058, 90% CI: 0.021, 0.086; CFI = 0.963; TLI = 0.955; SRMR = 0.044). Together, the EFA and CFA results suggested that a three-factor solution was optimal in terms of interpretability and fit to the data. The three factors were named Nonclosure, Twists, and Cognitive Challenge. Table 15.1 shows the EFA and CFA loadings of each item in the final three-factor solution.

Also presented in Table 15.1 are the means, skew and kurtosis values for the three scales. Notably, the Twists scale had the higher mean, skew and kurtosis, suggesting that most people have a preference for twists in films. This supports the position that preference for twists may not be a strongly discriminating indicator of complexity preference (cf. Kiss and Willemsen 2017: 50). Preferences for a lack of narrative closure, on the other hand, were the lowest endorsed items, suggesting

Table 15.1. PNC scale factor loadings for EFA and CFA, factor means, skew and kurtosis.

Scale item	Nonclosure	Cognitive challenge	Twists
I enjoy films that end ambiguously.	.78/.75		
I am frustrated when movies have an unclear ending.	.74/.90		
I am annoyed by endings of films that leave a lot of gaps to fill in.	.71/.86		
Open endings in films spark my interest.	.69/.76		
I am frustrated by films that make you put the pieces of the story together.		.70/.85	
I enjoy films that require some thinking to understand the story.		.41/.60	
Films that are difficult to understand annoy me.		.72/-	
I get annoyed when a film overloads me with information.		.75/-	
I find films that have many different plotlines frustrating.		.76/.88	
Complexity in a film's story raises my interest.	.39/-	.57/-	
I enjoy films that feature many different plotlines.		.62/.75	
I get frustrated when films have many different timelines.		.73/.79	
I find it interesting when a film story is told out of order.		.65/.72	
It annoys me when a story frequently jumps in time.		.75/-	
I enjoy films that experiment with the order of time or story events.		.61/-	
I enjoy stories with unforeseen twists and turns.			.72/.67
I am annoyed by twists in a story.			.55/.73
Twists in a story frustrate me.			.60/.83
Unforeseen twists and turns in a story spark my interest.			.77/.78
I enjoy stories with mysterious and seemingly impossible events.		.66/-	.56/-
It annoys me when it is not exactly clear what is going on in a story.			
A paradox in a story sparks my interest.			.49/-
It frustrates me when it is unclear how the elements of a story connect to each other.		.63/-	
Factor mean	3.23	4.19	5.03
Factor skew	0.11	-0.68	-0.93
Factor kurtosis	-0.58	0.41	1.38

Note: The first number represents the loading from EFA and the second is from CFA. Only items from the final scale have CFA loadings. Only loadings above .30 are presented.

that Nonclosure could be a better indicator of preference for the more complex types of narrative, which commonly refuse cognitive closure.

The Nonclosure, Twists and Cognitive Challenge subscales were interrelated with each other. Particularly, the Cognitive Challenge subscale was strongly related to both the Twists ($r = .57, p < .001$) and the Nonclosure scale ($r = .57, p < .001$), while the Twists and Nonclosure scales were only weakly related to each other ($r = .22, p = .03$). These findings suggest that preferences for narratives that feature Twists and Nonclosure are both related to preferences for Cognitive Challenge in narratives, but that preferences for Twists and preferences for narrative Nonclosure are distinct from each other.

Reliability of the PNC Scale

The internal consistency of the total PNC scale was excellent ($\omega = .91$). Internal consistencies were also excellent for the PNC-Cognitive Challenge scale ($\omega = .90$), the PNC-Nonclosure scale ($\omega = .89$), and good for the PNC-Twists scale ($\omega = .84$). Together, these findings suggest that the PNC scale and its subscales display excellent internal consistency.

Demographic Variables and the PNC Scale

There were no significant relationships between age and the full PNC scale ($r = .05$, $p = .66$), the Nonclosure scale ($r = .04, p = .70$), the Cognitive Challenge scale ($r = .04, p = .67$), or the Twists scale ($r = .02., p = .86$). Although males had higher scores on the total, Nonclosure, and Cognitive Challenge PNC subscales, none of these differences reached significance ($p > .05$ for all). Thus, the PNC scale was independent of age and gender.

Given that some of the educational levels had very small samples, we collapsed the variable into four broader categories: no college experience; some college but no degree; bachelor's or associate degree; and master's or doctorate degree. ANOVAs testing the differences in PNC between these four educational levels revealed that the differences in the PNC total scales were significant – $F(3,97) = 2.81, p = 0.04, \eta^2 = 0.08$ – and that these differences were driven by the PNC Cognitive Challenge scale – $F(3,97) = 5.04, p = 0.003, \eta^2 = 0.14$. Further analysis of the pairwise differences between the four levels was done with Bonferroni adjustment to the criterion for significance ($p = 0.05/6 = 0.008$).

Pairwise comparisons revealed that people with no college degrees had lower PNC Cognitive Challenge levels compared to people with some college experience and those with master's and doctorate degrees, but not with bachelor's or associate degrees. This implies that seeking cognitive challenges in real life is somewhat associated with a higher level of preference for narrative complexity.

Personality and Preference for Narrative Complexity

The current sample measured two indicators for preference for complexity: the PNC scale; and behavioural and emotional engagement with complex narrative films. The relations between personality, the PNC scale and its subscales are presented in Table 15.2. As predicted by hypotheses 1–3, the PNC scale was strongly and significantly related to Openness, Tolerance of Ambiguity and Need for Cognition. As predicted by hypothesis 2, the strongest relation between NFC and PNC was observed in the Cognitive Challenge subscale. The hypothesis regarding the relations between ToA and Nonclosure was not directly supported, given that the strongest relation of Nonclosure was with Cognitive Challenge. Notably, ToA did have the largest relation with Nonclosure out of all the other measures, while NFC had its lowest relation with Nonclosure. This supports the idea that those higher on ToA have higher preferences for open endings.

Next, we tested whether NFC and ToA independently predicted PNC. Results of the multiple regression analyses are presented in Table 15.3. The two variables explained substantial variance in the PNC total (39 per cent), Cognitive Challenge (37 per cent), Twists (23 per cent) and Nonclosure (18 per cent) scales. The ToA

Table 15.2. Correlations between PNC scale and personality traits.

Variables	PNC Total	PNC Nonclosure	PNC Cognitive Challenge	PNC Twist
Tolerance of Ambiguity	.62***	.42***	.59***	.45***
Need for Cognition	.49***	.25*	.51***	.42***
Openness	.45***	.30**	.43***	.35**
Conscientiousness	.04	−.01	.06	.04
Extraversion	.21*	.11	.23*	.17
Agreeableness	.13	.02	.12	.19
Neuroticism	−.1	−.08	−.11	−.03

Note: * p <.05, ** p <.01, *** p <.001.

Table 15.3. Regression models predicting PNC scales with NFC and ToA.

Predictor variables	PNC Total	PNC Nonclosure	PNC Cognitive Challenge	PNC Twists
Tolerance of Ambiguity	.52***	.46***	.45***	.31*
Need for Cognition	.14	−.06	.21⁺	.21⁺
R2	.39	.18	.37	.23

Note: ⁺ p <.10, * p <.05, **p <.01, **p <.001; Statistics are standardized regression betas.

scale was a significant predictor of the total and all subscales. The NFC scale did not predict additional variance in the PNC subscales, but the notable regression weights for the Cognitive Challenge and Twist subscales suggest that a bigger sample would render these tests significant. Of further interest is the possible suppression effect for the relation between Closure and NFC by ToA. Suppression effects should be interpreted carefully, preferably post-replication of such effects (Paulhus et al. 2004), and thus should be tested in follow-up studies.

The other dimensions of the Big Five, apart from Extraversion, had no significant relations with the PNC scale. Extraversion had a weak but significant relation with the total PNC scale, and this was particularly driven by the Cognitive Challenge subscale. Within the current sample, Extraversion was positively related to both ToA and NFC, suggesting that extraverted people have a higher ToA and NFC – an overlap that could be driving this unexpected result. To test this speculation, we conducted two regression analyses with Extraversion and either ToA or NFC as predictors of the PNC scale. In both models, our speculation was confirmed, with NFC and ToA being almost fully responsible for the relation between Extraversion and PNC.

Personality and Behavioural and Emotional Engagement with Complex Films

The relations between personality traits and behavioural and emotional engagement with complex films are presented in Table 15.4. We report the relations between movies seen and personality scales via the exponents of negative binomial and Poisson regression coefficients. The coefficients can be interpreted as the increase in the number of movies seen with a one unit increase in the personality scale score. For example, a person scoring one unit higher on the Tolerance of Ambiguity scale is predicted to have seen 1.23 times (or 23 per cent) more films compared to the other person.

Table 15.4. Correlations between behavioural and emotional engagement and personality.

Variables	Enjoyment	All movies seen	Puzzle seen	Impossible seen	Art seen
Tolerance of Ambiguity	.26*	1.23*	1.15	1.30	1.33
Need for Cognition	.21*	1.23**	1.15*	1.28*	1.40*
Openness	.26*	1.13	1.08	1.11	1.39
Conscientiousness	-.07	1.10	1.09	1.10	1.15
Extraversion	.11	1.08	1.09	1.07	1.09
Agreeableness	-.06	1.02	0.96	1.04	1.20
Neuroticism	.09	0.92	0.94	0.86*	1.02

Note: * p <.05, **p <.01, ***p <.001. Relations between personality traits and enjoyment are based on a reduced sample of 88 people (those who have seen at least two of the films). The coefficients for movies seen variables are exponents of negative binomial regression coefficients (all movies seen) and Poisson regression weights for puzzle, impossible puzzles, and art movies seen.

In line with our predictions, ToA, NFC and Openness all predicted greater enjoyment of complex films, with slightly weaker effects for Openness compared to the others. NFC was the strongest predictor of behavioural engagement with complex films, both overall and within the three film categories. Tolerance of Ambiguity was also a significant predictor of total movies seen, but did not reach significance for any of the separate categories – notably, the relations of movies seen to ToA and NFC were very similar in magnitude; the difference in the significance of these parameters was that the relations with NFC were more stable. Given the relatively small size of this sample, we would expect that the relations with ToA would also be significant in larger samples.

Openness did not predict overall behavioural engagement or any of the categories, but the magnitude of the relation with art cinema films was substantial and would likely be significant in a bigger sample. Additionally, the short Openness scale was not very reliable in itself; thus, the relation between Openness and PNC should be further investigated in future studies. Finally, Neuroticism was associated with having seen fewer impossible puzzle films.

Emotional and Behavioural Validity of the PNC Scales

Relations between the PNC and its subscales with behavioural and emotional engagement are presented in Table 15.5. The total PNC scale and its subscales all positively predicted enjoyment of complex films, with the total and Cognitive

Challenge scales having the strongest associations, while the Twists subscale had the lowest correlation. Relations between movies seen and the PNC scales are reported via the exponent of negative binomial and Poisson regression coefficients. The coefficients can be interpreted as the increase in the number of movies seen with a one-unit increase in the PNC scale score. For example, a person scoring one unit higher on the PNC total scale is predicted to have seen 1.39 times (or 39 per cent) more complex films compared to a person with an average PNC total score. The PNC total and PNC Cognitive Challenge scales were associated with the highest numbers of films seen, with stronger relations for more complex movie types. Results regarding the Twists and Nonclosure variables were not as consistent. Both scales predicted the total number of movies seen, but the Twists scale was not associated with impossible puzzle movies seen, and the Nonclosure scale did not predict the number of puzzle films seen.

Given the substantial overlap between the Cognitive Challenge scale and the Twists and Nonclosure scales, we explored whether these different peripheral aspects of preference for narrative complexity would predict enjoyment and behavioural engagement. Multivariate regression models revealed that the Cognitive Challenge scale was consistently driving the results, while the Twists and Nonclosure scales did not add to the predictions. While these two scales did not contribute to the predictions in models that included the Cognitive Challenge scale, we further explored whether they differentially predict enjoyment and behavioural engagement in the absence of the Cognitive Challenge scale. Both Twists (Beta = .32, t = 2.08, p = .04) and Nonclosure (Beta = .23, t = 3.00, p = .004) significantly predicted enjoyment independently. Likewise, Twists (25 per cent more movies for one point on the scale, p = .03) and Nonclosure (12 per cent more

Table 15.5. Correlations between behavioural and emotional engagement and PNC scales.

Variables	Enjoyment	All movies seen	Puzzle seen	Impossible seen	Art seen
PNC Total	.47***	1.39***	1.25***	1.55***	1.79***
PNC Nonclosure	.36***	1.14**	1.08	1.23**	1.28*
PNC Cognitive Challenge	.48***	1.34***	1.22***	1.47***	1.65***
PNC Twist	.22*	1.23*	1.17*	1.21	1.38*

Note: * p <.05, ** p <.01, *** p <.001. The coefficients for movies seen variables are exponents of negative binomial regression coefficients for all movies seen, and exponents of the Poisson regression coefficients for puzzle, impossible puzzle, and art movies seen.

movies for one point on the scale, p = .02) predicted having seen more movies. However, only Twists predicted having seen more puzzle films (16 per cent more movies per point increase on the scale, p = .04), while only Nonclosure predicted having seen more impossible puzzle (21 per cent more movies per point increase on the scale, p = .04) and art cinema films (24 per cent more movies per point increase on the scale, p = .04).

Together, these findings indicate that the Cognitive Challenge subscale is clearly central to understanding individual differences in the emotional and behavioural engagement with various types of complex narratives. However, the Twists and Nonclosure scales can be differentiated in terms of their associations with types of complex film engagement. While preferences for Twists predict liking of puzzle films, they are not central to engagement with the other complex narrative forms. Preference for Nonclosure, on the other hand, is particularly relevant to preferences for the more complex types of narrative (like impossible puzzle or art cinema narratives), which more commonly tend to refuse cognitive closure.

To further demonstrate the predictive validity of the PNC scale, we tested whether this scale could explain added variance in enjoyment and behavioural engagement over and above personality (hypothesis 6). To this end, we used the full PNC scale as a predictor of the enjoyment and behavioural engagement measures alongside the strongest personality predictor. The results of the negative binomial (all movies seen) and Poisson (rest of behavioural indicators) regressions models are presented in Table 15.6. For every behavioural engagement variable, the PNC scale explained a significant amount of variance, and, in every case, it rendered the personality predictor non-significant. This suggests that the PNC

Table 15.6. Regression results predicting behavioural and emotional engagement with the PNC scale and the best personality predictor.

Predictor variables	Enjoyment	Movies seen	Puzzle seen	Impossible seen	Art seen
Best personality predictor	−.05	1.08	1.05	1.09	1.13
PNC Total	.49***	1.34***	1.22**	1.49**	1.69**
R^2	.22				

Note: * $p < .05$, ** $p < .01$, *** $p < .001$. The coefficients for movies seen variables are exponents of negative binomial regression coefficients (all movies seen) and Poisson regression coefficients for puzzle, impossible puzzle, and art movies seen. The best personality predictor was ToA for enjoyment, and NFC for the movies seen variables.

scale is the best predictor of behavioural engagement with complex films compared to the personality measures.

Conclusions and Perspectives

The Structure of Preference for Narrative Complexity

In this study, we developed a new scale to measure Preference for Narrative Complexity (PNC), and investigated the construct's interrelations with various measures of personality and behavioural engagement in an online survey. Of the six factors of PNC initially hypothesized (Puzzling, Complexity, Temporality, Nonclosure, Twists and Incongruities), our results provided support for a stable 3-factor structure and 14-item scale – together making up the single overall construct of PNC.

The data did not differentiate between the first three hypothesized factors (Puzzling, Complexity and Temporality), as the items of all three loaded significantly onto a single factor, suggesting that these three factors should be seen as one construct. This seems reasonable from a theoretical perspective: all three pertain to the experience of dealing with cognitively challenging information during the narrative comprehension process, be it as a result of a need for extensive inferencing (Puzzling), an overload or multiplicity of narrative information (Complexity), or fragmented or alternative timelines (Temporality). Consequently, these three factors were merged into a single composite factor that we labelled 'Cognitive Challenge', using the two most discerning items of each to create a 6-item subscale.

Nonclosure and Twists, however, were supported by the data as distinct and stable factors. In both cases, all four items formed a consistently differentiating factor of preference for narrative complexity. The hypothesized factor of Incongruities, on the other hand, was removed from the final PNC scale as its items did not form a consistent factor but rather loaded onto the Cognitive Challenge factor and Twists (see Table 15.1). This suggests incongruities and paradoxes may not form a distinct aspect of complex narrative experiences but can rather be subsumed under the construct of dealing with cognitively challenging story information or encountering surprising twists. It could also be that the items were not phrased clearly enough, and therefore failed to present a relatable, distinctive construct.

Taken together, the findings resulted in a final, 14-item PNC scale, with excellent reliability and internal consistency, comprising three distinct subscales: Cognitive Challenge (six items), Nonclosure (four items) and Twists (four items). Among the three factors, Cognitive Challenge was most central to overall Preference for Narrative Complexity. This is also in line with theoretical expectations, as cognitive challenge has frequently been identified as the key determinant of narrative complexity (e.g. Kiss and Willemsen 2017; Grishakova and Poulaki 2019; Magliano, Higgs and Clinton 2019). The Cognitive Challenge factor was also most strongly interrelated with the other two factors of Twists and Nonclosure, meaning that people who have a preference for cognitively challenging storytelling also tend to prefer surprising twists and open endings. By comparison, the Twists and Nonclosure subscales were only weakly related to each other, suggesting that people who like twists do not necessarily like ambiguous endings, and vice versa. This finding was also reflected in the behavioural engagement scores, where preferences for Twists predicted having seen more puzzle films, while Nonclosure predicted having seen more impossible puzzle films and art films.

Preferences for Twists seems to be the least central to PNC in general. This can also be seen in the large mean scored on this subscale, and the degree to which it was skewed (Table 15.1), suggesting that the majority of people have a preference for twists in a story. This finding shows this factor is less suited for differentiating preference for narrative complexity. Moreover, it appears to support the suggestion that twists are not necessarily a 'complex' narrative device but are better subsumed under the more universal category of narrative surprise (Sternberg 2003; Tobin 2018), as they are strategically 'misleading' rather than 'confusing' their viewers (Kiss and Willemsen 2017: 50).

Narrative Complexity and Personality

The hypothesized relations between PNC and personality were largely confirmed. All three personality constructs that were hypothesized to predict PNC – Openness to Experience, Tolerance of Ambiguity, and Need for Cognition – were associated with higher scores on the PNC scale and its subfacets. In other words, people who are more tolerant of ambiguity in everyday situations, or tend to seek out more cognitively effortful activities and sensory and abstract information, also show a preference for cognitively demanding narratives that stimulate these traits. These results appear to be particularly driven by the ToA scale, although the possibility of NFC predicting additional variance in PNC could not be ruled out due to the small sample size. The enjoyment of complex narratives was also associated with all three personality scales, with similar magnitudes in the strength of relations. Behavioural engagement (i.e. having seen more complex narrative films) was primarily associated with a higher NFC, though the size of the parameters for ToA in relation to more complex types of narratives (impossible puzzle films, art cinema), and for Openness to art cinema, were both substantial enough to be followed up with larger samples.

The finding that all three predicted personality constructs were associated with a preference for narrative complexity is not surprising, because all three variables can be considered part of the broader Openness/Intellect personality domain. They do, however, point to different aspects of Openness. ToA is particularly associated with the intellectual curiosity (rather than aesthetic sensitivity) aspect of Openness/Intellect (Jach and Smillie 2019). Given that NFC is predominantly a measure of the Intellect aspect, it is not surprising that the effect sizes for ToA and NFC were similar, and larger than those for the broader Openness scale.

However, while ToA and NFC are closely related constructs, they can be differentiated in terms of their relations with a type of intellectual curiosity called 'curiosity as a sense of deprivation' (Litman 2008). Deprivation curiosity describes the tendency to seek relief from negative emotions associated with a lack of knowledge. This form of curiosity can certainly be experienced in response to films that end ambiguously. While NFC is positively associated with deprivation curiosity (Mussel 2010), ToA is negatively associated (Litman 2010). Given these differential relations to deprivation curiosity, it could be expected that those high in NFC may have less preference for complex films that end ambiguously (as this can cause the negative feelings associated with deprivation of information), whereas those high in ToA are more comfortable coping with a lack of information. Future studies could prod the distinction between these three constructs by studying relations between these personality traits and live (as opposed to recalled) experiences in response to films with different levels of ambiguity.

The Validity and Utility of the PNC Scale

The validity of the PNC scale was further confirmed in relation to the other measures in the study. High scores on the PNC construct were associated with more behavioural engagement (having seen more complex narrative films) and emotional engagement (reporting higher enjoyment scores in response to the complex films seen). The relations with behavioural engagement also increased as a function of film complexity (puzzle films, impossible puzzle films, art cinema), all of which suggest that the scale is a particularly relevant indicator of preferences for forms of complex storytelling, and offers a more targeted and context-specific complex story engagement than the more general personality constructs.

This finding underlines that the PNC construct can have various uses. Firstly, it highlights and reveals the role of individual differences in engagement with complex stories, acknowledging how the same narrative forms can entail different (behavioural, emotional or aesthetic) effects on different people. The PNC scale can also be used to select participants specifically for their preference or dislike for complex narratives or to cluster participants by this predisposition: for instance, in research on states such as interest, flow, absorption, or narrative engagement. For researchers interested in the experience of narrative complexity, the PNC scale will be instrumental in further studying what factors are involved in the preference for or dislike of such stories (e.g. personality, expertise, exposure). Moreover, while the present PNC scale has been tailored to the medium of film, it can be relatively easily rephrased to study story complexity in other narrative media, such as literature and television.

Future Directions

The current study marked only a first inquiry into the connection between personality and preference for complex narrative engagement, and so the findings warrant further exploration. Follow-up work should, first of all, confirm the structure of the PNC in a larger sample. Due to the limited number of participants in the current study, both the exploratory and confirmatory factor analyses were derived from the same sample; ideally, these should be established independently. Replication with a larger sample size could also help to provide a more refined understanding of the relations between the various personality factors and PNC – particularly to see whether ToA and NFC can predict PNC independently, as well as to differentiate between facets of Openness (e.g. aesthetic responsiveness versus intellectual curiosity), as engaging with stories can be characterized as both a cognitive-intellectual and a perceptual-aesthetic endeavour. The present findings also pave the way for future work that tests whether coping with complex narratives could have any 'transfer effects' to everyday situations (for instance, by 'training' one's tolerance for ambiguity).

An additional factor (though not strictly a personality trait) that warrants exploration is *expertise*. Expertise, in the context of the PNC scale, would refer to a person's repeated exposure to films and their knowledgeability about cinema and related aesthetic domains. Previous work on film preferences (Silvia and Berg 2011) provided indications that viewers high in expertise not only had more resources to cope with challenging films but also typically showed more interest in stimuli they deemed complex. In other words, experts seem to be more reactive to complexity per se (regardless of coping potential). For this reason, we would predict expertise to also positively relate to PNC, particularly in relation to the category of art cinema. Art films, after all, typically display the highest degrees of narrative and stylistic novelty and complexity.

Finally, the PNC scale can, together with the findings on the relevant personality factors, form a basis for further exploration of the dynamic processes that underlie experiences of narrative complexity. Do some spectators become more engaged as a story becomes highly confusing? Do some find exactly the same point to be frustrating? Or do they get more excited when a surprising conclusion resolves the standing uncertainties? While the PNC scale is itself a static measure, combining its findings with dynamic measures (e.g. continuous self-report, psychophysiology) can deepen understanding of the dynamics of engagement with storytelling, and show how different people respond to different narrative forms.

Steven Willemsen is Assistant Professor in Arts, Culture and Media at the University of Groningen, and Senior Researcher at the Max Planck Institute for Empirical Aesthetics in Frankfurt. He is co-author of *Impossible Puzzle Films: A Cognitive Approach to Contemporary Complex Cinema* (with Miklós Kiss, Edinburgh University Press, 2017).

Katalin Bálint is an Associate Professor specializing in Media Psychology at the VU Amsterdam, Department of Communication Science. She researches psychological responses to fictional narratives, social cognition of film viewers and the psychological effects of cinematography.

Frank Hakemulder specializes in the psychology of literature and media. His research pertains to the effects of stories on well-being, self-concept and social perception. He is Assistant Professor at the Department of Media and Culture Studies, Utrecht University, and affiliated full professor at the Reading Centre, University of Stavanger.

Miklós Kiss is Associate Professor of Audiovisual Arts and Cognition, and Chair of the Arts, Culture and Media department at the University of Groningen, the Netherlands. His research intersects the fields of narrative and cognitive film studies. He is co-author of the books *Film Studies in Motion: From Audiovisual Essay to Academic Research Video* (with Thomas van den Berg, Scalar, 2016) and *Impossible Puzzle Films: A Cognitive Approach to Contemporary Complex Cinema* (with Steven Willemsen, Edinburgh University Press, 2017).

Elly Konijn is Full Professor in Media Psychology, Department of Communication Science, VU Amsterdam. She chairs the Media Psychology Program Amsterdam, integrating her multidisciplinary background in psychology, media studies and computer science. Her research covers: relating to media figures, virtual humans, social robots; emotions and media-based reality perceptions and adolescents' media use. She publishes widely, including several books, and was editor of *Media Psychology*.

Kirill Fayn is a Senior Researcher at the Max Planck Institute for Empirical Aesthetics. His work focuses on understanding the processes underlying individual differences in experiences with complex information, particularly the link between the personality trait of Openness to Experience, and interest in confusing stimuli and situations.

References

Bálint, Katalin, et al. 2016. 'Reconceptualizing Foregrounding: Identifying Response Strategies to Deviation in Absorbing Narratives', *Scientific Study of Literature* 6: 176–207.
Bordwell, David. 1985. *Narration in the Fiction Film*. Madison: University of Wisconsin Press.
Buckland, Warren (ed.). 2009. 'Introduction: Puzzle Plots', in Warren Buckland (ed.), *Puzzle Films: Complex Storytelling in Contemporary Cinema*. Oxford: Wiley-Blackwell, pp. 1–12.
———. 2014. 'Introduction: Ambiguity, Ontological Pluralism, and Cognitive Dissonance in the Hollywood Puzzle Film', in Warren Buckland (ed.), *Hollywood Puzzle Films*. London: Routledge, pp. 1–14.

Buhr, Kristin, and Michel J. Dugas. 2002. 'The Intolerance of Uncertainty Scale: Psychometric Properties of the English Version', *Research and Therapy* 40: 931–45.

Cacioppo, John T., and Richard E. Petty. 1982. 'The Need for Cognition', *Journal of Personality and Social Psychology* 42(1): 116–31.

Cacioppo, John T., et al. 1996. 'Dispositional Differences in Cognitive Motivation: The Life and Times of Individuals Varying in Need for Cognition', *Psychological Bulletin* 119(2): 197–253.

Cameron, Allan. 2008. *Modular Narratives in Contemporary Cinema*. Basingstoke: Palgrave Macmillan.

Campora, Matthew. 2014. *Subjective Realist Cinema: From Expressionism to Inception*. New York: Berghahn Books.

Carleton, R. Nicholas, Peter Norton and Gordon Asmundson. 2007. 'Fearing the Unknown: A Short Version of the Intolerance of Uncertainty Scale', *Journal of Anxiety Disorders* 21: 105–17.

Cohen, Arthur R., Ezra Stotland and Donald M. Wolfe. 1955. 'An Experimental Investigation of Need for Cognition', *The Journal of Abnormal and Social Psychology* 51(2): 291–94.

Costa, Paul T., and Robert R. McCrae. 1992. 'The Five-Factor Model of Personality and its Relevance to Personality Disorders', *Journal of Personality Disorders* 6(4): 343–59.

DeYoung, Colin. 2014. 'Openness/Intellect: A Dimension of Personality Reflecting Cognitive Exploration', *APA Handbook of Personality and Social Psychology: Personality Processes and Individual Differences* 4: 369–99.

Elsaesser, Thomas. 2009. 'The Mind-Game Film', in Warren Buckland (ed.), *Puzzle Films: Complex Storytelling in Contemporary Cinema*. Oxford: Wiley-Blackwell, pp. 13–41.

———. 2018. 'Contingency, Causality, Complexity: Distributed Agency in the Mind-Game Film', *New Review of Film and Television Studies* 16(1): 1–39.

Fayn, Kirill, Carolyn MacCann, Niko Tiliopoulos and Paul J. Silvia. 2015a. 'Aesthetic Emotions and Aesthetic People: Openness Predicts Sensitivity to Novelty in the Experiences of Interest and Pleasure', *Frontiers in Psychology* 6: 1877.

Fayn, Kirill, Niko Tiliopoulos and Carolyn MacCann. 2015b. 'Interest in Truth versus Beauty: Intellect and Openness Reflect Different Pathways towards Interest', *Personality and Individual Differences* 81: 47–52.

Fayn, Kirill, et al. 2017. 'Interested in Different Things or in Different Ways? Exploring the Engagement Distinction between Openness and Intellect', *Journal of Individual Differences* 38: 265–73.

Fayn, Kirill, et al. 2019. 'Confused or Curious? Openness/Intellect Predicts More Positive Interest-Confusion Relations', *Journal of Personality and Social Psychology* 117(5): 1016–33.

Furnham, Adrian, and Joseph Marks. 2013. 'Tolerance of Ambiguity: A Review of the Recent Literature', *Psychology* 4(9): 717–28.

Gardner, William C., Edward P. Mulvey and Esther C. Shaw. 1995. 'Regression Analyses of Counts and Rates: Poisson, Overdispersed Poisson, and Negative Binomial Models', *Psychological Bulletin* 118(3): 392–404.

Grishakova, Marina, and Maria Poulaki (eds). 2019. *Narrative Complexity: Cognition, Embodiment, Evolution*. Lincoln: University of Nebraska Press.

Hodson, Gordon, and Richard M. Sorrentino. 1999. 'Uncertainty Orientation and the Big Five Personality Structure', *Journal of Research in Personality* 33(2): 253–61.

Hu, Li-tze, and Peter M. Bentler. 1999. 'Cutoff Criteria for Fit Indexes in Covariance Structure Analysis: Conventional Criteria versus New Alternatives', *Structural Equation Modeling* 6(1): 1–55.

Hven, Steffen. 2017. *Cinema and Narrative Complexity: Embodying the Fabula*. Amsterdam: Amsterdam University Press.

Jach, Hayley K., and Luke D. Smillie. 2019. 'To Fear or Fly to the Unknown: Tolerance for Ambiguity and Big Five Personality Traits', *Journal of Research in Personality* 79: 67-78.

Kiss, Miklós. 2012. 'Narrative Metalepsis as Diegetic Concept in Christopher Nolan's Inception', *Acta Film and Media Studies* 5: 35-54.

———. 2013. 'Navigation in Complex Films: Real-Life Embodied Experiences Underlying Narrative Categorisation', in Julia Eckel, Bernd Leiendecker, Daniela Olek and Christine Piepiorka (eds), *(Dis)Orienting Media and Narrative Mazes*. Bielefeld: Transcript, pp. 237-56.

Kiss, Miklós, and Steven Willemsen. 2017. *Impossible Puzzle Films: A Cognitive Approach to Contemporary Complex Cinema*. Edinburgh: Edinburgh University Press.

Klecker, Cornelia. 2011. 'Chronology, Causality ... Confusion: When Avant-Garde Goes Classic', *Journal of Film and Video* 63(2): 11-27.

———. 2013. 'Mind-Tricking Narratives: Between Classical and Art-Cinema Narration', *Poetics Today* 34(1-2): 119-46.

Kovács, András Bálint. 2007. *Screening Modernism. European Art Cinema, 1950-1980*. Chicago, IL: University of Chicago Press.

Lim, Sangdon, and Seungmin Jahng. 2019. 'Determining the Number of Factors Using Parallel Analysis and its Recent Variants', *Psychological Methods* 24(4): 452-67.

Lins de Holanda Coelho, Gabriel, Paul H.P. Hanel and Lukas J. Wolf. 2018. 'The Very Efficient Assessment of Need for Cognition: Developing a Six-Item Version', *Assessment* 27(8): 1870-85.

Litman, Jordan. 2008. 'Interest and Deprivation Factors of Epistemic Curiosity: Personality and Individual Differences', *Personality and Individual Differences* 44(7): 1585-95.

———. 2010. 'Relationships between Measures of I-and D-Type Curiosity, Ambiguity Tolerance, and Need for Closure: An Initial Test of the Wanting–Liking Model of Information-Seeking', *Personality and Individual Differences* 48(4): 397-402.

Magliano, Joseph P., Karyn Higgs and James Clinton. 2019. 'Sources of Complexity in Narrative Comprehension across Media', in Marina Grishakova and Maria Poulaki (eds), *Narrative Complexity: Cognition, Embodiment, Evolution*. Lincoln: University of Nebraska Press, pp. 149-73.

McLain, David. 2009. 'Evidence of the Properties of an Ambiguity Tolerance Measure: The Multiple Stimulus Types Ambiguity Tolerance Scale-II (MSTAT-II) 1', *Psychological Reports* 105(3 Pt 1): 975-88.

McNeish, Daniel. 2018. 'Thanks Coefficient Alpha, We'll Take It From Here', *Psychological Methods* 23(3): 412-33.

Mittell, Jason. 2015. *Complex TV: The Poetics of Contemporary Television Storytelling*. New York: New York University Press.

Mussel, Patrick. 2010. 'Epistemic Curiosity and Related Constructs: Lacking Evidence of Discriminant Validity', *Personality and Individual Differences* 49(5): 506-10.

Panek, Elliot. 2006. 'The Poet and the Detective: Defining the Psychological Puzzle Film', *Film Criticism* 31(1-2): 62-88.

Paulhus, Delroy, et al. 2004. 'Two Replicable Suppressor Situations in Personality Research', *Multivariate Behavioral Research* 39: 303-28.

Petty, Richard E., et al. 2009. 'The Need for Cognition', in Mark R. Leary and Rick H. Hoyle (eds), *Handbook of Individual Differences in Social Behavior*. New York: The Guilford Press, pp. 318-29.

Poulaki, Maria. 2011. *Before or Beyond Narrative? Towards a Complex Systems Theory of Contemporary Films*. Amsterdam: Rozenberg Publishers.

———. 2014. 'Puzzled Hollywood and the Return of Complex Films', in Warren Buckland (ed.), *Hollywood Puzzle Films*. London: Routledge, pp. 35–54.

Rentfrow, Peter J., Lewis R. Goldberg and Ran Zilca. 2011. 'Listening, Watching, and Reading: The Structure and Correlates of Entertainment Preferences', *Journal of Personality* 79(2): 223–58.

Rochow, Kathrin. 2010. 'Show Me Your Playlist and I Tell You Who You Are': An Investigation of the Social Psychological Foundation of Musical Playlists. Unpublished thesis, Uppsala University.

Rocklin, Thomas. 1994. 'Relation between Typical Intellectual Engagement and Openness: Comment on Goff and Ackerman (1992)', *Journal of Educational Psychology* 86(1): 145–49.

Schutte, Nicola S., and John M. Malouff. 2004. 'University Student Reading Preferences in Relation to the Big Five Personality Dimensions', *Reading Psychology* 25(4): 273–95.

Silvia, Paul J., and Christopher Berg. 2011. 'Finding Movies Interesting: How Appraisals and Expertise Influence the Aesthetic Experience of Film', *Empirical Studies of the Arts* 29: 73–88.

Silvia, Paul J., Robert A. Henson and Jonathan L. Templin. 2009. 'Are the Sources of Interest the Same for Everyone? Using Multilevel Mixture Models to Explore Individual Differences in Appraisal Structures', *Cognition and Emotion* 23(7): 1389–1406.

Silvia, Paul J., et al. 2015. 'Openness to Experience and Awe in Response to Nature and Music: Personality and Profound Aesthetic Experiences', *Psychology of Aesthetics, Creativity, and the Arts* 9(4): 376–84.

Soto, Christopher J., and Oliver P. John. 2017. 'Short and Extra-Short Forms of the Big Five Inventory–2: The BFI-2-S and BFI-2-XS', *Journal of Research in Personality* 68: 69–81.

Sternberg, Meir. 2003. 'Universals of Narrative and their Cognitivist Fortunes (I)', *Poetics Today* 24(2): 297–395.

Swami, Viren, et al. 2010. 'The Disinterested Play of Thought: Individual Differences and Preference for Surrealist Motion Pictures', *Personality and Individual Differences* 48(7): 855–59.

Tobin, Vera. 2018. *Elements of Surprise: Our Mental Limits and the Satisfactions of Plot*. Cambridge, MA: Harvard University Press.

Verplanken, Bas, Pieter T. Hazenberg and Grace R. Palenéwen. 1992. 'Need for Cognition and External Information Search Effort', *Journal of Research in Personality* 26(2): 128–36.

Wiersema, Daphne, Job Schalk and Gerben van Kleef. 2012. 'Who's Afraid of Red, Yellow, and Blue? Need for Cognitive Closure Predicts Aesthetic Preferences', *Psychology of Aesthetics, Creativity, and the Arts* 6(2): 168–74.

Willemsen, Steven, and Miklós Kiss. 2017. 'Resistance to Narrative in Narrative Film: Excessive Complexity in Quentin Dupieux's Réalité (2014)', *Global Media Journal: Australian Edition* 11(1): 1–18.

———. 2020. 'Keeping Track of Time: The Role of Spatial and Embodied Cognition in the Comprehension of Non-Linear Storyworlds', *Style* 54 (2): 172–98.

Xu, Xiaowen, and Jordan B. Peterson. 2017. 'Differences in Media Preference Mediate the Link between Personality and Political Orientation', *Political Psychology* 38: 55–72.Cimi, tem. Um quod

Index

A

abduction, 329–30, 347n1
acceptance, 291, 295–97, 298
acousmatic, 179
active discovery
  in *Philadelphia Story*, 31–37
  topics addressed, 5
aesthetic fluency, 198
aesthetic functions, 328–29
aesthetic pleasure. *See also* "Conspiracy Theories and Interior Design"
  cognitive challenge and, 16–21, 144–45
  complexity and, 198
  counter cinema and, 144–46
  empirical studies, 19–20
  epistemic value and, 256n1
  hedonic value and, 256n1
  from incongruity, 145–46
  Mittell and, 281
  synaesthesia and, 151–53
aesthetics
  confusion and, 3
  fluent processing and, 3, 198
  operational, 227, 239–42
Afrosurrealism, 268
agreeableness, 356, 359, 365, 370, 372
Alber, Jan, 322n1
Aldouby, Hava, 123
alien invasion narrative
  Arrival as, 86–89
  origins, 83–84
  Other as threat in, 83–89
Alsop, Elizabeth, 265
ambiguity. *See also* Morally Ambiguous Character drama
  counter cinema and, 145
  spatio-temporal reasoning and, 177–78
  techniques, 52–53
  tolerance for, 360–61, 362, 365, 370–72, 376–77
anthology format, 220–21
Anthropocene, 97
anti-hero drama, 284, 285–86. *See also* Morally Ambiguous Character drama
The Antihero in American Television (Vaage), 285
anti-hero movies, 25
Antonioni, Michelangelo, 163
  The Eclipse and, 164–66, 167, 168
  Godard compared with, 182
  mobile framing used by, 185
  The Passenger and, 166–69, 170–71, 192n4
  Resnais compared with, 171
  style of, 164–69, 170–71, 191n2, 192n4
Aristotle, 58
Arlington Road (1999), 246
Armstrong, Thomas, 20–21
Arnheim, Rudolf, 191
Arnold, Gordon, 249
Arrival (2016), 69, 86–89, 90
art-cinema narratives. *See also* counter cinema; *8½*; embodied-cognitive perspective
  cognitive appeal of, 157–58
  time and, 158–59
  topics addressed, 6–8
asa nisi masa (pig Latin for soul), 119–21, 129, 133n10
Asimov, Isaac, 77–78, 79
Atlanta (2016–), 262, 268, 274, 275
Atwood, Margaret, 319
Austen, Jane, 336

auteur, 125–30, 133n17, 133nn13–15
author film, 202

B
Babel (2007), 217
background textual structures, 332–33
backward reference, 314–18
Ball, Alan, 222
Band of Outsiders (1964), 188
Bartlett, Frederic C., 310
Bateson, Gregory, 250
batshit TV, 9
   Atlanta as, 262, 268, 274, 275
   complex TV versus, 263–65, 266–67
   conclusions, 275
   Dadaism and, 267
   inferred author function and, 269–70
   The Leftovers as, 262, 265, 270, 271–73
   Legion as, 265–66, 267, 275
   mental illness and, 266
   other traditions and, 264
   perplexion of, 264
   term origins, 262
   trance-like viewing of, 267–68
   Twin Peaks (2017) as, 264, 265
   unnatural narrative compared with, 262–63, 276n3
   viewing mode of, 265
   Watchmen as, 270, 273–75
Bazin, André, 133n13
Beardsley, Monroe, 17, 23
beautiful objects, 20–21
Beckett, Samuel, 309
Being John Malkovich (1999), 228
Benson-Allott, Caetlin, 268
Bergson, Henry, 322n5
Berliner, Todd, 241, 256n1
Berlyne, Daniel E., 3, 22–23
Bharucha, Jamshed, 25
Bierce, Ambrose, 319–20
Big Five, 359–60, 365, 370–71
The Blind Assassin (Atwood), 319
The Body Snatchers (Finney), 91n5
Bogart, Humphrey, 282–83
Bondanella, Peter, 121–22, 130

Booth, Wayne
   ambiguity techniques identified by, 52–53
   narration types and, 50–53
   unreliability and, 44
Bordwell, David, 218, 225, 226
Braly, Kenneth, 310
Branigan, Edward, 122
Breathless (1960), 184
Brecht, Bertolt, 139, 147, 183
Bresson, Robert, 161
   Godard compared with, 178, 182
   image exchanged for off-screen sound and, 179, 180–82
   A Man Escaped and, 179–80
   metonymic minimalism of, 178–79
   Mouchette and, 180–82
   style of, 178–82
Brütsch, Matthias, 44
Byford, Jovan, 249

C
Carhart-Harris, Robin L., 149
Carroll, Noël, 18, 21
Carruth, Shane. *See Primer*; *Upstream Color*
Carter, Jimmy, 260
Casablanca (1942), 282–83
Castiglione, Davide, 338–39
Caughie, John, 243, 247
causality, 314, 322n3
Cavell, Stanley, 30
Chakrabarty, Dipesh, 97
Chaney, Jen, 271
character integrity, primacy of, 205–7
Chion, Michel, 179
cinéma vérité (documentary style), 182
Clark, Andy, 306, 322n2
climate change. *See* ecological crisis
clue scanning, 244–45, 257n3
CMT. *See* Conceptual Metaphor Theory
cognitive categories, 46–49
cognitive challenge
   aesthetic pleasure and, 16–21, 144–45
   Deux ou Trois Choses Que Je Sais d'Elle and, 140–44
   engaging effects and, 4

cognitive challenge (*cont.*)
  entropy and criticality, 149–51
  knowledge/threat interplay in, 74–79
  mass art and, 21–25
  in narrative, 2–4
  personality/preferences and, 356–57
  politics and, 140
  in SF, 68–69
  topics addressed, 15–16
cognitive dissonance, reduction of, 311, 322n1
cognitive theory of film narration, 226
Coherence (2013), 201, 204, 209
Community (2009-2015). *See* "Conspiracy Theories and Interior Design"; "Epidemiology"
compartmentalizing, 201, 202–5
complex film. *See also specific films*
  asa nisi masa and, 119–21
  behavioural and emotional engagement with, 364
  cognitive processes and, 117, 132n2
  diegesis and, 118–19, 132n6
  narrative environment of, 116–19, 133n9
  viewer-as-organism and, 117, 132nn3–4
  wide-scale enjoyability limited in, 195–96
complexity. *See also* Preference for Narrative Complexity scale
  aesthetic pleasure and, 198
  decomplexification, 121–24
  factors, 357–59, 376–77
  interest in, 4
  knowledge and threat enhancing, 76–77
  personality/preferences and, 357–61, 370–71, 376–77
  in SF, 68–69
  varieties of, 95–96
complex plot, 58
complex TV
  attention to detail watching, 265
  batshit TV versus, 263–65, 266–67
  comprehension and, 261–62
  inferred author function and, 269–70
  Lost as, 270–71
  topics addressed, 8–9
  WandaVision as, 268–69

conceptual breakthrough
  higher knowledge via, 71
  Interstellar and, 72–73
  narrative configuration types, 73–74
  novum/expanded perception and, 71–74
  wonder and, 71–72
Conceptual Metaphor Theory (CMT), 158–59, 180, 192n8
confusion
  aesthetics and, 3
  in "Conspiracy Theories and Interior Design," 246
  Twin Peaks (1990-1991) and, 262
connoisseurship, 297–98
conscientiousness, 356, 359, 365, 370, 372
"Conspiracy Theories and Interior Design" (*Community* episode), 217
  archetypical genre roles and, 248–49
  B plot of, 254–55
  breathing room erased in, 242–43
  chase scene, 254–55, 257n11
  climax of episode, 236–42
  clue scanning as irrelevant in, 244–45, 257n3
  conclusions, 255–56
  confusion and, 246
  conspiracies enumerated in, 240, 245–46, 257n4
  double-crosses in, 247
  fake night school courses in, 257n9
  genre parody appeal of, 244–51
  homage appeal of, 253–55
  introduction, 236–37
  low stakes in, 242, 249–50, 254–55, 257n8
  murder and, 250
  music used in, 254, 257n10
  non-climax scenes appeal in, 253
  operational aesthetic in climax of, 239–42
  parody and, 239, 244–51, 254
  plot twists in, 242–44, 247–48
  recursive structure of conspiracies in, 246
  retrospective significance in, 241
  serial knowledge and, 241, 242, 251–52
  suspicion and, 244
  synopsis, 237–38

topics addressed, 8
CONTAINER schema logic, 160–61, 164, 167
containment principle, 164–67, 192n5
Contempt. See Le Mépris
conversational implicature. *See* pragmatic theory of conversational implicature
"The Conversation of Prayer" (Thomas), 326–27, 329, 330, 331
cooperative narration, 5, 51
Cooperative Principle, 43, 46–47, 51–52, 54–55
counter cinema. *See also* Godard, Jean-Luc; specific films
   aesthetic pleasure and, 144–46
   ambiguity and, 145
   challenge for attention in, 143–44
   entropy and criticality, 149–51
   heterogeneity of elements in, 143–44
   incongruence and, 145–46
   language, role of, in, 142–43
   montage used in, 140–41
   topics addressed, 7
critical state, 149–51
Csikszentmihalyi, Mihaly, 3
cumulative format, 221
curiosity, 341, 348n6

D

Dadaism, 267
Danto, Arthur, 317
Dargis, Manohla, 103–4
Dark Ecology (Morton), 99–100
"Dave" (*Lost* episode), 270–71
deception, 49
deceptive narration
   features of, 51
   of *Lost Highway*, 58–64
   topics addressed, 5
   unreliable narration compared with, 44–45, 66n2
deceptive puzzle film. *See also Lost Highway*
   character of, 58
   conclusions, 64–66
   conversational implicature and, 45–49
   filmic narration and, 49–50
   implied author and, 44–45, 66n1

narration types related to, 50–53
topics addressed, 43
deduction, 329, 347n1
defamiliarization, 308. *See also ostranenie*
Deleuze, Gilles, 133n13
deliberate reflection, 286
Denby, David, 217, 233
Detweiler-Bedell, Brian, 20–21
Deux ou Trois Choses Que Je Sais d'Elle (1967)
   aesthetic pleasure and, 144–46
   cognitive challenge and, 140–44
   from conflict to relation, 147–48
   description and, 139
   epilogue about, 153–54
   imagination related to, 140
   object/subject abolished in, 155n3
Dewey, John, 17
Dexter (2006–2013), 219, 282
   emotion regulation in watching, 288–94
   "Love American Style" episode, 288–90, 291, 292–93, 294–97
   moral challenge of, 284–86
Dick, Philip K., 73–74
diegesis, 118–19, 132n6, 230
diegetic sounds, 161
direct meaning, 45–46
discrepant narration, 5, 51
Dissanayake, Ellen, 307
distancing effect, 182–83, 184–85, 192n9
Donnie Darko (2001), 15, 201, 202–3, 204–5, 209
Donovan, Barna William, 247, 249
double-crosses, 247
DST. *See* dynamic systems theory
dual epistemic functions, 329–30
dwelling silently, 341–42, 348nn7–8
dynamic systems theory (DST), 149

E

The Eclipse (1962), 164–66, 167, 168
ecological crisis
   awareness loops and, 99–101
   narrative challenges of, 97–98
Edge of Darkness (1985), 243
8½
   asa nisi masa and, 119–21, 129

8½ (cont.)
  auteur and, 125–30, 133n17, 133nn13–15
  categorization of, 131n1
  cognitive-formalist analysis of, 122
  conclusions, 130–31
  critic, demise of, and, 127–30, 133n18
  emotional landscapes in, 124–25
  fantasy versus reality and, 123–24
  introduction, 115–16
  judgment criteria for, 120
  narrative complexity and decomplexification, 121–24
  narrative environment of, 116–19
  opening scene, 115
  reality bleeding and, 224
  topics addressed, 6–7
Eisenstein, Sergei, 147–48, 152–53
Eitzen, Dirk, 250
Elsaesser, Thomas, 50, 65
embedded viewpoints, 335
embodied-cognitive perspective
  conclusions, 189–91
  introduction, 157–59
  radical continuity and, 163–78
  radical discontinuity and, 178–89
  time and, 158–59
  topics addressed, 7
Embodied Simulation Theory (EST), 190, 192n10
Emma (Austen), 336
Emmott, Catherine, 313, 315–16
emotion
  8½ and, 124–25
  engaging, 364, 371–72
  MAC and negative, 287–88
  PNC scale and, 372–75
emotion regulation
  costs/benefits associated with, 291–94
  strategies, 289–91
  in watching *Dexter*, 288–94
Empson, William, 145
enactive, 117, 132n4
Enlightenment, 75, 76, 90
Enrico, Robert, 205
entropy, 149–51
"Epidemiology" (*Community* episode), 257n7
episodic format, 221
epistemic functions, 328–30
epistemic value, 256n1
EST. *See* Embodied Simulation Theory
Eternal Sunshine of the Spotless Mind (2004), 217, 234
exhilarated pleasure, 20
experiential sets, 332
explanation-centred reflection, 331
explanation-seeking
  difficulties that motivate, 335–37, 338
  embedded viewpoints and, 335
  superimposed viewpoints and, 336
  temporal intervals and, 335–36
explication-centred reflection, 331
expressive enactment, 10
  inexpressible realizations and, 343–44
  integrative comprehension contrasted with, 327, 343–46
  linguistic structures, difficult, and, 342–43
  metaphor comprehension and, 344–45
  sublime disquietude and, 345–46, 348n9
expressive explication, 327
extradiegetic, 230
extraversion, 356, 359, 365, 370, 371, 372

F

fabula (story), 226
Fargo
  aspect ratios used in, 259–60
  coherent narrative of, 264
  second season opening scene in, 259–61, 264, 276n1
Fellini, Federico. *See 8½*
fiction, as game of make-believe, 282–84
fictional relief, 285–86
Field, Syd, 205
Fight Club (1999), 133n9, 202, 203, 209, 219, 232, 272
filmic narration
  deceptive puzzle film and, 49–50
  invisible narrator and, 44–45
  mainstream, 54–57
  types of, 43, 50–53
Finney, Jack, 91n5

first-degree puzzle films, 200–201
flouted narration, 5, 51
fluent processing, 3, 198
Ford, Hamish, 142
foregrounding, 332–33, 347n3, 347n5
framing, 201, 202–5
Frankenstein (Shelley), 75
The French Connection (1971), 254
Freud, Sigmund, 86
Fuller, Bryan, 264

G

Le Gai Savoir (1969), 140
Gallese, Vittorio, 190, 192n10
Game of Thrones (2011–2019), 223
Genette, Gerard, 224
Ghosh, Amitav, 100
Gilliam, Terry. *See Twelve Monkeys*
Godard, Jean-Luc, 7. *See also specific films*
  Antonioni compared with, 182
  Bresson compared with, 178, 182
  cinéma vérité and, 182
  distancing effect and, 182–83, 184–85, 192n9
  Eisenstein compared with, 147–48
  epilogue about, 153–54
  introduction, 138–39
  mobile framing used by, 185–87
  montage used by, 140–41
  pleasure and, 140
  politics and, 139–40
  polyphony and, 148
  shot-reverse-shot related to, 183, 185, 188
  sound used by, 188
  style of, 182–89
  synaesthesia and, 151–53
Grice, H. P., 5, 43
  conversational implicature and, 45–49, 66
  narration types and, 50–52
Grodal, Torben, 190
Groundhog Day (1993), 228
Gunning, Tom, 44–45, 234

H

Hamlet on the Holodeck (Murray), 220
Hannibal (2013–2015), 262, 263, 266, 267

Harmon, Dan, 243, 246
HBO. *See* Home Box Office
"Head of Woman" (Picasso), 198–99
hedonic value, 256n1
Hepburn, Katharine, 26, 27, 32–37
Heyduk, Ronald, 19
hindsight bias, 318
Hiroshima Mon Amour (1959), 171, 176–77
Hitchcock, Alfred. *See Rear Window; Stage Fright*
Home Box Office (HBO), 221
  freedom enjoyed by, 222–23
  Six Feet Under, 222, 224–25
  The Sopranos, 219, 220, 223–24
  style, 222–25
Hopkins, Manley, 316
humor, 23–24
Huron, David, 24, 312
Husserl, Edmund, 330, 347n1
Hutcheon, Linda, 254
hypothetical intentionalism, 270

I

image schemata, 109n2
implied author, 44–45, 66n1
impressionist art, 199
Inception (2010), 72, 73, 200–201
incongruity
  aesthetic pleasure from, 145–46
  as complexity factor, 358
  logical, 27–31, 37
Incongruity Theory, 23–24
Independence Day (1996), 84, 86
induction, 329, 347n1
inexpressible realizations, 339–40
inferred author function, 269–70
inferred meaning, 45–46
information load, 357
Inland Empire (2006)
  coherence versus paradox in, 209
  opening scenes of, 207–8
  uncompensated identity paradox of, 207–11
insight, 24
instrumental sets, 332
integrative comprehension, 10

integrative comprehension (*cont.*)
    expressive enactment contrasted with, 327, 343–46
    linguistic structures and, 342
interpretive explanation, 327
Interstellar (2014), 69
    Arrival and, 88–89, 90
    conceptual breakthrough in, 72–73
    knowledge/threat interplay in, 79–81
intradiegetic, 230
intuition, categorial, 330
Invasion of the Body Snatchers (1956), 78–79, 85–86, 91n5
inverted-U model, 22, 38n2
invisible narrator, 44–45
It Came from Outer Space, 85

J

Jacob's Ladder (1990), 202–3, 204–5
James, Henry, 205
JFK (1991), 245
Johnson, Mark, 118
The Joy of Learning. See Le Gai Savoir
Jung, Carl Gustav, 120, 133n10

K

Kaaronen, Roope Oskari, 311
Kael, Pauline, 128–29
Kafka, Franz, 311
Kahneman, Daniel, 25, 313, 322n2
Kant, Immanuel, 17, 18
Katz, Daniel, 310
Kelly-Romano, Stephanie, 244, 249
Kermode, Frank, 23
Kesner, Ladislav, 308
Kharkhurin, Anatoliy V., 151–52
Kintsch, Walter, 318–19
Kiss, Miklós, 81, 203, 320
    complexity and, 95, 106, 244
    dissonant experiences and, 308
    formal play and, 244
    Zen way of reading and, 267
knowledge
    brain and, 76
    complexity and, 76–77
    conceptual breakthrough and, 71
    Interstellar and, 79–81
    schema-based, 226
    serial, 241, 242, 251–52
    tacit, 313–14
    threat interplay with, 74–83
Kovács, András Bálint, 158–59, 163, 178. *See also* radical continuity; radical discontinuity
Kubovy, Michael, 25
Kubrick, Stanley, 1
Kukkonen, Karin, 322n4

L

Lampert, Jay, 317
Landa, Garcia, 317
Landy, Joshua, 129
Last Year at Marienbad (1961), 171–76, 192n6
"Learning from Text, Levels of Comprehension" (Kintsch), 318–19
The Leftovers (2014-2017), 262, 265, 270, 271–73
Legion (2017-2019), 265–66, 267, 275
"Let the Mystery Be" (*The Leftovers* episode), 271
Levinson, Jerrold, 16, 17–18, 47–48
Libet, Benjamin, 317
Lindelof, Damon, 270–71, 273. *See also specific TV shows*
linguistic structures, difficult
    expressive enactment, 342–43
    functionally coordinated, 337–38, 347n4
    integrative comprehension, 342
    open reflection and, 341–42, 348nn7–8
    range of, 327–28
    reflective engagement modes and, 341–43
literary reading
    attentional dispositions and, 330–31
    conclusions, 346–47
    differential openings for creative response, 330–32
    difficulty, other sources of, in, 338–39
    dual epistemic functions and, 329–30
    epistemic and aesthetic functions, 328–29
    explanation-seeking and, 335–37, 338
    functionally coordinated linguistic structures, 337–38, 347n4
    introduction, 326–27

metaphor and, 327–28
Openness to Experience, 330–31
resemblance-seeking and, 332–35, 338
stylistic deviations and, 328
traditional dualities revisited, 328–39
logic
  CONTAINER schema, 160–61, 164, 167
  defined, 39n4
  incongruity in, 27–31, 37
Looper (2012), 69, 73
  Arrival and, 88–89
  knowledge/threat interplay in, 79–80, 81–83
loops
  ecological crisis and, 99–101
  Upstream Color and, 101–7, 109n8
Loschky, Lester C., 143–44
Lost (2004-2010), 270–71, 275
Lost Highway (1997), 43, 269
  deceptive narration of, 58–64
  doppelganger theme, 63
  dream in, 63–64
  murder scene, 59–64, 66n4
  omniscient narration in, 61–62
"Love American Style" (*Dexter* episode), 288–90, 291, 292–93, 294–97
lying, 49
Lynch, David, 1, 58, 262, 264, 269. *See also specific films*

M

MAC. *See* Morally Ambiguous Character drama
The Manchurian Candidate (1962), 242, 246
A Man Escaped (1956), 179–80
Maniac (2018)
  alternate ontologies within, 218–19
  complex narrative of, 229–31
  conclusions, 233–34
  metadiegetic narrative of, 230–31
  as multiform narrative, 219–20
  Russian Doll compared with, 231
  topics addressed, 217–18
Manovich, Lev, 192n6
The Man Who Could Work Miracles (Wells), 70
Martindale, Colin, 198

Massacre at Sioux Falls (fictional film in *Fargo*), 259–61, 264, 276n1
mass art
  cognitive challenge and, 21–25
  topics addressed, 16
material anchors
  image schemata and, 109n2
  Upstream Color and, 94, 103, 105, 109n5
McKenna, Chris, 257n10
Memento (2000), 15, 72, 132n5, 234
Menninghaus, Winfried, 3
Le Mépris (1963), 144, 183, 184, 186–87
metadiegetic, 230
metalepsis, 224
Metamorphosis (Kafka), 311
metaphor
  CMT and, 158–59, 180, 192n8
  comprehension, 344–45
  literary reading and, 327–28
  nominal, 333
  visual field and, 180, 192n8
metonymic minimalism, 178–79
Metz, Christian, 127, 129, 133n17, 161
Meyer, Leonard, 24
Millis, Keith, 19
mind-game films, 50, 65. *See also* deceptive puzzle film
mind-wandering, 314
Mittell, Jason, 218, 221, 243
  narrative special effect and, 236
  operational aesthetic and, 227, 239, 250–51, 252
  parody and, 254
  pleasure and, 281
mobile framing, 185–87
"The Mockingbird" (Bierce), 319–20
Mole, Christopher, 320
moral disengagement, 289–90, 292–93
Morally Ambiguous Character drama (MAC). *See also Dexter*
  acceptance and, 291, 295–97, 298
  challenge and reward balance in, 299–300
  challenge in game of, 284–88
  discussion, 300–301
  emotions, negative, and, 287–88

Morally Ambiguous Character drama (MAC) (*cont.*)
    introduction, 281–82
    make-believe game and, 282–84
    playful reward in, 294–97
    reappraisal and, 289–91, 292–93
    relatedness needs and, 298–99, 302n3
    rewards of, 286
    suppression and, 289, 291–92, 294
    terminology and, 286–87
    topics addressed, 9
    viewer expertise and, 297–99
Morin, Edgar, 119
Morton, Timothy, 99–100
"The Most Powerful Man in the World" (*The Leftovers* episode), 271–72
Mouchette (1967), 180–82
Mr. Robot (2015–2019), 266, 267
    complex narrative of, 231–33
    conclusions, 233–34
    as multiform narrative, 219–20
    ontologically fragmented narrative of, 219
    topics addressed, 217–18
    unreliable narration of, 231–33
Mrs Dalloway (Woolf), 335
Mulholland Drive (2001), 201, 202, 203, 209, 228, 269
multiform television. *See* television
Murray, Janet H., 220
music, 254, 257n10, 312

N

Nabokov, Vladimir, 332–33
narrative. *See also specific topics*
    cognitive challenge in, 2–4
    cognitive theory of film, 226
    coherence axioms, 197–98
    complex, understanding, 226–33
    complexity and decomplexification, 121–24
    ecological crisis and, 97–98
    hierarchy of, 5
    mental continuity related to, 196–97
    postdiction in complex, 318–20
    as problem solving process, 197
    puzzle prototype and, 196–200

    trend in modern, 2
    unnatural, 262–63
Need for Cognition (NFC), 360, 362, 370–72, 376–77
Nehamas, Alexander, 17, 18
neuroticism, 356, 359, 365, 370, 372
NFC. *See* Need for Cognition
Nielsen, Henrik Skov, 276n3
"Nightfall" (Asimov), 77–78, 79
Night of the Living Dead (1968), 257n7
Niven, Larry, 86
noise, 150
Nolan, Christopher, 72, 200
nonclosure, narrative, 358
noun–noun compounds, 333
novum
    defined, 6
    expanded perception from, 70–74
    narrative configuration types related to, 73–74

O

Occurrence at Owl Creek Bridge (1961), 205
Odin, Steve, 152–53
O'Faolain, Sean, 331
The Old Bridge (Nabokov), 332–33
omniscient narration, 61–62
Openness to Experience
    as attentional disposition, 330–31
    NFC and, 360, 362
    personality and preferences and, 359–61, 362, 370–72, 376–77
    ToA and, 360–61, 362
operational aesthetic, 227, 239–42, 250–51, 252
ostranenie (defamiliarization), 339–40

P

Pallasmaa, Juhani, 124–25
parody. *See* "Conspiracy Theories and Interior Design"
The Passenger (1975), 166–69, 170–71, 192n4
Pepper, Stephen, 152
Perlmutter, Ruth, 140–41
perplexion, 264
personality and preferences. *See also* Preference for Narrative Complexity scale

behavioural and emotional engagement, 371–72
cognitive challenge and, 356–57
complexity and, 357–61, 370–71, 376–77
conclusions, 375–79
empirical studies on, 19–20
engagement and, 361
introduction, 355–56
for narrative complexity, 370–71
narrative complexity factors influencing, 357–59, 376–77
NFC and, 360, 362
Openness to Experience and, 330–31, 359–61, 362, 370–72, 376–77
study aims, 362
study hypotheses, 362–63
study measures, 364–66
study methods, 363
study results, 366–75
ToA and, 360–61, 362
topics addressed, 10
The Philadelphia Story (1940), 5, 16
  active discovery in, 31–37
  challenge in, 25–37
  classical structure of, 26
  Hepburn performance in, 26, 27, 32–37
  logical incongruities in, 27–31, 37
  synopsis, 27
A Philosophy of Mass Art (Carroll), 21
Picasso, Pablo, 198–99
Pierrot le Fou (1965), 142, 144
pleasure, 20, 140, 308–9. *See also* aesthetic pleasure
plot. *See* syuzhet
plot twists, 242–44, 247–48
PNC. *See* Preference for Narrative Complexity scale
Poetics of Unnatural Narrative (Alber, Nielsen and Richardson), 276n3
Pollmann, Inga, 132n8
postdiction, 307
  backward reference and, 314–18
  in complex narratives, 318–20
  Libet and, 317
  in neuroscience, 317–18
  re-entry and, 317, 322n5
pragmatic theory of conversational implicature, 5, 43, 45–49, 66
precision, 315, 322n4
Predestination (2014), 201, 203, 209
prediction
  failure, 308–9
  role of predictable, 309–12
  stereotype and, 309–10
  surprise and, 308–9
predictive processing framework
  art experience and, 306–7
  conclusions, 320–21
  low-level predictions and, 312
  topics addressed, 9
Preference for Narrative Complexity scale (PNC), 356
  conclusions, 375–79
  demographic variables and, 369–70
  emotional and behavioural validity of, 372–75
  future directions, 378–79
  item selection, dimension reduction, and psychometric properties, 365–66
  measures, 364–66
  narrative complexity and personality, 376–77
  personality and preference for narrative complexity, 370–71
  perspectives on, 375–79
  reliability of, 369
  structure and psychometric properties, 366–69
  utility of, 377–78
  validity, 366–69, 377–78
prettiness, 20, 21
Primer (2004), 15, 79, 93
Probability Designs (Kukkonen), 322n4
protagonist identity
  coherent, 200–201, 209
  coherent versus paradoxical, 209
  conclusions, 211–12
  degrees of, 200–202
  integrity primacy of, 205–7
  introduction, 195–96

protagonist identity (*cont.*)
   paradoxical, 201–2
   paradoxical, framing and compartmentalizing, 202–5
   topics addressed, 7–8
   uncompensated identity paradox, 207–11
prototype
   aesthetic fluency and, 198
   impressionist art and, 199
   Picasso and, 198–99
   of puzzle, accommodating, 196–200
Przbylski, Andrew K., 283, 302n1
"Psychology of Art" (Vygotsky), 145–46
Pulp Fiction (1994), 217
puzzle film, 357. *See also specific topics*
   characteristics of, 57–58
   complex plot compared with, 58
   complex versus complicated, 122, 133n11
   degrees of, 200–202
   enjoyability limited in, 195–96
   narrative coherence axioms and, 197–98
   prototype of, accommodating, 196–200
   solver/viewer and, 117–18

Q
quasi-metaphoric markers, 334

R
radical continuity, 163–78
radical discontinuity, 178–89
Reagan, Ronald, 259–61
reality bleeding, 224
reality check moments, 286, 290
real-world interrelations, 6
reappraisal, 289–91, 292–93
Rear Window (1954), 43, 54–57
re-entry, 317, 322n5
reflective engagement modes, 328, 341–43
resemblance-seeking
   difficulties that motivate, 332–35, 338
   foregrounding and, 332–33, 347n3, 347n5
   structures, 334
Resnais, Alain, 162, 163, 202
   Antonioni compared with, 171
   Hiroshima Mon Amour and, 171, 176–77

Last Year at Marienbad and, 171–76, 192n6
   mobile framing used by, 185
   style of, 169, 171–78, 192n6
rhetorical focusing principle, 313
Richardson, Brian, 276n3
Robbe-Grillet, Alain, 202
Romanticism, 75–76, 90
Rouch, Jean, 182
Rumelhart, David, 197
Russian Doll (2019–), 266
   complex narrative of, 227–29
   conclusions, 233–34
   foldback structure in, 229
   as game-like puzzle narrative, 218
   Maniac compared with, 231
   as multiform narrative, 219–20
   ontologies used in, 227–29
   topics addressed, 217–18

S
Sanford, Anthony, 313, 315–16
Sartre, Jean-Paul, 147
Sbragia, Albert, 126–27
scenario-mapping, 313
schema, 309–11
schema-based knowledge, 226
science fiction (SF)
   alien invasion narrative, 83–89
   cognitive challenge and complexity in, 68–69
   conceptual breakthrough and, 71–74
   conclusions, 89–90
   defined, 71, 91n4
   knowledge and threat interplay in, 74–79
   novum and expanded perception in, 70–74
   topics addressed, 5–6, 69
Sconce, Jeffrey, 218, 220–21
Scorsese, Martin, 161
Screening Modernism (Kovács), 163. *See also radical continuity; radical discontinuity*
second-degree puzzle films, 201
Seitz, Matt Zoller, 263
serial format, 221
serial knowledge, 241, 242, 251–52
series/serial hybridity, 221–22

"Seven Types of Ambiguity" (Empson), 145
SF. *See* science fiction
Shelley, Mary, 75
Shimojo, Shinsuke, 317–18
Shklovsky, Viktor, 320, 338, 339
shot-reverse-shot, 183, 185, 188
The Singing Detective (1986), 225
Six Feet Under (2001–2005), 220, 222, 224–25
The Sixth Sense (1999), 219
Solaris (1972), 228
Sontag, Susan, 83, 84
The Sopranos (1999–2007), 219, 220, 223–24, 267
soul. *See* asa nisi masa
spatio-temporal reasoning
   ambiguity and, 177–78
   cinema and, 159–63
   embodying radical continuity, 163–78
   embodying radical discontinuity, 178–89
   of modern form, 163–89
   of shot, 161–62, 191n1
Stage Fright (1950), 57, 66n3
stereotype
   cognitive load and, 312, 314
   prediction and, 309–10
   schema and, 312–13
story. *See* fabula; *specific topics*
Stubbs, John C., 133n14
Der Student von Prague (1913), 204
superimposed viewpoints, 336
suppression, 289, 291–92, 294
surface tension, 96
surprise
   fast/slow thinking related to, 313, 322n2
   in music, 312
   prediction failure and, 308–9
   sense-making triggered by, 312–14
   tacit knowledge leading to, 313–14
suspicion, 244, 256n2
synaesthesia, 151–53
syuzhet (plot), 226

T

Tate, R. Colin, 223
Taxi Driver (1975), 161
"Teddy Perkins" (*Atlanta* episode), 268
television. *See also* batshit TV; complex TV; *specific shows*
   case studies, 218–20
   complex, 220–22, 226–33
   complex narrative, understanding, 226–33
   comprehension and, 261–62
   conclusions, 233–34
   confusion in, 262
   formats, 220–21
   introduction, 217–18
   topics addressed, 8
temporal intervals, 335–36
temporalities, alternative, 357–58
temporal montage, within a shot, 192nn6–7
text stratification, 315
textual structures, difficult
   curiosity and, 341, 348n6
   immediate attentional responses to, 339–41
   inexpressible realizations and, 339–40
theory of mind (ToM), 205, 206–7
third-degree puzzle films, 201–2
"The Thirty Years' War began in 1618" (Danto), 317
Thomas, Dylan, 326–27, 329, 330, 331
Thompson, Kristin, 21, 225
Thoreau, Henry David, 104, 107
threat
   alien invasion narrative invoking, 83–89
   brain and, 76
   complexity and, 76–77
   knowledge interplay with, 74–83
   Looper and, 79–80, 81–83
time. *See also* spatio-temporal reasoning; temporal intervals; temporalities, alternative; temporal montage, within a shot
   conceptualization of, 159–60
   embodiment and, 158–59, 171–78
   temporal montage within a shot, 192nn6–7
The Time Machine (Wells), 70, 73
Time-Reference-Point (Time-RP), 160–61
Titanic (1997), 200
ToA. *See* Tolerance of Ambiguity
Todorov, Tzvetan, 218, 228

Tolerance of Ambiguity (ToA), 360–61, 362, 365, 370–72, 376–77
ToM. *See* theory of mind
Triangle (2009), 201, 202, 204, 209
The Trout (O'Faolain), 331
Twelve Monkeys, 100, 108
Twin Peaks (1990-1991), 217, 225, 227, 267
    atom bomb in, 1–2
    confusion and, 262
    2001: A Space Odyssey compared with, 1
Twin Peaks (2017), 267
    as batshit TV, 264, 265
    coherent narrative and, 264
    episode 8 of, 263
    unnatural narrative of, 263
twist films, 26
twists, 242–44, 247–48, 358
2 or 3 Things I Know about Her. *See Deux ou Trois Choses Que Je Sais d'Elle*
2001: A Space Odyssey (1968), 1, 72, 74

U

The Uncanny (Freud), 86
uncompensated identity paradox, 207–11
unnatural narrative, 262–63, 276n3
unpredictability, pleasure and, 308–9
unreliable narration, 44–45, 66n2, 231–33
Upstream Color (2013), 6
    complexity varieties in, 95–96
    conclusions, 107–8
    forensic viewership and, 102, 109n4
    human–nonhuman interconnectedness in, 103–4, 105
    looping upstream in, 101–7, 109n8
    material anchors and, 94, 103, 105, 109n5
    plot of, 93–94, 101–2
    topics addressed, 93–95

V

Vaage, Margrethe Bruun, 299
    anti-hero drama and, 284, 285–86
    connoisseurship and, 297–98
    MAC drama costs and efforts, 287
    MAC drama rewards and, 286
    reality check moments and, 286, 290
Vanelli, Marco, 133n15
Vanilla Sky (2001), 200, 219
Le Vent d'Est (1970), 142, 143
Vertov, Dziga, 147
ViewPoint Identification Procedure (VPIP), 338
villains, 25–26
visual field is a container metaphor, 180, 192n8
VPIP. *See* ViewPoint Identification Procedure
Vygotsky, Lev, 145–46

W

Waiting for Godot, 261
Walsh, Richard, 98
Walton, Kendall, 282
WandaVision (2021), 268–69
"The War of the Ghosts" (American folk tale), 318
The War of the Worlds (Wells), 83
Watchmen (2019), 270, 273–75
Wells, H. G. *See The Man Who Could Work Miracles; The Time Machine; The War of the Worlds*
Willemsen, Steven, 81, 203, 320
    complexity and, 95, 106, 244
    dissonant experiences and, 308
    formal play and, 244
    Zen way of reading and, 267
Wind from the East. *See Le Vent d'Est*
The Wire (2002–2008), 222, 223
Witness for the Prosecution (1957), 24
Wollen, Peter, 140, 142, 143, 150
A Woman Is a Woman (1961), 183, 184, 186–87
Woolf, Virginia, 335

Z

Zen way of reading, 267
Zettl, Herbert, 161
Zunshine, Lisa, 335

www.ingramcontent.com/pod-product-compliance
Lightning Source LLC
Chambersburg PA
CBHW071329080526
44587CB00017B/2778